METAPHYSICAL APORIA
AND
PHILOSOPHICAL
HERESY

SUNY SERIES IN
CONTEMPORARY CONTINENTAL PHILOSOPHY
DENNIS J. SCHMIDT, EDITOR

METAPHYSICAL APORIA

AND

PHILOSOPHICAL HERESY

Stephen David Ross

STATE UNIVERSITY OF NEW YORK PRESS

Published by
State University of New York Press, Albany

For information, address State University of New York
Press, State University Plaza, Albany, N.Y. 12246

Library of Congress Cataloging-in-Publication Data

Ross, Stephen David.
    Metaphysical aporia and philosophical heresy/Stephen David Ross.
        p. cm.—(SUNY series in contemporary continental
philosophy)
    Includes index.
    ISBN 0-7914-0006-9. ISBN 0-7914-0007-7 (pbk.)
    1. Metaphysics—History.   2. Methodology—History.   3. Belief and
doubt—History.   I. Title.   II. Series.
BD111.R66 1989   88-24773
110.9—dc19   CIP

CONTENTS

PREFACE

The purpose of this book is not to "save philosophy" from its critics who say it is at its end, not to dissipate the violence of their rejection of metaphysics. It is not to leave the metaphysical tradition somehow whole at a time of its disruption. To the contrary, it is to acknowledge the forcefulness of the critiques by absorbing them into a view of metaphysics as both aporetic and heretical. Heresy here is disruption. It is not a way in which philosophy preserves itself through repetition, but a way in which it tears itself apart to fly again. Metaphysical aporia is neither a site of tribulation over which philosophical reason must eventually triumph nor an impasse in which reason halts at its limit, but the mark of truth tearing itself asunder, emerging in the form of heresy. It is the disruptive side of a tradition that needs both repetition and its annihilation for intelligibility. It is a site at which same and other dance their unending gavotte of life and death, in which they are themselves both other and the same.

The heresies discussed here fall into two main groups, one of which marks recurrence and repetition, the continuing resurgence of the play of same and other that defines the metaphysical tradition—more accurately, one reading of that tradition characterizing its historical locality— the other of which marks the heretical side of heresy, irreducible to repetition. The first reads as a grand narrative of philosophic history; the second resists succumbing to the authority of an overarching story, demands that we continually read each philosophic work anew, redefining the tradition, even repudiating the works that define its canon. Heresy demands a continual rereading of individual works and philosophers as they depart from any greater form under which we may subsume them, including even that of metaphysical aporia and philosophical heresy.

The course chosen here is to preserve the canon with many of its major works but to argue against the reduction of their singularities to a uniform tradition. I read works as works and authors as authors, not to bring them under a principle of the same, but to find heresies within them.[1] In a heretical reading, the author and his *oeuvre* are principles of disruption more than of totality.

1 INTRODUCTION: THE APORIA OF THE END

Viewed from a sufficient distance, all systems of philosophy are seen to be personal, temperamental, accidental, and premature. . . . In a word, they are human heresies.[1]

Santayana

1. What does it mean that philosophy in the present age has entered its final stage?
2. What task is reserved for thinking at the end of philosophy?[2]

Heidegger

FROM its beginnings, philosophy, especially metaphysics, has been said to be at its end: the cease of dogmatism and folly, the emergence of a new and better understanding of the world, even of a better human life. We may ponder this millenial thesis. For such an end has never been reached and, short of the extinction of human life, never will be, any more than science, art, or politics will reach their end. They are among the pervasive forms of human life and reason. They will change in important ways: relativistic and quantum physics have replaced Galilean and Newtonian mechanics; twentieth-century art has transformed our understanding of representation; contemporary technologies have changed human life and practice. What such changes manifest is the deepest truth of every tradition: that it endures through massive changes, incorporating them into itself. *Plus ça change, plus c'est la même chose,* but

1

also, conversely, *plus c'est la même chose, plus ça change:* the endless round of same and other. Every tradition endures through manifold changes, including those that would transform it wholly; every tradition changes as it endures. Repetition and variation are the forms whereby a tradition is able to relate to itself through a past and future that inevitably divide it. Every tradition, however homogeneous and orthodox in certain respects, is deeply divided by established norms and submerged variations, by recurrent heresies. The truth is that reason is heretical.

Science has profoundly changed, but we cannot doubt that science will continue, even more powerfully for its heresies. Art has deeply changed, but we can be sure that art will continue, even more sublime for its heresies. Human practices have also changed, but we cannot imagine their disappearance while life goes on, enriched by its heresies. Our assurances here are themselves divided by the threats and promises of the future. If our convictions are strong, it is because science, art, and politics are able to transform themselves through heresy. In the case of art, heresies include a return to superseded forms. When variation and novelty themselves become orthodox, heresy requires older orthodoxies. The heretical side of reason disrupts even the norm of heresy. It follows that reason is as deeply manifested in conflict as in agreement. It demands heresy as well as consensus, demands that every rule be challenged, including the rule of heresy.

The question is whether the claim that the end of metaphysics is at hand belongs to philosophy dividing against itself as a mark of its rationality, or whether one tradition, definitive of philosophic reason, has reached fulfillment, to be replaced by another. Yet, however radically philosophy may change, it cannot come to an end provided it is an expression of divided human reason. It will change as it must to respond to whatever forces impel it. Similarly, metaphysics will not and cannot end to the extent that it has established a living tradition. Such a tradition, such a discourse, is one that incorporates its divided interrogations into itself, disrupts itself through heresy.

The question is whether reason can think its own limits without disruption, if only in the form of heresy. The idea of the end of the metaphysical tradition includes within itself the premise that philosophy has hardened into a tradition incapable of interrogating itself, that cannot think the limits of its own intelligibility. Metaphysics will end in being replaced by another form of thought that achieves what it promises and avoids its dogmas.[3] Yet every such claim of the death of metaphysics denies its capacity to disrupt itself heretically under its own interrogations. Moreover, every such claim ascribes to itself the capacity to seize the essence of the tradition whole. Each defines an orthodox view of the metaphysical tradition, neglecting its manifold heresies.

One of the striking aspects of philosophical modernity, a reflection of the rise of science, is the repeated sense that a true understanding requires a new beginning. Despite their disagreements, earlier philosophers frequently shared the sense of a common enterprise. It required empiricism's brand of heresy, the rejection of a shared inheritance, to suggest that the tradition rested on a number of pervasive dogmas. Critical philosophy continued this self-understanding, rejecting the philosophic attempt to reach the ultimate springs of nature.

What then arose was a new orthodoxy: the conviction that every major philosophical innovation requires a break with its past. Few contemporary philosophers still understand themselves to belong to a shared philosophic activity, however heretical. There is then the irony in contemporary philosophy that among the philosophers who regard themselves as inhabiting a shared field of philosophic activities, there are far-reaching differences amounting to heresy, while among the philosophers who regard themselves as representing major departures, there is a shared orthodoxy, however iconoclastic. This irony is a manifestation of the dividedness that belongs to philosophy as one of its recurrent moments.

Heidegger speaks of "the end of philosophy and the task of thinking," suggesting that philosophy either has reached its end in a "scientific-technological world and of the social order proper to this world" or is to be replaced by a thinking that is not so forgetful of being.[4] He speaks of the destruction of a metaphysical tradition which is both forgetful of being and "ontotheological."[5] Derrida calls this side of the tradition "logocentric."[6] Rorty calls it a "mirroring of nature," seeking to supplant a foundational view of knowledge by "the conversation of mankind."[7] These authors share a view of the metaphysical tradition as the subordination of beings to propositional language as if they might be fully manifested there. Such a subordination entails a denial of beings' finiteness, consequently of their inexhaustibility. It entails a denial as well of the inexhaustibility of language and representation. Yet the limits of representation—consequently of reason and intelligibility—also have their limits. The limits of limits, and of those limits as well, comprise inexhaustibility. Its consequences for truth are aporia and heresy. The possibility is that propositional reason and science depend as much as art and philosophy upon the limitations of intelligibility. If so, then science is also inexhaustible, filled with aporia and heresy.[8]

The notions of aporia and heresy are fundamental to the ensuing discussion. By *aporia,* I mean the moments in the movement of thought—including but not restricted to metaphysics—in which it finds itself faced with unconquerable obstacles resulting from conflicts in its understanding of its own intelligibility. Such conflicts cry out for a resolution that cannot be achieved within the conditions from which they emerge. The result is either the termination of thought or heresy: a break in the limits of intelligibility. The question is whether such heretical disruptions are at the limits of reason or, aporetically, its fullest expression.

While the forms aporia may take are inexhaustible, three recurrent forms are worth noting. One is that of contradiction, the antinomic side of the tradition that culminates in Hegel's dialectic. To say that paradoxes and antinomies are aporias is to deny both their contradictoriness and their resolvability. The second form is that of multiplicity dividing identity, same and other. A famous example is Spinoza's sense that God is one substance divided by infinite attributes, including thought and extension. No distinction can resolve this aporia of many and one. Rather, metaphysical thought must play within this aporia endlessly, manifesting its own inexhaustibility. Here, finiteness *is* inexhaustibility and inexhaustibility *is* aporia: in particular, the aporia of the limit of every limit, the indeterminateness in every determination and the determinateness in every indetermination. The third recurrent form, then, is that of limitation, the limits of every limit, the reciprocity of determinateness in every indeterminateness.

The claim that philosophy has reached its end, that it must be replaced by thinking or by conversation, rests on several assumptions. One is that new truths are now available that contradict major presuppositions of the tradition. Yet these are not alternative truths about human beings and the world, but concern the nature of truth and intelligibility — traditionally metaphysical subjects. A second assumption is that the tradition homogeneously rests on a number of widely if not universally accepted premises. Yet there have always been philosophers who rejected established norms, especially the greatest metaphysicians. Closely related is the third assumption, that the tradition, despite its richness and complexity, can somehow be thought completely, to the point where its entire supersession might be intelligible. Yet every tradition, every major text, transcends any reading, however authoritative. Every reading is in this sense coercive, including every heretical reading. A fourth assumption is that it would be intelligible to foster an alternative form of thought free from the errors ascribed to the tradition. The criticism seeks to replace one view of truth by another while rejecting the traditional conflicts involved in truth. It would, for example, repudiate unconditioned transcendence, replacing it with unconditioned finiteness. Closely related here is the dispersal of the subject that constitutes "postmodernism"'s rejection of the modern tradition from Descartes to Hegel. Ironic here is the radical dispersal of the subject to be found in the metaphysical theories of Whitehead and Dewey as well as in Leibniz and Spinoza. The centering of the subject belongs to the metaphysical tradition as but one of its orthodox moments. A fifth assumption is that metaphysics will be overthrown by a thought at the limits of thought itself. Yet it is metaphysics that, traditionally, has brought thought as close as possible to its limits. If there is thinking at the limits of representation and intelligibility, it must lie as much within metaphysics as without (though, indeed, without exteriority, the limits of metaphysics cannot be thought). If our task is to make language strange—or abide within its strangeness[9]— metaphysics has traditionally faced the deepest resistances of language and thought. The strangeness of metaphysics is aporia. Its manifestation is heresy.

Among the themes in the iconoclastic side of the tradition is a denial that the systematic side of that tradition is worth paying attention to.[10] What we must seek are heretical forms of discourse. We should disdain any attempts to philosophize systematically and to listen only to marginal voices. This theme, that minority voices are fundamental within a dialogic philosophical practice, can be found in many contemporary writers. There is much to admire in this position, especially its recognition that orthodoxy is a form of power and that every great achievement works through heresy. What must be added is that such minority voices manifest the only form of reason that we will ever know, the only reason compatible with local human being.

Dewey, Heidegger, and Rorty share the sense that the metaphysical tradition has fostered mistaken assumptions about knowing and being that can be pervasively criticized and rejected. What is more questionable is their further suggestion that the tradition is sufficiently homogeneous to be brought to an end. For the claim that it is at an end belongs to the tradition as one of its orthodox moments. The claim is one of the ways in which the tradition tames its heretical side.

What is missing in these different writers is a certain sense of the philosophic tradition, deeply present in Santayana: an understanding that the major works that define the philosophic tradition are powerful because they were and still are profoundly heretical. In philosophy, greatness is heresy. This is as true for the systematic philosopher—Aristotle or Hegel—as for the iconoclast—Nietzsche or Derrida. Conversely, however, heresy is blunted as a work becomes a fixture in a canonical tradition. If every tradition is deeply divided, every tradition seeks to overcome its internal divisions through the exercise of authority.[11] The production and regulation of heresy are the pathways through which judgment and reason work. So important is this truth that every form of thought that claims to escape regulation must be regarded as suspect. Orthodoxy is antagonistic to heresy. Yet, the two are inseparable. All thought is coercive, imposing orthodoxy on the aporetic fragments that escape any stable reading; all thought is heretical, transcending any interpretation, however rich and complex. All philosophic thought is aporetic—including the thought of aporia itself.[12]

We come to two understandings of tradition. Every tradition includes and synthesizes within itself manifold divisions and differentiations.[13] Every tradition is filled with negations and discontinuities, and seeks to establish rules to control their risks and dangers.[14] Every tradition endures through the development of heresies, but every tradition seeks to control its development by exercising control over its heretical departures. Nowhere is this pattern more evident than in the metaphysical tradition, for that tradition is filled with works of singular grandeur that, when taken seriously, utterly transform our worlds, while the very presence of the tradition works to blind us to the heresies that pervade it. Works and schools that become established define orthodoxies incompatible with further heresies. Ironically, among the recurrent forms in which heresy has been regulated is in the claim that philosophy has reached its end. The contemporary form of heresy proclaims its authority by disdaining all other heresies. Here the expression of contemporary heresy manifests a coercive orthodoxy toward the heresies in the tradition that preceded it. To deny a tradition its heresies is to entomb it. It is to misunderstand the nature of one's own heresies.

Philosophy is not alone in being heretical. Art and practice typically, and science frequently, are deeply heretical, departing profoundly from established rules and governing principles. The most well known contemporary claim to scientific heresy is based on the claim that science undergoes "revolutions" that transform the norms of scientific intelligibility.[15] Implicit here is a denial that there is a definite "scientific method" that, properly employed, leads to truth. Rather, there are novel theoretical insights, experimental departures, heretical variations in established norms. To many readers, that there should be such heresy in science is incompatible with the image of its progress. Yet it is important to distinguish the claim that science lurches its way through history by heretical departures that violate the most sacred of established canons from the claim that there are no standards in science of legitimacy and truth. There are such standards, but they are neither immutable nor sacred. And they were produced as a consequence of the greatest act of secular heresy in human experience: the establishment of human reason as an arbiter against the established powers of tradition. The reason that opposes orthodoxy is an embattled, agonistic reason, one that can never rest in its unceasing opposition to established powers and its unceasing pursuit of heresy, constantly seeking to overthrow itself.

A metaphysics that preserves within itself a striving for heresy is a local metaphysics—limited itself and based on limitation. Only orthodoxy can hope to attain universality, by political means. The deepest flaw in Hegel's understanding of the dialectical process, which otherwise unmistakably manifests the force of heresy, is that its movement provides its own overcoming, passing from heresy into orthodoxy. In Hegel's system, heresy passes into triumphant culmination devoid of regret at the loss of its dialectical powers. Similarly, in Marx, heresy belongs to alienated practice, to be overcome by dialectical reconciliation. Marx, too, is devoid of regret at the loss of the very principle that makes his system intelligible.

Where heresy remains at the heart of metaphysical activity, along with its importance for art and practice, both being and truth are regarded aporetically. The reality that heresy manifests is aporetic. The form in which heresy realizes itself in the tradition is by unceasing interrogation of the aporias that define it. The universality of both being and truth must be called into question wherever heresy remains a viable alternative — a heresy untamed by permanent doctrine. In the sciences, for example, progress moves through one great discarded theory after another. A theory defines scientific understanding for a time, only to be supplanted by another that heretically disdains the definitions that inspired it. It is said that poets murder their ancestors.[16] Scientists commit far more devastating acts of destruction, discarding universes, large and small, upon the wreckage of heretical history. Nevertheless, the greatest heresy of science is science itself: the form of reason that proclaims consensus as its only norm while filled with conflict and controversy, even violence.

Metaphysical heresy remains heretical beyond the heresy of science. This truth substantiates the view that the metaphysical tradition is ontotheological, guided by a quest for certainty,[17] or based on a mirroring view of nature.[18] Yet, two important inadequacies are found in such a view of the tradition: the one that these writers are calling to our attention by characterizing the tradition so monolithically, suggesting that it has not adequately understood its own heretical nature; the other that the tradition has nevertheless been profoundly heretical, through and through, and remains so despite regulation. The major works in the metaphysical tradition remain deeply heretical even while orthodoxy rules within the tradition. Moreover, these works frequently manifest within themselves deep understandings of their own heretical nature and of the aporias they are enlisted to combat. The works that characterize the metaphysical tradition not only were heretical in their time but remain so. This truth lies at the heart of the deepest division in the tradition: it reveres as orthodox works that deeply call orthodoxy into question. Both the established philosophic tradition and its iconoclastic offspring share this aporia, manifesting the failure within any tradition to achieve control over its heretical nature.

What is important is not so much repeating the argument that Plato and Aristotle display heretical departures from prevailing Greek orthodoxy, a claim almost tiringly repeated in the Platonic dialogues. What is essential is coming to terms with the truth that Aristotle and Plato are, for most of us, the Greeks themselves, expressions of a culture from which they profoundly departed. Moreover, as a consequence, a new orthodoxy has emerged that masks the still relevant heresies present in both Plato and Aristotle. The question is how we are to understand a metaphysical tradition that has recurrently engaged, implicitly or explicitly, in heresy against itself, a tradition whose own intelligibility, even intelligibility itself, is always profoundly in question.

What is required is a theory of heretical reason based on an aporetic metaphysics. Heresy is the epistemic side of a local ontology for which being is aporetic. Together they comprise metaphysical inexhaustibility. In response to the strains in modern thought that emphasize the poverty of the metaphysical tradition, we may consider Santayana's and Whitehead's insights that a metaphysical theory can be both systematic and heretical. Our goal is to develop a systematic and aporetic theory of philosophic heresy, a theory that, however aporetically, can acknowledge its own heresies, aporias, disruptions, and limitations.

2 THE HERESY OF THE BEGINNING

THE heresy with which philosophy began is, without doubt, the greatest of which it is capable, a miracle surpassed only by that of Creation. It is the heresy of a divided reason, consequently, of aporetic being. The heresy of philosophy itself may be thought of minor importance, with little influence and power. What is mistaken is the equation of heresy with influence, as if philosophy were merely a form of practice. For philosophy and its major works, along with science and art, would be heretical possessing little influence. Spinoza is a supreme example. Philosophy is heretical simply by dividing reason, by being other, in this case at first, to religion and myth, later, to science and art. That there are manifold forms of reason is heretical: the singularity of each in relation to the others. Not all heresies strongly influence the course of human history. Yet without their dividedness, even recessively, other, more important heresies would be impossible.

The heresy with which philosophy began was repeated in a minor key 2,000 years later when Descartes sought again to establish rational foundations for truth independent of established authority. That reason should be able to exercise authority is heretical in the context of established institutions that define the seat of power and legitimacy. That human beings might think that first principles of explanation could be accessible to them through their own activities contains the deeper heresy that intelligibility belongs to thought itself.

Three heresies shape the beginnings of philosophy: that it should be capable of truth; that it should exist alongside mythology and science; and that reason should be capable of epistemic authority when devoid of political power. The third heresy passes into the hegemony of

9

science and appears to lose its heretical nature. Certain forms of reason become canonical, calculating reason based on repeatable observations and proofs. Mythology and emotion are displaced to the peripheries of rational activity where they can no longer exercise their heretical energies. A paramount example of such displacement occurs in Socrates' account of art as founded on inspiration rather than technique. What is implied on a standard reading is that an art that is founded on divine inspiration is at best true opinion and never knowledge, that science and philosophy are knowledge while art is frenzy. Overlooked is the possibility that such an art is a felicitous paradigm for reason, the possibility that knowledge is always in some sense beyond proof. There is always something miraculous, heretical, in any understanding.

What is heretical, then, in the origins of philosophy is the intelligibility of a form of truth very different from science. Given that science began at the same time as philosophy, it may appear odd to emphasize their differences. Yet there is a continuing heresy that orthodoxy has not been able to conquer in the unbreakable resistance of science and philosophy to each other. Science is natural philosophy, except that science achieves consensus while philosophy rejects it. Philosophy seeks truth along with science, but philosophy is more iconoclastically self-critical than science. The two are not the same but are inseparable. There is aporia in any position we take toward them. Their individual truth imposes upon us the aporia of their coexistence.

The threefold heresy of the beginning of philosophy includes two additional, far-reaching heresies that have shaped the course of subsequent thought. One is the heresy of aporia itself, the focus of our entire discussion. The early Greek philosophers invented aporia—it was not waiting in the wings to be discovered—in conjunction with their understanding of limit and unlimit. They profoundly grasped the affinities between aporia and inexhaustibility. The second heresy that accompanied the beginnings of philosophy was the idea of an origin, of the *archē*.[1] If there is disagreement among commentators about whether Thales' water was an *archē*, as Aristotle suggests (*Metaphysics*, 963b),[2] there is no doubt that the early Greeks developed the idea of the origin, whether a first principle, cause,[3] or ground, and that within their polemics lies a profound intuition of the aporias of any beginning. The question of the origin is the undying question of philosophy precisely because it is the question of aporia, of the inseparability of intelligibility from its other.

Science—or philosophy—began, we are told, with Thales, who according to Aristotle thought the first principle of all things was water.

    . . . getting the idea, I suppose, because he saw that the nourishment of all things is moist, and that warmth itself is generated

> from moisture and persists in it . . . . (Nahm p. 38; Aristotle, *Metaphysics*, 983b)[4]

Aristotle suggests that Thales must have been struck by a powerful analogy between the role of moisture in living things and the first principle of all things. Yet, to say that the first principle of all things is water is not to draw an analogy with an unknown principle. It is to take water itself as primary. Plausible or not, such a view is disturbing in two fundamental respects. One is the idea that there might be a singular first principle of all things, all falling under a common *archē*. Even today, such an idea of the same surpasses any credibility. The other is that such a principle might be common in everyday experience, another idea of the same. For the gods, who work in mysterious ways, are not accessible to us, nor can we expect their laws to be manifest.

We do not find it plausible today to suppose that the origin of all things is water. The closest we come to such familiar mechanisms is in empiricism and behaviorism, where we are asked to understand experience in terms of repetition and representation. In both cases, however, what is presupposed is that there are unrestricted principles under which all things fall, and that such principles are familiar and ordinary. There is profound heresy in such inflation of familiarity. Were such a view to become orthodox, then contemporary science would be a recurrent heresy in its repeated appeal to alien worlds. And it is such a heresy relative to everyday experience, for science recurrently asks us to understand familiar things in alien terms. This alienness of science deeply contributes to the hatred many contemporary writers betray toward it: a yearning for more congenial conditions; a hatred for the unyielding strangeness that cannot be eliminated from science. What remains as an alternative is to welcome heresy as the condition that makes reason possible.

There is an unmitigated conflict in the heresy of familiarity rooted in our philosophical beginnings. Thales proposes both an absolute unity of understanding under a single principle and a totally familiar basis of that understanding. In a natural but heretical response, Anaximander claims,

> . . . that the first principle and element of all things is infinite (*apeiron*), . . . neither water nor any other one of the things called elements, but the infinite is something of a different nature, from which came all the heavens and the worlds in them. (Nahm, p. 39; DK 12 A 9)

while in return, Anaximenes suggests

... that the essential nature of things is one and infinite, but he regards it as not indeterminate but rather determinate, and calls it air. (Nahm, p. 43; DK 13 A 5)

For Anaximenes, understanding presupposes familiarity—in this case, air—because an unknown principle lying behind familiar things remains unintelligible. For Anaximander, familiar things cannot provide satisfactory understanding *because* of their familiarity.[5]

It is heretical in relation to lived experience that all things present to us might rest on a single principle that is absolutely beyond experience, but it is equally heretical that anything present to us in experience might be the source of so many things altogether different. On the one hand, the first principle of all things must be entirely unfamiliar, utterly indeterminate; on the other hand, it must be altogether determinate. Now nothing can be altogether determinate or altogether indeterminate. The aporia of determinateness in relation to indeterminateness pervades the tradition. What is determinate is too familiar to be explanatory; what is indeterminate is unintelligible. The relationship between determinateness and indeterminateness demands heretical insights for its appropriation.

The differences among the views of Thales, Anaximander, and Anaximenes are significant in relation to our understanding of heresy because what constitutes intelligibility is in question among them. To differ on the conditions of intelligibility is unavoidably heretical. Shall we seek within familiar things for understanding or behind them in something altogether different? Shall we seek understanding in one principle that, undivided, is unintelligible, or in many principles that cannot all be intelligibly related? Can anything be intelligible if it is not altogether determinate? Can anything be altogether determinate and be variable enough to constitute an intelligible basis for variable experience? Can same and other be thought without aporia?

To these questions of intelligibility around which most philosophic heresies turn may be added the aporetic nature of the form of understanding implicit in Anaximander's and Anaximenes' writings. The elements— the hot, the cold, the dry, the moist, and the rest (Robinson, p. 25; DK 12 A 9)—are opposites. In part, this means that they destroy each other, so that something is required beyond each of them as their foundation. In further part, however, the oppositions of the elements comprise a dynamic, divided principle. Here the heresy is that many first principles work by conflict and strife. This principle of aporia is explicit in Heraclitus.

What is in question in the beginnings of philosophy is reason itself, not only what it is, but the conditions of its intelligibility. What is heretical about the earliest philosophers, still today, is present in the differences among them that constitute undecidable questions of intelligibility.

Crudely put, we have no basis for deciding upon the intelligibility of a metaphysical theory apart from the determinations by that theory of what intelligibility is. The heresy inherent in most metaphysical theories lies in this middle region between being and intelligibility, as if we must somehow entirely reconstitute our relationship to metaphysical understanding every time we seek to attain it, although such a reconstitution is unintelligible. We inhabit this midworld both aporetically and heretically.

Where this great heresy of intelligibility is clearly manifest is in the polarity of positions represented by Heraclitus and Parmenides, the reason why so many understandings of the tradition go back to them. The Western philosophic tradition may consist of but a series of footnotes to Plato,[6] but that is already a truth about traditional orthodoxy, taming Plato's own heretical nature. There can be no similar taming of Heraclitus and Parmenides: they confront the heresy of metaphysical intelligibility directly.

For Heraclitus, opposites and flux are aporetic principles.

All things come into being through opposition, and all are in flux like a river. (Robinson, p. 89; DK 22 A 1)

Cool things become warm; what is warm cools; what is wet dries out; what is dry becomes moist. (Robinson, p. 90; DK 22 B 126)

Plato describes Heraclitus' position paradoxically:

Heraclitus, you know, says that everything moves on and that nothing is at rest; and, comparing existing things to the flow of a river, he says that you could not step into the same river twice. (*Cratylus*, 402a)

We have, including Plato's account, three different versions of the river fragment:

. . . you could not step into the same river twice.

Upon those who step into the same rivers flow other and yet other waters. (Robinson, p. 91; DK 43 B 12)

In the same rivers we step and we do not step. We are and are not. (Nahm, p. 73; DK 44 B 49)

The third emphasizes the aporetic nature of Heraclitus' position, emphasizes the strife and opposition inherent within it.[7]

The second reading of the fragment tames its heresy by interpreting it to say that we can step into the same river twice, but not into the same waters. What is neglected in such a reading is the continuing emphasis in Heraclitus on the aporias of experienced reality: justice is strife; opposition is good; war is the father and king of all. (Robinson, p. 93; DK A,B) Suppose we were to grant, with Plato, the full measure of Heraclitus' aporetic view of things, setting aside our own rational prejudices concerning intelligibility. Aporia and difference would be the fundamental conditions of being. But the greatest aporia of all is that amidst their differences they are the same.

> Listening not to me but to the *logos*, it is wise to acknowledge that all things are one. (Robinson, p. 95; DK 22 B 50)

> The way up and the way down are the same. (Robinson, p. 94; DK 22 B 60)

We may read Heraclitus as a somewhat aberrant member of an established tradition seeking a rational common basis in public experience for variable phenomena. Yet the tradition, in its wisdom, has tended to affirm the heretical nature of his understanding of the world. Indeed, two forms of aporia mark the heretical side of Heraclitus: between and among ordinary things, in conflict and strife, where justice (*dikē*) is antagonism and opposition is rational; between the flux of experienceable things and the unchanging *logos*. All things are in flux, all are changing, in conflict; opposition is the source of all determinateness. But truth lies in commonality. In this sense, things are unintelligible in themselves and in their movements, but they are intelligible in the order that underlies them—an order that is absolutely inaccessible in experience.

This is extraordinary enough, but the aporias go deeper. For there is nothing whatever in Heraclitus' view that mediates between the unending warfare of the flux and the unqualified sameness of the *logos*— nothing that mediates and nothing that can mediate. Heraclitus effectively denies that the *logos* "explains" ordinary experience with its variability and oppositions. Truth and wisdom lie in the *logos*, but experience is altogether different. This prime heresy is shared by very few philosophers in the tradition: intelligibility lies in a oneness that lies behind everyday events but that does not and cannot intelligibly explain them, while the conflicts and disruptions of everyday events comprise their intelligibility. Such a view is so antiempirical, so antiscientific, that it can barely be considered in a modern age. It marks the heresy of a remote and hidden truth that bears no rational relationship to experience but bears every important relationship to being and understanding.

Heraclitus makes one effort to characterize the sameness of the *logos* and its relationship to the conflicting flux.

> Men do not understand how what is divided is consistent with itself; it is a harmony of tensions like that of the bow and the lyre. (Nahm, p. 71; DK 22 B 51)

The analogy is apt to the extent that a many-stringed instrument can be harmonious, that one harmony is many voices, even that many voices can be represented as one moving principle. The analogy is less plausible to the extent that a stringed instrument can be heard as one harmony—or, if we are to accept the analogy strictly, that the *logos* can be felt and heard, thought and understood, though it cannot be derived from experience.

The issue here is of the one and many: the one of the *logos*, the divided many that comprises the flux. The oneness of the *logos* is its intelligibility; the manyness of the flux comprises the content of lived experience. The profound insight in Heraclitus, the heresy that has never been resolved, is that the same, though it comprises intelligibility, does not take absolute precedence over the flux. Each possesses its own intelligibility. What is unintelligible is the relationship between the flux and *logos*. Heraclitus expresses a profound lacuna between determinateness and indeterminateness, same and other. The heresy is that there is no way to resolve the difference, no way to make indeterminateness into determinateness. Opposition and conflict are not resolved into the *logos*, but coexist with it. Moreover, the aporia is continued at the second level of analysis, between the flux and the *logos*. Same and other, indeterminateness and determinateness, are conjoint and equal principles of being and intelligibility.

Parmenides and Zeno are frequently thought to be deeply opposed to Heraclitus, the latter emphasizing the flux, the former, undivided Being. For Heraclitus, there is both a one and many; for Parmenides, Being cannot be divided in any way. Such a reading makes much of emphasis, in Heraclitus' case, an emphasis upon the flux, in Parmenides', an emphasis upon undivided Being. Yet both share an aporetic view of ordinary experience and an unqualified view of the unity of what lies behind it.[8] Parmenides maintains that aporia must be absolutely avoided, at any cost, including any capacity whatever to understand everyday experience. Heraclitus maintains that everyday experience is aporetic, therefore intelligible, but that in addition intelligibility lies in the *logos*. These views are different in how they relate intelligibility to aporia. In other respects, they are in deep affinity. They are in affinity concerning the profound aporia between being and reality.[9]

Parmenides is not the only philosopher to propose the heresy that the world of human experience is aporetic, beyond all intelligibility. Nor is he alone in suggesting that there lies, beyond aporia, a perfect, undivided Being.[10] This heresy is important enough in making us aware of the irresistibility of the strife and conflict in the only reality we will ever encounter. But it is even more striking and important when we consider Parmenides and Heraclitus together.

For the Way of Truth is not the only way, and Parmenides, who has forbidden us to speak of what is not must also propose a Way of Opinion. Whatever we might say to neutralize this inexplicable aporia, that what we have been forbidden to say about being we may say of the things of opinion, we are left with its aporia untouched: that there is at once nothing and everything between being and opinion, just as there is in Heraclitus nothing and everything between the *logos* and the flux.

The fundamental heresy in Heraclitus and Parmenides is that despite their commitment to the quest for understanding and wisdom, their views rest on a fundamental gulf between everyday experience and its ground of intelligibility. Intelligibility is not rejected, skeptically, but affirmed joyously, amid a clear sense of its own unintelligibility. Not only is there something unintelligible at the heart of experience: intelligibility itself is unintelligible, and conversely.

The heresy in Heraclitus and Parmenides entails the unintelligibility of the unity of being amid the plurality. Within this remarkable view of the nature and limits of reason, there is an assumption that has so completely dominated the Western tradition as to surpass any sense of its heresy. While the flux is aporetic, incomplete and divided, the *logos* is unified and intelligible; while the things of ordinary experience are variable and divided, being is undivided and unchangeable. The assumption is that only a whole, unified, self-sufficient, therefore unchanging and undivided being can be intelligible and real. Aporetic reality is not and cannot be thought real. The assumption that what changes requires explanation in terms of what does not change, that what is dependent requires explanation in terms of what is self-sufficient, and, generically, that what is indeterminate is intelligible only in terms of what is determinate, but not conversely, is so characteristic of the Western philosophic tradition that to challenge it is to commit outright heresy.

Against this assumption, there is the explicit heresy in Heraclitus, still present in his view of the *logos*, that intelligibility and being are aporetic through and through, but are not any less intelligible and real for their aporias. Intelligible being is aporetic, and nothing is more intelligible; nothing is less aporetic.

In the tradition, aporia has been interpreted as contradiction, therefore irrational. To say that A is not A is to commit every absurdity because anything whatever follows. Here we can do no better than to admire Parmenides on the one hand but Hegel and Bradley on the other, for helping us to understand, if indirectly, the inexhaustible difference at the heart of aporia that distinguishes it from contradiction. For the principle that being cannot be divided entails, in Parmenides, that it can stand in no intelligible relation to ordinary experience. The intelligibility demanded by undivided and self-sufficient being imposes an absolute sacrifice in intelligibility in relation to everything else in experience. Similarly, in Bradley, the "absolute criterion" of reality is consistency:

> Ultimate reality is such that it does not contradict itself: here is an absolute criterion.

What follows, again, is that except for the ultimate reality, *Experience*, everything else is aporetic, therefore Appearance.

> Appearance must belong to reality, and it must therefore be concordant and other than it seems. The bewildering mass of phenomenal diversity must hence somehow be at unity and self-consistent; for it cannot be elsewhere than in reality, and reality excludes discord.[11]

Thus, everything *appears* many, divided, aporetic; but everything *is* one, unified. Under the name of Appearance, Bradley ignores the aporia between appearance and reality. It is impossible that any intelligible relation might exist between them. The "absolute criterion" of intelligibility, based on a total rejection of aporia, rests on the sweeping aporia that the intelligibility so defined is empty.

We may seek to tame Heraclitus' heresy that reality is inescapably aporetic, but only by the heresy that reality is beyond intelligibility. Parmenides' heresy is that nothing whatever in human understanding or experience can be intelligible, a heresy that is incompatible with any philosophy or science, including itself. Heraclitus' heresy is that aporetic reality is intelligible, although intelligibility also demands the unity of the *logos*. If we take Heraclitus seriously, we cannot avoid the possibility that the aporetic reality is as intelligible as it can be, that aporia *is* intelligibility. With the qualification that aporia is not contradiction, Heraclitus' enduring contribution is that reason will forever war with aporia, not to attain an absolute and undivided being, but to divide aporia from unintelligibility. We may reread the line that "Nature loves to hide" not as emphasizing the obscurity of nature, not even that underlying the surface there is an absolutely intelligible reality, but that reason is the inexhaustible activity of uncovering the hidden aporias of nature, only to fall into still others. Aporia is the soul of intelligibility.

With such heresies in mind, Zeno's role in the history of philosophy is clear. He is a prime exemplar of aporetic thinking, a role Plato assigns to him unequivocally.

> If you want to be thoroughly exercised, you must not merely make the supposition that such and such a thing *is* and then consider the consequences; you must also take the supposition that the same thing *is not*.[12]

No wonder young Socrates replies, "There would be no end to such an undertaking": there are unending ways in which something may be not—everything else, actual and possible. I return to *Parmenides* in the next chapter to discuss Plato's heresies, in my view as well as that of others the greatest of the tradition. Here the point is that he, through the voice of Parmenides, expresses a thoroughly positive role for aporetic thinking. One must consider both that something is and that it is not: therefore, everything is always both. This is Zeno's general argument, although it strikingly affirms what Parmenides' goddess has disdained. What we are considering is that to be both is not a mark of unintelligibility. Given the tradition's position on contradiction, the notion sounds absurd. Yet the young Socrates says in *Parmenides*, about things other than the Ideas,

> I see nothing strange ... in a proof that all things are one by having a share in unity and at the same time many by sharing in plurality.
> ... what is there surprising in someone pointing out that I am one thing and also many? (*Parmenides*, 129c)

Of course, he is correct, except that such a mundane view is heretical in relation to a strong interpretation of consistency such as Bradley's or Parmenides'. Moreover, there is implicit the profound heresy that this conjunction of same and other that characterizes ordinary things pertains to beings in general. What follows is that the formal properties of intelligibility—consistency, order, succession, distinction, explanatoriness, clarity—are always aporetically in question.

Zeno's paradoxes dramatize the aporias of the relationship between determinateness and indeterminateness, same and other. If space exists and is something, then it will be in something else. If an arrow has a definite location, then it cannot move, for motion involves indeterminateness of place. To move, one must traverse a finite distance in a finite time, but every distance is infinite (infinitely divisible). In all these cases, the reality requires aporetic descriptions, examples of the generic aporia of determinateness and indeterminateness: every being is determinate in certain ways and indeterminate in others, and there is a reciprocal relationship between determinateness and indeterminateness. What makes Zeno's arguments paradoxical is the implicit suggestion that things — here space and time — cannot be indeterminate as well as determinate. Directly or indirectly, Zeno expresses the pervasive aporia of the tradition: the circling minuet of same and other. The aporia is presented compellingly in the paradox of the grain of millet. If the fall of a grain of millet makes a noise, then does not the fall of a thousandth of a grain of millet make a noise, and so on? The answer is that no property of any thing can be considered to belong to it universally and unequivocally under division or aggregation, for these are forms of transformation and relation. Some properties are constant under division, others are not. More generally, properties are always local, and none belongs to any being without qualification. There is an irresistible otherness in every being in virtue of its parts and relations.

This otherness in the same pertains to space as well as time. Yet the tradition, except perhaps for Leibniz, has always regarded space as definite, restricting aporia to time. A striking expression of this aporia, deeply reminiscent of Zeno's paradoxes, is McTaggart's famous argument.[13] Time falls under two descriptions: a continuum from earlier to later and a continuum from past to future. The former is infinitely divisible and not intrinsically temporal because it does not involve change. The second involves a constantly changing present, so that what was once future becomes present and then past. McTaggart argues that this second sequence is self-contradictory because it assigns incompatible determinations to the same event. An alternative is that time is aporetic but not self-contradictory, not only in the presence of different determinations in the same event, but in the copresence of two incompatible descriptions. The aporia of time is that it requires incompatible determinations. We may add the heresy that such an aporia is as much a mark of intelligibility as of unintelligibility. Aporia does not collapse reason into unintelligibility but presents us with intelligibility as an inexhaustibly divided project. Aporia requires unending heresies. Intelligibility is as indeterminate (as well as determinate) as is being. From this vantagepoint, Kant's antinomies are not expressions of the (absolute) limits of reason, but of the aporetic limits that make reason possible.

The greatest heresies in philosophy involve profound transformations in our understanding of both being and intelligibility. At the beginning of philosophy, such transformations were of necessity frequent; in later centuries, only the greatest works could be profoundly heretical. In earliest philosophy, the questions not only of what is, but of how we can grasp it intelligibly, were in constant turmoil. We may briefly consider some of the remaining figures of the period to note just how remarkable even minor positions may be understood to be.

In Aristotle's words, the Pythagoreans

> ... took numbers to be the whole of reality, the elements of numbers to be the elements of all existing things, and the whole heaven to be a musical scale and a number. (Aristotle, *Metaphysics*, 985b)

> They construct the whole heaven out of numbers. Not, however, out of numbers considered as abstract units; for they suppose the units to have magnitude. But how the first "one" was constructed so as to have magnitude, they seem to be unable to say. (Aristotle, *Metaphysics*, 1080b)

Such a view defines a reality without matter. Thus, on Aristotle's account the Pythagoreans repeat the heresy that the intelligible reality underlying experienced reality might be so altogether different as to bear no resemblance to it. This heresy continues in contemporary physics, in quantum mechanics especially, but also in microbiology and astronomy. Major changes in scale produce radical transformations in being. Moreover, there is the further heresy here, carried into the theory of Ideas, that mathematics is uniquely intelligible, therefore that intelligible being must be number. What is not number is not intelligible or real—it is, we may say, unmeasurable and unmeasured. The mark of (intelligible) being is measure—a rule of the same within the play of same and other. It was not for thousands of years that such a view of intelligibility could be effectively challenged—a challenge central to Whitehead's metaphysical theory. What is essential is understanding the notion of limit.

> They say plainly that when the "one" had been constructed—whether from planes, or surface, or seed, or something else which they are unable to express—that straightway the nearest part of the unlimited began to be drawn in and limited by the limit. (Aristotle, *Metaphysics*, 1091a)

There is a deep insight in this Pythagorean view. Being is limitation, and number is limitation. Yet limitation must itself be limited, and the Pythagoreans cannot explain how number can be limited except by number. Measure cannot be its own limit.

If what is unfamiliar cannot establish a determinate basis for ordinary things, and if division and aggregation are transformations introducing important changes into experience, then it is natural to seek within them for the intelligibility required in being. Instead of regarding division and aggregation as threats to intelligibility, we may regard them as intelligibility itself.

> There is no origination of anything that is mortal, nor yet any end in baneful death; but only mixture and separation of what is mixed, but men call this "origination." (Nahm, p. 117; DK 31 B 8)

One of the most remarkable insights concerning these matters is found in Anaxagoras:

> For neither is there a least in what is small, but there is always a less. For being is not non-being. But there is always a greater than what is great. And it is equal to the small in number; but with reference to itself each thing is both small and great. (Nahm, p. 140; DK 59 B 3)

Division and aggregation here are pervasive conditions of being—not, as in Zeno, threats to intelligibility. It follows that there is no end to either division or aggregation, that every being is both divisible and aggregatable, and that these are not contradictory but always copresent. Smallness and greatness are not properties of things in themselves, nor are there any such properties in themselves, but only in relation to other things. Being here is relational and inexhaustible. Inexhaustibility here is not unlimit but limit and the limit of limit together.

The conjunction of three of Anaxagoras' principles has been regarded by many commentators as contradictory. They are certainly aporetic:

1. There is no smallest or greatest, but always a smaller and a greater. (DK 59 B 3)
2. There is something of everything in everything. (DK 59 B 11)
3. Everything is composed of smaller units like itself. (Aristotle, *De Caelo*, 302a)

The first and second principles are explicit expressions of the conjunction of limit and unlimit that inhabits every being. The apparent contradiction is between the second and third principles.[14] If everything contains everything, then it does not contain only homoionerous units like itself. Moreover, if there is something of everything in everything, we cannot distinguish things from each other. Both of these ways of establishing the contradiction ignore the manifest aporia of the indeterminateness inherent in every being: no being is merely itself, but both potentially and even actually other beings. Every being is similar to every other being in some ways, although also different from every other in other ways. The particles that make up a being are the same particles that make up other beings. Aggregation and division are forms of indeterminateness. Simples and complexes tell us nothing entirely determinate about their aggregates and elements. In generic terms, sameness and difference are the same—and different. There is no absolute difference that does not involve similarity and conversely.

Nothing is more orthodox today than atomism, though it is virtually bankrupt in contemporary science. Orthodoxy never frees itself from heresy. This truth is manifest even in Greek atomism.

> [Leucippus, Democritus, and Epicurus] said that the first principles were infinite in number; and they supposed them to be uncuttable and indivisible and impassive because of their solidity, and without any share of the void. For division, they maintain, takes place because of the void which is in bodies. (Robinson, p. 198; DK 67 A 14)

A scientific interpretation of this void, nonbeing, is as empty space, where space *is something*. Even on this interpretation, the atomists maintained that the void is *in* bodies, not around them. The atoms, then, are indivisible and pervaded by empty spaces; in the aggregate, they comprise compound bodies. Now the view that solid bodies are filled with empty space is one of the heresies that comprises modern physics. Empty space is really full; solid bodies are really empty; bodies comprise differing fields of influence and location.

The standard view is aporetic. But there is a more aporetic thought in Greek atomism: the void is not empty space—full, at best, of geometric relationships—but nothing. And the nonbeing is required for the divisibility of bodies. Now divisibility (and aggregation) are forms whereby bodies are intelligible. Therefore, the intelligibility and determinateness of bodies are functions of both their being and their nonbeing. There is, here, a foreshadowing of one of the most important insights in the philosophic tradition: that intelligibility and determinateness require nonbeing as well as being. Determinateness is inseparable from indeterminateness, and conversely.

Atoms, to the Greeks, "jostle and move in the void" but do not change. (Robinson, p. 198; DK 68 A 37) The atomists were satisfied that change could, in this way, be grounded on changelessness, although without changes in position and order among the atoms, there could be no such grounding. At best, atoms might not change in certain respects, but must change in others. Similarly, the immutability of mechanistic natural laws obscures the truth that particles do indeed change (in position), that change is a first principle of things despite the immutability of the laws that govern them. The assumption is that the intelligibility in changing things is given by what does not change—solid atoms or immutable natural laws. What is overlooked is that natural laws without changing states of material conditions would be unintelligible, not laws at all, and that solid particles that did not change in any way would not be atoms, for they would neither comprise any compounds nor participate in any activities.

The heresy is that while change is intelligible only in terms of what does not change, what does not change is unintelligible except in terms of what changes. More generally, again, same and other are inseparable. To be is to be determinate in certain ways and indeterminate in others, each intelligible only in terms of the other. We cannot associate such an insight with the atomists, but may at best ascribe it to Heraclitus among the Greeks. Nevertheless, the insight pertains directly to their theory. Atoms may not change in certain respects, may not be materially divisible, but they must be changeable in other respects, divisible by their states and locations.

Appearance is intelligible only in terms of an underlying reality; but such a reality, if not reciprocally determined by appearance, is indeterminate. This is the difficulty on which Parmenides and Bradley founder. But there is a greater difficulty: the assumption that intelligibility entails culmination in an ultimate principle of determination. To be intelligible, events must rest on a foundation that does not itself require a foundation. The most famous example of such an argument is in relation to Aristotle's unmoved mover. But it is present in Parmenides' view of being, full and complete, in Heraclitus' view of the *logos*, and in the indivisibility of the atoms. Only in Heraclitus and perhaps Anaxagoras directly, although in all the others indirectly, can we discern the reciprocal movement that requires that oppositions and conflicts, aporetically, belong to intelligibility. Especially in Anaxagoras, there is explicit affirmation of the inexhaustibility that being requires to be intelligible.

Yet, the implicit indications of this insight are sweeping. One example is the recognition in Parmenides that the Way of Truth lacks both credibility and standing without the Way of Opinion. Similarly, the changeability of atoms, in place and movement, shows that changelessness is not intelligible of itself, that only by changing can a being manifest itself, including changing relationships to changing things. An even more striking manifestation of this insight, however, lies in the fragmentary nature of early Greek writings.

That the earliest philosophic writings are fragmentary is a contingent historical fact. We have no fragments left from Thales, only descriptions of his position. We have fragments left from most of the others, but if there had ever been a continuous doctrine, it is no longer available to us. The historical fact is one of fragmentariness, and it is important to recognize its influence and relevance. We are turning for the first time to the question of philosophic style.

The early fragments present us with the truth that philosophic influence and importance may be functions less of coherent doctrine than of fragmentariness and condensation, less of unitariness than of dividedness and aphorism. If we had a complete systematic work from Heraclitus or Anaxagoras, could it be as influential and important as the fragments? It is impossible to say. But such a work would compete directly with Plato and Aristotle (although Plato is a special case because of his dramatic style). It is felicitous to consider the possibility that the fragmentariness of early philosophic writing lends itself to aporetic reading. In contrast with the prosaic forms of later philosophic writing, the fragmentariness of early philosophy remains iconoclastic. There is aporia in the fragmentary style of early philosophy that supports the other sources of aporia evident there. Following Heraclitus, we may conclude that not only does nature love to hide, but philosophy and even science love to hide, and that hiding is an essential condition of intelligibility. Heresy is an irresistible component of reason.

Such an emphasis upon the aporias of the beginnings of philosophy cannot overlook the Sophists. A traditional view is that philosophy could achieve legitimacy only by severing itself from eristic. On this view, the central and recurrent movement in Plato, from *Republic* to *Sophist*, is to distinguish true philosophy from rhetoric and sophistry. Leaving Plato for the moment, with his own remarkable heresies, we may consider briefly some of the known Sophists' teachings. There are, of course, few fragments known to us directly, and the Sophists are measured less by what they said and taught than by what the characters in Plato's dialogues say about them. We cannot in this light avoid questioning Socrates' claim in *Phaedrus* about written words, that:

> . . . . if you ask them anything about what they say, from a desire to be instructed, they go on telling you just the same thing forever. And once a thing is put in writing, the composition, whatever it may be, drifts all over the place, getting into the hands not only of those who understand it, but equally of those who have no business with it; . . . . (Plato, *Phaedrus*, 275e)

All of this may be true, but it loses much of its force when we consider that we have no writings left from the Sophists and have no basis upon which to evaluate what they said and taught. Their own writings might distort what they said and taught, but Plato's writings do so unmistakably.

There is one premise on the basis of which what Socrates says here can be plausible given the difficulties we have with hearsay, especially over historical time. Truth is not a function of person or milieu, but of an entirely autonomous understanding. There can be no regret at having lost the words of the Sophists, or even of Plato, if we understand that neither authors nor words matter: truth is a living reality. We later consider whether it is plausible to ascribe such a position to Plato (already a heretical act in this context), but in present terms it may be more useful to consider Protagoras' famous maxim:

> Of all things the measure is man; of existing things, that they exist; of nonexistent things, that they do not exist. (Robinson, p. 245; DK 80 B 1)

The maxim does not tell us whether it is human beings collectively or individually who are the measure, although in *Cratylus*, Socrates interprets Protagoras entirely in individual terms. This proves little, because that work is filled with irony. Yet, if we accept Socrates' interpretation, then it is essential to ascribe interpretations to individual human beings because they are the measures of their truths and existences. We find the remarkable suggestion here that we are to understand a philosophical work in terms of its author, opening the possibility of so personal and idiosyncratic a vantagepoint as to make heresies and departures unavoidable, only to impose upon the author so unified and coherent a role as to make heresy unintelligible. In either case, whether it is humanity individually or collectively who determines the basis of truth and existence, there can be no independent standard of reality and truth.

Far more important is the notion again that intelligibility is measure. This is a shocking notion if we only stop to consider it. Poetry is intelligible even when we have no relevant measures applicable to it. And there is a tradition of wise men and women whose actions surpass any relevant measures. Far more important, that being and practice are intelligible only in relation to measure entails a system of equivalences within which all things may be located. This, although it has become modern orthodoxy, is one of the major heresies of our tradition.

The heresy of the Sophists to which Plato is least sympathetic lies in their emphasis on the human or variable element in determinations that seem to require universality. They emphasize the worldly side of limit and determinateness; indeterminateness and the limits of limits are moved from the edges of intelligibility, as in Parmenides and Heraclitus, to the everyday, from the divine to the mundane. In the case above, truth is a human measure. Antiphon makes a similar claim with respect to justice, but with the kind of conclusion that we typically identify with sophistry:

> A man will be just, then, in a way most advantageous to himself if, in the presence of witnesses, he holds the laws of the city in high esteem, and in the absence of witnesses, when he is alone, those of nature. (Robinson, p. 250-51; DK 87 B 44)

Such a claim may be interpreted to entail that human beings should act unjustly whenever they can benefit from doing so and act justly only to sustain their public reputations. As a moral doctrine, such a position does not sustain justice over injustice, and Plato is properly contemptuous of it. Yet what he has difficulty taking seriously, although there is no escaping it in *Republic*, is the possibility that justice is in fact disadvantageous, that there is a profound sacrifice involved in acting justly. The sophistic heresy confronts us with a deep living truth from which we have never found escape: there is no way to live in an aporetic reality without far-reaching sacrifices. The consequence of this aporia for practice is the unavoidability of failure in all our undertakings.

A standard view is that the views of the Sophists entail relativism and skepticism. Such an interpretation is supported by what we know of Gorgias' teachings:

> For in his book entitled *Concerning the Non-existent or Concerning Nature* he tries to establish successively three main points—firstly, that nothing exists; secondly, that even if anything exists it is inapprehensible by man; thirdly, that even if anything is apprehensible, yet of a surety it is inexpressible and incommunicable to one's neighbor. (Nahm, p. 233)

Such a position is reminiscent of Parmenides and Zeno. Why, then, has Gorgias been so reviled while they have been admired faithfully? Perhaps Gorgias used his dialectical tricks to praise injustice and to lead Athens into disaster. But in fact, he is famous for seeking to unify a divided Athens.

The most plausible answer is that Gorgias is a primary exemplar of the style and position against which the formidable forces of Platonic argument are arrayed. Yet Platonic doctrine became orthodoxy, especially the distinction between philosophy, concerned with truth, and rhetoric, concerned with opinion. Virtually the entire philosophic tradition, despite its heresies, accepts the principle that the goal of reason is to win truth not merely from falsity, but from opinion, and that it does so by following logical and rational methods and avoiding methods of confusion and deception. It is a distinction involving method.

The distinction between philosophy and rhetoric, in modern terms passing into a distinction between science and nonscience, may be more definitive of orthodoxy than any conclusions of fact or substance. It is a distinction between legitimate and illegitimate methods and acceptable and unacceptable styles. It is continued in the Platonic dialogues in the related distinction between philosophy and poetry and between acceptable and unacceptable forms of narrative—continued there despite the dramatic form of the dialogues and the continual eristic in which Socrates engages. Legitimate and illegitimate discourses are distinguished less by whether they actually say or manifest plausible and defensible positions than by their style. It is part of the established reading that Plato consistently maintained such a distinction of form and method. I question the standard reading based on Plato's own dramatic style. What cannot be denied is how important that reading has been to the tradition.

There are two fundamental heresies that characterize not so much the positions of the Sophists—who followed many of their predecessors in substance and style—but the distinction between philosophy and eristic. One pertains to the autonomy of standards of truth in contrast with their human relevance—Protagoras' maxim. The other pertains to any distinction involving the legitimacy of discursive forms. It is not simply that what the Sophists advocated was wrong or destructive, but that their style, as with that of the poets, was deficient. That we might take the Sophists seriously (or the poets instead) suggests that philosophy has no absolute authority in virtue of its voice or style, but only whatever authority and legitimacy it is able to establish through its own activities. Combining these two views we conclude that there is no unique relation of philosophy or science to truth, in virtue of their style, only the manifold determinations of knowledge and truth that human beings can establish through their diverse activities.

There is a related consideration. Gorgias' argument is clearly skeptical, although not so clearly relativistic. Yet the skepticism without the relativism does not entail that anyone may do anything he chooses to do with impunity. Even if there were no reality or understanding free from aporia, it would not follow that there is no life or practice with legitimacy and standing. Even with relativism taken to considerable lengths, understood to entail that there are no standards that are invariable with context and situation, it does not follow that there is no difference between truth and falsity, or rightness and wrongness, only that differences are not independent of conditions. What is involved is the possibility that truth and understanding are not grounded in autonomous and universal rules, but must be reinterpreted and reestablished in every local situation.

This is a staggering heresy, one which has returned in contemporary writings that are critical of the tradition. The philosophy that might be brought to an end is one that makes universality and autonomy orthodox. Thus, rereading the Sophists, we find a heresy that is at the center of many present heresies.

The heresy is that philosophy and science have no singular and unique legitimacy. It is not that they have *no* legitimacy, have no right to speak in the name of truth or goodness, but that there is nothing unique to their form or style, their distinctive voices, that gives them greater authority than that of marginal voices. The heresy is that discourses are not marginal because they are intrinsically illegitimate, but because they have been displaced by superior powers.

Does skepticism entail a relativism without credible standards or norms? Must truth be autonomous relative to changing finite conditions? When Gorgias argues that nothing exists and that nothing can be known, but continues to make beautiful speeches and to support noble causes, is the only plausible alternative that his position is contradictory? When a philosopher argues against absolute standards, but denies that he is a relativist without standards, is it legitimate for us to say that he *must* be such a relativist because that is the only alternative to absolute standards? What we do is to impose a certain orthodoxy on the relations among truth and finite conditions that makes it impossible to heed any genuine heresy.

What is at stake is nothing less than the nature of reason itself, especially its heretical nature. Heresy always sounds like sophistry, because the tradition defines its orthodoxy by displacing heresy. Orthodoxy imposes not only standards of truth and falsity, legitimacy and illegitimacy, but generic standards that apply to competing forms of discourse and thought. The alternative is that truth arrives wherever it does and can, in any voice or form, provided that voice has succeeded in rendering itself valid, but there are no universal standards of validation. The weaknesses of the Sophists lie not in their heresies but in their limited sense of aporia. Compared with Heraclitus and Parmenides, their sense of heresy is restricted to the mundane, lacking all sense of the aporetic plenitude of being. Nevertheless, this flattened sense of aporia is itself heretical, despite its limitations, in contrast with the yearning within the tradition for the infinite. What it called for, in the subsequent tradition, was a deeper sense of aporia and inexhaustibility.

The fundamental heresy in the beginnings of philosophy is that being and truth are aporetic. Determinateness is inseparable from indeterminateness and conversely. So deep is this heresy that it has never faded from the tradition, but returns recurrently, countermanded by the sweeping heresy, which later became orthodoxy, that aporia may be overcome by displacing certain voices. This latter heresy is that of orthodoxy. Among the inexhaustibly manifold discourses in which human activities transpire, some have unqualified legitimacy. We must question the assumption that orthodoxy succeeds in obliterating heresy. To the contrary, no tradition can maintain itself without dividing itself. This fundamental truth of reason applies most of all to Plato, the most heretical philosopher of all, who has thoroughly passed into philosophic orthodoxy.

3 PLATO: THE HERESY OF REASON

THE greatest heresy in the history of philosophy, after that of philosophy itself, is found within the works of Plato, the greatest philosopher of all, whose greatness is due in no small part to the presence of this continuing heresy, yet who is all too frequently read neglecting it. Even Whitehead, among the most heretical of philosophers, whose often-quoted line expresses profound admiration for Plato and his influence, does not acknowledge the heresy in question.

> The safest general characterization of the European philosophical tradition is that it consists of a series of footnotes to Plato.[1]

Whitehead goes on to explain that,

> I do not mean the systematic scheme of thought which scholars have doubtfully extracted from his writings. I allude to the wealth of general ideas scattered through them.[2]

It is not, then, Plato's "doctrine" that has defined the philosophical tradition, but the suggestive ideas found throughout his writings.[3] What Whitehead never explicitly recognizes is that these writings are dramatic dialogues. His own acknowledged debt to Plato is expressed entirely in doctrinal terms:

> The things which are temporal arise by their participation in the things which are eternal.[4]

31

This is, indeed, one of the greatest heresies in the history of philosophy, a sublime scene in the drama of same and other. It is the extraordinary view that what is found in ordinary experience is given its reality by something permanent and unchanging that can be grasped only in a magnificent intuition of both being and the good. It is a view that in related forms pervades much of Eastern thought, that expresses what Whitehead calls the "religious intuition." Yet, what is missing even in Whitehead's deep recognition of Plato's importance is any sense of Platonic irony and of the dramatic form of Plato's writings. Although Whitehead doubts that we may find a systematic doctrine within the dialogues, certain doctrinal ideas take precedence. This is the established view of Plato, colored by Whitehead's own profound unorthodoxies. It is the view that within the Platonic dialogues is a view that can be expressed in doctrinal terms.

Even Kierkegaard, whose admiration is unmatched for philosophical irony in general, and Socratic irony in particular, cannot bring himself to ascribe the dramatic and ironic character in the dialogues to Plato.[5] Yet the unbroken dramatic form of the dialogues poses questions that the doctrinal view of Plato cannot answer. One alternative is to distinguish Plato from Socrates, allowing the heretical moments to pass entirely into the latter while the former largely retains his orthodoxy.

Another strategy whereby Platonic heresy may be tamed without denying its irresistibility is to ascribe to Plato a secret doctrine.[6] Such a view conforms to the famous passage in the *Seventh Letter* in which Plato denies that he has ever written anything expressing his most serious thoughts. It is supported by the suggestion, following Aristotle and Simplicius, that Plato had an unwritten doctrine based on number and the indefinite dyad.[7] The difficulty with such a reading is that despite Plato's denial that he has ever written "seriously," the passage is taken entirely "literally." Against such a view, we must consider the alternative that Plato is no more (or less) "literal" and "serious" in any of his writing, including the letters. This alternative is to be conceived, not as limiting Plato's heresy, but as extending it.

What makes the view that Plato's dialogues are written under masks antiheretical is that it leaves him with a doctrine that could have been expressed in explicit form. It finds in Plato the heresy of eternal truth and reality but neglects the heresy that reason has no singular, authentic, and transparent form.

The heresy suggested by the Platonic writings is that the dramatic dialogue form is not a device whereby a more profound doctrine is somehow either obscured or rendered palatable, but is reason itself. Truth belongs to philosophy in a divided and aporetic way. Dialectic here is simply dialogue; philosophy is conversation in all its forms, including arguments and logical proofs but also speeches, irony, and figuration: displacements as well as affirmations; decenterings as well as centerings. It includes written dramatic dialogues as well as the conversation embodied within them. These various forms, interacting and interfering, comprise the authentic forms of truth and reason. No particular form takes precedence over the others.[8]

From the standpoint of the established tradition, such a heresy is almost unintelligible, because it altogether opposes the principle that there is a singular authentic voice in which truth may be spoken.[9] The doctrinal views ascribed to Plato emphasize both the priority of speech over writing and the priority of proof over storytelling. They quite overlook the constant displacements within the dialogues of the allegedly primary voice. That philosophic truth may not lie in positions taken, defended by repeatable and formalizable arguments, is not merely heretical within the established tradition, but unintelligible. Yet the heresy is quite as unacceptable from a "postmodern" point of view because it is virtually unthinkable from such a point of view that Plato himself, who defines the philosophic tradition, quite undermined what became orthodox within it. The tradition carries within it its own countermanding. It is as if there never were an established tradition, at least from the standpoint of its major progenitor.[10] Postmodernism must define the tradition's orthodoxy if it is to be able to posit that tradition's radical revision. It is as essential to postmodernism to define an orthodox view of modernism as it is essential to modernism to define an orthodox view of classicism.

What must be done to establish a heretical reading of Plato is to avoid the temptation to relegate the dramatic moments and ironies to a marginal status. What must be done is to avoid reading the dialogues from the standpoint of later doctrine. There are proofs and doctrines aplenty, but they function within, not apart from, the dramatic structure. Moreover, they are associated with incessant ironies. We find ourselves placed within a dramatic, ironic movement without doctrinal resolution or conclusive proof, as if this movement were philosophy itself. It is as if the millions of words written after Plato by even the greatest philosophers, written in plodding, argumentative prose, were not themselves philosophy, but some moribund form of dogma antagonistic to rational thought.

In this context, we may again consider the famous lines of *Phaedrus* on the defects of writing:

> It is the same with written words: they seem to talk to you as though they were intelligent, but if you ask them anything about what they say, from a desire to be instructed, they go on telling you just the same thing forever. (*Phaedrus*, 275e)[11]

Several ironies are present. One is that the Plato of the theory of ideas, who held that only eternity could be intelligible, is found objecting to the stability of writing over living speech. The mutability of discourse ought to be ascribed to the changeableness of opinion. An alternative is that the "living speech" that Socrates refers to a few lines later is characterized by its dynamism (*dynamis*) more than its stable truth, a movement countermanded by an unchanging contemplative knowledge of eternal forms. A profound incompatibility exists between the notion of a living, mutable speech and the imperatives of a doctrine of unchanging forms. A similar incompatibility exists between Plato's rejection of mimetic narrative in Book II of *Republic* and the fundamentally repetitive movement of the theory of ideas.

A second major irony is that writing does not and cannot in fact tell us the same thing forever. Rather, always reading philosophic writing in the same way constitutes orthodoxy. A third, related irony is that speech cannot escape from the defects of writing, but, as the dialogues constantly tell us, language and even thought suffer from the same dangers of becoming moribund in repetition. One suggestion is that Plato is advocating a heretical over a doctrinal discourse. Writing tends to become orthodoxy. A fourth irony, however, the irony of history, is that without the writings of Plato, the ironies of Socrates would be totally lost. Without the writings of Plato, the heretical movement of Platonic thought would be unavailable to us.

> And once a thing is put in writing, the composition, whatever it may be, drifts all over the place, getting into the hands not only of those who understand it, but equally of those who have no business with it; it doesn't know how to address the right people, and not address the wrong. And when it is illtreated and unfairly abused it always needs its parent to come to its help, being unable to defend or help itself. (*Phaedrus*, 276)

Read as criticism of writing compared with speech, this is entirely untenable. Read as ironic acknowledgment of the aporetic conditions of discourse—not of writing alone, but of any epistemic activity—it is profoundly true, qualified by the irony that there is no parent to defend any such orphan from abuse. There is nothing we can do to avoid the misunderstandings that pertain to any shared, public activity (nor, for that matter, to preclude the discoveries that are the result of alternative readings of established texts). A further irony is that no one has been more subject to such abuse than Plato and no one has been more immortalized than Socrates by the Platonic writings.

The issue defined in *Phaedrus* recurs throughout the dialogues. It is that of truth and representation, of the indeterminateness of the relationship between reason and any of its manifestations—speech, writing, or thought.[12] In the extreme, essential to heresy, there is the possibility that the indeterminateness pertains to reason as well as to its manifestations. The question is whether there is an authoritative form of discourse in which truth may be spoken or written. Socrates' caveats concerning writing suggest far less the primacy of speech over writing and more the denial that any representation carries authority of itself. The question Plato poses concerns not a contrast of rhetoric with philosophy or writing with speech, but of the corruption of truth by its other. What the dialogues present us with are manifold forms of such corruption conjoined with manifold forms of redemption, with the qualification that no form of representation can distinguish these from each other. Corruption and redemption, error and truth, cohabit incessantly in the Platonic dialogues. The question of how to distinguish reason from unreason is at the center of the dialogues, and functions there dynamically and changeably without stable resolution. Platonic doctrine offers a naive and defective view of truth compared with the variations on truth and error embodied in the dialogues themselves. Rather, the movements toward epistemic authority in the dialogues are always accompanied by heretical displacements, as if only the two together might constitute truth.[13]

To write on all or many of the Platonic dialogues at once poses a special difficulty, the suggestion that only by reading the dialogues together can one develop a fair reading of Plato. What is presupposed is that there is a unified doctrine, at least a unified reading that opposes doctrine. The alternative is that no unified reading of the dialogues may be appropriate—or a unified reading of the history of philosophy. Nor may a selective or disunified reading be appropriate instead. Only a detailed reading of one or two dialogues can convey the force of Platonic irony. Only applications of such a reading to other, "doctrinal" dialogues can indicate how such irony must influence a doctrinal reading. What is needed is to understand the dialogues collectively without "making sense" of them "as a whole."

Before undertaking a detailed dramatic reading of *Meno* with applications throughout other dialogues, we may consider a brief characterization of the Platonic doctrine. It is stated succinctly in *Phaedo* and *Republic*, not, however, without major displacements.

> If all these absolute realities, such as beauty and goodness, which we are always talking about, really exist, if it is to them, as we rediscover our own former knowledge of them, that we refer, as copies to their patterns, all the objects of our physical perception—if these realities exist, does it not follow that our

souls must exist too even before our birth, whereas if they do not exist, our discussions would seem to be a waste of time? (*Phaedo*, 76e)

> This image then, dear Glaucon, we must apply as a whole to all that has been said, likening the region revealed through sight to the habitation of the prison, and the light of the fire in it to the power of the sun. And if you assume that the ascent and the contemplation of the things above is the soul's ascension to the intelligible region, you will not miss my surmise, since that is what you desire to hear. But God knows whether it is true. (*Republic*, 517c)

There are important ironies in these passages and throughout these dialogues—the recurrent hypothetical suggestions in the first, the appeal to God and to what Glaucon desires to hear in the second. Leaving the ironies aside, we may crudely summarize the Platonic doctrine as follows, always emphasizing the same in its agon with its other:

1. What is intelligible must be eternal and undivided, while what is sensible is changeable and divisible.
2. True knowledge of any reality, sensible or otherwise, depends on knowledge of the eternal form or idea in which it partakes; therefore, what is intelligible in divided experience always rests on a unitary, undivided form.
3. Such knowledge cannot be acquired from sensible experience, but must always have been possessed by the immortal soul, and is but recollected as the result of sensible experience.
4. Sensible experience is divided, aporetic; eternal reality is absolutely consistent with itself, indivisible, independent, and self-sufficient: a supreme triumph of the same.
5. Both knowledge and being are mimetic, the repetition of unchanging, eternal forms.
6. Absolute reality is utterly beyond sensible experience, but is nevertheless knowable by the immortal soul.
7. The highest idea is that of the good; virtue is knowledge of the good.
8. Everyone pursues the good; no one intentionally acts to harm himself.[14]

Missing in the above list is any reference to the gods, without whom little understanding of the Greeks is possible. Here different orthodoxies give us different readings:

9a. The gods inhabit unchanging eternity with the forms.
9b. The gods define the limits of reason and experience.

That such a doctrine appears recurrently in the Platonic dialogues is unquestionable, although it appears in full-blown form in very few of the dialogues and is always surrounded by ironic displacement. More questionable are the idea of doctrine in Plato and how such a doctrine actually functions in the dialogues.

To read a dialogue as a dialogue, rather than in terms of certain doctrinal passages, is to consider its setting and events intrinsic. Closely related is an awareness of the reader as an invisible interlocutor to whom the dialogue presents itself. The opening speeches of any dialogue define who is speaking, under what circumstances, and to whom. It is important that *Apology* and *Phaedo* transpire in the shadow of Socrates' impending death, not least because his references to the immortality of the soul are counsels of reassurance to his friends more than they are proofs of immortality. It is important that Euthyphro is leaving the Athenian court after having brought charges against his father while Socrates is on the way to the same court to answer his accusers. Similarly, *Laws* is said to be an entertainment to occupy the time involved in the long walk taken by the interlocutors. (*Laws*, 625b)

Meno begins with a question:

Can you tell me, Socrates—is virtue something that can be taught? (*Meno*, 70a)

Who is Meno, and what kind of interlocutor is he? Plato places him for us immediately. (70b) He has returned to Athens from his studies with Gorgias. We may assume he is young and brash ("confident") to approach Socrates to try out his newly learned argumentative tricks on him. His name means "stay put," but rings of memory and recollection (*anamnēsis*).[15] He represents the rule of the same. We may also know that the historical Meno was regarded by Xenophon and Ktesias as an unscrupulous and vicious person.[16] Twice in the dialogue are references to Meno as a tyrant. (*Meno*, 76b, 86d) We need not suppose that his full character is manifested in the dialogue. What we must consider, instead, is the relationship established in the dialogue between him and Socrates.

We may surmise that Meno's question is one to which he has a memorized answer. The dialogue turns repeatedly on the relationship between memory and wisdom. Whatever Socrates says, Meno has a prepared "move" ready. But Socrates will not play the game. Indeed, he shows nothing but contempt for such "moves" when not concomitants of genuine inquiry, and constantly refers to his own lack of knowledge to empha-

size this point. The game here is that of philosophy. More accurately, it
is that of reason. Philosophic truth is far closer to ignorance than to skill.

> The fact is that far from knowing whether it can be taught, I
> have no idea what virtue itself is. (*Meno*, 71a)

Everybody knows what virtue is, or at least claims to know it. Meno is
taken aback. And with this unsettling displacement, he runs the risk of
losing the confidence that inspired his opening question.

> But is this true about yourself, Socrates that you don't even know
> what virtue is? Is this the report that we to take home about
> you? (*Meno*, 71c)

Socrates, of course, replies,

> Not only that, you may say also that, to the best of my belief, I
> have never yet met anyone who did know. (*Meno*, 71c)

Gorgias, among others, is the referent.
    Shall we suppose that Socrates blithely lies to his interlocutors, or
may we assume instead that he means what he says: he does not know
anything, and certainly does not know what virtue is? He recurrently
claims to be ignorant, even in the later dialogues.

> I am so far like the midwife that I cannot myself give birth to
> wisdom, and the common reproach is true, that, though I ques-
> tion others, I can myself bring nothing to light because there is
> no wisdom in me. (*Theaetetus*, 150c)

Closely associated with this famous image of a midwife is Socrates'
emphasis on the exorcism of false doctrines more than the revelation of
truth. He is barren, and cannot bring forth a child. The compensation is
that he will not bring forth a monster.

> Perhaps when I examine your statements I may judge one or
> another of them to be an unreal phantom. If I then take the
> abortion from you and cast it away, do not be savage with me
> like a woman robbed of her first child. (*Theaetetus*, 151c)

> Then supposing you should ever henceforth try to conceive
> afresh, Theaetetus, if you succeed, your embryo thoughts will be
> the better as a consequence of today's scrutiny, and if you remain

barren you will be gentler and more agreeable to your compan-
ions, having the good sense not to fancy you know what you do
not know. For that, and no more, is all that my art can effect;
nor have I any of that knowledge possessed by all the great
admirable men of our own day or of the past. (*Theaetetus*, 210c)

How can so explicit a rejection of doctrine be compatible with the doctrines ascribed to Plato in the standard readings? What is involved is the
question of doctrine itself—whether "knowledge" is something that can
be possessed and utilized upon call; whether, indeed, all claims to truth
are not more monstrous than they are productive. In this context, the
rejection of writing in *Phaedrus* may be given a different meaning. The
greatest philosophic sins are doctrine and proof; both produce monsters
more than wisdom.

There is a striking early passage where Socrates explicitly rejects a
major part of the doctrine typically ascribed to him.

How will wisdom, regarded only as a knowledge of knowledge or science of science, ever teach him that he knows health,
or that he knows building? (*Charmides*, 170c)

A science of science has no object, effectively knows nothing. In this
way, it resembles philosophy and art. How could knowledge of the good,
of virtue, even of oneself, resolve this difficulty? To the contrary, in this
agnostic and agonistic form, Socrates' affirmation of ignorance expresses
the conviction that no form of truth can exercise authority over other
forms of truth. Reason divides into diverse sciences and arts, and there
is no knowledge over them, whether of knowledge itself, of virtue, or
the good. Knowledge of the good is knowledge of nothing. Refutation
and contention are the purifying moments in the activity of understanding that opposes doctrine and self-satisfaction.

The questions of what virtue is and whether it can be taught permeate the dialogues, typically ending both inconclusively and contentiously. *Protagoras*, for example, raises the question of whether virtue
can be taught (*Protagoras*, 119) and concludes with its return without
resolution. (*Protagoras*, 361d) That we cannot inquire into whether virtue can be taught without knowing first what virtue is presents the traditional reading of the dialogues. It presupposes that Plato (and his
protagonist Socrates) actually believe they know what virtue is. The
alternative is that virtue is not something that can be known determinately.
This alternative is supported by the inconclusiveness of the dialogues
wherever virtue is in question. There is no dialogue where virtue is
explicitly defined, though there are dialogues that discuss different vir-

tues and their interrelations. The heretical alternative is supported by the ironies in even the latest dialogues where they concern virtue.

> The life of the aspirant to victory at Olympia or Pytho leaves no leisure for any other tasks whatever, . . . the whole day and night is verily not long enough for one who is engaged on this sole work of getting the full and perfect benefit from these pursuits . . . . In fact, that any citizen whatsoever should spend the whole of any night in unbroken sleep, and not let all his servants see him always awake and astir before anyone else in the house, must be unanimously pronounced a disgrace and an act unworthy of a free man, ... (*Laws*, 807ce)

It is among the worst lives, not the best, to be obsessed by virtue, not only because such an obsessive person will lead a driven, guilt-ridden life, but because such a person will be a torment to those around him.

The drama in *Meno* lies not so much in Meno's question concerning virtue, not even in Socrates' counter, but in their interaction on the question of the acquisition of knowledge. The entire dialogue turns on the characters that inhabit it. On the reading I am suggesting, Meno is just returned from a course in eristic, eager to try it out on any passerby. On these terms, the dramatic question becomes, what is the appropriate response from Socrates to such an accostation?

Similar dramatic beginnings define the reading of other dialogues. The dialogues may be classified by their principal interlocutors: young, inexperienced Greeks in *Crito, Phaedo, Phaedrus, Theaetetus*, even *Cratylus*; experienced ordinary citizens in *Meno, Euthyphro, Charmides*, but especially *Republic*; serious and frequently famous philosophers, in *Gorgias, Protagoras, Parmenides*, but including most of the later dialogues: *Sophist, Statesman, Philebus*, and *Timaeus*. These differ in many ways, among themselves in each group as well as among the groups. But a striking similarity exists within each group: the students are genially and encouragingly confronted with the need to think for themselves; ordinary Greek citizens are either shown their ignorance almost contemptuously or, where they display openmindedness, are subjected to lectures and told stories of great persuasiveness but little philosophical profundity; the major discussions are restricted to the dialogues with established philosophers, known or unknown.

It follows that the setting of *Republic* is all-important. It is a gathering of ordinary young Greeks after a festival, rather like a celebration by alumni after a college football game. It takes place between two festivals, almost an entertainment—as is *Symposium*. There is not a single interlocutor present, including Thrasymachus, toward whom Socrates must show the slightest philosophic respect. On the other hand, the setting requires from him great social tact and courtesy. If we ask ourselves what kind of dialogue on the subject of justice would be appropriate in the home of a wealthy businessman and his well-educated son and his friends, the answer must be, a catchy speech with uplifting moral overtones, but not too much deep philosophical thought. By way of contrast, where the young Socrates carries on philosophical discussions on the subject of his own theory of ideas in the company of two major philosophers, the issues are treated far more seriously. *Parmenides* is indeed, as Hegel recognized, among the most important of the Platonic dialogues, not least because it is where the theory of ideas is brought under strenuous criticism, where both philosophy and being are shown to be profoundly aporetic.

Furthermore, there are dialogues whose settings are of grave importance, but which suggest reassurance and encouragement more than deep philosophic thought. The theory of ideas is present in a pure form in very few of the dialogues, but specifically in *Phaedo*. What must be added is that the setting requires not philosophy from Socrates, but consolation.

> You are afraid, as children are, that when the soul emerges from the body the wind may really puff it away and scatter it, especially when a person does not die on a calm day but with with a gale blowing.
>
> Cebes laughed. Suppose that we are afraid, Socrates, he said, and try to convince us. Or rather don't suppose that it is we that are afraid. Probably even in us there is a little boy who has these childish terrors. Try to persuade him not to be afraid of death as though it were a bogy.
>
> What you should do, said Socrates, is to say a magic spell over him every day until you have charmed his fears away. (*Phaedo*, 77e)

What is required are magic spells and potions rather than propositional proofs.

The question in *Meno* is whether virtue can be taught, raising two fundamental issues of the Platonic doctrine: what knowledge is and whether it can be acquired. There are, however, the equally important questions of what and who Meno is, indicated by his name but also by an important dramatic movement. (*Meno*, 70b)[17] Who or what one is pertains fundamentally to the questions of what virtue and wisdom are as well as how they are to be acquired.

There is a repeated irony in *Meno* that although Socrates would like to consider the question of what virtue is, the discussion returns repeatedly to the acquisition of knowledge. The irony is compounded by Socrates' recurrent denial that he knows what virtue is. One possibility is that he knows but will not say. This is analogous to the position that there is a Platonic doctrine hidden behind the dialogue form. Another possibility is that knowledge of virtue cannot be possessed. Generalizing, knowledge lies not in what is known, but in the activity whereby we know it—in unceasing dialectic rather than the ideas, in the dialogues rather than in their doctrines. The reason is that both being and knowledge are aporetic, and that the only positive response to aporia is unending philosophic activity, neither skepticism nor doctrine.

If so, then the hidden purpose of the dialogue is not to teach Meno anything he does not already know—any principles, facts, or methods of argument—but to transform the way he thinks about the practice of philosophy. The dialogue concerns knowledge and wisdom not as they might be possessed, but as they might be pursued. It must be contrasted, then, with the very different treatment of the acquisition of knowledge in *Republic*. By comparison, the latter cannot be taken very seriously.

What is essential is to get Meno to participate in ongoing inquiry, represented by conversation and dialogue. An important heresy, then, is that possession of arguments and counterarguments, proofs and counterproofs, doctrines and counterdoctrines, is not philosophy. Rather, philosophy is conversation in all its forms, one that requires a spirit of openminded participation. For a major part of the philosophic and scientific tradition, the attitude of the participant is relatively minor, as long as he is honest, for the arguments and evidence work independent of his relationship to them. It is worth noting, in this context, Whitehead's rejection of proof as second-rate:

> The thesis that I am developing conceives "proof," in the strict sense of that term, as a feeble second-rate procedure. When the word "proof" has been uttered, the next notion to enter the mind is "half-heartedness." Unless proof has produced self-evidence and thereby rendered itself unnecessary, it has issued in a second-rate state of mind, producing action devoid of understanding. Self-evidence is the basic fact on which all greatness supports itself. But "proof" is one of the routes by which self-evidence is often obtained.[18]

Self-evidence will not do, and is reminiscent of the worst features of apriorism, although it is essential to any understanding. What is heretical here is the suggestion that logical proof in philosophy (and even science) is second-rate, deceptive, even misleading. Philosophic truth is not won by argument as such, but by participation in complex and divided philosophic activities.

A singular feature of Platonic irony now presents itself. The question, never answered in the dialogue, which Socrates claims must precede the question of whether and how virtue may be acquired is what virtue is. This is, doctrinally speaking, the fundamental Platonic question. Dramatically speaking, the only function of this question in *Meno* is to frame the discussion of truth. Yet, we must suppose that it is essential because it both begins and ends the dialogue. It therefore is both fundamental to the dialogue and misleading within it. The irony is that truth is used to obscure as much as to clarify.[19]

The question of what virtue is passes in virtually every dialogue in which it is broached into the question of its relationship to knowledge. It is in part a question of the relationship of wisdom to practice, but also of knowledge to opinion. The striking possibility, represented by the conclusion in *Meno* that virtue is a divine gift, therefore only true opinion, is that knowledge cannot be distinguished generically from opinion, just as reason cannot be distinguished from unreason by forms and rules. Neither virtue nor knowledge here follows by rule, nor is the relationship of virtue to knowledge one of form. The law of the same does not hold. There is rather an extraordinary sense of the indeterminateness of the good life and of virtuous practice, later expressed by Aristotle in terms of *phronēsis*. Plato suggests, moreover, that this indeterminateness in practice can be represented only in dialogue form, that of conversation. If virtue is knowledge, it is not science, neither *theōria* nor *epistēmē*.

No one knows what virtue is, including Socrates. To Meno, however, it is a simple matter. Yet he commits all the standard Platonic mistakes: offering a list of virtues instead of one essence (72a); defining a whole by its part (73d). Two of Meno's comments in this context are worth noting. When Socrates suggests that there must be something common to bees and to health that defines them, and analogously, to the many virtues, Meno says that:

> I somehow feel that this is not on the same level as the other cases. (*Meno*, 73a)

Apart from the Platonic doctrine, this is what almost anyone would say: there is nothing in common among the virtues, justice, courage, honesty, etc. They are not the same. Concepts such as mass and velocity may have essences, but not normative concepts. We might add Wittgenstein's argument that no concepts have essences, but are defined by networks of family resemblances.[20] On the Platonic doctrine, every concept is intelligible only in terms of its essence or form. Yet in *Meno*, there are suggestions that there is no form of virtue though there may be a form to bees and health. Virtue, Meno wants to say, is different from the others, and he says it twice.

> I cannot yet grasp it as you want, a single virtue covering them all, as I do in other instances. (*Meno*, 74b)

Meno quite understands the nature of essences in other cases. Virtue, he wants to say, is somehow different. It is indeed different, and Plato knows it. For, the second half of the dialogue presents the explicit conclusion that we cannot have knowledge of virtue, only true opinion. Quite apart from this, Socrates surely knows that virtue is different from the other cases. Yet he never replies to Meno on this point. Where we may find a reply is in *Philebus*, where pleasures are shown to be as different as possible despite their common name. (*Philebus*, 13a) Surely the same heterogeneity pertains to virtues. Yet the general Platonic reply to the question of what virtue is lies not within any dialogue, but among them: virtue is the result of practicing human excellences through unending dialogue. Here the image of Socrates in *Symposium* is fundamental: his courage and fortitude are unexcelled, but they inhabit his life as part of its nature. Courage is no virtue apart from the constant interrogation of its nature. *Symposium* is philosophy itself.

The explicit reply Socrates gives to Meno on whether there is a common essence to virtue is through the example of shape, quite ignoring the issue of whether virtue is unique. Shape is the only thing that always accompanies color. (75c) Meno clearly is not satisfied, casts about for some kind of reply, and asks:

> If somebody says that he doesn't know what color is, but is no better off with it than he is with shape, what sort of answer have you given him, do you think? (*Meno*, 75c)

Socrates' answer is one of his harshest and most significant. It requires detailed consideration. We may approach it by noting that Meno's question is ambiguous. Its form may express genuine puzzlement: you have explained something in terms of something else that I do not understand. But its form may also close off all interrogation and explanation by opening up an infinite regress. We can define something only in terms of something else which must also be defined. Moreover, everyone knows what color is, although it may be extraordinarily difficult to define explicitly.

Socrates' reply is one of a handful of comments in the dialogue that express the central movement of its dramatic structure. These occur in a circular movement after every significant theoretical advance. The context here is that Meno has refused, either out of genuine puzzlement or duplicitous obstinacy, to pursue the interrogation. The possibility that he is more contentious than puzzled must be confronted. The possibility that dialogue is more agonistic and adversarial than consensual is central within the dialogue form itself. Socrates does not reply to Meno's question, but to what lies behind it.

> A true one, and if my questioner were of the clever, disputatious, and quarrelsome kind, I should say to him, "You have heard my answer. If it is wrong, it is for you to take up the argument and refute it." However, when friendly people, like you and me, want to converse with each other, one's reply must be milder and more conducive to discussion. By that I mean that it must not only be true, but must employ terms with which the questioner admits he is familiar. (*Meno*, 75cd)[21]

First, the answer must be true. Second, where the discussion is agonistic, of a polemical nature, then it is up to the interlocutor to refute it. But of course, we are not engaged in such a polemic, but engaged in a friendly discussion. What is required is a beginning in familiar notions. Therefore, Socrates defines shape "à la Gorgias" as "an effluence from shape commensurate with sight and perceptible by it." (76d) Meno finds this an excellent answer, because, as Socrates notes, "No doubt it is the sort you are used to." (76e) Rhetorically, he displaces the possibility that Meno is a disputatious, contentious sort of person by demanding that if he can, he may refute Socrates' definition. If he cannot, perhaps he will return to the discussion with an open mind.

What is at stake, dramatically more than doctrinally, is a fundamental truth: knowledge can be acquired only through a movement from same to other. Both sides of this principle must be emphasized. The relationship between heresy and orthodoxy is at the center of the dialogue. Meno approaches Socrates with a mind closed to any possibility of learning from him, closed to novelty. What is required is that his mind be opened. That will only happen if Socrates can speak in terms familiar to him. Socrates' recurrent denial that he possesses knowledge is both intelligible and significant in this context: doctrinal knowledge closes off any possibility of learning anything that may challenge the doctrine. Heretical knowledge, even the acquisition of novel insights, is incompatible with any sense of doctrine.

Meno accepts Socrates' definition of shape because it is "high-minded" and familiar, and is eager to continue the discussion. (77a) Socrates' purpose has been in part fulfilled. What must be noted are his extraordinary remarks concerning this definition:

> Nevertheless, son of Alexidemus, I am convinced that the other is better, and I believe you would agree with me if you had not, as you told me yesterday, to leave before the Mysteries, but could stay and be initiated. (*Meno*, 76e)

Meno does not notice these words nor does he notice similar self-denials when they recur.

This form of recantation is among the most important devices whereby Plato signals ironic displacement in the midst of a dramatic discussion. It typically occurs where Socrates has succeeded in making a persuasive argument against a weaker interlocutor, frequently utilizing eristic devices and duplicity. Whoever looks to Socrates himself for proof of the efficacy of the Socratic method cannot but be struck by how duplicitous he typically is, as if his own method could not possibly establish rational thought in his interlocutors, but effectively coerces them to his point of view. Nevertheless, after having made his point, having won his argument, Socrates frequently recants in an ironic aside. "You are convinced, but I am not so sure." After Meno has indicated that he would stay if he is given more answers like the definition of shape, Socrates replies,

> You may be sure I shan't be lacking in keenness to do so, both for your sake and mine, but I'm afraid I may not be able to do it often. (*Meno*, 77a)

The reason is that these are not Socrates' answers but those of others.

Such explicit recantations—"I am not so sure"; "I am not convinced"; "I preferred the other formulation"—manifest a recurrent form of Platonic irony where the dialogue and its activity take precedence over doctrine, where the other is acknowledged within the same. In this case, Socrates clearly displaces the definition of shape preferred by Meno: the other was better. What must be noticed is that after the most important argument of the entire dialogue, ostensibly proving the doctrine of recollection through the questioning of Meno's slave, Socrates says something very similar. To Meno's words, "Somehow or other I believe you are right," Socrates replies:

> I think I am. I shouldn't like to take my oath on the whole story, ... (*Meno*, 86bc)

The ironies are so strong here because we are not to take any part of the slave sequence as true except for its conclusion, explicitly stated by Socrates entirely independent of the doctrine of recollection.

... one thing I am ready to fight for as long as I can, in word and act—that is, that we shall be better, braver, and more active men if we believe it right to look for what we don't know than if we believe there is no point in looking because what we don't know we can never discover. (*Meno*, 86c)

We cannot doubt that we can acquire knowledge, and its discovery is, like memory, miraculous. We cannot doubt the miracle of heretical discovery.

There are similar displacements throughout the dialogues, almost always at crucial moments. In the midst of his most outrageous arguments to Hermogenes in the *Cratylus* on the truth of names, Socrates tells him

... you had better watch me and see that I do not play tricks with you. (*Cratylus*, 393d)

He says a bit later on,

I dare say that I am talking great nonsense . . . .
My good friend, I have discovered a hive of wisdom.
    Of what nature?
Well, rather ridiculous, and yet plausible. (*Cratylus*, 401e)

He also says that

... if I am not careful, before tomorrow's dawn I shall be wiser than I ought to be. (*Cratylus*, 399a)

To Hermogenes' comment,

Indeed, Socrates, you make surprising progress,

Socrates replies,

I am run away with . . . .
But I am not yet at my utmost speed. (*Cratylus*, 410e)

But most important of all, when he turns to Cratylus, toward the end of the dialogue, to take the opposite position, Socrates says,

I am by no means positive, Cratylus, in the view which Hermogenes and myself have worked out, ... (*Cratylus*, 428b)

And the dialogue concludes with Cratylus' words, after Socrates makes a speech suggestive of the theory of Ideas:

> Very good, Socrates. I hope, however, that you will continue to think about these things yourself. (*Cratylus*, 474e)

That he must and does think about them reveals itself in the constant return in the dialogues to the question of language in relation to both reality and wisdom. If *Cratylus* is the only dialogue in which language is considered in the modern context of names and reference, most of the dialogues concern the nature of representation.

In a striking passage in *Charmides*, Socrates introduces his favorite image of a philosopher-statesman as pilot with the words,

> I dare say that what I am saying is nonsense, ...
> Hear, then, I said, my own dream—whether coming through the horn or the ivory gate, I cannot tell. (*Charmides*, 173b)

Even in *Republic*, to the question of whether the guardians will not be miserable, Socrates replies,

> . . . while it would not surprise us if these men thus living prove to be the most happy, yet the object on which we fixed our eyes in the establishment of our state was not the exceptional happiness of any one class but the greatest possible happiness of the city as a whole. (*Republic*, 420b)

What would not suprise us is the truth, but Socrates is not prepared to argue for it. In an even more striking passage, after exiling the poets for their deceptions and remoteness from truth and reality, Socrates suggests:

> Then may she not justly return from this exile after she has pleaded her defense, whether in lyric or other measure? (*Republic*, 607d)

The poets may plead their case in lyric form; others may plead their case in prosaic form. But the lyric form is intrinsically incapable of truth. Alternatively, the entire discussion of art as imitation is pervaded with ironic displacement.

Similarly, in the context of his own death and the reassurances required by his friends, Socrates comments on his own arguments concerning recollection,

> And if you don't find that convincing, . . . see whether this
> appeals to you . . . , (*Phaedo*, 56)

a strange remark where truth is involved. Similarly, he speaks in a hypothetical mode after he has apparently given a formidable proof of the
doctrine of recollection.

> Well, how do we stand now, Simmias? If all these absolute
> realities, such as beauty and goodness, which we are always
> talking about, really exist, ... (*Phaedo*, 76e)

Socrates is required in *Phaedo* to offer a proof on impossible terms.
What we may suppose he offers instead is no proof at all, but consolation.

> . . . no one but a fool is entitled to face death with confidence,
> unless he can prove that the soul is absolutely immortal and
> indestructible. Otherwise, everyone must always feel apprehen-
> sion at the approach of death, for fear that in this particular
> separation from the body his soul may be finally and utterly
> destroyed. (*Phaedo*, 88b)

Socrates' answer is no answer at all, because he openly admits that he
must offer it even if it is false.

> If my theory is really true, it is right to believe it, while, even if
> death is extinction, at any rate during this time before my death
> I shall be less likely to distress my companions by giving way to
> self-pity . . . . (*Phaedo*, 91b)

Even more important, the proof is hypothetical.

> I am assuming the existence of absolute beauty and goodness and
> magnitude and all the rest of them. If you grant my assumptions
> and admit that they exist, I hope with their help to explain causation
> to you, and to find a proof that the soul is immortal. (*Phaedo*, 100b)

For he can never explain causation on these terms. Tallness and short-
ness do not explain why particular things are tall and short. (*Phaedo*,
100d) The wonderful story Socrates tells, after all the arguments have
done their work, includes the comment, transparent in its irony,

> Of course, no reasonable man ought to insist that the facts
> are exactly as I have described them. But that either this or

> something very like it is a true account of our souls and their future habitations—since we have clear evidence that the soul is immortal—this, I think, is both a reasonable contention and a belief worth risking, for the risk is a noble one. (*Phaedo*, 114d)

The presence of the stories in *Phaedo* is very important because it suggests both that the arguments are not conclusive and that the stories are. To those who claim that the stories Socrates tells are persuasive while the arguments are rationally compelling, the reply is that such readings do not pay close enough attention to the dramatic structure and its displacements. No "knock-down" arguments exist in the dialogues except, agonistically, to knock down a stubborn opponent or charm an interlocutor into submission.

Returning to *Meno*: Meno must again attempt to define virtue unitarily rather than plurally. His second efforts are more sophisticated, but they succeed no better than the first. Virtue is the "power of acquiring good things." (78c) Socrates' criticism is that such a power is not virtuous unless it is accompanied by virtue, therefore that we have substituted a part for the whole. (79c) Here we cannot help but be struck by the similarity between this argument and Meno's previous question concerning color.

> If somebody says that he doesn't know what color is, but is no better off with it than he is with shape, what sort of answer have you given him, do you think? (*Meno*, 75c)

> Don't you agree that the same question needs to be put? Does anyone know what a part of virtue is, without knowing the whole? (*Meno*, 79c)

Socrates says that he and Meno "rejected the type of answer that employs terms which are still in question and not yet agreed upon." (79d) But they did nothing of the sort. Rather, the point of the example was to show that there is no avoiding a familiar beginning in pursuing knowledge. Virtue cannot be defined in terms of anything more familiar than itself. There is no analysis of virtue that does not begin with virtue, no knowledge of justice that does not presuppose it, no knowledge of anything that does not begin with something known.

Not only does Socrates have no compunction about utilizing eristic arguments when it suits him, but such arguments are employed less to prepare the way to more theoretical matters than to coerce Meno agonistically to submit to the Socratic method. What is altogether missing to this point in the dialogue is any acknowledgment that Meno has in

fact made progress, that he has attempted a genuine definition, whatever its limitations (leaving aside the question of what it would mean
here to make progress toward understanding virtue). Instead, Socrates
tells Meno to go back to the beginning. No wonder Meno breaks out
exasperatedly in one of his two major images:

> I think that not only in outward appearance but in other respects
> as well you are exactly like the flat sting ray that one meets in
> the sea. Whenever anyone comes into contact with it, it numbs
> him, and that is the sort of thing that you seem to be doing to
> me now. (*Meno*, 80ab)

He goes on to note that such behavior is regarded as criminal by most
people.

> In my opinion you are well advised not to leave Athens and live
> abroad. If you behaved like this as a foreigner in another coun-
> try, you would most likely be arrested as a wizard. (*Meno*, 80c)

Setting aside the irony that Socrates was arrested in Athens for such activities, we must pause to consider the images of a stingray and a wizard
(*goēteyeis*).[22] For Meno surely means that the numbness that he feels is
destructive and should be avoided. Yet what he is discussing is heresy, an
encounter with a genuinely novel point of view. The traditional model
of reason is that whatever is discovered fits into the mind like an old
shoe, familiar and comfortable. Socrates is instead encountered like a
catastrophe. The result is a divided sense of philosophic reason: magic,
trickery, and illumination. The complexity of the image is repeated in the
pharmakon, both a poison and a medicine.[23] The subject is that of rational
heresy: the thought of something so unfamiliar that the mind is numbed
and one feels that everything one has ever known has been shaken.

> I have spoken about virtue hundreds of times, held forth often
> on the subject in front of large audiences, and very well too, or
> so I thought. Now I can't even say what it is. (*Meno*, 80a)

The subject of *Meno* here is heresy itself, the discovery that what
one thought one knew, familiarly, one no longer knows. It is the radical
side of *phronēsis*. On one hand lies despair. On the other, it is Socrates'
purpose in life to confront those who claim to possess wisdom to show
them that they lack it. The first discovery essential to further discovery
is that what one thought one knows is not knowledge. Socrates speaks
directly to this in his *Apology*.

> The wisest of you men is he who has realized, like Socrates, that in respect of wisdom he is really worthless. (*Apology*, 23b)

In order to know, we must be ignorant and know that we are ignorant. Meno has travelled a rocky course to an essential discovery: what he thought he knew about virtue he does not know. We must only add that following Socrates' example, there is no end to such ignorance. Skepticism does not follow: what follows is heresy. True knowledge is always heretical.

> It isn't that, knowing the answers myself, I perplex other people. The truth is rather that I infect them also with the perplexity I feel myself. (*Meno*, 80d)

Such perplexity is inseparable from, even indistinguishable from knowledge and even wisdom. For what it makes possible is inquiry and investigation, impossible within the law of the same.

> So with virtue now. I don't know what it is. . . . I am ready to carry out, together with you, a joint investigation and inquiry into what it is. (*Meno*, 80d)

There is no form of knowledge that is not an obstacle to further knowledge, no knowledge that does not inhibit (but also facilitate) discovery. Knowledge is inseparable from true rhetoric, a fusion of poetic, religious, and erotic madness.[24] Reason and desire dance around each other inescapably. That is why knowledge is of necessity heretical.

Meno is still not ready to capitulate. His last defense is the paradox of learning, bringing us to the doctrine of recollection, a supreme return of the same.

> But how will you look for something when you don't in the least know what it is? . . . even if you come right up against it, how will you know that what you have found is the thing you didn't know? (*Meno*, 80e)

Socrates calls this a trick argument. But he never explains why it is a trick. Indeed, he takes it so seriously that he spends the next nine pages addressing it. (80d-86d) It is time for a story, the one place in the dialogue where the gods appear:

> Thus the soul, since it is immortal and has been born many times, and has seen all things both here and in the other world, has learned everything that is. (*Meno*, 81bc)

That there are such stories in the Platonic dialogues, typically ascribed to poetic, priestly, or divine authority, is among their striking features, as captivating as their dramatic form and significant in the same ways. In the midst of some of the most technical and demanding philosophic discussions and arguments known, recurrently, Socrates breaks off and tells a fascinating story. Why does he do this? The answers, analogous to those we considered in relation to the dramatic form, are that the stories are masks obscuring a deeper truth that can be known and understood only by the elect, that the stories are rhetorical, persuasive forms to replace philosophical argument where that would be inappropriate given the dramatic circumstances, and that the stories *are* philosophy—not perhaps its only form, but not a second-rate form either.

We may pause here to consider briefly several of the other famous stories in the dialogues. Even in *Apology*, there is a reference, if not quite a story, to the authority of the god at Delphi, who in answer to Chaerephon's question as to whether anyone is wiser than Socrates, "replied that there was no one. Except that Chaerephon is dead, so his brother will testify in his place." (21a) Such an appeal is of no value as evidence. But that is certainly among the points of these stories: to serve in place of evidence and proof. A doctrinal reading of Plato is that the irony goes no further than to juxtapose the emptiness of mythology against the veracity of philosophy. A heretical reading would be that there is no greater veracity to proof and argument than to inconclusive dialogues and the stories within them. The heretical reading is supported by the crucial role played by so many of the stories. Indeed, wherever the discussion becomes important, we may expect a fascinating story that stands on its own apart from any prior proofs. The gods appear at the limits of intelligibility.

In Phaedo, after Socrates has given his major arguments for the immortality of the soul, he tells the story of how such an immortal soul is guided by its guardian spirit and how it participates in divine company if it has been pure. The issue is that of fear of death, and the discussion has shown that logical proofs will not suffice to calm the soul. The beautiful story serves to calm the restless fears and passions that inhabit the subject of death. What we must ask, given the expressed fears of Simmias and Cebes, is whether any logical argument about immortality could reassure them, or whether a story is not essential. The implicit question is whether the issue of immortality could be settled propositionally.

The great myths of *Republic* are the myth of metals, to be told to the guardians to encourage them to accept their inner being, and the myth of Er. The myth of metals is unabashedly fictitious, and succeeds the argument that the guardians must be purified but immediately precedes the question of whether they will be happy. (414-415) It mediates between the formal ideality of the guardians' way of life and the proposed moral ideality that they are to attain. It is tempting to treat it as an outright lie, but its role then becomes perverse. Socrates has argued strenuously that poets both deceive and corrupt; yet when it suits his purposes he is deceptive and poetic. Shall we say that he is deceitful but not corrupting, that those who know the good and true may lie to bring others to see the light? Such an account lies behind the not uncommon view of Plato as authoritarian. What is overlooked are the ironic variations Plato performs on the most authoritarian of his suggestions. For the issue within the myth of metals is that of the specialization in virtue that defines justice. If the one is fraudulent, may not the other be? If so, then the entire discussion of the just state in *Republic* is equally fraudulent.

We may add that the myth of Er is another beautiful story of the adventures of the immortal soul. If Adeimantus and Glaucon are not convinced by the preceding arguments and speeches, perhaps they may be convinced by the eloquence of a moving story. If this hypothesis is plausible, another must be considered: that the fraudulence of the first story may contaminate the second. Each, within the dramatic structure of the dialogue, displaces itself ironically. The earlier myth immediately follows the rejection of fictitious stories, the later myth immediately follows the expulsion of the poets from the state. There are, moreover, deep ironies within the myth of Er, indicated by its name—*er* means pertaining to the earth while the forms pertain to the heavens—but perhaps more important, the story of the soul that chooses unwisely *because* of its many years in heaven, suggesting that knowledge of eternal forms provides no protection from injustice. (*Republic*, 619c)

The doctrinal reading is that the argumentative voice in which Socrates sometimes speaks is the authentic philosophic voice, overlooking the fact that Plato never wrote in such a voice. Rather, he wrote in a dramatic form in which propositional proofs cohabit with ironies and stories. The heretical reading is that the dramatic form is authentically philosophical, along with the didactic, sophistic, poetic, mythic, and other voices Socrates adopts where appropriate. Mythology and poetry are authentically philosophical; they are not equivalent with the other forms. In the manifold voices in the Platonic dialogues, there are both aporias and antagonisms. The heretical possibility is that these belong intrinsically to the philosophic movement. Carrying this possibility further, the heresy is that we must regard each of the dialogues as a good story, told to us by Plato, that may enlighten and move us, but whose purpose is not to replace a more authentic philosophical activity, found within the dialogues. Each is philosophical reason itself, a reason divided within and without. The suggestion is that *Republic* is not the didactic account it appears to be of the just state and just soul, but is a story, told to us, about a story told to a group of intelligent and well-meaning Greeks about the best way to live. It is, moreover, a narrative by Socrates in the mimetic form he explicitly rejects in the dialogue.

What is at stake here is whether reason is limited, divided intrinsically into many equally legitimate forms and, if so, whether these different forms may be conjoined into an overarching form. The issue among the different stories, conversations, and arguments in the dialogues, is of the unity of truth, of how it is a site at which same and other play. That the telling of stories might be persuasive rather than as truthful and rational as propositional argument avoids dividing truth by dividing it from persuasion. The presence of stories as voices of truth entails that truth is divided into many different voices, that many different kinds of truth always pertain.

There are many other well-known stories in the dialogues. Three are worth explicit notice. Of these, two—*Symposium* and *Timaeus*—are stories themselves, narrated to the reader; the third is the wonderful story in *Phaedrus*. Each of these dialogues must be read not only as a philosophical account of the nature of truth or reality, supported or contaminated by a beautiful story, but as a story itself. Together, they confirm the suggestion that philosophy has no more authentic form. Philosophy is the telling of stories, and there is no privileged form that marks the most authentic or truthful stories. Yet to deny such a privilege is to commit so great a heresy against one side of the tradition as to make unintelligible most contemporary forms of iconoclastic criticism. These require the privileged voice of the tradition to establish their legitimacy.

The stories within *Symposium* are about the nature of love (more generally, of desire). There is, in Plato, no thought or activity without desire.[25] The structure of *Symposium* is of a story within a story within a story. It matches the structure of many of the dialogues: a story told about Socrates by Plato containing stories Socrates (or another character) tells as part of the philosophic activity. What we may consider, in addition, is the festival setting: *Symposium* is an entertainment of storytelling in which everyone tells a story about love, with the irony that the most important story is not Socrates' tale of Diotima, but Alcibiades' story about Socrates offsetting the transcendent powers of the ideas. *Symposium* is where, in the dialogues, we find storytelling itself present most forcefully, where truth and fiction present themselves inseparably in relation to philosophy, dramatized by the model presented by Socrates to us. What is worth adding is the striking indication within the dialogue of the intimate relationship between *logos* and *eros*; and, conversely, the suggestion that to understand love is to tell a story about it. Desire requires a form of expression suitable to it.

Another theme of the dialogue is the infinite nature of desire—more accurately, the inexhaustibility within the finiteness of desire. This inexhaustibility is what requires the storytelling form, and is the theme toward which the stories told within the dialogue move. Love is first characterized as a restricted form of practice: what lovers should and should not do for and with each other. Practice and desire are regarded as entirely determinate in form, neglecting their undying restlessness. In particular, Aristophanes' famous story of love as the desire to rejoin what Zeus has set asunder contains a severely restricted sense of both desire and its fulfillment, thereby of both humanity and what moves it. With Agathon's speech, love becomes an inexhaustible source of creativity—but not an inexhaustible longing for something higher. Socrates' speech under Diotima's tutelage defines desire as inexhaustible both in longing and in fulfillment. Here the same of eternity reaches its highest moments in the dialogues, matching the restlessness of desire to the infinite. Desire is where the gods appear in human form. It takes Alcibiades' story of Socrates to restore to us the realization that it is not among eternal forms where inexhaustibility and transcendence are to be found, but in the worldly forms virtue takes, manifested in individual human examples.

> It is difficult, my dear Socrates, to demonstrate anything of real importance without the use of examples. Every one of us is like a man who sees things in a dream and thinks that he knows them perfectly and then wakes up, as it were, to find that he knows nothing. (*Statesman*, 277d)

The love that lacks all tenderness, trust, and care for human beings, which is merely love of the ideal within them, is transformed into a love for Socrates himself, warts and all. Despite the striking emphasis on the ideal as form, love is realized in Socrates' person, not abstractly.[26] His sobriety reflects a far greater passion than Alcibiades' drunkenness.[27] In his supreme individuality, he is other within the same. We must not ignore the recurrent images of lust and sexuality that pervade the representation of the highest forms of *eros* in both *Symposium* and *Phaedrus*.

Phaedrus not only contains several stories on the subject of love, but is expressly on the subject of story itself. In this way it surpasses even *Symposium* in its complex relationship to storytelling and in the complex relationship of storytelling to love. Both, in *Phaedrus*, are a form of *mania*.[28] While *Symposium* is a story within a story within a story, *Phaedrus* is this and more, for one of the stories is about the form and legitimacy of stories, establishing a close parallel between the inexhaustibility of truth and that of desire. Moreover, Socrates professes to prefer listening to stories to admiring the beauties of nature—indicating the intimate relationship between *logos* and *polis* that parallels the relationship between *logos* and *eros*. (*Phaedrus*, 230d) In such a dramatic context, Socrates' critique of writing must be read with irony. For not only is Phaedrus in possession of a story which he reads to Socrates, but Socrates throughout the dialogues typically tells stories that he claims to repeat from memory—tantamount to being written—and inhabits a story written by Plato. Whatever relationship Socrates may bear to writing, that is, to words that

> . . . seem to talk to you as though they were intelligent, but if you ask them anything about what they say, from a desire to be instructed, they go on telling you just the same thing forever (*Phaedrus*, 275e),

Plato's relationship is very different. Socrates did not write his words; Plato did. Plato wrote stories about Socrates containing Socrates as a character—and the two Socrateses are by no means identical. Plato also wrote stories about stories containing stories—and these stories are by no means the same.

Once we take for granted the extent to which stories inhabit Plato's writings, in multiple roles, there is no escape from the implication that philosophy is telling stories, if not telling stories alone, with the qualifications that telling a story is a complex phenomenon and that there are inexhaustibly manifold forms and styles of philosophical storytelling. The implication is that it is in the telling of stories, but not within any story in particular, that philosophical activity transpires. If the discussions in the dialogues about speech and writing reflect the transition in Greek life from an oral to a written tradition,[29] then the dialogues both express and display a divided and sensitive awareness of the nature and importance of storytelling, oral and written. It is within the displaced voices of storytelling and drama that philosophy is to be found. For Socrates concludes his criticisms of writing in *Phaedrus* by restoring it to favor.

> The conditions to be fulfilled are these. First, you must know the truth about the subject that you speak or write about; . . . secondly, you must have a corresponding discernment of the nature of the soul, discover the type of speech appropriate to each nature, and order and arrange your discourse accordingly. (*Phaedrus*, 277bc)

The second condition matches the structure of the dialogues; the first is belied by Socrates' recurrent profession of ignorance. Also present in the discussion is Socrates' famous image of the organic unity of *logos*, more like a living creature than scientific demonstration. (264c) What is suggested is the possibility that philosophy can be nothing but dialogue itself, including whatever stories advance the discussion, attaining only the temporary unity of dialogic resolution. Here the view that philosophy is the love of wisdom presents us with a striking sense of the parallels between desire and truth. What is further suggested is the collapse of the distinction between legitimate and illegitimate forms of expression, rendering the entire discussion in Book III of *Republic* ironic.

There is a striking parallel between Socrates' criticisms of mimesis in Book III of *Republic* and the end of *Phaedrus* where he criticizes writing. In the latter case, he criticizes writing as "dead discourse" and compares it with "living speech," but goes on to describe what might make writing an art, entirely neglecting its intrinsic defects. Moreover, he goes on to speak of truth "veritably written in the soul of the listener." (*Phaedrus,* 278a) The structure of the discussion entirely displaces the explicit criticisms of writing by first, suggesting that there is a legitimate art of writing, and second, by interpreting speech as a writing upon the soul. The ironies are analogous to those in *Meno* where the doctrine of recollection is described as the soul having learned all things. In *Republic*, Socrates rejects all forms of "imitative" or "dramatic" art in which anything and everything is imitated. Yet Plato wrote only dramatic dialogues, wrote only in a mimetic narrative mode. There is no stronger displacement possible for the position evinced by Socrates than that it is told exclusively within dramatic writing. Moreover, it cannot be overemphasized in this context that the theory of ideas is entirely a mimetic theory.

What we must conclude is that no one more thoroughly indicates the displacements that pertain to representation in all its forms than Plato. In this sense, the Platonic dialogues, in their dramatic, ironic, and mimetic forms, including polemical and agonistic exchanges, but also storytelling and figurative displacements, present us with a thoroughly divided relationship to philosophic thought and writing. Writing is a figure that simultaneously expresses both philosophic activity—"written on the soul"—and entombed and moribund thought in contrast with a "living understanding." The suggestion is that writing is philosophy itself *and is heresy*, that there is no nonheretical form of philosophical understanding, no undisplaced relationship of thought to truth. The sense that writing becomes moribund, "dead," saying the same thing forever is the sense of a living thought passing into orthodoxy. To remain alive and active, philosophic thought must be heretical, must transcend any reading.

No dialogue manifests this sense of philosophy as heresy more powerfully than *Meno*, once we allow for its dramatic structure. The story is Socrates' response to the paradox of learning, that the acquisition of knowledge is impossible because if we are ignorant we cannot tell whether what we have discovered is true while if we already have knowledge, we cannot acquire it. The doctrine of recollection cannot answer this paradoxical objection. Moreover, it is typically stated by Socrates as that the soul, because it is immortal, "has learned everything that is"; (81c) "All nature is akin, and the soul has learned everything." (81d) Even in *Phaedo*, in a much more serious context, "we must have obtained knowledge of all these characteristics before our birth." (75d) Obtaining knowledge is acquiring it. Moreover, in both *Meno* (86d) and *Phaedo*, Socrates argues *from* recollection to the immortality of the soul, not the reverse. Every presentation of the doctrine of recollection in the dialogues is similarly displaced. Among such displacements is the discussion in *Euthydemus*. For that immensely ironic dialogue explicitly addresses Meno's question and presents an explicit refutation of the doctrine of recollection.

> It is clear therefore that you knew as a child, and when you were born, and when you were begotten, and that before you came into being, and before heaven and earth came into being, you knew all things, since you always knew. (*Euthydemus*, 296d)

There is no way around the paradox of learning from within the doctrine of recollection, and there are countless signals that Plato (with Socrates) is fully aware of it. Immortality does not resolve the impossibility of acquiring knowledge from ignorance, but only compounds it. If Socrates were to say, as he must, that the soul *always knows* the eternal truth, then it could never acquire knowledge. Inquiry would be unintelligible. Yet Socrates' purpose, repeated frequently, is to engage in inquiry with Meno. Reason here is inquiry, and there can be no argument against reason that does not derive from reason itself. The difficulty of the paradox of learning is that it contains a profound truth: the acquisition of knowledge is miraculous, the invasion of the same by another. Every discovery is heretical; every discovery transcends any foundations that preceded it; knowledge is not reducible to antecedent conditions or to measures and calculations. Reason is profoundly aporetic.

This is clear in the interrogation of Meno's slave. If Socrates' argument based on this interrogation has any cogency at all, it is that the slave "learned" what he did by himself, that is, he acquired an understanding that transcends what Socrates showed him.

> This knowledge will not come from teaching but from questioning. He will recover it for himself. (*Meno*, 85d)

In all learning, whenever knowledge is acquired, there is a discovery that goes beyond the available materials, beyond sensible experience. In every discovery, there is something abnormal, the breaking of some rule or prior expectation. Between what is familiar and what is discovered, there is always something inexplicable. Unintelligibility belongs intrinsically to intelligibility, heresy to reason.

The interrogation of Meno's slave is ostensibly Socrates' defense of the doctrine of recollection. Meno is captivated by the idea as an answer to the paradox of learning—although it is not a very good answer—and asks Socrates to explain it to him.

> But what do you mean when you say that we don't learn anything, but that what we call learning is recollection? Can you teach me that it is so? (*Meno*, 81e)

Socrates notes the contradiction in such a teaching, although he does not acknowledge the similar contradiction in his own claim that the soul "acquired" knowledge of all things. These recurrent displacements are unmistakable indications that Plato cannot have failed to notice the absurdity of the doctrine of recollection as an answer to the paradox of learning. It appears in the dialogues in the context first, in *Phaedo*, of a profound concern with death, then, in *Meno*, in the context of an obstinately resistant student. In the first case, extraordinary measures are necessary to overcome the fear of death. In the second case, the issue is less theoretical than pedagogical, one of learning, although pedagogy is not less philosophical. The suggestion is that the doctrine of recollection cannot serve its assigned theoretical function, but serves a practical purpose wherever it is found. The further suggestion is that this is not a practical function contrasted with a rational truth, but that practice requires its own rationality, given by the telling of good stories where appropriate. Philosophic reason requires adaptation to different purposes and different audiences, as described in *Phaedrus*.

In the dialogue, Meno is on the verge of accepting Socrates as his teacher, with the qualification that Socrates will refuse to teach him anything in particular—that is, any doctrine or position. All that Socrates is prepared for him to learn is the art of inquiry—philosophy itself. What is involved is heresy: to learn from Socrates anything but the art of inquiry is to acquire a form of orthodoxy. The paradox of learning is an expression of a practical obstruction to inquiry: a student may be unprepared to inquire and unable to learn from his inquiries. Theoretically, the possibility is that we cannot tell, due to ignorance, what is true from what is false. Inquiry can be justified only by inquiry—a fundamental aporia. Practically, the possibility is that a person may be unwilling or unprepared to participate responsibly in inquiry. The practical difficulty requires a practical resolution, represented by the doctrine of recollection and the interrogation of the slave.

This interrogation is ostensibly a proof that the slave learns nothing from Socrates, but always knew what Socrates teaches him. The proof consists of Socrates drawing diagrams in the sand and asking fifty-three questions, all of which but eleven are leading questions of the form: (82b-86b)

> Now boy, you know that a square is a figure like this?

> It has all these four sides equal?

> Then the side of the eight-foot figure must be longer than two feet but shorter than four?

The eleven are mostly of the form:

> And how many feet is twice two?

When Socrates asks the slave,

> Now then, try to tell me how long each of its sides will be. The present figure has a side of two feet. What will be the side of the double-sized one?,

he answers, incorrectly,

> It will be double, Socrates, obviously.

Socrates turns to Meno and says,

> You see, Meno, that I am not teaching him anything, only asking. Now he thinks he knows the length of the side of the eight-foot square.

This is hilarious. First, Socrates offers the boy the words "double-sized," elicits from him the answer "double," and then claims to Meno that all these answers come from the slave himself. But the entire exchange is just as hilarious, containing a great majority of leading questions to which the slave answers only "yes" and "no," except for a small number of direct questions, several of which he gets wrong. Most of the exchange goes like this,

> Tell me, boy, is not this our square of four feet? You understand? Yes.

Now we can add another equal to it like this?
Yes.

And a third here, equal to each of the others?
Yes.

And then we can fill in this one in the corner?
Yes.

Not a single one of the drawings could have been produced by the slave. At best we may say he can understand the proof although he cannot produce it. But Socrates makes no effort to show that this is the case. When the slave is asked

How big is this area?

He answers,

I don't understand.

At the end, Socrates turns to Meno, while we collapse with laughter, and says,

What do you think, Meno, has he answered with any opinions that were not his own?

Meno's answer is

No, they were all his.

There are two types of conclusion:

Then if he did not acquire them in this life, isn't it immediately clear that he possessed and had learned them during some other period?

The only thing that is clear is that the slave acquired whatever geometric opinions he has on the subject from Socrates; moreover, they are of relatively little value. Knowledge can indeed be acquired, and its acquisition is like remembering, not in the sense of repetition, but in the sense that there is something miraculous about it. No mediation can produce understanding by rule. The doctrine of recollection is incompatible with acquiring knowledge by rules.

The second conclusion, to Meno's comment,

Somehow or other I believe you are right;

Socrates replies, in one of his most telling displacements:

> I think I am. I shouldn't like to take my oath on the whole story,
> but one thing I am ready to fight for as long as I can, in word
> and act—that is, that we shall be better, braver, and more active
> men if we believe it right to look for what we don't know than if
> we believe there is no point in looking because what we don't
> know we can never discover. (*Meno*, 86c)

Socrates won't take an oath on the story or on the doctrine of recollection because they are indefensible. What the stories entail, however, is that we cannot subscribe to the position that it is impossible to acquire knowledge. To the contrary, it is essential to the entire dialectic, to philosophy and to the dramatic form of the dialogues, that we are able to acquire knowledge, however we do so. Nevertheless, as suggested by the interrogation of the slave and the doctrine of recollection, there is something unintelligible about the acquisition of knowledge. It remains an other within the same. There is no method for connecting what is familiar with what is unfamiliar. We recall the wonderful aviary example in *Theaetetus* where pieces of knowledge are compared with birds in a cage. How, on such a model, is error possible?

> ... are we to understand that a man knows both a piece of knowledge and a piece of ignorance, and then supposes that one of these things he knows is the other which he also knows? Or does he know neither, and then judge that one of these unknown things is the other? Or does he know only one, and identify this known thing with the unknown one, or the unknown one with the known? ... (*Theaetetus*, 200bc)

One interpretation is that Socrates is arguing against an internal criterion for perceptual knowledge. The heretical suggestion is that this argument, in all its imagery, applies to the entire Western epistemological tradition, because it is incompatible with epistemological foundations of any kind. We can never "possess" a knowledge that achieves certainty. It is impossible to eliminate error. Recollection and memory, like all forms of knowledge, involve difference as much as similarity. (*Phaedo*, 73d)

Theaetetus' suggestion, to which the above is Socrates' reply, was that

> Perhaps, Socrates, we were wrong in making the birds stand for
> pieces of knowledge only, and we ought to have imagined pieces
> of ignorance flying about with them in the mind. (*Theaetetus*,
> 199e)

Despite Socrates' reply, there is no alternative if we are to hold that
error is always possible. Knowledge and ignorance are inseparable.
Analogously, what is familiar and what is unfamiliar, same and other, are
thoroughly inseparable. There is always something in anything known
or experienced that transcends our expectations. Heresy is both the promise of great discoveries and the threat of folly, and the two are only
locally distinguishable. Heresy here belongs to any important discovery
as the alien other that makes further discoveries possible, that threatens
truth with absurdity as much as aporia.

The slave scene occupies the exact center of *Meno*. It is framed at
its beginning by the paradox of learning and at its end by the only resolution possible in the dialogue, that Meno is convinced to participate in
the inquiry. (86d) He becomes actively interested in being instructed by
Socrates. Even here, however, he will not recognize Socrates' question
concerning the nature of virtue, and would rather have his own (familiar)
question answered. Despite his changes, he remains within the same. His
resistance is largely overcome, but what remains is a need to be instructed
rather than to inquire. He never learns that learning is not instruction.
We may add that what he might learn from Socrates is but the Socratic
method. Because what Meno wants is to be told, rather than to discover,
this is an altogether heretical idea, one he cannot bring himself to accept.
He cannot overcome the resistance to heresy embodied in his name.

What Socrates has to offer, throughout the dialogues, is not knowledge as a possession but participation in philosophic conversation. The
suggestion is that there is no other form of instruction. The doctrine of
recollection masks this heresy behind the immortality of the soul, but it
cannot be avoided: even an immortal soul must have acquired what it
knows at some time, and such an acquisition is inseparable from error
and ignorance. Inquiry as an ongoing practice is a mixture of error and
understanding. What follows is that we never acquire knowledge, but
endlessly participate in its pursuit by overcoming error locally. Error
cannot be overcome permanently, only in this or that context of inquiry.
As explicitly stated by Socrates, contexts of inquiry vary with the partic-
ipants and their circumstances, and there is no legitimate or authentic
form in which it occurs or is expressed. The dialogues are inquiry, and
there is no form superior to them.

Against his better judgment, now, in the interests of good pedagogy, Socrates accepts Meno's question rather than his own as the basis

of inquiry. They will investigate together how virtue may be acquired without knowing what it is. (86e) They begin by assuming that if it is knowledge, then it is teachable. (87c) The question is whether it is knowledge. This hypothesis is what Plato's doctrine requires to be true: virtue is a form of knowledge possessed by the philosopher. Therefore, indirectly and obliquely, we are considering "Plato's doctrine of virtue." The conclusion of the first discussion is that,

> If we accept this argument, then virtue, to be something advantageous, must be a sort of wisdom. (*Meno*, 88d)

If we accept this argument. For it is not a very good one, although it expresses the doctrinal view. There are goods that are beneficial without being knowledge—good fortune, for example. But Socrates has a more telling objection: there are no teachers of virtue whose students, no parents whose children, reliably acquire virtue from them. There is no guaranteed perpetuation of the same. This objection, we may note, runs counter to the earlier rejection of routine methods of acquiring or transmitting knowledge. If knowledge is always aporetically mixed with ignorance, then there can be no routine methods of gaining knowledge, only inquiry, with its successes and failures, and without secure resolution. The image is again of knowledge as a possession, which can be transferred at will, an image inappropriate with the form of the dialogue. Knowledge is not a thing or possession, but an inexhaustible and aporetic activity.

An extraordinary dramatic event occurs at this point. Socrates breaks off the discussion with Meno to discuss with Anytus the question of whether there are teachers of virtue. Why does Plato introduce him at this point? We remember that Anytus is one of the plaintiffs in the suit against Socrates that costs him his life. Socrates even suggests that without Anytus, Meletus' suit would have failed. (*Apology*, 36b) Moreover, Meno is Anytus' house guest, indicating the darker side of Meno's opening arrogance. (92d)

When Socrates asks Anytus, to whom should Meno go to acquire virtue, and suggests the Sophists, Anytus' reply is one of revulsion, (91c) although he admits that he has never had anything to do with them. One point, then, is that Anytus has no compunction about having strong opinions concerning people whose lives and teachings he knows nothing about directly. This is an excellent point in criticism of people who moralize about matters they keep themselves ignorant about. Yet there is a far greater irony than Plato's mocking portrait of a smug and self-important man whose dogmatic opinions brought about Socrates' death.

Anytus gives the same answer Meletus gives to the question of who can teach virtue: any Athenian citizen. Socrates' criticism is that sons of such citizens are often not virtuous. Anytus' answer is a threat:

> You seem to me, Socrates, to be too ready to run people down. My advice to you, if you will listen to it, is to be careful. I dare say that in all cities it is easier to do a man harm than good, and it is certainly so here, as I expect you know yourself. (*Meno*, 95a)

Threat aside, this is not a bad answer. Virtue is difficult to acquire and to maintain. Therefore, that the sons of virtuous people should not be virtuous is no surprise and not a compelling criticism of their parents' virtues.

Plato does not need Anytus to make his point convincing. Socrates could have mentioned the same examples to Meno of parents whose children were not virtuous. Anytus functions here at several dramatic and ironic levels. One is to remind us of the dogmatism that lay behind Socrates' trial. Another is to show how moral indignation is frequently founded not on knowledge but on dogmatism. A third is to give an example of how not to discuss virtue, a reprise of the closedmindedness with which the dialogue begins. A fourth serves to clarify Meno's character by association. None of these, however, seems enough to justify the disruption of the dramatic structure of the dialogue.

We remember the earlier interpolation with the slave. This discussion took place to show Meno that even a slave could acquire knowledge through interrogation and discussion. By analogy, the possibility is raised that Meno is himself a slave to the same, that the only freedom worth having is that of free and open inquiry. Here, we may consider the hypothesis that Anytus is another such slave, but one who, unlike Meno's slave and even Meno himself, cannot recognize that he does not know what he thinks he knows. What and who Meno and Anytus are, as well as who Socrates is, express dramatically two fundamental principles: to claim to know is slavery; virtue is acquired by example. Meno is a creature of memory while Socrates admits his bad memory openly. (*Meno*, 71cd)[30] Meno's thought is a collection of recollections and repetitions, and repetition is neither inquiry nor knowledge. Recognition of error, even of ignorance, is a first condition of freedom and understanding, because without it, inquiry is impossible. Knowledge is not repetition but heresy. Ignorance is closer to knowledge than any present truth. Aporetically, only one who "knows" he is ignorant can acquire or possess knowledge. He who claims to know does not know. This returns us deeply to the paradox of learning but to a position counter to the doctrine of recollection. Recollection is to be interpreted not as always knowing everything, but as never knowing anything, in the sense that we are always suspended within ignorance, incompleteness, and aporia. In this context, recollection is heresy.

The dialogue pursues this conclusion with the argument that there are neither teachers nor students of virtue, so it would appear that virtue cannot be taught. (96d) Nevertheless, there are virtuous human beings, and they become virtuous rather than having been born so. A fundamental irony, here, is that such acquisition is incompatible with the doctrine of recollection. Yet despite the paradox of learning and the doctrine of recollection, the evidence is unmistakable that virtue is acquired. There remain two possibilities. One is that virtue is acquired through inquiry, a position Socrates has maintained consistently throughout the dialogue. The other is the position with which the dialogue concludes.

> On our present reasoning then, whoever has virtue gets it by divine dispensation. (*Meno*, 100b)

We may hazard the presumption that the two positions Socrates maintains consistently throughout the dialogue are essential to it. They are that virtue is acquired through inquiry and that inquiry into its nature is essential to possessing it. We may combine these into the single principle that inquiry into the nature of virtue is virtue. But we must add that inquiry is grounded in ignorance more than possession. Alternatively, the search for essences is dialectic, with the qualifications that dialectic is dialogue, including ironization and storytelling, and that understanding is not different from the practice of conversation, dialogue, and storytelling. In this sense, human *aretē* is dialogue and storytelling. The good life is the life of philosophy, carried on in the diverse practices of conversation. The life of reason is never quieted.

If this is our conclusion, it is never explicitly stated in the dialogue and is a product of its dramatic and ironic structure more than of any explicit thesis. If this is so, then the activity and structure of the dialogue are more authentically reason and virtue than any conclusions to which we may come. The inconclusiveness of the discussion manifests this point: what we know is less important than the activities involved in pursuing it and the aporias that engender it. Even this formulation is deficient. The extreme possibility is that there is *nothing* to be known, and *no way* of acquiring either virtue or knowledge, only dialogue itself, the diverse activities that comprise reason and virtue. The dialogues end inconclusively wherever the issues are important because the dialogues are philosophy and can terminate only dogmatically in the same where dialogue itself concludes. In this profound sense, Plato's heresy concerns heresy itself. Every doctrinal conclusion lacks acknowledgment of aporia and inexhaustibility.

In this context it is worth noting the explicit conclusion of the dialogue: virtue comes by divine dispensation. On the standard reading of Plato, this cannot be his view. On the reading provided here, the possibility is that this is a truth inherent in the dialogue. It is a perfect expression of the only defensible form of the doctrine of recollection. Recollection can be no answer to the paradox of learning if the soul learned everything in its many immortal travels. It can be an answer only if the soul always knows all things—that is, if knowledge comes miraculously, as by divine gift. What must be added is that virtue is not unique in this miraculous sense, for it is shared by all forms of knowledge. Knowledge is not a thing or condition. Instead there is dialogue itself, divided by interlocutors and conversations. We may add that dialogue has no authoritative form, that storytelling and myth are as much part of dialogic reason as proofs and interrogations. The conclusion of *Meno*, that virtue cannot be distinguished from true opinion, and cannot be acquired with certainty, is represented by the dramatic form. The apparent contradiction in the conclusion that virtue, which Socrates maintains is knowledge throughout such dialogues as *Republic* and *Gorgias*, here is but true opinion miraculously based on a divine gift, follows from the premise that knowledge is a state or condition, in which form it is disastrously vulnerable to the paradox of learning and the aviary argument. What we are left with are far-reaching aporetic implications in the dialogues, emphasizing their dramatic form and style. There is a profound parallel between the aporias of being and knowing and the dramatic displacements of the dialogues.

Extending this possibility further, we recall the argument in *Ion* that rhapsodes—and, by extension, poets and other artists—do not base their gifts on knowledge, but on divine inspiration. (*Ion*, 536c) The doctrinal reading is that Socrates is arguing against the art of the rhapsode and even the poet as based on a miraculous gift rather than science or knowledge.[31] *Meno* concludes with a similar claim concerning virtue. Shall we conclude, on the doctrinal reading, that virtue is similarly a divine gift, or merely that in *Meno*, Plato is presenting a paradoxical conclusion while in *Ion* the analogous argument is to be taken seriously? Such a reading presupposes an absolute and unqualified distinction between knowledge and opinion, science and inspiration. This view is supported in *Ion* by the contrast between the rhapsode's divine inspiration and the artisan's *technē*, although in *Meno*, there is no corresponding contrast with a *technē* of virtue. In both cases, the contrast effectively calls this *technē* into question as the only relevant knowledge. If the poet does not know how to win battles as well as the general or how to cure disease as well as the physician, the poet does know something about war and health, something that may be opinion but is not empty, something that may fall more within the other than the same. Reason and knowledge are divided, here, by variations that comprise heresy.

The doctrinal view is belied by the structure of the dialogues as well as by much of what we find in them. The alternative possibility is that virtue is indeed (like) a divine gift, similar to recollection, a form of madness, and not based on science, because there is no science of virtue — that is, a stable method of either acquiring or demonstrating virtue. Reason here is heresy. Dialectic takes precedence with the qualification that the only manifestations we have of dialectic are the dialogues themselves, including the stories within them and the stories that they tell. This reading entails that the conclusion of *Ion* is by no means destructive. The fact that rhapsodes function by divine dispensation is typical of all forms of science and art. Without such divine possession they are empty. Both the acquisition and the demonstration of knowledge are heretical, departures from rules, and there is no reliable method of either acquiring or displaying knowledge. Despite this, the possibility of knowledge and truth is not to be denied, although it is always aporetically in question. No science or art can be without miraculous inspiration on the one hand or can reach settled conclusions free from aporetic results on the other. Again, the dramatic dialogue form, in all its complexity and inconclusiveness, manifests both halves of this principle of reason.

We should not overlook Socrates' description of dialectic in *Republic*, dominated by two fundamental images: the continuing and unrelenting process that pertains to it and the freedom from sensible experience and hypothetical thought that it brings. Emphasizing the latter image, ignoring its irony, gives the doctrinal reading. Emphasizing the former, but equating dialectic with the dialogues themselves, gives us a more heretical reading. Such a reading is deepened and strengthened when we reflect the dramatic structures of the dialogues upon the doctrinal interpretation. For the images that support the identification of the good with the sun, the divided line leading to timeless knowledge, and the otherworldly Platonic strain, always occur in dialogues whose dramatic form counters the otherworldly emphasis. *Phaedo* is concerned with the fear of death, and to counter that fear must make use of images and devices that far exceed what propositional discourse requires. *Republic* is a dramatization of a discussion on justice after a festival involving only Socrates as a serious philosopher — the Socrates who virtually without exception, even in *Republic*, claims his ignorance of wisdom and virtue. When we emphasize the dialogues and specific polemics, we may be led to a doctrinal conclusion. When we consider the many dialogues and their dramatic structures, we are led to a more heretical reading. What we must add is that it is part of the heretical reading to deny that any one reading, including its own, is the truth about Platonic doctrine.

For there is no such doctrine, only a body of dialogues with complex dramatic as well as propositional structures. There are proofs and conclusions in the dialogues, but only as moments in the dialectical activity. Far more important, the relationship of the doctrine to the activity within the dialogues, with their ironies and displacements, is fundamentally aporetic: the aporia of heretical reason.

It is necessary to consider briefly some of the later dialogues in terms of this reading. What we may add here is the suggestion that just as the many dialogues together comprise no single coherent doctrine, that such a doctrine is incompatible in spirit with the pursuit of wisdom, which is aporetic and present in no privileged form, the many great works in the history of philosophy—but especially of metaphysical philosophy—comprise no doctrine and lead to no doctrine. Rather, metaphysical truth lies in the many works themselves, collectively, in spite—or in virtue—of their incompatibilities. If reality is inexhaustible, then incommensurateness belongs to it intrinsically, and it can be known only in aporetic terms.

What must be done to enrich the reading here of *Meno*, and to deepen its heretical nature, is to consider the discussions in other dialogues. Such considerations must be brief, and no one reading of such complex dialogues can be regarded as definitive. A reading that emphasizes Platonic style can claim consensus no more than can interpretations of Shakepeare and Homer. More generally, philosophy lends itself to consensus no more than do painting and poetry—indeed, consensus is hostile to any deeper understanding or truth. Aporia and heresy belong to truth intrinsically.

The doctrinal reading of Plato owes an overriding debt to *Republic*, neglecting not only its dramatic setting and overt ironies, but the complexity of storytelling within it. We may begin by noting that it is a story told by Socrates in mimetic form, representing his and others' conversations. Second, it occurs between two festivals, not an optimal time for serious discussion. Third, Socrates' interlocutors are not philosophers, but ordinary Greek citizens. Given Socrates' eristic skills, we may suppose that he could convince such a group of almost anything, and does so. Fourth, the structure of the dialogue is a repetition of the structure of Socrates' exchange with the slave in *Meno*: what Adeimantus and Glaucon say most of the time is "Assuredly"; "Right"; "Of course"; "That is true"; and so on. It is difficult to believe that Plato's greatest truths would be expressed in such a company and based on so empty an interrogation.

To this we must add, fifth, Socrates' recurrent refrain that he does not know what justice is and does not profess to know. (337e, also 605b and 450e) In the other dialogues where he professes ignorance, the discussion concludes without resolution. We may also note, sixth, that the dialogue opens with the presentation of the question of justice to Cephalus, a man who has lived honorably and well and who is an object of Socrates' admiration, not his contempt. "Cephalus" (or his namesake, with "Adeimantus" and "Glaucon") appears as the narrator of *Parmenides*, and there is little justification there for believing that Socrates is prepared to subject him to ridicule. The parallel is with *Phaedo*, where Socrates is far more concerned with encouragement and reassurance in the face of death than confrontation with hard truths. Why should an older, generally virtuous man like Cephalus be subjected to the indignity of acknowledging that he has not lived a virtuous life because he does not know what virtue is? And why should his sons and their friends, during a festival? More important, perhaps, than Cephalus' conception of justice is its cerebral nature (after his name), altogether lacking desire. No human justice or knowledge can be free from *eros*. If so, then the entire middle books of *Republic* are ironic.

There are other considerations. One of Socrates' remarks, in Book I, concerns a disputatious form of conversation.

> If then we oppose him [Thrasymachus] in a set speech enumerating in turn the advantages of being just and he replies and we rejoin, we shall have to count up and measure the goods listed in the respective speeches and we shall forthwith be in need of judges to decide between us. But if, as in the preceding discussion, we come to terms with one another as to what we admit in the inquiry, we shall be ourselves both judges and pleaders. (*Republic*, 348b)

Here Socrates considers two very different paradigms of discourse: one agonistic or contentious, the other consensual.[32] On the doctrinal view, Plato clearly opts for the paradigm of the same. Yet without exception the dialogues dramatize a competitive, agonistic discourse, nearly always resolving inconclusively, and manifest consensus only where a weaker interlocutor has been overcome by a stronger. Almost all the ironies exemplified in the dialogues manifest the readiness of a weaker interlocutor to agree with a stronger one—the danger inherent in the teachings of the Sophists. There is recurrent reference throughout the dialogue to bouts and strength, and *Republic* opens with the question of whether Socrates is strong enough to escape from Polemarchus' clutches. (327c) We must consider whether *Republic* is not more than anything else the agonistic coercion by Socrates of Adeimantus and Glaucon, even more than of Thrasymachus, to agree with him concerning the superiority of the just life. The just life is better than the unjust life. But there are no conclusive arguments to produce that result, and it is a continuing theme in the dialogues that those who claim to know what virtue is always delude themselves.

Even more important, most of the images pertaining to desire, entailing that justice demands that it be controlled by reason, are incompatible with the principle that virtue is not control of *eros* but a manic passion for the highest things.[33] Finally, images of worldliness, even of the *under*world, Hades, frame the dialogue, from the festival of Bendo—a goddess of Hades—to the myth of Er. The discussion of eternity is framed inescapably by the sensible world, as the philosopher-king cannot escape from worldly rule and the ideas require embodiment.[34] There is a downward pull in *Republic* that opposes the upward pull of the ideas. The dialogue as a whole inhabits the midworld between heaven and hell, caught between the attractions of each, but to neither of which can we escape.[35] The center of *Republic* is the escape from the cave to the idea of the good. The center of *Meno* is the ironic exhibition of *anamnēsis* by the slave. The center of *Meno* is flanked on both sides by a positive but fallible view of inquiry. The center of *Republic* is flanked on both sides by the complex practical conditions of social life—education, procreation, and family.

The crucial part of the opening book is clearly a combat between Socrates and Thrasymachus. Perhaps the better man wins, but philosophy does not. The transition to the rest of the dialogue produced by Adeimantus' and Glaucon's questions is crucial. Yet what they request is not that justice be shown to be the highest good, as *nous* and *logos* are shown to be the highest goods in *Philebus*—that is, mixed goods— but that it be praised "pure" and in itself, grounded in the rule of the same. Both of these requests—that justice be praised and that it be regarded in itself— are extraordinary, suggesting that what follows also is equally extraordinary.

> What I desire is to hear an encomium on justice in and by itself. (*Republic*, 358d)

Socrates remarks that Glaucon purifies both justice and injustice to the point where they cease to be human

> How strenuously you polish off each of your two men for the competition for the prize as if it were a statue! (*Republic*, 361d)

So extreme are Adeimantus' and Glaucon's demands that Socrates disavows them.

> I do not know how I can come to the rescue. For I doubt my ability for the reason that you have not accepted the arguments whereby I thought I proved against Thrasymachus that justice is better than injustice .... The best thing, then, is to aid her as best I can. (*Republic*, 368c)

Such a defense may well be not through propositional argument but through storytelling. We may note that the arguments against Thrasymachus are not very convincing. But Glaucon has explicitly rejected the persuasiveness of arguments.

> Do not, then, I repeat, merely prove to us in argument the superiority of justice to injustice, but show us what it is that each inherently does to its possessor . . . . (*Republic*, 367e)

The rest of the discussion is this "showing"—not a proof at all, and certainly not the lesser. Showing, in storytelling and dialogue, is the preeminent form of philosophical discourse.

On this kind of reading, emphasizing the displacements, ironies, and dramatic setting, the decision to write justice large, in the state, is unpersuasive. The principle that an individual can be virtuous only in public terms does not require justice writ large, only the social and political concomitants of virtue, realized through the association of knowledge with practice. It is clear in Socrates' presentation, in both *Republic* and *Laws*, that a perfectly just state would be abominable to those who inhabited it. But there is an important reason for this conclusion in *Republic*: justice in the state is blithely interpreted to be for the good of the objects served rather than for the human beings involved. The work (*ergon*) of human beings is both objectified and unitary. Human excellence is represented as both inorganic and inhuman. It is overwhelmed by the law of the same, incompatible with the fundamental principle of justice as an order among a multiplicity of desires. It is also incompatible with the inexhaustible plenitude of things as well as human beings that they should have one overarching excellence. Involved here is a view of *technē* that has dominated much of the Western tradition, although it is incompatible fundamentally with Plato's own sense of *eros* and truth. This interpretation of *aretē* as *technē*, on which the following discussion turns, is passed off in but a few lines, although it imitates the refutation of Thrasymachus. That refutation is acknowledged to be flawed and incomplete. What is involved is the explicit sacrifice of human beings to the state in the name of justice, corresponding to the sacrifice of human virtue to the ends served by human beings. No wonder *Republic* has been regarded by many readers as authoritarian.

The irony is that the different "ideal" states Socrates describes are quite awful. The reason for this awfulness is unclear to Glaucon, who bemoans the lack of salt and cushions in the ascetic life. The just life is the simple life. (*Republic*, 372) One objection is that such simplicity is unpleasant. Another, far deeper, is that human life is a complex life because reason and virtue, not to mention reality, are complex. Too simple a life is not a human life—not a life of reason and virtue. The members of the state described would not be happy because they would not be living a truly human life in all its complexity. The ascetic city is not human or ideal because it lacks *eros*. The city Socrates describes sacrifices the happiness of its members to the state. The *aretē* he describes involves the sacrifice of human fulfillment to a sense of *ergon* constricted by the same. Human beings no longer useful to the city are to be destroyed like implements and possessions. (407de) The sense in which the ascetic state Socrates describes is "perfect"—perfectly just—is not a human excellence. For, dramatically speaking, there is no perfect sense of human virtue, only mixed virtues in varied hues. This mixing is analogous to the mixing of styles of discourse and forms of truth. Neither virtue nor truth is credible "pure."

Given such an ironic beginning, we may expect ironies throughout. Thus, despite the supreme importance of truth to the gods (382d), the rulers may lie in the interests of the state—its justice. (389c) Socrates confesses embarrassment at telling the myth of the metals, (414c) for he has already indicated that its purpose is not to achieve truth but to help his guardians avoid fear of death. (386) We have seen how far he is prepared to go in *Phaedo* to help his friends overcome their fear of death.

An explicit reference is made at a juncture where the argument falters to the style of Socrates' arguments in *Republic*. Adeimantus becomes uneasy at the implausibility of the picture Socrates is promoting, but knows that he is unable to provide counterarguments. Socrates is the master of disputation.

> No one, Socrates, would be able to controvert these statements of yours. But, all the same, those who occasionally hear you argue thus feel in this way. They think that owing to their inexperience in the game of question and answer they are at every question led astray a little bit by the argument, and when these bits are accumulated at the conclusion of the discussion mighty is their fall, and the apparent contradiction of what they at first said, and that just as by expert draughts players the unskilled are finally shut in and cannot make a move, so they are finally blocked and have their mouths stopped by this other game of draughts played not with counters but with words; yet the truth is not affected by that outcome. (*Republic*, 487bc)

This is an apt description of Socrates' agonistic style. Why should we not accept it? Socrates' response is to tell a story. However, this story, of the pilot of a ship, although it succeeds in reassuring Glaucon, reminds us of the similar "dream" in *Charmides* that Socrates himself characterizes as "nonsense." (173) The image Socrates uses to describe his imaginary opponents is again one of bouts and contention rather than of persuasion and understanding. (*Republic*, 501e) He also refers to what he has been saying as "audacities" (503c) and continues with a striking displacement.

> We were saying, I believe, that for the most perfect discernment of these things another longer way was requisite which would make them plain to one who took it, but that it was possible to add proofs on a par with the preceding discussion. And you said that that was sufficient, and it was on this understanding that what we then said was said, falling short of ultimate precision as it appeared to me, but if it contented you it is for you to say. (*Republic*, 504b)

Adeimantus may be contented, but not the reader. The proofs "on a par" with the preceding discussion are unsatisfactory, but that is because the preceding discussion, from a conclusive philosophic point of view, is unsatisfactory. Only the stories in, and the story that is, *Republic* are truly satisfactory, *because* they lack precision. These stories include not only *Republic* itself and the myths of metals and of Er but the stories of the infinite and the good. The discussions of the divided line and cave are preceded by the same kinds of disclaimer that typically mark Socrates' most remarkable flights of imagination.

> Have a care, however, lest I deceive you unintentionally with a false reckoning of the interest. (507a)

The movement, within the divided line and out of the cave, is toward an intelligibility in ideas alone, although a knowledge of pure form would be altogether useless. The gods constantly return to the earth to play their roles.

The issue is whether the philosopher should rule the state. There are several qualifications: philosophy is a divine gift, a possession (532c); the philosopher who returns from having seen the good is dazzled by it to the point where he cannot discern ordinary things (517a); he is forced to cease living a life in the light of the good and required to return to the shadows to rule the state; and, finally, the ideal state declines precisely where the ruler cannot adequately cope with ordinary events like phases of the moon and procreative cycles. (546) Ruling a state requires ordinary gifts and empirical skills. There is nothing otherwordly about Socrates' view of practical politics. Yet there is no proof whatever in *Republic* that the otherwordly philosopher will have such practical skills,

and recurrent argument throughout the dialogues that knowledge of philosophy, even of the good, does not make one competent in a particular
art. We may recall the discussion in *Charmides* that neither a science of
science nor knowledge of virtue, by implication neither self-knowledge
nor knowledge of the good, has any value, because it provides knowledge of no particular art. (171de) The knowledge of philosophy is like
the knowledge of the rhapsode—without any content whatever.

The ironies and recantations continue throughout *Republic*. Socrates' description of dialectic is hard both to accept and to reject; (532d)
Glaucon will not be able to follow Socrates further, followed by another
recantation; (533a) Socrates says that he is jesting, and "spoke with too
great intensity." (536c) To these we may add that one may study philosophy freely only after age fifty, closely approaching the age of Cephalus
with whom the work begins. Such a view "is not altogether a daydream."
(540d) But it is perhaps mostly one. And again, Socrates describes his
activity as a wrestling bout that one must win or lose. (544b) Although
justice is described as a harmony in the soul, it is the mirror image of
tyranny, one part ruling absolutely over the other. The sole difference
between the tyrant and the philosopher-king rests on which part of the
soul commands the others. If Cephalus is cerebral, representing a deficient ideal in which the head rules the passions, the philosopher-king is
far more so. The life without *eros* is a life without philosophy. The aporia
at the center of *Republic* is that of the emptiness of the vision of the good
in relation to a complex human life[36] and of the meaninglessness of a
human life without a vision of the good. Read this way, *Republic* is as
much caught up within the war between the giants and the gods over the
nature of being and intelligibility as is *Sophist*. (*Sophist*, 246c) The implication in both cases is of the reciprocity of power.

The myth of Er concludes, not with an overt claim to truth, but
with another recantation:

> And so, Glaucon, the tale was saved, as the saying is, and was
> not lost. And it will save us if we believe it . . . if we are guided
> by me we shall believe that the soul is immortal and capable of
> enduring all extremes of good and evil, ... (*Republic*, 621d)

We will believe it, and that is what is important. For we must return to
the irony of lyric poetry that appears just before the myth of Er: despite
the argument that poetry is deceptive in virtue of its form of mimesis, we
will permit the poet to make his defense in lyric poetry. (607d) Such a
defense is the myth of Er but also *Republic* itself.[37] Er is of the *earth*
although his story is of the heavens. The ancient quarrel between philosophy and poetry is not resolved in *Republic*. (607b)

In relation to *Republic*, then, what we must consider is that it *both* presents a transcendent vision of the good, and of a society based on it, and at the same time pervasively and deeply ironizes it, displacing our relationship to it. If we now ask what Plato is saying in the dialogue as a whole, and seek an answer in doctrinal terms—either that *Republic* is a utopian vision of an ideal state or that it is a criticism of such utopianism—we seek to tame one of the most heretical philosophic visions ever produced. Such domestication occurs if we suppose that Plato could have written and defended his doctrines in the form of argumentative discourse although he has Socrates constantly tell us that such doctrinal writing is inappropriate to philosophy. What we may emphasize instead is that *Republic* (with the other dialogues) *is* the only philosophy Plato wrote or thought, with its visions and its arguments, its stories and its displacements. It is philosophy, reason itself, with its doctrines and myths and the ironies that displace them. It includes both proofs and doctrines and their ironic displacements. It is among the greatest forms of rational thought in human history precisely because it provides a form in which "literal" and "figurative" expression interrogate each other endlessly, expressing the deepest understanding of the metaphysical enterprise with its heresies and aporias. In Plato's writings we find both the striking contrast between eternal and temporal and a recurrent, aporetic ironization of that contrast. Rather than regarding this ironization as a flattening of the theory of ideas, we may regard it as a deepening of its rationality, realized in aporia.[38]

Before we ask what difference the reading presented here makes to our understanding of Plato and of philosophy itself, we may briefly consider the remaining, deeply philosophic dialogues. We may come to terms with *Parmenides*, that most difficult of dialogues to interpret in canonical terms, by noting its close affinities with *Sophist*, *Statesman*, and *Philebus*. Although their proximate concerns are very different, the four dialogues share a common theme: the one (*to hen*) and many, limit and unlimit (*peras* and *apeiron*), determinateness in relation to indeterminateness. We may hypothesize that these dialogues are to be taken together dramatically and thematically, concerned among other things with the aporias of being and knowing.

The dialogue divides in two. In the first part, Parmenides and Zeno present to the younger Socrates most of Aristotle's important criticisms of the theory of ideas: that there must be ideas not only of beauty and the good, but of mud and excrement, undermining their ideality; forms must be divided over their instances, and cannot then be absolutely self-sufficient, undivided; the third-man argument that if similar things participate in forms by resemblance, then with their form they constitute another class that must participate in still other forms by resemblance, and so forth in an infinite regress; and finally, that forms are entirely other and therefore unknowable. These criticisms are so devastating that it is difficult to see how readers can still ascribe to Plato belief in a theory of ideas, at least of the sort criticized.

Socrates' reply to the aporetic nature of ordinary things is that

> ... if anyone can prove that what is simply unity itself is many or that plurality itself is one, then I shall begin to be surprised. (*Parmenides*, 129c)

But that is precisely what we find in the longer, second part of the dialogue.

> To this we may add the conclusion. It seems that, whether there is or is not a one, both that one and the others alike are and are not, and appear and do not appear to be, all manner of things in all manner of ways, with respect to themselves and to one another. (*Parmenides*, 166c)

This conclusion is intensely aporetic. A doctrinal resolution is that Plato is concerned to show that logical contradictions entail anything whatever. A more sophisticated interpretation is that Plato is defending the theory of ideas against Eleatic criticisms by showing that Parmenides' own views are subject to similar criticisms. A still more sophisticated interpretation is that he is criticizing a weaker version of the theory of ideas. The difficulty is that even the strongest version of the theory is still subject to the Parmenidian criticisms. The alternative is that the aporetic dance of same and other profoundly belongs to both truth and being.

The later discussion in the dialogue follows an earlier description of philosophic method. First, Zeno acknowledges that:

> ... the book is in fact a sort of defense of Parmenides' argument against those who try to make fun of it by showing that his supposition, that there is a one, leads to many absurdities and contradictions. This book, then, is a retort against those who assert a plurality. It pays them back in the same coin with something to spare, and aims at showing that, on a thorough examination, their own supposition that there is a plurality leads to even more absurd consequences than the hypothesis of the one. (*Parmenides*, 128d)

This passage supports the interpretation that the entire dialogue is an inverted imitation of the method described, defending the theory of ideas by showing that Parmenides' own theory is contradictory. However, Zeno concludes his description of his method with a striking figure:

> . . . you imagine it was inspired, not by a youthful eagerness for controversy, but by the more dispassionate aims of an older man, ... (*Parmenides*, 128e)

Given that the dialogue includes the younger Socrates as well as the older Parmenides, we are led to ask what these older, less contentious aims might be. A suggestion is that where youth regards opposition polemically and contentiously, age recognizes the profound importance of aporia. Where youth impatiently expects a quick resolution of philosophic difficulties, age understands that philosophy never ends, but participates in unending heresies. The theory of ideas is youthful exuberance. Age affirms the aporias within it without rejecting it. The theory of ideas is not refuted by its aporias, but enriched through them.

After the critical discussion of the theory of ideas, Parmenides offers another description of Zeno's method, apparently quite different from the first, and incompatible with his own rejection of nonbeing:

> If you want to be thoroughly exercised, you must not merely make the supposition that such and such a thing *is* and then consider the consequences; you must also take the supposition that the same thing *is not*. (*Parmenides*, 136a)

We have noted Socrates' reply that "There would be no end to such an undertaking." (*Parmenides*, 136d) And no wonder, for the method entails that we not only adopt certain hypotheses and determine their implications, but consider everything else ("what is not"), unendingly and inexhaustibly. Philosophy is the endless ballet of same and other. If we consider the aporias of being, there may indeed be no end to philosophy. Yet neither the indeterminateness nor the determinateness of ideas is the last word on the subject of being, for there is no last word. Metaphysics is an unending, heretical activity of reason.

It is worth comparing this definition of philosophic method with one in *Philebus*.[39]

> All things, so it ran, that are ever said to be consist of a one and a many, and have in their nature a conjunction of limit and unlimitedness. This then being the ordering of things we ought, they said, whatever it be that we are dealing with, to assume a single form and search for it, for we shall find it there contained; then, if we have laid hold of that, we must go on from one form

> to look for two, if the case admits of there being two, otherwise
> for three or some other number of forms. And we must do the
> same again with each of the "ones" thus reached, until we come
> to see not merely that the one that we started with is a one and
> an unlimited many, but also just how many it is. (*Philebus*, 17d)

While this account is given in the form of a story, it is among the most
important passages in the dialogues. It tells us that to be is to be together
one, many, and some determinate number, and we cannot stop until we
have determined the exact manyness, although that determination is inexhaustible. The play of same and other is itself a play of same and other.
There is neither undifferentiated oneness nor indeterminate manyness.
But we cannot deny such oneness and manyness—limit and unlimit—in
the name of measure. The aporetic nature of being and reality requires
an unending quest for the precision that, along with aporia, constitutes
truth. What Aristotle says about the indefinite dyad may be understood
here to be a moment in the unending dialectic of same and other: the
great and small of unlimit, indefinite manyness, and the determinateness
of number, measure.[40] The unending dialectic between these is truth:
aporetic, heretical, and inexhaustible.

What the "late" dialogues present us with are variations on the
aporias of one and many, limit and unlimit, same and other. What they
express, in the two descriptions of philosophic method, is that determinateness in being is both aporetic and inexhaustible, that as a consequence, reason is also aporetic and inexhaustible. In this sense, the
dialogues themselves, in their aporetic plurality, are reason itself, and
there is no superior form of philosophical thought. Where reason passes
beyond everydayness, beyond *technē*, it can have no definite form.

We may note some other features of these later dialogues, for example, the presence of the younger Socrates in addition to the Socrates we
know, suggesting a double relationship of Socrates' critical philosophy
to his own doctrines. We may note as well that even in these very late
dialogues, refutation—"the greatest and chiefest of purifications"—is
more important than is doctrine. The result is a profound sense of the
diversity and complexity of things.

> And the man who can do that discerns clearly *one* form
> everywhere extended throughout many, where each one lies apart,
> and *many* forms, different from one another, embraced from
> without by one form, and again *one* form connected in a unity
> through many wholes, and *many* forms, entirely marked off apart.
> That means knowing how to distinguish, kind by kind, in what
> ways the several kinds can or cannot combine. (*Sophist*, 253d)

The Eleatic Stranger corresponds to Parmenides and Zeno. When he is asked by the younger Socrates to explain his method of division, described in *Statesman*, he never complies. (262c) He suggests that the time to give a full account of dialectic has not yet arrived (284d) (and never does). He tells a story, "to relieve the strain," (268e) of the reversal of time, a speculation reminiscent of Philo's exercises in *Dialogues on Natural Religion* and Hegel's inverted world. Even more important, in *Statesman*, are the parallels with *Republic*, (293d) followed first by a recantation—"I was just going to cross-examine you to see if you really accepted all I have said" (294a)—and then by the claim that this "best" form of government degenerates into tyranny, the worst form of government, when "one man rules but does not govern his actions either by laws or by ancient customs, ..." (301b) The conclusion is that:

> The rule of one man, if it has been kept within the traces, so to speak, by the written rules we call laws, is the best of the six. But when it is lawless it is hard, and the most grievous to have to endure. (*Statesman*, 302e)

The "best" form is, then, also the "worst"; the "second-best" form is a democracy under law. (303b) The discussion so closely matches the dramatic form of *Republic* that it appears again in displaced terms. To this we may add that *Laws* begins with an extended discussion, not of justice and virtue, but of drinking. The second virtue is sobriety. (631c) The conclusion is that drinking will be prohibited to boys younger than age eighteen, permitted in moderation to men up to age thirty, and permitted in those older than age forty with suitable genuflections, (666b) a parody of the education of the philosopher in *Republic*. Additional parodies abound. The Athenian suggests that singers be educated in ways parallel to the education of the guardians. We remind ourselves that *Laws* is described as an entertainment during a walk in the heat of the day. It is an entertainment that constantly refers to earlier dialogues. It is Plato ironizing himself.

> Men are perpetually fancying they have discovered some splendid creation which might have worked wonders if only someone had known the proper way—whatever it may be—to use it. (*Laws*, 686d)

As for the doctrine of forms, not only is it subjected to devastating criticisms in *Parmenides*, it is far more profoundly refuted in *Timaeus*, that greatest of cosmological stories, described by Socrates as a "feast of discourse," a "banquet." (20c) The crucial criticisms of the theory of ideas lie first, in the recognition that two kinds of causes are required, beyond the forms, in the creator and in the "variable cause" (48a) that require a new beginning—an explicit recantation; then, second, in the reference to the receptacle that so captivated Whitehead. To recognize the importance of efficient causes and of a place where real things can exercise their powers is to give up any simple view of the relation between forms and things. But we could go on indefinitely with the ironic and dramatic displacements in the later dialogues.

We find in these dialogues several recurrent themes. One is the ironization of earlier dialogues, especially *Republic*. Second is a devastating criticism of the theory of ideas. Third is an increasing emphasis on both technical discussions and elaborate storytelling. Fourth is emphasis upon the aporias of knowing and being. Aporia imposes upon us, not mere acceptance, but unending dialectic. In *Parmenides*, not only must we pursue the (inexhaustible) consequences of the same, but the (inexhaustible) possibilities of otherness. Philosophy is a *première danseuse* in the unending ballet of same and other.

This interpretation explains the function in *Philebus* of measure, proportion, and reason in relation to the highest goods. The doctrinal position, following the Pythagorean strain in Plato and, later, after modern science, is that there is a determinate measure to being that makes it intelligible. What Socrates says, however, quite specifically, is that being is aporetic in conjoining one and many because there is no such conjunction that has a precise and stable measure. To the contrary, amidst the one there is an inexhaustible many; amidst the indeterminate many, there is a determinate "intermediate" number. The analysis of manyness in both cases is inexhaustible. Socrates is critical of both Parmenides' undivided One and of Heraclitus' disunified multiplicity, of both unqualified determinateness and unqualified indeterminateness. Yet he is also critical of a determinate number that defines the precise otherness in the same. There is neither an indefinite and unqualified multiplicity nor a determinate number that defines any being, for it is *both* one and a definite intermediate, aporetically. The pursuit of these intermediates is philosophy, but it is unendingly engaged amidst aporia in both being and knowing.

Conforming to this inexhaustible play of one and many, limit and unlimit, is an inexhaustible play of language and ideas, of art and science, rhetoric and philosophy. Each of the oppositions defines a distinction that requires an inexhaustible play of dialectic. The result is Plato's dramatic method, where aporia is exhibited dramatically and precision is expressed argumentatively. It is because the dialogues pay attention to the intermediates that they are philosophical. Philosophical method is not scientific experiment or logical proof *instead* of storytelling and dramatic irony, but is them all together, aporetically and agonistically. Even here, the choice between rhetoric and philosophy, or opinion and truth, is not unqualified, but requires inexhaustible intermediates. Certain questions provide the center of philosophic activity, changing their forms inexhaustibly, but nevertheless remaining indefinitely aporetic and unresolvable.

What we want to do, finally, is to ask what such a reading of the dialogues implies. What, after all, is Plato's philosophic position, given that he wrote dialogues and not tracts, given that irony pervades even the most technical arguments? The question is misconceived, supposing that there is an alternative form of expression that Plato might have employed instead. What I am suggesting is that what we find in the Platonic dialogues is philosophy itself, that the only philosophy that can be found within the dialogues is the result of reading them as dialogues, as stories. Storytelling is philosophy. There is no deeper or more precise form of knowledge that can evade storytelling, dramatic interaction, conversation, and dialogue. Philosophy is where language employs every means at its disposal.

The ironies and displacements found in the Platonic dialogues, with their stories, suggest a doctrinal revision of the theory of ideas. It might go something like the following:

1. What is intelligible must be understood jointly in terms of eternity and changeability, between the intelligibility of forms and the intelligibility of sensible experience. However, the relationship between what is eternal and what is changeable, what is indivisible and what is divisible, is aporetic. Moreover, unchanging forms and sensible things are themselves aporetic.

2. Two things follow: (a) there is no form of metaphysical understanding free from aporia, only a thinking and rethinking of aporia, especially in relation to time; (b) aporia is compatible with both knowledge and science. The continuing interplay between aporia and scientific determinateness comprises reason. There is no undivided knowledge, but there can be no knowledge without the intelligibility given by its undivided form. This form is then aporetically disruptive of the intelligibility that defines reason.

3. There is no determinate method for acquiring knowledge, and there are no rules for understanding. In this sense, all knowledge is, like memory, a divine inspiration. The pursuit of knowledge is an unending dialectic filled with aporias and heresies. The two extremes must equally be avoided: that knowledge is impossible in virtue of aporia and that knowledge can overcome aporia.

4. Both sensible experience and intelligible reality are aporetic.
5. Both knowledge and being are aporetic: inventive and creative. Mimesis is unintelligible without heresy.
6. Intelligible reality can be determinate only in relation to sensible experience and only known in virtue of its relations to
   such experience, although all such relations are aporetic.
7. Virtue is knowledge of the good. But all such knowledge is
   heretical. Virtue is therefore the unending heresy of the good
   in relation to every established rule or principle.
8. Virtue and self-knowledge are aporetic, pervaded by heresy.
9. Wherever one turns one finds the gods, expressing inexhaustibility, the infinite in the finite, limitation in unlimit, reason in
   unreason, and in every case, conversely.

There is a theory of ideas in Plato, as there is a view that the best
life for human beings is a life of virtue inseparable from reason. There is
also a deep and abiding sense of the aporias of being and knowing, including the ideas, accompanied by what may be the deepest sense known to
humanity of the limitations of every philosophical doctrine, including
even the explicit rejection of doctrine. The dialogues express a profound sense not only of the aporias of determinateness and indeterminateness—limit and unlimit—but of the ways in which determinate
measure and proportion are required for understanding and the good
life. There are doctrines and arguments in the dialogues, but they are
not simply the doctrines and arguments *of* the dialogues, and certainly
not simply Plato's. Rather, reason is a matter of telling stories and myths,
in dramatic form, under divine inspiration, concerning the deepest
thoughts that reason allows, concerning being, reality, and the good.
Doctrines and proofs *belong to* philosophy; they are not identical with
it. Moreover, there is no canonical form for the true expression of philosophy, no particular form of legitimacy and authority.

It follows that we cannot say in other words what Plato tells us in
his own, not without imposing a doctrine upon him. What we can do
instead is to tell a story.

There is a tale often told about a city of human beings who understood, more deeply than any before them and possibly any after, what a
life of reason might be. We must imagine such a city, because we cannot
be sure if there have ever been such human beings or ever will be. But
even if we are not sure, we should consider the possibility of their existence. We should even more deeply consider the possibility of the life of
reason that they embodied.

What made them deeply philosophical was that they did not wor-
ship knowledge but simply lived it. It took no specialized gifts but was

inseparable from human life itself—a life that prided itself on understanding and truth, that sought to know its own limits and to transcend them, marked by a sense of the constant presence of the gods. Philosophy and science were the thinking that human beings did in all their activities, practical and political, as they sought to live the best human life they could. Reason was manifested in the unceasing discussions, conversations, and stories in which the citizens of that city participated every waking moment of their lives except when urgent practical matters took priority.

What the citizens of our state opposed most passionately was every effort to curtail reason by defining its limits absolutely. They saw two dangers, so to speak, on the left and right: that reason should become a specialized form of discourse, of great exactness, that contributed little to human excellence; or, on the other hand, that reason might become a mindless matter of diverse opinions, without depth and rigor, that being and the good should be regarded as absolutely transcendent conditions of sensible experience, available only to the chosen few, and that sensible experience should utterly lack transcendence. In order to steer their ship between these reefs, they avoided every citizen who proclaimed himself a philosophic leader, capable of piloting the ship of state to virtue and to truth, subjecting every such candidate to withering sarcasm. They opposed those who proclaimed the absolute limits of finite experience, lacking a profound sense of the miraculous and the divine, and those who sought to escape from aporia to an undivided absolute. They equally opposed those who attempted to tread a middle line and those who attempted to think at the limits of thought itself. They followed the path of thought wherever it might lead, constantly probing within it, seeking the limits of limits and the limits of those limits. They discussed issues of being, truth, and excellence as they walked, while they talked, at their festivals, late at night, whenever they could. They endlessly discussed every question that they could think of, and awarded prizes to those who thought up new questions that inspired further discussion. Above all, they mocked each other for dogmatism and closedmindedness, especially including those who claimed moral rectitude and extreme virtue. Yet they displayed equal contempt for those who had no convictions concerning virtue. To them, the human life was the virtuous life, in all its discursive and divided plenitude. It was, they believed, both aporetic and heretical, its greatest aporia that it demanded the stability of determinateness while it found itself forever divided by indeterminateness. This dividedness was regarded as the origin of reason, which would terminate with the overcoming of aporia. Ideals were understood to be aporetic moments in a reason that had to find itself divided in order to think itself: mimetic reason surrounded by heresy; inventive reason inescapably repetitious.

The city we are told about was far from perfect. At times, it fostered slavery, engaged in acquisitive wars, treated women as second-class citizens, and brought about great injustices. Its citizens emphasized the profound interrelationship between philosophy and politics, but found it impossible to establish a perfect harmony between them. They opposed injustice but found themselves surrounded by it. They understood this imperfection in human life as one of its inescapable conditions. To such imperfections, they responded deeply, sometimes tragically, sometimes comically, always with a sense of a future pregnant with both terror and exhilaration, and of the limits of intelligibility and being that constitute human life.

What was unique about the city was the importance of philosophy and art within it: these were regarded as capacities of every citizen. Every human life was lived at the edges of both reason and unreason. What was also unique about the city was that it encouraged the production of the greatest poetry and art as well as philosophy ever known, to the point where many of those who followed, in later generations, could not imagine the production of equally great works. Philosophy, and even poetry, these followers said, can do no more than adumbrate the work of those great writers. The irony in such reverence for the past—if it really was the past—is that the people who wrote the works that inspired such reverence had little admiration for them except as transitory moments in a heretical process of life and thought.

Among the favorite topics of discussion in this city was philosophy itself, particularly amusing to those who asked it given that they regarded everything they did as philosophy. They would divide themselves into groups, by lot, one side taking the position that philosophy was poetry and poetry philosophy, the other criticizing poetry for its divine inspiration and lack of technical rigor, a third criticizing philosophy for its lack of proof, a fourth criticizing science for its sterility and oppressiveness, a fifth criticizing philosophy for being useless in politics, a sixth rejecting every possibility of philosophy, a seventh arguing that philosophy provides the only knowledge possible of a divine, transcendent being. To amuse themselves even more, they would require those who defended the first position to argue in technical, almost hermetic language, based on mutually agreed on logical principles, while those who defended the second position were required to express their views in rhyming couplets. The third were required to critize poetry by devising experiments; the fourth had to criticize science by telling stories; the fifth had to show that philosophic questions could be answered through public works, the sixth had to combine all the others into a single form, the seventh had to defend themselves through dance and dramatic performances. They gave arguments, made speeches, wrote poetry, even painted and sang. They also engaged in many forms of experimentation and observation, with corresponding entertainments, in which great debates took place as to whether discussion without experimentation was empty or whether observation without storytelling was blind. Sometimes they divided themselves into groups to discuss whether one particular form of expression was more truthful than another, more authentic, or more sincere. Such debates were regarded as the greatest spectacles available. These were spectacles, they thought, where truth appeared in its most visible form, aporetically and heretically. Each expressed position imposed itself coercively on those who listened. Each displacement revealed the dividedness in every position.

One of the joys of life in this mythical city were biannual festivals at which great public discussions and performances took place, before thousands of people, sometimes merely watching, sometimes joining in the activities by shouting questions from the audience or by encouraging one side against the other. When first begun, the discussions were carried on close to the audience while great dramatic and religious spectacles took place on a stage raised high above. Later, the stages were divided, and some performances took place down below while at the same time, discussions and spectacles were joined on the raised stages. These festivals were enjoyed so much because they were understood to be the public, celebrative form in which the many discussions and conversations that had taken place during the preceding years could be shared among those who had not participated in them. They were also regarded as the sites at which the gods, who defined both the limits and disruptions of reason, made themselves most forcibly present.

It was considered the greatest form of entertainment to establish a position at one festival and to criticize it at the next, to philosophize in one form—say lyric poetry—at one festival and to display another form at the next. The most spectacular of philosophic entertainments presented themselves as timeless and necessary at one festival, only to repudiate their necessity and eternity at the next, aporetic moments in a continuing activity of reason interrogating itself. The citizens of the state were expected to remember earlier festivals and to recognize later variations upon them. Although there were constant discussions about the rigidity of written discussions, and a constant debate over the superiority of speech over writing, there were those who kept detailed records of the debates as aids to memory.

What happened to this city, if it ever existed, is largely lost in the mists of time. Some say that it was replaced by autocratic regimes that demanded absolute agreement in the name of power, divine authority, or science. Others say that the weaknesses of the city—its ambitions and greed—led to its fragmentation. Still others say that we are not to believe that it ever existed, that it is but a dream, a vision for the future. Some think that its transitoriness manifests the impossibility of any enduring, stable form of human life. One of the outcomes of its disappearance was that the few written works that have come down to us from that city, if they have indeed done so, and were not written by others who pretended to have discovered them, seem to have entirely lost the qualities that inspired them. The doctrines that were accepted only to be criticized have entered recorded history as authoritative positions, and the sense that philosophy is profoundly heretical, constantly challenging its own forms and conditions, has passed into dogma. Those few who continue to tell the story of this city revere it as the ideal life for which all human beings should strive, perfection itself.

Whether or not this city ever existed, and whether or not it is to be taken as the model of an ideal human life, we will be better for believing that both natural and human reality, including human virtue, have no particular essence, but are always manifold and variable, yet that variability is not itself without limit, and both being and human being are determinate as well as indeterminate. We will profit from believing that the highest human life consists in the unending project imposed by limitation, making what is indeterminate determinate and what is determinate indeterminate, to the limits of our imaginations and capabilities.

4 ARISTOTLE: THE HERESY OF ORTHODOXY

OF the philosophers who define orthodoxy in the Western tradition, Aristotle is certainly the most orthodox. This is still true despite the complete repudiation of his physics and astronomy, even his biology, and the widespread rejection of his theory of substance. It is true despite the unceasing admiration of many of the most heretical philosophers for Aristotle's own heretical greatness. And it is true despite unceasing controversy among his admirers over the nature of his orthodoxy.[1] Part of the reason lies in the style of Aristotle's extant work: the voice of propositional reason. Argument triumphs over storytelling and drama. Yet even in Aristotle, the preeminent purpose of discourse is to triumph. We cannot escape the will to power in Aristotle. We cannot escape the will to heresy.

Aristotle has never lacked defenders, of both his orthodoxy and his heresy. Of those in recent times who have emphasized the unorthodox side of Aristotle, three may be singled out. Giovanni Reale finds in Aristotle unremitting concern with the supersensible. If this is Thomistic orthodoxy, it nevertheless is profoundly heretical: the heresy of "ontotheology."[2] Nevertheless, despite such ontotheology, Heidegger finds in Aristotle's view of nature, of *physis*, a plenitude, an inner source of enrichment and change,[3] quite lacking in modern, Galilean thought.[4] Yet, if we regard the Greek view as antithetic to a "technomorphic" view of nature, based on *technē*, then Aristotle cannot be said to hold it consistently if at all. His teleology gets in the way.

> Nature belongs to the class of things which act for the sake of something. (*Physics*, 198a)[5]

Nature is a productive power, and what it produces is the end for which it strives. These concepts of production and end pertain more to *technē* than to *physis*.

John Herman Randall Jr.'s reading of Aristotle emphasizes a different heresy:

> Aristotle's aim is to understand, to find out why things are as they are. It is not to control things, not to make them different from what they are. And that seems strange to us, for we are all confirmed Baconians.[6]

Randall describes a side of Aristotle that in modern terms is indeed heretical. For knowledge is regarded as a form of power, even, within late modernity, the most important form. That there could be a view of knowledge apart from power is either remarkably singular or self-deluded. To this we must add that among the most striking of the heresies in late modernity is the suggestion that knowledge, especially including science, is a form of power and deception. Knowledge, even in science, is ideology.[7]

What could it mean to pursue knowledge independent of power and control? One answer, partly Aristotle's, is that scientific knowledge mirrors the nature of things without distortion, presenting truth uncontaminated by power and desire. Another answer, also partly Aristotle's, is that theoretical knowledge is something to be had, or pursued, for its own sake independent of its outcomes or influences. We are far too empiricistic and pragmatistic today to accept such a view without question. What is required, if we separate these two answers, is a need to think that theory can be pursued regardless of its practical results without assuming that knowledge can mirror reality.

Aristotle's *Metaphysics* opens with the line, "All men by nature desire to know." (980a) Randall gently mocks the plausibility of this claim.[8] Yet, what is implausible is not that human beings strive to know, strive for truth, but that they strive for it only so far and primarily in relation to practical ends. That human beings might desire a knowledge with no practical consequences whatever, or a knowledge with only debilitating consequences, is implausible. That human beings might desire knowledge even if it could be shown to be destructive is even less plausible. Dostoievski's Grand Inquisitor argues that most human beings would choose to give up their freedom and knowledge to be contented. The more likely explanation is that most human beings are able and willing to set aside their practical concerns only partially and with mixed success, rather than that they do not esteem knowledge for its own sake. Human beings desire knowledge, but it is not for all the highest good, and certainly not an unmixed good.

The emphasis in the tradition is that Aristotle's view of nature, contrary to Heidegger, is based almost entirely on his view of explanation and intelligibility. To Aristotle, "Wisdom is knowledge about certain principles and laws." (*Metaphysics*, 982) Knowledge is of the causes and principles to which nature conforms. The alternative strains Heidegger discerns in Aristotle's sense of *physis* are marginal in relation to his strong emphasis on demonstrative necessity, although they reflect the inconsistencies that make Aristotle's sense of aporia so enthralling. Randall's sense of what may be heretical in Aristotle is as plausible. Yet even he neglects what may be the greatest heresy in Aristotle: that of orthodoxy itself.

The idea that orthodoxy is heretical is susceptible to different interpretations. One is that too much orthodoxy is, like all extremes, perverse and becomes heretical in its extremity. This may well be true of Aristotle, but is more a function of the orthodoxy of the tradition than of his own excessive claims to orthodoxy. Aristotle here is always heretical in refusing to be subsumed under the tradition as its primary progenitor. His views cannot be taken whole, but must be transformed into orthodoxy to comprise a tradition. The second interpretation follows the image of domestication more closely. A great, systematic philosopher is like a wild beast who can only be tamed at great risk, for he may at any time revert to his blood lines and threaten us with violence. The image here is of a grand and unruly thinker who can be tamed only by neglecting the singularities in his view of things. Aristotle is frequently regarded as among the sanest of philosophers—sanity here is orthodoxy. Yet throughout his writings prominent strains are found that cannot be subsumed under normal standards of intelligibility.

A striking example concerns the notion of aporia in Book III of Aristotle's *Metaphysics*. His solutions, if they exist at all, have no equivalent textual integrity, but scatter throughout other discussions. If aporias here are "problems," crying out for solution as a traditional view would have it, Aristotle's style of presentation is counterproductive. Moreover, in his most explicit explanation of his treatment of aporias, he does not speak of resolving them.

> We must, as in all other cases, set the observed facts before us and, after first discussing the difficulties, go on to prove, if possible, the truth of all the common opinions about these affections of the mind, or, failing this, of the greater number and the most authoritative; for if we both refute the objections and leave the common opinions undisturbed, we shall have proved the case sufficiently. (*Nicomachean Ethics*, 1145b)[9]

The sometimes violent controversies over the unity or inconsistency of his thought frequently turn on assumptions concerning the nature of his problem-solving.[10]

The alternative I propose is that Aristotle's aporias are not problems and have only aporetic resolution. The controversies in Aristotelian scholarship embody a more fundamental question than they seek explicitly to address, concerning not so much what were Aristotle's views and what they mean, but the nature of philosophic intelligibility. The first four aporias in Book III address whether there is one or many sciences concerned with causes and substances in general. Aristotle's own answer, manifested in his understanding of being *qua* being, has occasioned enormous controversy because he denies that being is the highest genus.

> But it is not possible that either unity or being should be a single genus of things; for the differentiae of any genus must each of them both have being and be one, but it is not possible for the genus taken apart from its species (any more than for the species of the genus) to be predicated of its proper differentiae; so that if unity or being is a genus, no differentia will either have being or be one. (*Metaphysics*, 998b)[11]

If first philosophy (*protē philosophia*) is a science of sciences, it cannot rule over the other sciences demonstratively. The controversies over Aristotle's view of *protē philosophia* tend to obscure the possibility that there is no decisive answer to whether there is a science of being *qua* being. There is such a science, but it is an extraordinary one bearing extraordinary relations to local sciences and substances. Not only is the nature of metaphysics itself aporetic on this reading—highly plausible given its subsequent history—but so is the nature of science in relation to many local sciences.

The aporias of one science in relation to many sciences are aporias of intelligibility: one and many, same and other. The question of intelligibility is that of aporia itself, and returns throughout the other aporias of Book III: whether what is fundamental concerns substance or its (many) attributes, whether there are many (kinds of) substances, many kinds of being. In every case, the answers Aristotle gives elsewhere in his *Metaphysics* have occasioned continuing controversy. The reason is that he does not resolve the aporias without aporia. The most pervasive form of Aristotelian argument is that there is a multiplicity—many substances, many kinds of substance, many fundamental principles, many causes—but among the many, one is primary—primary substance, the unmoved mover, separated substance. Yet this ontological primacy is always arbitrary relative to Aristotle's own understanding of the multiplicity. His thought retains aporia throughout, both in its "aporematic" and in its "doctrine."

The most prominent notion in Aristotle is that of *nous*. As important as this notion is in Plato, it is overshadowed by the dramatic exchanges and the storytelling. In Aristotle, however, *nous* is the first principle of understanding and reason. All human beings by nature desire to know. What they desire to know, among other things, is being *qua* being.

Briefly setting being aside, we may divide knowledge here in two. One is largely orthodox in relation to modern science. Knowledge is of causes and principles: explanatory. Knowledge is science.

> We suppose ourselves to possess unqualified scientific knowledge of a thing, . . . when we think that we know the cause on which the fact depends, as the cause of that fact and of no other, and, further, that the fact could not be other than it is. (*Posterior Analytics*, 71b)

Such a view of the parts of animals and of heavenly motions may appear plausible. It is implausible, as it stands, in relation to organic and inorganic nature in general, and especially in relation to philosophy. With respect to the former, some hints of implausibility reveal themselves in Aristotle's view of science. Where there are many intrinsically local sciences, each with distinct subject matters and principles, there is no manifest procedure for relating one local understanding with another — relating animals to the heavens, for example — or for connecting different local spheres together. It is, then, essential that there be a science of sciences, however latent or potential, that the many sciences be the same if all explanations are finally to be necessary.

Aristotle's view, however, is that there are many sciences, not one, each based on a different *archē*, with a different "origin," although there is also a science of being *qua* being. Moreover, his epistemology parallels his ontology, for similarly, there are many kinds of substance, but within the many, one is primary. This conjunction of unity and plurality is among his most striking features. It is a form of philosophic "common sense," and he is perhaps the most commonsensical of great philosophers. Carried to great lengths, however, common sense is heresy. There are limits that define the boundaries of familiarity and heresy in broaching those limits. An example we have noted in relation to the preSocratics is the suggestion that all is water or air. These are too mundane to serve as originary principles and can do so only by heretical significations.

There is, in Aristotle, a common sense view of science that remains unorthodox within the age of modern science. It is a combination of almost total acceptance of the possibility of a science—necessary, demonstrative, and explanatory knowledge—conjoined with an almost total rejection of what may be called its *legitimation*.[12] One form in which a demand for legitimation has traditionally been expressed is that of skepticism. Yet Aristotle has no interest in refuting skepticism. Far more important, however, there are deep disparities between this commonsensical acceptance of the form of science and the general conditions that make an empirical science possible. Relative to contemporary scientific practices, there is too great an emphasis in Aristotle on ordinary observations rather than on the more arcane and subtle forms of observation that are made possible by technical instruments. Common sense, carried to an extreme, in relation to technical scientific methods, is aporetic. We cannot take science whole in relation to such common sense. One reason is the heresy within science that common sense gives us a distorted view of things.

There is, in Aristotle, both a view that there are many sciences, based on different origins, with distinct subject matters and forms, and a view that there is a science of sciences—the view rejected in Plato's *Charmides*. There is a view of science as the form knowledge takes, in connection with any subject matter or activity, and there is a view of science as comprising demonstrative, necessary proof. Throughout these views runs Aristotle's commonsensism, which in the present context involves the rejection of a science of sciences as the basis of any particular science. In connection with both *logos* and *nous*, however, Aristotle's commonsensism is abandoned. What we may say, if we do not insist on consistency, is that throughout his view of intelligibility and rationality, there are irresistible aporias.

For the other side of Aristotle's view of knowledge, beyond that of science, although related to it, lies in his view of *logos* on the one hand and *nous* on the other. If it is implausible that all human beings desire to know being *qua* being, it is certainly true that there can be no human life that is not based on knowledge, practical if not deeply theoretical. Less plausible is that the knowing self that constitutes the condition of practical human experience might have the qualities Aristotle ascribes to *nous*. For his view of *nous* is among the most extraordinary conceptions ever devised.[13] It is one of the impoverishments of the modern period to have rejected it without recognition that it remains a mainstay of every significant theory of knowledge.

The knowing mind must be able to become its object. It must, then, be both pure and possess no nature of its own. (*De Anima*, 429a) If we interpret the identity of knower and known here as a mirroring, suggested by Aristotle's language, then we may regard his view as foundational. Relevant criticisms are that there is no mind that fails to possess a nature of its own, biological, historical, and cultural, and that there is no intelligible identity possible between mind and object. Here we may discern the power of the theory of ideas, in either Platonic or Aristotelian terms, for *eidos* is precisely what is identical in both object and thought, knower and known. Following a mathematical analogy, we may say that the identity between knower and known is entirely formal: the idea common in mind and object is the basis on which it may be known. Intelligibility rests in the same. We sacrifice any intelligible sense of the knowledge of individual things. It is for this reason that a more empiricistic epistemology, based on generalization from individual things, must reject too formalistic an epistemology. The purity and generality of *nous* is incompatible with the concreteness required for determinate knowing.

This issue, of the determinateness required for knowing and being, appears in Aristotle in a variety of forms, but especially in relation to the identity of essence and being in any individual substance or *ousia*. He seeks to establish the possibility of knowing upon a determinate identity of knowing and known. On the one hand, then, *nous* must be pure and have no nature of its own, so that it may take any form required. On the other hand, what makes a being determinate, its essence, also *ousia*, must be identical in formula and being. What is clear on Aristotle's account is that the plurality of ways of being that pertain to *ousia* is only incompletely, if at all, equivalent with any essence in thought or language.

Aristotle's thought has two predominant strains: understanding being in relation to what can be said about it, requiring that *logos* be the expression of being itself; and understanding beings in terms of the natural processes that comprise them and that make them determinate. Similarly, two relevant forms of determinateness or intelligibility are present: that belonging to the *logos* or *nous*, and that belonging to beings in their natural relations. The *ousia* that is the essence of a determinate individual being is the concept that links these different senses of being. Aristotle both establishes an identity in essence and being and acknowledges its aporetic nature. Only form can be one in thought and being, but if essence is form, then it cannot be determinate. Form can be the identity of thought and being only in relation to mathematical objects, and never in relation to physical or observable objects. This disparity passes into the tradition in the realization that finite knowledge is always incomplete. The alternative, suggested by Aristotle himself, is that this incompleteness pertains to knowledge intrinsically and that an infinite knowledge would be no knowledge at all.

The principle that *nous* or the knowing mind can have no nature of its own without distorting its object has passed into the tradition to the point where any contrary view is regarded as Kantian: to say that the nature of the knowing subject pertains to the known object is to abandon naturalism and realism.[14] Aristotle speaks of *nous* as a "bare capacity" and as "pure," akin to the receptacle in *Timaeus*. Yet the notion of a substratum in which qualities inhere without possessing a determinate nature, similarly, that space and time are similarly "bare" and "pure," is incoherent, rejected by Aristotle himself in relation to matter.[15] Space and time, metrical or not (as in Whitehead),[16] can be intelligible only if they are determinate (although they are also indeterminate), divided by their relations. The point is that *nous* must be able to take on any qualities or properties, must be able to "become" all things, *and* must possess a determinate nature of its own. Here we pass from Aristotle not to Kant, but to Spinoza and Hegel. Form is thinkable only because thought has a determinate historical and teleological nature. Form requires an other to be determinate.

The mirroring relation between noetic mind and noematic object suggests a correspondence epistemology. That side of Aristotle is simply unacceptable. It becomes heretical only in Spinoza, among his greatest heresies as he is among the most heretical of philosophers. *The order and connection of ideas is the same as the order and connection of things.* (*Ethics*, II, Prop. VII [discussed in Chapter 5 herein]) Far more plausible is to interpret Aristotle's view of *nous* in relation to how the mind can be said to know rather than in relation to how a science can be said to achieve certainty. Aristotle's view, here, is that the mind must be able to receive all characters, to think all things, and must be pure, cannot have a nature of its own. We may divide these claims in two.

We are still almost as ignorant as Aristotle was of how the brain might be able to know all things, even any things. However, we may avoid problems of internal representation by following the "linguistic turn." The question of how the mind can know all things is analogous to the question of how a language can express all things, however incompletely. The two sides of Aristotle's characterization of *nous* apply to language. On the one hand, we must accept the principle of expressibility, that whatever can be thought can be said.[17] On the other, we must acknowledge the specificity of any particular language, that it fosters certain forms of expression and inhibits others. These two principles conflict in every act of translation, a continuing drama of same and other.

The latter formulation of the principle of expressibility is too weak for our purposes and suffers from presupposing *nous*: thought before language. We may redefine it as follows: if language is to be a universal medium of expression—although not the only such medium[18]—then we must be able to express knowledge of any kind in linguistic form. We may qualify this principle however we choose. Linguistic expression of certain truths may not be as effective or informative as expression in other forms: pictorial or symbolic. Still, that knowledge should be possible through language requires that language, with or without other forms of representation, must be able to serve as a medium of any knowledge. Here we may consider not only the modest force of the principle of expressibility above, but the far more sweeping claims by Gadamer concerning language:

> In reality, language is the single word whose virtuality opens up the infinity of discourse, of discourse with others, and of the freedom of "speaking oneself" and of "allowing oneself to be spoken." Language is not its elaborate conventionalism, or the burden of pre-schematisation with which it loads us, but the generative and creative power unceasingly to make this whole fluid.[19]

> While we live wholly within a language, the fact that we do so does not constitute linguistic relativism because there is absolutely no captivity within language—not even within our native language.[20]

Such claims appear inflated where we are concerned with the transparency of language, analogous with the purity of *nous*. That mind and language should possess determinate natures suggests distortion. If, instead, we emphasize the adaptability and malleability of language, its capacity for novelty and expressibility, so that we can find a way, somehow, to say whatever we need to say, then Aristotle's view of *nous* and Gadamer's view of language are far more plausible. What must be emphasized is that language's expressibility, and the mind's ability to think, *somehow* achieve their goals. There is a miraculousness to knowledge and language that corresponds to heresy. As soon as we attempt to define the universal conditions of expression and thought, we face aporias and indeterminatenesses. There is here the heresy of heresy itself.

We may define the traditional position as that in order for mind and language to be epistemic, they must be undistorting mirrors of the same capable of reflecting anything whatever. Such a view is incompatible with any empirical understanding and the social and cultural determinants of thought and language. The question is whether we can accommodate an understanding of the specific determinants of thought and language without a skeptical epistemology. The answer, suggested by Gadamer but by no means incompatible with Aristotle's view of *nous*, is that it is precisely *because* language possesses a determinate nature that knowledge and expression are possible. It is *because* the mind possesses determinate structures and pathways that it is able to gain knowledge—by overcoming its antecedents. We must postulate the first of Aristotle's principles, the "identity" of mind and object, universally, but reject the second, the transparency and purity of thought. Even the first, however, reinterpreted not to involve mirroring, is strikingly heretical.

What we find in Aristotle's view of the mind and its epistemic capacities are two principles that, in the tradition, have been reduced to one: (1) a potentiality in thought that it may be expanded and enriched to pertain to any object whatever, of any kind, acknowledgment of inexhaustible otherness; (2) an identity between knower and known based on the rule of the same. The latter principle faces us with both a mirroring view of knowledge and an identity of mind and world. It was natural that empiricism should have transformed such an unintelligible identity into internal representation: any object, to be knowable, must be representable internally in terms of the mind's forms and structures. Effectively neglected is the far more heretical first principle: anything whatever is knowable, *somehow*. Knowledge and the knowing mind are together inexhaustible.

The inexhaustibility of knowing and thinking is obscured within the tradition in part by too great an emphasis upon the identity of knowing and known, suggesting a finitely knowable world in relation to a finite mind, in part by the medieval tradition's denial that anything whatever is knowable through the finite mind because God is not finitely knowable. The tradition chose to emphasize the limits of the finite knowing mind in relation to an infinite God. Yet, in Aristotle, no such sense of limitation is present. To the contrary, he holds that the inexhaustibility of *nous* requires that it be able to become *anything* whatever. The Judeo-Christian tradition could not regard such a view of the finite intellect as anything but sacrilege. What it is instead is heresy.

For it is not only unnecessary to postulate that the mind has no nature of its own in order to "become" or know all things: it is mistaken to do so. Without a nature, the thinking mind cannot begin to know anything at all. More precisely, without prior knowledge, whatever its limitations, no subsequent knowledge can be acquired. This, more than anything, is the principle embodied in the doctrine of recollection, stripped of its mythic resonances. New knowledge can be acquired only from older knowledge. The two inescapable conditions of knowing are prior forms of knowledge and the development of new, heretical forms. Obscured by Aristotle's view of the inexhaustible potentialities of *nous* is the implication that it may transform itself where necessary to take on whatever new forms are required by the epistemic conditions of thought and expression. The denial that *nous* has a nature of its own makes the acquisition of knowledge unintelligible, because there is no intelligible origin, but also makes the development of new forms of knowledge unintelligible, because they do not affect *nous* itself.

To the contrary, it is only because reason has a determinate nature — however it acquires it: biologically, historically, genetically, or empirically — that it can acquire knowledge; and it is only because reason can change its nature that it can acquire knowledge. Knowledge requires that the knowing mind and reason be inexhaustible, but one side of inexhaustibility is the possibility of heresy. There is, here, a side of empiricism from which no epistemology can escape: what is known is at any time a function of the experienced conditions of the knowing subject. The other side, however, is that within every local knowing condition there are inexhaustible potentialities of local transcendence.

Aristotle's view of *nous* is heretical, but not on the side of his epistemology that later became orthodox, that is, the mirroring tradition. Indeed, there is something remarkably implausible about the view that the mind is capable of becoming its object, however radically we reinterpret the identity. So great is the implausibility, indeed, that this deeply foundational epistemological principle has, throughout the Western tradition, recurrently flirted with skepticism, whether in relation to knowledge of a God unknowable to an infinite intellect or in relation to the repetition involved in internal and external representations. Even in Kant, the representational view of knowledge is preserved throughout the first *Critique* only to be effectively supplanted, in the third, by a view of judgment based on the breaking of rules. This heretical view of genius, closely related to Aristotle's view of *phronēsis*, is denied epistemic legitimacy by Kant. Aristotle here is the greater heretic. Far more important, however, is the recognition that there is another side to Aristotle's view of *nous*, quite unrelated to his view of the same. The knowing mind must be capable of becoming inexhaustibly other.

This is a profound metaphysical heresy, found in the preSocratics in the form of aporia, in Plato in the form of dialogue and dialectic, but in Aristotle in his view of *nous* and substance, although so thoroughly mixed with other principles as to obscure both its power and heresy. Aristotle's view of *ousia* is always divided within itself into a plurality of ways of being and a primary way. His view of knowing is always divided within itself into a plurality of ways of knowing and a primary way. Only one side of this view has been adopted in the orthodox tradition — except, perhaps, in Spinoza, who has always remained heretical, marginal. Even here, however, Aristotle's sense of inexhaustible reason, of both *logos* and *nous*, far surpasses Spinoza's. The latter interprets all knowledge in relation to God, and all adequate knowledge shares the same geometrical form. Where Aristotle speaks of the inexhaustible nature of *nous* and of the plurality of sciences and forms of knowledge, he suggests that there is no privileged epistemic form, even in science, and certainly no privileged form for knowledge in general, just as there is no single form taken by being.

The identity of knowing and being, distinct from that of knowing and known, is one of the most striking features of Aristotle's writings. It is not that what we know must correspond to its object as that the forms of knowledge must *be* the forms of being. The ways of thinking being are the categories of being. Aristotle's causes are less forms of explanation than they are forms of being.

Even here, the heretical point is not so much that knowing and being are the same as that they are divided into many forms—although within the many forms one is primary. The ontology is divided by the plurality of the metaphysical categories. The epistemology and the theory of mind are divided into different forms and sciences. Overlaid upon this diversity is a view of science that has become orthodox, although it plays only a marginal role in Aristotle himself. What offsets it in his view, compared, for example, with Descartes for whom the question of method is all, is Aristotle's sense of the plenitude of *nous* and *logos*. Reason is inexhaustible because beings are inexhaustible. We must be able to think anything whatever, in some form, and we must be able to develop new forms of thought and reason wherever necessary.

The notion of "knowledge for its own sake" is, then, in Aristotle, anything but what that notion became in the tradition after Descartes, closely allied with notions of method and exclusion. One example is that of dialectic, regarded by Aristotle as essential to science.[21] In today's world, "pure" knowledge is often contrasted with "applied" knowledge, not because the former has no applications or results, but because the applications are not present in it throughout as proximate aims. One of the reasons for such a view of knowledge for its own sake is based on the economic conditions of scientific research. If society must pay, then it may demand measurable results. From the standpoint of practice, consequences are imperative. Yet to subordinate all forms of knowledge to such accountability is to regard knowledge in practical terms alone. In Aristotle, by way of contrast, not only is practical knowledge—*phronēsis*—contrasted with *epistēmē* and *theōria* as well as *technē*, but knowledge for its own sake—*theōria*—closely conforms to the plenitude inherent in *nous*: that is, the capacity of thought to manifest and express, represent and symbolize, whatever is available to be known, including itself. Even more important, these latter terms—"manifest," "express," "represent," "symbolize"—cannot be methodological terms, for they would then overdetermine the forms in which knowledge can be realized. There is no form that we can be sure knowledge will take. It falls as much out of the same as it must fall within. The essential capacity of *nous* is to be able to adopt whatever form is required by its own epistemic requirements. Even traditional representation is too limited a notion because there are forms of knowledge in which nothing stands for anything else, but either simply "is" or "brings about."

That mind should be inexhaustibly malleable is implausible where every other being is regarded as entirely determinate and limited. We have replied that this inexhaustibility of thinking is possible only because every being is inexhaustible. What is different is that the mind thinks other beings inexhaustibly while they do not think each other, but simply *are* inexhaustible. This point may be emphasized in relation to one of Aristotle's most opaque notions, the capacity of *nous* to know itself. For if it has no nature, how can it think itself?

> ... if *nous* is simple and unaffected and as Anaxagoras says has nothing in common with anything else, how will it think, if to think is to be acted upon? (*De Anima*, 429b)

The answer Aristotle gives is that *nous* is already potentially all things, thereby determinate. This poses the problem of why it does not always think all things. Again, he does not appear to appreciate the full force of his own understanding of the inexhaustibility of *nous*. That *nous* might already "be" all things, however potentially, makes a mockery of history and time, the development of new forms of understanding and thought. For *nous* to be potentially all things is not to have a nature of its own, and is to be unknowable. Nevertheless, the capacity of *nous* to think all things, including itself, somehow, is fundamental to reason. Moreover, it knows itself through its thinking of other things.

> Once the mind has become each set of its possible objects, as a man of science has, when this phrase is used of one who is actually a man of science (this happens when he is now able to exercise the power on his own initiative), its condition is still one of potentiality, but in a different sense from the potentiality which preceded the acquisition of knowledge by learning or discovery: the mind too is then able to think itself. (*De Anima*, 429b)

For Aristotle, the major issue is not the unknowability of a *nous* without a nature of its own, but why *nous* does not always think all things if it "is" them all potentially. The answer leads to one of Aristotle's most difficult passages concerning the passive and active intellect.

> And in fact mind as we have described it is what it is by virtue of becoming all things, while there is another which is what it is by virtue of making all things: this is a sort of positive state like light; for in a sense light makes potential colors into actual colors.
>
> Mind in this sense of it is separable, impassible, unmixed, since it is in its essential nature activity (for always the active is superior to the passive factor, the originating force to the matter which it forms). (*De Anima*, 429)

Again, two themes dominate this account: the openness of *nous* to other forms of being, its inexhaustibility, and its activity. Here, Aristotle speaks unequivocally, if obscurely, against a purely passive view of *nous*, that it merely mirrors or follows its objects. We may compare his language with that of Plato, but also with that of Coleridge:

> The primary IMAGINATION I hold to be the living Power and prime Agent of all human Perception, and as a repetition in the finite mind of the eternal act of creation in the infinite I AM. The secondary Imagination I consider as an echo of the former, co-existing with the conscious will, yet still as identical with the primary in the *kind* of its operation. It dissolves, diffuses, dissipates, in order to recreate; or where this process is rendered impossible, yet still at all events it struggles to idealize and to unify. It is essentially *vital*, even as all objects (*as* objects) are essentially fixed and dead.
>
> FANCY, on the contrary, has no other counters to play with, but fixities and definites. The Fancy is indeed no other than a mode of Memory emancipated from the order of time and space; . . . .[22]

Within the knowing and thinking mind, if there is to be knowledge, there must be more than a repetitive power—fancy—but an originative power. The active intellect shines upon its objects and illuminates them, rather than merely being shined upon and illuminated by them. *Nous* does not think all things passively, although it is them all potentially, but thinks only what it has constituted by its creative powers. Repetition is not knowledge.

We may interpret Aristotle in Kantian terms, although such an interpretation would be no more felicitous in relation to Kant than to

Aristotle. The relevant principles are that if knowledge is to be possible, the knowing mind must be able to know all things, must be in that sense inexhaustibly malleable, and that such an inexhaustibility in the knowing mind must be interpreted as an active, not a passive principle. That *nous* might be, like the receptacle, pure and eternal, unmixed and separate, that it might have no nature of its own, that it might be eternal along with the eternality of truth, that it might fall entirely under the rule of the same, would make its activity unintelligible. Activity and power require determinateness. The question is whether we must interpret such determinateness in the knowing mind as distortion, as incompatible with the inexhaustible potentialities of reason. The tradition has frequently understood knowledge as a mirroring without distortion. Yet in the greatest philosophers, including Aristotle and Plato, important alternative strains are present.

For being to be inexhaustible, it must be aporetic, thereby determinate but also indeterminate. Inexhaustibility is aporia, the indeterminateness in determinateness and conversely. Analogously, the knowing mind or reason must be similarly aporetic and inexhaustible. The former entails that there is no knowing that is not, in Heidegger's language, as concealing as it is revealing, concealing while it reveals. The latter gives us both of the principles we are examining: the openness of the knowing mind and its specificity. These derive from the necessity that it play an active role, that it illuminate its objects by constituting them, by making them present to it. A purely passive mind can know nothing. An active mind determinately illuminates its objects, thereby revealing them, more like a searchlight than a mirror—a light whose spectrum falls upon its objects, constituting their visibility. Alternatively, thought is a prehensive relation, impressing itself upon its object.[23] It follows that what is known is as much a function of the knower as the known. It does not follow that knowledge is intrinsically defective. Rather, being and knowing are always limited, and such limitation—understood to entail specificity as well as variability—is necessary to any knowing or being.

The active intellect, then, expresses a heretical view of knowledge that, historically, could not have been restored to consideration until, having passed through Kant's transcendental turn, could be thought to contribute to its own achievements without self-destruction. Nevertheless, Aristotle goes far beyond Kant to at least Hegel's understanding that the knowing subject determines itself, thereby its object. Without the development of effective and powerful instruments, the scientific intellect would be impotent. Without the coercive effects of language and culture upon human conditions, the invention of new theories would be inhibited. Without an intellect capable of actively transforming itself as well as its object, knowledge would be impossible. An active intellect is a transforming intellect. But transformation enriches knowledge, even scientific knowledge, and does not nullify it.

The theme of the active intellect appears in Aristotle in relation to many other themes than that of the creative mind. It appears, in particular, in Book X of *Nicomachean Ethics* as the highest form of human virtue, *eudaimonia*. (*Nicomachean Ethics*, 1177a) *Nous* here is activity but not practice, that is, not concerned with any end lying outside its own activity.[24] It is thought thinking itself: no other form of knowing can be continuous and self-sufficient. "Now if you take away from a living being action, and still more production, what is left but contemplation?" (*Nicomachean Ethics*, 1178b) If you take away from a rational being all practical and fabricative judgments, what is left is either entirely passive or is the active process in which reason thinks itself.[25] In thinking itself, however, because its nature is given by what it knows of other things, *nous* thinks other things as truly as they can be thought.

This is perhaps the most far-reaching sense of knowledge for its own sake to be found in the tradition, exceeding even Spinoza's. If we reject, as we must, the purity and self-sufficiency of *nous*, which in Aristotle is deeply qualified by the fact that it is nothing without its objects, we must conclude that knowledge for its own sake must be equated not with the purity of *nous*, but with its ability to think itself more and more deeply. If knowledge is equated with activity, with interrogation, then the culmination of reason is reason interrogating itself: thought thinking itself. The thinking, here, is unending interrogation in the same, reason unceasingly examining its own precepts and forms. We return to the notion of the active intellect with the understanding that the activity lies in the power inherent in both *logos* and *nous* to transform themselves unendingly. It is the capacity of a heretical reason to think its own heresies, to think the aporias within aporia.

We find in Aristotle, recurrently, in connection with every subject matter, an aporetic emphasis on both determinateness and specificity and indeterminateness and plurality. We find two reciprocal levels of aporia: of same and other, and of an unceasing plurality of modes of being and knowing, joined throughout with singular, unifying moments that are incompatible with Aristotle's pluralism.

Just as there are many sciences and ways of knowing in Aristotle, there are many causes and many substances—many ways of being. Among the central strains is a pluralism that is manifested less in the view that the universe is composed of many individual things or substances—although he certainly holds that view—and more in the multiplicity of categories or ways of being. The most obvious form of this plurality lies in the multiplicity of causes, for such causes mediate between how things are and how we know them. They are the forms that constitute any particular area of knowledge as a science, but they are also the ways in which we are able to say that things "are." To be is to be an individual substance, a process, but each such individual "is" form, matter, by origin, and by end.

This pluralistic theme is repeated throughout Aristotle's categories and forms of understanding. It is not the only such pervasive theme, however, but is conjoined with an almost strident emphasis on singularity amidst the plurality, frequently if not always defined in terms of primacy: the primary way of knowing, the primary form of substance. This emphasis on primacy—metaphysical and epistemological—has entered the Western tradition as a major component of its orthodoxy. Yet there is nothing quite corresponding to it in Aristotle's predecessors and in most of his successors. There is, for example, no question that in the traditional reading of the doctrine of forms, forms are ontologically and epistemologically primary over ordinary, changing things. But Plato never says this, either in his orthodox or heretical mood. Rather, the doctrine of forms claims only that unchanging forms are fully knowable and intelligible, full being, whereas changing things are only half knowable and midway between being and nonbeing. Similarly, the preSocratics do not assert the primacy of their *archai* beyond claiming that they are first principles. Such a first principle is first in knowledge and even being, but not first in all ways, as Aristotle claims for individual substance. Likewise, Spinoza claims that all things follow from God or Substance, but leaves untouched the explicit question of God's primacy. Hegel is a similar example.

The notion of ontological primacy is Aristotelian, not even Platonic. It requires, if we accept it as orthodox, that we read backward into Plato and the preSocratics the notion of ontological primacy in relation to first principles. The important distinction in the doctrine of forms between appearance and reality is indeed a distinction of ontological priority, but contains and requires no additional claim that reality is prior to appearance in every way. The priority here is one of intelligibility first, of being second. What Aristotle claims is that among the multiplicity of substances one form is prior in *all* respects: epistemologically but also ontologically, chronologically, and logically. Such a view has become so entrenched in the metaphysical tradition that we may associate some form of ontological primacy with metaphysics itself. What characterizes orthodoxy in the metaphysical tradition is not so much what Heidegger calls its attempt to bring being to presence, but its attempt to define some type of being as primary without qualification.[26] The alternative is that being is inexhaustible.

Inexhaustibility here is plurality, but not simply a plurality of beings, congenial with a mechanistic ontology, but a plurality of kinds of being, ways of being, not all of which are commensurate with the others. We may again see in Aristotle's metaphysics two central movements: the one toward primacy, the other toward a generic plurality in being that manifests its plenitude. The former is reductive in the explicit sense that it denies that being is inexhaustible, imposes a hierarchical ontological structure on the plenitude of inexhaustible ways of being, falls within the shadow of the same.

There is another movement toward oneness in Aristotle that is incompatible with his ontological pluralism, expressed in his emphasis on an ultimate unmoved mover. The argument for such a mover runs throughout his metaphysics, but has far greater generality. It is paralleled by the argument in the *Nicomachean Ethics* that a single end underlies all human actions and in *De Anima* by the argument that there is a single source of organic movement: desire. Amidst many changing beings, there must be a single cause of all their motions that does not itself change or move. Amidst many proximate goods and actions, there must be a single end toward which they all strive and which is the measure of their intelligibility.

Such a view of ends and intelligibility in relation to all things taken together gives us the metaphysical tradition's cosmological emphasis upon a single universe based on a single ground of unity. It is repeated in Spinoza's view that an inexhaustible universe containing inexhaustibly diverse modes and attributes follows from one absolutely infinite substance, in Leibniz's view that the inexhaustible plurality of monads is the manifestation of a single principle of plenitude that follows from the principle of sufficient reason, and in Whitehead's view that the inexhaustible diversity of actual entities is unified in a single divine experience. Yet Aristotle's conformity to such a cosmological principle is far less explicit than the others. If the idea of cosmology is derived from Aristotle—although we should not overlook Timaeus' story about the universe that is the result of a single divine act of creation—it functions in his theory in a complex and divided way. The remarkable thing about Aristotle's orthodoxy in what became the Christian theological and philosophical tradition is that there is always another side to his orthodoxy.

In this case, the other side lies in the insistent plurality that cohabits with his cosmology. There are diverse individual substances with diverse causes and ways of being. These diverse natural processes require causes of their motion that are not themselves moved because there would otherwise be a infinite regress of causes for any motion. Leaving aside the question of why such an infinite regress of motion and its causes should be problematic, we note that the force of Aristotle's argument, assuming its plausibility, establishes only that for any motion there must be an unmoved cause, for example its formal *telos*, and quite fails to establish a single cause for all events and processes. Certainly there is no straightforward or plausible argument that a single object of desire serves to direct all sentient activities. Similarly, not only does Aristotle's argument concerning the final end required for all human actions—happiness or *eudaimonia*—not demonstrate that a single end is required for all human activities: he explicitly notes that there may be many such ends or goods, and that if so we must consider the greatest good among them. (*Nicomachean Ethics*, 1097a)[27]

We may therefore understand his otherwise perverse view that although a final unmoved mover is required for metaphysical intelligibility, there are many such movers moving in a circle, constituting the heavens. (*Metaphysics*, 1071b, 1073) What would be perverse would be to suppose that although one unmoved mover is required for the unity of different motions in the universe, many such movers may constitute the heavens. To the contrary, Aristotle's argument establishes only that any motion requires some unmoved mover, some end. Similarly, any action, directed toward the good, requires some *telos* that is not itself directed toward anything else. Such an end, however, may be local. It is an independent question whether, among all the ends in view of human practice, one is supreme. Practically speaking, the question is whether one and only one life is to be regarded as the supreme human life, or whether many such lives are equally supreme and effectively incomparable. It is the question of whether virtue is one or many. Given many human excellences, the latter is the only plausible conclusion. That is, there is no way to compare different "styles" of rational, contemplative life, only comparisons among different (incomplete) realizations of any particular form of such a life.

The most important and potentially heretical dimension of Aristotle's view of movers and causes lies not so much in either its rational or organic side, that which moves the living creature to activity or *nous* to understanding, but in relation to desire. He offers perhaps the most generic theory of desire found in the Western tradition, matched only by Spinoza, closely corresponding to the unmoved cause of motion in every natural process. Every substance, every *ousia*, functions according to an end, *hormē*, that moves it, teleologically, because there always is, in every process, a cause of its movement that in one sense lies "within," in another, because it is not moved, lies "without." Substance, here, is always and of necessity changing, although it does not change in being substance, because a substance cannot change into something that is not substance, only into a different substance, only "in respect of quality and quantity and place; for each of these admits of contrariety." (*Metaphysics*, 1068b) Movement and change pertain to individual substances intrinsically, and desire is the organic form of the cause of motion in every living natural process as its *telos*, although it cannot be part of that process, changing with it.

> ... it is the object of desire that moves, and through this reasoning moves, since the object of desire is the starting-point of reasoning. ... Therefore, while in kind the mover will be one, the power of desiring as desire, and ultimately the object of desire (this moves without itself being moved, through being thought of or imagined), in number there is a plurality of movers. (*De Anima*, III:10)

Desire is both the same in other and the other in the same.

There is therefore a pervasive and important ambiguity in Aristotle's view of *ousia* and its movements: it is both what remains unchanging throughout change, in that nothing can transform it into its contrary, and it is precisely *what* changes in any movement, the logical subject to which different predicates apply. In both cases, the movement is intrinsic, and the form in which movement is originated in living creatures is through an object of desire.

Three features of desire are worth emphasizing. One is the pervasiveness of desire in relation to living movement and activity. Nature, including human activities, reason as well as sentience, is teleological, and there is no living natural process that is not a function of desire. Nature is effectively a form of *praxis*—but not *technē*—given by the form within it of desire. Desire, however, is fundamentally local, an end within each process. There is no overarching sense that one form of teleology—certainly not desire—is common to all processes or all human processes.

A second feature of desire is that it both belongs to the processes and activities that it governs and is external to them. Every local process is defined by an end that both is within it and transcends it, locally. Desire, here, the end within a local organic movement or activity, is both internal and external, local and transcendent. We may compare two sides of Freud's understanding of desire. Taken narrowly, desire is local, a function of specific historical antecedents, so that every human activity is interpreted in terms of individual biography. Taken generically, desire is the form in which libidinal energies are released, and is undifferentiated by individual person. The locality and generality of desire in Freud—for example, in relation to sexuality—are entirely unmediated. The great insight in Aristotle's view of desire is that it can be local, within any individual process, only by being external to that process—that is, unmoved. What must be added is that the immovability of the mover is as local as its causality.

It follows, third, that the immovability of the end of any process, the desire that defines its object, is both essential to its locality and a threat to its activity. What is suggested is that desires are both infinite and infinitely unsatisfiable, in that sense immovable and unmodifiable. Such a view is implausible in relation to both reason and competing desires, which define limits in relation to each other. Moreover, it is the basis of the Western tradition's inability to define an acceptable understanding of practice. Infinite desires are beyond all practical satisfaction. To the contrary, then, the immovability of desire is always local, and a mover immovable relative to one process is movable relative to another. Desires are reciprocal and diverse forms of limitation. What must be added is that the immovability of ends and desires is not equatable with eternity. The side in Aristotle that emphasizes eternity is incompatible with his understanding of local desire.

We may return from desire to consider the cause of motion in general. Aristotle's argument for the necessity of an unmoved mover, whether one or many, is based on three arguments: (1) individual, changing substances require a cause of their motion, but should every cause of motion be itself moving, then motion itself would continue to be unintelligible; (2) changing things are contingent and destructible, and, if so, it is possible that all might be destroyed, while motion is necessary; (3) time cannot come into existence or pass away because it would require a before and after.

Let us imagine, following Whitehead, an epochal theory of time and natural laws. Relative to the second argument, it is not that changing *things* are necessary, but that motion is a determinant for any natural thing. All such things might be contingent. One alternative would be a principle of emergence, perhaps from a "nothing" sufficiently unstable as to produce epochs of contingency. Another alternative is that while all things are contingent, it does not follow that they are together contingent: the destruction of one might involve the production of another. Relative to the third argument, that time cannot come into existence or pass away, an epochal theory entails that a temporal metric may come and go, but that the succession of events may not cease, although its measures and laws may change radically. What Whitehead asks us to consider is that even natural laws may be epochal. What is required is that they change with a different rhythm than the events they move.

The entire case depends on the first argument: that change is unintelligible without an unchanging ground. It is the fundamental principle of the theory of ideas. Whitehead ascribes this principle to Plato, although our reading negates most of the force of such an ascription. Perhaps we may ascribe it to Aristotle, at least in relation to his unmoved mover. It nevertheless inhabits many of the writings before Aristotle in some form, aporetic or undivided, and many of the writings after, up to Hegel. It is a fundamental principle of orthodox intelligibility, not only in philosophy but in science. That there might be no form of being, including natural laws, immune to epochal variation is still regarded by many scientists as unintelligible.

We may consider here an unspoken, far-reaching heresy that Aristotle probably would not have found acceptable. Following Whitehead's line of thought, we may formulate the traditional position as that changing, temporal things are intelligible only in terms of something unchanging and eternal, an absolute principle of the same. If everything changes, then time and motion become unintelligible. What is assumed is that eternity is intelligible in and of itself, and not by contrast. Changing things require changelessness for their intelligibility; changelessness is intrinsically intelligible. This is remarkably implausible. Natural laws are intelligible only to the extent that we can perceive and measure the changes that they govern. Forms are intelligible only to the extent that we can observe the changing objects in which they participate. What follows is that natural laws and forms cannot be simply eternal and unchanging, indivisible and without magnitude (*Metaphysics*, 1073a), but, as Plato's *Parmenides* makes clear, may be indivisible in some respects but must be divisible in others (over their exemplifications), may not be changing in certain respects, but must change in others (in relation to their applications). These notions of change and changelessness, eternity and temporality, divisibility and indivisibility, are not opposing forms but manifestations of the complementarity of same and other.

There are, in Aristotle, both four causes and four ways in which something may be said to be something: it may be said to "be" matter, form, its essence, or the result of its cause. If we think of things as individual, enduring beings, then the efficient cause is external: something outside it that causes the individual thing. The other three causes are "what it is." However, if we think of *ousia* as an individual process, including its principle of movement, then it "is" all its causes, and they are the ways in which it is: it moves from its efficient cause to its final cause; it is its matter and form. If we are to understand Aristotle's ontology as an explication of what it is to be determinate, then what *makes* a being so determinate and what it *is* determinately coincide. Naturally enough, Aristotle's epistemology and his metaphysics, his ontology and his science, coincide as well.

The categories of being, here, are ontological, ways in which an individual process may be said to be. But there is a complete (if aporetic) identity among what we may say a process is—how we speak of it (perhaps in Greek)—how we may know it, and what it is. The ways of being-something are both ways in which we speak of being determinate and ways in which a being is determinate. One interpretation is that Aristotle's is a mirroring theory, that he assumes that things are ontologically determinate first and that language mirrors the forms and modes of their reality. The alternative, supported by the ways in which he emphasizes the logical structure of (the Greek) language, is that what we may understand being to be is inseparable from what we may say about the ways it is, that what must be accepted as true is a reciprocal function of what we may say with authority and legitimacy—that is, scientifically—is true. Such an interpretation is consonant with the corresponding interpretation of the active intellect: reason is active in the sense that it constitutes its object. It does not follow that this constitution divides knowing from its object. Rather, what follows is that a being is in the ways we may know it to be, although these ways are actively constituted by thought and language, *nous* and *logos*.

We have, here, a relationship of the same between language and being, logic and nature, *logikos* and *physikos*, that pervades Aristotle's writings, methodologically and ontologically. The primary movement is from an account of what we say about things to how things are.[28] Two features of such a method are worth noting, one, largely traditional, that language is an origin for philosophical understanding, the other, far more unorthodox, that a natural or physical origin is required as well. We may characterize this method generically, setting the emphasis on origins aside, as that every form of truth is incomplete. The reason is that being is inexhaustible. A corollary is that there are many senses of being and no single, essential meaning.

There is a deeper point within the pluralism: not simply that there "are" many modes and forms of being, many beings and many categories of being. Aristotle's ontology is functional, not merely in its teleology of final causes but in the very meaning of being itself. To be is to function in certain ways. The different senses of *ousia* are the different functions that they serve. The primacy of individual substance is based on the logical function that it serves. The different causes are not simply forms of explanation and intelligibility, but manifest functional distinctions among beings in relation.

It follows that intelligibility is neither stable nor a given, but is inseparable from a view of being. Each metaphysical view includes a view of what constitutes its own intelligibility. Our understanding of things implicitly or explicitly includes an understanding of intelligibility, its *logos*. Thus, we find in Aristotle a far-reaching plurality of intelligible causes that, by comparison with most later understandings of intelligibility, is both more pluralistic and more sweeping in how it defines intelligibility. Far more heretical, however, is the suggestion that the causes are entirely contingently four, that there is no necessity to any particular number. The tradition has tended to reduce the number in ways that may be identified with its theology: to God or Substance, to natural law and matter. The heretical possibility in Aristotle is that different beings may require different *kinds* of intelligibility, multiplying causes in some cases, reducing them in others, but, in the extreme, expressing the otherness in the unity of being. The heresy is that being has no definite form or number in terms of which it makes itself intelligible, that the number and kinds of causes are constantly under revision, manifesting inexhaustibility.

Closely related to the notion of a plurality of causes, thereby of intelligibility, is the notion of a plurality of powers, the understanding that power may take diversely inexhaustible forms. Such a view is certainly Aristotelian on one side.

> The actual is to the potential as a man building is to a man who can build, as waking is to sleeping, as one who is seeing to one who possesses sight but has his eyes closed, as that which has been separated out of the matter is to the matter, and as the accomplished to the unaccomplished. To one of the terms in each case let us assign operation or functioning, to the other power. Not all things are said to be functioning in the same way, but only by analogy: as that is in that or to that, so this is in this or to this. For some are as motion is to power, others as *ousia* is to some matter. (*Metaphysics*, 1048)

Following *Sophist*, Aristotle defines being as power, with the qualification that there is a plurality of powers and no overarching power or end for which all things exist potentially. The pluralism here has no correlative ontological priority.

Another example of Aristotle's far-reaching pluralism, incompatible with his view of ontological primacy, is his understanding of chance or coincidence. Each individual process has a natural end, but not all processes comprise an overarching world process with a single natural end. The result is the introduction of "incidental causes" into the internal causes of any individual process.

> It is clear then that chance is an incidental cause in the sphere of those actions for the sake of something which involve purpose. (*Physics*, 197)

Aristotle's view here must be contrasted with Spinoza's, for whom there can be no incidental causes—there is but one causal order of the universe—and with Hume, for whom experience is entirely regular. Within each process, according to Aristotle, there is a natural end as well as manifold determining causes. Relative to different intersecting processes, there is contingency and chance, incidental causes relative to a process viewed from within. Where all processes conjoin into a world process, there can be no chance or coincidence. It follows that coincidence divides the inexhaustible sameness of the world. Coincidence is perhaps the most important manifestation of inexhaustible plurality.[29]

Closely related is Aristotle's view of place. Everything that exists is *somewhere*. If we interpret this view of place in spatiotemporal terms, then all things exist together in a universe of space and time, and the possibility threatens that there is no coincidence or chance, but a single mechanistic order of the universe. Cosmology is entailed by too narrow a view of place. If, however, we accept the principle that to be is to be located *somewhere*, but conjoin it with the principle that processes and locations may intersect but do not comprise a universal order of locations, then location or place is local. Generalizing, locatedness includes processes and events in time and space, individual things, but also forms and qualities, located by predication and classification. Locatedness is local, not universal or generic; a universal system of locations makes coincidence impossible. Such a view of location gives an intelligible meaning to coincidence without undermining natural necessity. There is natural necessity in every being and process, its causes, but there is no universal necessity and no world process. From this point of view, ontological priority is unintelligible, based on a cosmic principle of hierarchical order.

There is in Aristotle a far-reaching and unbroken adherence to ontological plurality—a plurality of ways of being and modes of intelligibility—conjoined with an equally extreme emphasis upon the priority of individual substance—prior in every sense. I have suggested that this doctrine of ontological priority is Aristotelian, that there is no comparable doctrine in anyone prior to Aristotle. The search for first principles, *archai*, is not equivalent with ontological priority because it does not depend on a claim of absolute priority, in all relevant respects, amidst a plurality of forms of being. To say that all is water is not to deny the reality or importance of earth and fire, but to subsume the intelligibility of the latter under a single generic principle. To say that the forms are the only intelligible reality is not to assert their priority in time over changing temporal things.

Aristotle's claim is that individual substance is prior in *all* respects, in order of definition, knowledge, and time. (*Metaphysics*, 1028a) His arguments are:

> For (3) of the other categories none can exist independently, but only substance. And (1) in definition also this is first; for in the

definition of each term the definition of its substance must be present. And (2) we think we know each thing most fully, when we know what it is, e.g. what man is or what fire is, rather than when we know its quality, its quantity, or its place; since we know each of these predicates also, only when we know *what* the quantity or the quality *is*. (*Metaphysics*, 1028ab)

We can respond critically in two ways, by suggesting that there are other respects than those he considers, especially, all the ways in which something might be said to be, all the ways of intelligibility, or by denying that an individual being is in fact prior in the ways he describes it. What something is made of is typically prior to what it is, especially where, in the case of art, it is made out of something according to design. Similarly, what something is made for may be prior in time and definition to what it is. Generalizing, the claim that an individual being is prior to its causes is indefensible where what something is and what makes it intelligible are understood to be equivalent.

Each of the above arguments reduces to the first: that is, to speak of any of the other modes of being is to speak of a predicate of an individual subject: *its* form, *its* matter, *its* causes. Following Spinoza's language, each is a "modification" *of* substance. Yet that an individual is required wherever there is a form, so that the form cannot exist independently, does not entail that the individual exists apart from its form or matter. To the contrary, there can be no individual substance that has a form that is not made of something. It is not that form and matter are interdependent, but that individuals are not independent. The stronger form of Aristotle's recognition that there are many modes of being is that none can exist or be intelligible without the others. There is reciprocity of the ways of being and intelligibility.

We may add, then, that while any particular form must include that of which it is the form, so that the definition of the former must include the latter, the reverse is equally true: no individual being can be determinate without the determinateness of its form. It is not that either of these is more determinate than the other, but that each is determinate in certain ways and indeterminate in others, and that this complementarity of determinateness and indeterminateness inhabits every form of being, including individual substances. More strongly still, this complementarity of same and other defines being and its intelligibility. Finally, there is no temporal priority to individuals over their conditions and properties, not where beings arise and perish amidst multiple causes. Some of these causes must precede; others may follow. Temporal and logical priority cannot be mutually equivalent.

We find in Aristotle two intimately related principles: of multiple being and intelligibility, a plurality both of individual beings and of ways of being; and a unifying principle of ontological priority—individual substances are prior in all respects to other modes of being. Same and other dance their dance of being endlessly, but the same wins the prize. Aristotle recognizes that if individual substances were prior only in certain respects, then no doctrine of ontological priority could be defended. But he cannot sustain so strong a priority, for that would be incompatible with his pluralism of principles and causes. It follows that individuals are prior in certain respects while form and matter, efficient and final causes, structures and patterns, natural laws, are prior in others. The doctrine of ontological priority is and must be arbitrary in this sense, an explicit aporia.

Closely related is the aporia within first philosophy—*protē philosophia*—and explicit within the first four aporias in Book III as well as implicit within the others. It is of the study of being *qua* being where being is not the highest genus, of a most general science where there is no science of sciences.[30] Closely related also is his view of natural plenitude and *dynamis* conjoined with a continuing emphasis on demonstrative necessity—the aporia that aporia inhabits intelligibility. To attempt to resolve these aporias by either treating being as the highest genus nevertheless, or introducing another sense in which first philosophy can be both first and generic,[31] ignores the fact that the aporias are explicitly not resolved by Aristotle himself. Being *qua* being remains aporetic as does first philosophy, aporias that are to be found throughout the metaphysical tradition.

What we find in Aristotle's system of categories is either a straightforward and orthodox resolution of the relationship of one and many—that amidst multiple and plural causes and forms of being, one is first in all respects, and all others are its manifestations or modifications—or an aporetic and arbitrary imposition upon a plurality of forms of being and intelligibility the priority of the same. The orthodox view is the former. Yet Aristotle refuses to be orthodox, and frequently adopts an aporetic position. There is no entirely satisfactory resolution of the conflict of same and other. Rather, being is one in certain respects—expressed by individual *ousia*—and many in others—expressed by the plurality of other forms of *ousia*—and there is no satisfactory, nonaporetic resolution of the tensions between them. There is, in Aristotle, heresy amidst the metaphysical orthodoxy and inseparable from it.

What cannot be claimed is that these continuing aporias display defects that may be improved on. To adopt such a position is to assume that there is a form of improvement that would not itself be aporetic, that there is a form of metaphysical orthodoxy that would entirely eliminate aporia, that there will be a final heresy. The continuing heresy is that being is aporetic in its interplay of same and other. Being never entirely overcomes indeterminateness, for each overcoming occurs within being, rather than over it, generating new forms of indeterminateness. Unity never overcomes multiplicity without destroying it; multiplicity never overcomes unity without unintelligibility. Unity and multiplicity are among the major forms of the aporias of determinateness and indeterminateness that characterize the metaphysical tradition.

5 SPINOZA: THE HERESY OF HERESY

Few great philosophers have been regarded as heretics during their lifetimes, a fact that supports Marx's conviction that philosophy largely sustains the status quo. Yet if metaphysics is aporetic and philosophy is heretical, then they must either constantly find themselves in opposition to the status quo or be subjected to it. This subjection is the form that orthodoxy takes in the tradition, essential to its blindness to metaphysical heresy. Conversely, however, it is not necessary for philosophy to be explicitly moral and political to have important human implications.

Spinoza was excommunicated by the Ecclesiastical Council of the Congregation of Israel, in Amsterdam, on July 27, 1656, for "horrible heresies."[1] Although we should be outraged by the Ecclesiastical Council's actions, and its condemnation of the greatest and wisest of its members for his "atheism," perhaps we can respect them for recognizing heresy when they saw it.

That Spinoza should have been regarded as a heretic is all the more remarkable given what his most famous twentieth-century scholar has said about his work, an outright rejection of philosophic heresy:

> As for Spinoza, if we could cut up all the philosophic literature available to him into slips of paper, toss them up into the air, and let them fall back to the ground, then out of the scattered slips of paper we could reconstruct his *Ethics*.[2]

Despite devoting two volumes to such a reconstruction, Wolfson cannot ignore the fact that Spinoza made so radical a break with his predecessors as to be unassimilable in his time into the philosophic tradition.

> Now the long-envisaged truth which was established by the intre-
> pidity and daring of Spinoza was the principle of the unity of
> nature, which in its double aspect meant the homogeneity of
> the material of which it is constituted and the uniformity of the
> laws by which it is dominated.[3]

This was a great and remarkable heresy, in its time, repudiating the dividedness within the natural universe in relation to its divine active principle. What is omitted in such a backward-looking view of Spinoza is that the idea of the unity of nature eventually became commonplace but Spinoza has remained unique. He remains heretical even as his most obvious heresies have been assimilated into the tradition.

We may begin with perhaps the most striking feature of Spinoza's *Ethics*, its geometrical form. The entire work is constructed in the form of propositions proved from axioms and definitions. Shall we regard this as but a rhetorical feature of Spinoza's style, as if style and substance were separable? Or does it indicate a more unique perspective on the nature of things? Wolfson takes the conservative position, claiming that the geometrical form is no more than a rhetorical device.[4] Yet he must concede that Spinoza has a "mathematical way of looking at things" and, moreover, that such a way of looking at things does not require a geometrical presentation. Both Pythagoras and Plato have been described as taking what is intelligible in reality to be mathematical, but neither wrote in geometrical form. That Spinoza wrote his major work in such a form cannot be lightly dismissed. What he forces us to consider is the heresy that a geometrical view of nature is compatible with both its activity and its powers.

The orthodox view is nicely expressed by Wolfson: the geometrical method is a form of proof, a way in which a mathematical view of nature is to be given linguistic expression.[5] A more unorthodox view is that the geometrical form of the work *is* the order of nature. Indeed, it is difficult to imagine adopting any other position if we take Spinoza seriously. He claims, in his most famous proposition, that "The order and connection of ideas is the same as the order and connection of things." (II, Prop. VII)[6] This identity holds for all ideas, true or false, adequate or muti-lated (including the propositions of *Ethics*). It is a remarkable claim. Spinoza does not quite assert it, but surely means it when he says that: "Inadequate and confused ideas follow by the same necessity as ade-quate or clear and distinct ideas." (II, Prop. XXXVI) The proof makes clear that every idea is in God and as such is true. We have the double principle that inadequate ideas correspond to things as much as do adequate ideas, and that inadequate ideas correspond, in some other sense, to adequate ideas. To this we may add that ideas common to everything are necessarily adequate. (II, Prop. XXXVIII) By proposition VII, the order and connection among such adequate ideas is identical with the order and connection of things. Indeed, Proposition VII can be intelligible only if we take the relation to be more than a correspondence. Ideas and things "are the same." The attributes of thought and extension are identical expressions of substance. Spinoza's heresy is that of the same in the same.

That there might be an identity of idea and thing is among the most remarkable features of Spinoza's system. Among its implications is that what is true about things is identical with the adequate ideas in which it is expressed. If *Ethics* is a true account of the nature of things, if its propositions are adequate, the connections among these propositions are identical with the connections among the things described by them. Relations among things—geometrical and causal—are identical with the relations among the true ideas describing them. Things follow from each other as propositions follow from each other. It is no accident that we use the same phrase, "following from," to describe this relationship.

I have argued that the form in which Plato wrote is to be identified with philosophy itself: dramatic dialogues filled with figuration and irony, displacements along with arguments. What we cannot so easily argue in connection with Plato is that the aporetic nature of philosophy is the same as the aporetic nature of being. Yet we cannot ignore that possibility. In relation to Spinoza, there is no choice: the structure of adequate ideas is the structure of reality: geometrical.

This conclusion may not appear remarkable given the mathematization of modern physics and the Pythagorean background of Western thought. It nevertheless appears to be a striking example of what Derrida calls "logocentrism": that a particular voice or form of writing should be authoritative, a direct manifestation of reality. What cannot be so simply assimilated to Spinoza's position, however, what cannot be interpreted as logocentric, is that the identity holds for all ideas, adequate and inadequate. The heresy is that ideas "are" reality. On a traditional reading, we have no more than Aristotle's claim, regarding *nous*, that knowledge requires an identity of knower and known, *logos* and being. We have noted, however, even in Aristotle, a far-reaching heresy of active *nous* that makes it impossible to sustain this identity without qualification. In Spinoza, the identity is entirely unqualified, including all ideas, adequate and inadequate.

The geometrical method, in Spinoza, manifests the fundamental nature of both intelligibility and reality. Reality is geometrical. The structure of the world is geometrical. Things are related to each other geometrically, through God, as the ideas that "are" those things under the attribute of thought are related to each other—also geometrically. The structure of *Ethics* must be taken in the double sense that it both describes and displays the order and connection of things. Only in this way, through giving us adequate knowledge of God and the world, can it serve its moral purpose. In this sense, geometry is reality. More heretically still, God is geometrical, propositionally and extensively. Geometry, here, is the only analogue Spinoza had available to express the causal-logical structure of being. The causal nature of God, his active power, is geometrical. Rather than understanding Spinoza as reducing the plenitude of God and nature to its mathematical essence, we should understand him as presenting the infinite plenitude within geometrical thought and being. Alternatively, we may understand him to recognize that the inexhaustible plenitude of being is matched by an inexhaustible plenitude of mathematical thought.

There is, in Spinoza, a theory of causation that matches Whitehead's as an answer to Hume's critique, a view all the more notable for preceding it. We must distinguish here the question of how we may know that a causal relation between finite events or things obtains from the question of what causation *is*. Hume claims that we can have such knowledge only from experience and argues that causation can only be a constant conjunction, not merely because we cannot experience a natural connection, but because the idea of a necessary natural connection is unintelligible.

For Spinoza, however, causation is entirely intelligible, in two overlapping senses. One is that causation is mathematical in terms of two identities: the relation in which an event or thing "follows from" another is identically causal and geometrical; geometrical relations are identically both propositional and real. There is no distinction between a causal relation and its corresponding mathematical relation. In this respect, two, Spinoza's theory shares the form of a hypothetico-deductive system in which the natural laws and the propositions or ideas expressing them are identical and in which causation is identified with the workings of natural laws.

> Nothing happens in nature which can be attributed to any vice of Nature, for she is always the same and everywhere one. Her virtue is the same, and her power of acting, that is to say, her laws and rules, according to which all things are and are changed from form to form, are everywhere and always the same, so that there must also be one and the same method of understanding the nature of all things whatsoever, that is to say, by the universal laws and rules of Nature. (III, Preface)

There are differences. Certain natural laws, conservation laws for example, do not correspond to ordinary causal relations. Certain causal relations, involving volition and human action, do not have known natural laws corresponding to them. Spinoza associates the infinite side of causation with an absolutely infinite God rather than with universal laws. Nevertheless, his view of the causal universe is structurally identical with a mechanistic system, whatever his reservations concerning mechanism itself.

What Spinoza gives us is an understanding of the inexhaustible plenitude that pertains to any far-reaching mechanistic theory of the universe, showing us, heretically in relation to both his scholastic predecessors and scientific successors, the aporetic inexhaustibility of any comprehensive system of natural laws. His is the theory that mechanism ought to be, and the irresistible aporias in his theory manifest the plenitude, inexhaustibility, and dividedness that lie hidden within materialistic theories, obscured by their surface limitations.

It is no accident that his theory is entirely mathematical and deterministic, nor that its determinism is aporetic in relation both to God and to itself. The most famous and compelling aporia, in this context, is of the status of Spinoza's own theory in a deterministic world. If on the one hand it *is* the nature of things, geometrically, it is on the other hand unintelligible, in a deterministic context, as a human production. In the respect in which it is adequate it is infinite. In the respect in which it is a human work, it is finite. No voluntary production can be intelligible in a totally deterministic universe. No truth can be voluntarily produced in a deterministic universe. The identity between the propositions of *Ethics* and the natural world makes the production of such a work, as *text*, unintelligible in a universe without teleology or freedom.[7]

To the question of what causation is, Spinoza's answer—the second referred to above—is that it is the power of God from whom all things follow.

> A thing which has been determined to any action was necessarily so determined by God, and that which has not been thus determined by God cannot determine itself to action. (I, Prop. XXVI)

> In Nature there is nothing contingent, but all things are determined from the necessity of the divine nature to exist and act in a certain manner. (I, Prop. XXIX)

God is the absolute first and immanent cause of all things. In this sense, all things follow from God as, by analogy, all things follow from the laws of nature. Both of these relations are mathematical. Spinoza shows us what is entailed by a system of causation that includes the entire universe mathematically. Nothing finite follows from God directly, just as no natural event or thing can follow from the laws of nature alone. The causal relation is a double relation entirely distinct from the double aspect of nature under the two attributes of thought and extension.

> An individual thing, or a thing which is finite and which has a determinate existence, cannot exist nor be determined to action unless it be determined to existence and action by another cause which is also finite and has a determinate existence; and again, this cause cannot exist nor be determined to action unless by another cause which is also finite and determined to existence and action, and so on *ad infinitum*. (I, Prop. XXVIII)

Causation is a double relation: to God and to other finite things. There is a direct causation from God that produces infinite and eternal things (I, Prop. XXI) analogous to the mathematical sense in which theorems follow from other theorems: universally and necessarily (infinitely and eternally). But in relation to the finite events and things that comprise the "make of the universe" as we know and experience it,[8] causation is a double relation corresponding to two inseparable senses of "following from": natural laws follow from each other as theorems follow from other theorems and axioms; finite events follow from each other according to natural laws.[9] These senses are not distinct nor are they merely analogous: they are the same exactly but distinguishably. The natural laws "are" the powers that constitute both the reality and the intelligibility of natural things. It is no surprise that Spinoza explicitly claims that God is power. (I, Prop. XXXIV) Finite things are and are intelligible only in terms of two infinite relations: to God, absolutely infinite, and to other finite things, *ad infinitum*.[10]

We are dividing Hume's critique into its epistemological and metaphysical sides. To the latter, Spinoza has a deep and heretical answer, analogous to mechanism: causation is a double relation in which all finite things follow from God through each other (or, equivalently, from each other through God), while God is the active power in (or between) all things.[11] If there were nothing to the essence of any being but what it derived from God then God would be the only active power in the universe while finite things would be that upon which these powers work. Following this line of thought, Spinoza distinguishes between God as *natura naturans*, nature naturing, and finite modes as *natura naturata*, everything that follows from God's activity. (I, Prop. XXIX: Note) Spinoza's system is both structurally and thematically identical with a mechanistic system of natural laws, with the important and far-reaching proviso that God is *absolutely* infinite, in all ways and kinds. This view of God *and* of the natural world is deeply heretical, among the supreme conjunctions of same and other in the history of thought. Spinoza's theory is the expression of the heretical side of modern science, its inexhaustible plenitude, hidden within its orthodoxy.

The epistemological side of Hume's critique remains largely untouched within Spinoza's theory if we interpret him as a rationalist.

> Every idea which in us is absolute, that is to say, adequate and perfect, is true. (II, Prop. XXXIV)

> Those things which are common to everything, and which are equally in the part and in the whole, can only be adequately conceived. (II, Prop. XXXVIII)

If ideas are human ideas, then Spinoza is a rationalist who must face the question of how ideas that are common to everything, entirely universal, may be acquired from finite sensory experience. If, instead, ideas are God's ideas (the infinite intellect) concerning the human body, then it is immensely plausible that there should be adequate and true ideas (propositions) concerning finite things that follow with necessity from other adequate propositions, based on the power and order of the universe.[12] It is nothing less than the view that there is an (absolutely infinite) order to the universe that reason can strive to attain. It is a supreme view of the rule of the same. Yet, how we may acquire knowledge of specific causal relations remains unanswered. Indeed, it may be impossible for finite beings to *acquire* such knowledge adequately, for knowledge of individual things is always inadequate. Things bloom as individually other in the garden of the same.

> About the duration of our body we can have but a very inadequate knowledge. (II, Prop. XXX)

> About the duration of individual things which are outside us we can have but a very inadequate knowledge. (II, Prop. XXXI)

Implicit in any such knowledge, adequate or inadequate, are the truths that pertain to the order of the universe and its infinite powers.

> All ideas, in so far as they are related to God, are true. (II, Prop. XXXII)

> There is, in relation to every idea, regarded as part of the order and connection among natural things, a true and adequate idea. The

analogy with mechanism carries through even here. To any inadequate and confused idea or utterance produced by a human being, to any error or hasty conclusion, there corresponds a description of the state of that person's mind and body that simultaneously is true about that person and his surrounding circumstances and true about the errors he has made. Such a view of erroneous ideas is required by any system of the order of nature that includes its own intelligibility. There is a double causation ontologically and a double causation epistemologically that follows from it. Both of these relations are mathematical in structure.

There is in such a view of natural order a certain orthodoxy: an equivalence between knowing and known. But there is also so far-reaching a sense of this relation as to surpass any ordinary sense of orthodoxy: the relation is an identity. Thought and being do not coincide: they are the same. When we add to this the absolutely infinite nature of God, we must be struck by the sense that thought and being are equally infinite in their identity.

Spinoza's universe is comprised of three forms of being: substance, attributes, and modes, or, more accurately, substance, *its* attributes, and *its* modes. Attributes and modes belong to substance in complex ways. Substance is absolutely and unconditionedly self-caused, independent in all respects. It follows that substance, absolutely self-caused, and God, absolutely infinite, coincide. Most of the striking properties of substance follow from Spinoza's strong understanding of self-causation and independence. Were there two substances, each would limit the other, thereby defining it. Because each substance is conceived through itself, it cannot have anything in common (any attribute) with another, for that would require that each be conceived through the other. It follows that substance can have no external relations. Its internal relations, however, comprise attributes and modes. Similarly, substance or God must be *absolutely* infinite, not simply "infinite in its own kind," because any kind in which substance was not infinite would limit it. Substance is absolutely self-caused and absolutely without limits: these notions are the same. Such an identity is remarkable. It entails that the universe has an absolutely unlimited and unchanging, self-caused foundation immanent in every finite event.[13]

The natural question is whether there could be anything in the universe so self-caused. Suppose everything were finite, local and limited. Suppose every being were qualified by some relation, some other being. Such a view is largely held by Aristotle despite his emphasis on ontological primacy and unmoved movers. There is an ontological plurality of both beings and kinds of beings. For Spinoza, although there is as clearly a plurality of beings and kinds of beings, there is a single absolute and independent foundation.[14] Even thinking of such an extreme foundation is heretical.

Spinoza offers several proofs for the existence of substance in Part I, in Proposition VII and in Proposition XI. The argument of Proposition VII is that nothing other can produce substance, for it is absolutely self-caused; therefore, it must cause itself and must exist. The proof, taken from without, is unpersuasive, for although by definition substance can be caused by nothing else, it may not exist so as to cause itself. Nothing may in fact be absolutely self-caused, absolutely infinite and independent of anything else.

The proofs in Proposition XI are similarly unpersuasive. They all presuppose what they are designed to prove. For example, the first proof depends on the principle (which Spinoza claims to prove) that "if there be no cause nor reason which hinders a thing from existing it exists necessarily." In traditional terms, it is existence which requires a cause, not nonexistence. Either Spinoza assumes too strong a principle of sufficient reason, such that both the being *and* the nonbeing of anything must have a reason or cause, or, covertly, substance is a special case such that its existence can be denied only based on a sufficient reason. Through all these arguments, the existence of substance falls under the dominion of the same.

We may find it plausible to think of nature as a totality. If nature is comprised of all existing things in their unity and interconnections, then it is self-contradictory to deny its existence. If nature is comprised of whatever is in any way, then total nonexistence is unintelligible. Nonexistence is intelligible only in relation to existence, nonbeing to being (and conversely). It is meaningful to deny the existence of some things if what we mean is that something else might have existed instead. But it is unintelligible to deny the existence of anything or everything. The natural reply is that it is also meaningless and unintelligible to *assert* the existence of everything, of the totality of the universe. *All* things may not comprise a single being.

Nevertheless, God or substance is not without qualification *everything*. The double causation that pertains to every finite mode, in relation to God and in relation to other finite modes, entails that these cannot be identified. Spinoza indicates this in two separate passages. In one, he identifies God with *natura naturans*, nature's active principle, and modes with *natura naturata*, nature acted upon. Here, "Nature" is both together, but the two, activity and passivity, are distinguished. They are together because an active principle requires something to act upon. The double unity of the universe corresponds to the double causation pertaining to every finite mode. God is one; moreover, insofar as he is the active power in all things, their existence and their essence, they are the recipient side of that power. Each entails the other.

The second passage in which Spinoza denies that God is identical with what he acts upon is in the long Note to Proposition XVII:

> Since, therefore, God's intellect is the sole cause of things, both of their essence and of their existence (as we have already shown), it must necessarily differ from them with regard both to its essence and existence; for an effect differs from its cause precisely in that which it has from its cause. (I, Prop. XVII: Note)

It is difficult to imagine a more explicit denial that God is equivalent with the things that follow. What must be added is that although God is entirely different, in essence and existence, from anything that he acts upon, activity and passivity are inseparable. Spinoza offers a powerful sense of the unity of the universe based on a profound and far-reaching analysis of power. God here is the creative power in a deterministic universe without teleology. Spinoza may be an exception to Whitehead's striking criticism of the cosmological tradition that the world needs God but God does not need the world. God needs the world in Spinoza as the complementary object of his activities and powers.

With such an understanding of the central place of power and activity in Spinoza's theory, we may reinterpret the limitations of his proofs of God's existence. If there is no other cause of substance's existence, then it must be cause of itself, and must exist.[15] Spinoza presupposes that existence (and therefore nonexistence) requires an active cause. Thus, if we say that there is no such thing as substance, we deny that there are active powers in the universe. This is unintelligible. What we would have to mean instead is that there is no *unified* active power that can be distinguished from the local powers in finite things. Finite things are the only sources of activity and causation. Here the existence of universal laws of nature becomes problematic.

Similarly, Spinoza's arguments in Proposition XI that if substance does not exist there must be a cause of its nonexistence follow as well from the understanding that every determination must be the result of power. One reply is that nonexistence is not of itself a determination. Another, more relevant, is that the unity ascribed to substance is aporetic, that no cause could be sufficient in a universe of finite things to produce such a unified being. Spinoza recognizes the intimate relation between his view of power and the existence of substance in the other proof of Proposition XI:

> Inability to exist is impotence, and, on the other hand, ability to exist is power, as is self-evident. If, therefore, there is

nothing which necessarily exists except things finite, it follows that things finite are more powerful than the absolutely infinite Being, and this (as is self-evident) is absurd; .... (I, Prop. XI: Proof)

Again, we may reply that there is nothing self-contradictory about the greater power of (existing) finite things over a (nonexisting) absolutely infinite being. What is omitted in such a reply is that power must be determinate in order to be effective and that the source of all such determinations in Spinoza is God.

These proofs may lack credibility, but they indicate two important features of Spinoza's system and of metaphysics more generally. One is that despite the pivotal role played by the geometrical structure of the universe as exemplified in *Ethics*, the proofs fail at central points to carry conviction. The second is that the importance of Spinoza's view of things does not depend on the validity of these proofs.

We remember Whitehead's rejection of "proof" as "a feeble second-rate procedure."[16] He emphasizes self-evidence instead, although some of the most outrageous claims in the history of humanity have been made in its name. Yet there is something to his point, and it is evident in Spinoza.

I have called it "heretical." The heresy is that the supremacy of the same and the inexhaustibility of its others in Spinoza's conception of the universe lie indissociably within its geometrical structure—expressive of the nature of intelligibility—and outside the capacity of what can be proved by means of it.[17] Thus, the existence of substance cannot be proved, and Spinoza's proofs are weak gestures toward a closure that he neither achieves nor makes strenuous efforts to achieve. The forcefulness of the theory lies in something much closer to self-evidence than proof: the aporia of truth. Substance is conceived as the source of all activity, all creativity, of essence and activity: it is power itself. Everything follows from it, for there is no other active principle in the universe.

Spinoza's view of things entails the presence of inexhaustible powers: inexhaustible otherness within the unity of the same that is God. These powers are not separate from the finite things that they work upon and among, but belong to them immanently. Modes are what they are in virtue of the powers that are inherent within them. Both their being and their intelligibility are the result of the powers of God. There is, throughout Spinoza's entire system, a certain duality (but not a dualism) that maintains aporia at the forefront of every important consideration. How do two forms of causation coexist without mediation? How can nature be regarded as either identical with or different from God? How can power belong to God and not belong to finite things? The answer in each case is aporetic, a sublime movement in the unending ballet of same and other.

Take the question of how things follow from God. What follows from God or his attributes absolutely must be infinite and eternal.

> All things which follow from the absolute nature of any attribute of God must forever exist, and must be infinite, that is to say, through that same attribute they are eternal and infinite. (I, Prop. XXI)

There is again the analogy with universal propositions in logic or natural laws in science. What follows logically from any universal proposition or natural law is but another universal proposition or natural law. We can arrive at finite, existential propositions only through other existential propositions. The analogy is important, but it tames the heretical implication in Spinoza's formulation concerning what is eternally and infinitely the same. Setting that aside momentarily, the point is that he is explicit that while all finite things follow from God, they do not "follow from the absolute nature of any attribute of God." They follow through or qualified by other finite modes. There is therefore a "following" from God "directly" or without finite qualification, and there is a "following" from God qualified by other finite things. This is the aporia in finite things that they are *both* finite and infinite—infinite "under qualification" —and the aporia in the infinite that it may be qualified by what is finite. Both finite and infinite things are infinitely the same and infinitely other.

Within these aporias is an explanation of how modes are *of* substance, how they are substance's modes without being identical with substance. Modes follow from substance in the sense that substance is the only active power. Modes therefore could not be, in their existence or their essence—the strongest sense of their being—without God. But they also could not be without other finite modes, for they do not follow directly or from God, only under qualification. God's power works both absolutely, producing eternal and infinite things, generic powers, and, under qualification by finite things, producing other finite things.

The consequence is that finite things do not and cannot follow directly from God. Finite, temporal things qualify each other inexhaustibly. Although Spinoza associates contingency with inadequate ideas, there is a certain "contingency" (but not chance) that pertains to his view of the universe that qualifies it profoundly. Everything follows from God, but in relation to finite things, under qualification by other finite things. Everything follows from God necessarily, but, in relation to finite things, only in relation to other finite things. This means that finite things all together (or "as such") do not follow from God directly or mediately.

Each follows from God through other finite things, but all together cannot be said to be a necessary (direct) result of God's power. If we think of the universe as a succession of finite events, then each event follows from its predecessors through God, but the entire sequence of events does not. In this way, there is complete and universal necessity in Spinoza's system, relative to finite events, but it is nevertheless qualified. Such a necessity is, then, finitely qualified along with all finite conditions: that is what finiteness means.[18] By way of contrast, Leibniz attempts to transform the qualifications and contingencies that pertain to finiteness into unqualified necessity. At the center of both Spinoza's and Leibniz's theories is the question of the universe, whether all things can, together, be taken as a totality. Such a totality of the same is among the most remarkable aporias.

I am suggesting that Spinoza's theory is aporetic in its complex dualities, along with and within its sublime vision of the unity of the universe, and that the aporias are both heretical and among his greatest moments. That Spinoza fails to prove that all things follow directly from God is a defect only if we insist that all things should follow absolutely from God. That there might be a view of the complete intelligibility of the universe, unified and singular, without conforming to that absolute view of God's causality is among Spinoza's greatest insights.

We may now consider some of the other aporias in Spinoza involving the different modes of being: substance is self-caused; modes are other-caused. That should logically exhaust the universe. Yet there are also attributes of substance, "that which the intellect perceives of substance as constituting its essence." This is a famously ambiguous definition. Why does Spinoza introduce the "intellect's perception" of substance, and why is such a perception divided into attributes? Why may we not simply identify substance with its attributes? That would, of course, divide substance, which is undivided. It cannot be divided into different substances and cannot be divided into different modes because it would then be contingent. It follows, however, that substance is indeed divisible, simply not into other substances or into what is not of the nature of substance. Attributes *are* substance under qualification by the intellect.

Should we interpret the "intellect's perception" of substance to be subjective, therefore not of the nature of substance? That is among the most controversial questions of interpretation in relation to Spinoza. He never interprets attributes as distortions, but always as having the nature of substance in every respect save its unitariness and comprehensiveness. Attributes are themselves infinite and express the eternal and infinite essence of God. (II, Prop. I) The alternative is to take the attributes as "being" substance. The difficulty is to understand how they do not then divide it, although this may be no more of a difficulty than the comparable one pertaining to modes: if modes "belong" to substance, why do they not divide it over them? The answer to the latter question is given by Spinoza's distinction between *natura naturans* and *natura naturata*. There is no comparable distinction concerning attributes. The relation of attributes to substance is an embrace in the great dance of the same.

How are we to understand the emphasis upon the "intellect" in the definition of attribute if we reject the subjective interpretation? The questions are of *whose* intellect Spinoza is speaking and what kind of an intellect is involved. Here we must note his recurrent reference to the "infinite intellect." In one of his most important propositions:

> From the necessity of the divine nature infinite numbers of things in infinite ways (that is to say, all things which can be conceived by the infinite intellect) must follow. (I, Prop. XVI)

Here he effectively claims that all things exist in God both actually and potentially, and that the form of their existence is as conceived by the infinite intellect. This conception is closely related to what he calls "the idea of God" in Part II:

> In God there necessarily exists the idea of His essence and of all things which necessarily follow from His essence. (II, Prop. III)

> The idea of God, from which infinite numbers of things follow in infinite ways, can be one only. (II, Prop. IV)

The latter proposition refers backward to his discussion of the infinite intellect. The intellect here is divine and infinite. Spinoza's view is that all things follow from God as ideas in God's mind, which includes both existing and nonexisting things.

> The ideas of non-existent individual things or modes are compre-hended in the infinite idea of God, in the same way that the formal essences of individual things or modes are contained in the attributes of God. (II, Prop. VIII)

All things follow from God as ideas follow from other ideas. This plenitude includes not only existing, actual things but nonexisting, potential things. We may refer again to the analogy with mechanism to note that in a system of natural laws and finite material states (even of the entire universe), all possible states, actual or potential, must be mathematically embodied in the laws of nature. Mechanism and Spinoza's infinite intellect share a far-reaching sense of totality in which actuality is the exemplification of an infinite system that includes all states and conditions for all things, mathematically and potentially. There is an inexhaustible plenitude in mechanism that is obscured by its traditional formulations and is manifested clearly only in Spinoza (and possibly Leibniz).

If we understand that finite things follow from God mathematically and potentially in relation to God's infinite intellect, it is plausible to understand God's attributes similarly. It is not some finite being's intellect, subjectively, that conceives of God's essence in terms of infinite attributes, but God's own infinite intellect and conception. This is a remarkable idea: God's absolutely infinite nature is such that it can be conceived, ideally and infinitely—that is, even by himself—only in terms of infinite numbers of attributes, can be thought truly only in infinitely different ways. We have here a striking and far-reaching interpretation of the inexhaustibility of the universe. God is inexhaustible in the sense that he can be conceived, ideally and perfectly, only in terms of infinite difference. It follows, from God's immanence, that every finite mode is similarly inexhaustible. We leave behind all ordinary theories of mechanism and natural law, which are at best finite expressions of the inexhaustible plenitude of nature. Spinoza's sense of the infinite includes the plenitude of inexhaustibility everywhere. It lacks only the sense that inexhaustibility pertains to finite beings *because* of their finiteness, and, consequently, a corresponding emphasis upon the finiteness in inexhaustibility.

The term "infinite" has a double meaning. In its primary sense, it means unqualified, as Spinoza explains that he means by God something not merely infinite in a kind, but in all kinds—absolutely unlimited. In relation to the attributes, however, it follows from the absolutely unqualified nature of God that he will have infinite attributes. "Infinite" here is quantitative as it is not in the definition of God's absolutely infinite nature.

> The more reality or being a thing possesses, the more attributes belong to it, ... (I, Prop. IX)

> . . . the more reality or being it [each being] has, the more attributes it possesses expressing necessity or eternity and infinity. Nothing is consequently clearer than that Being absolutely infinite is necessarily defined, as we have shown, as Being which consists of infinite attributes, each one of which expresses a certain essence, eternal and infinite. (I, Prop. X: Note)

It follows that God or substance will have infinite numbers of attributes. More accurately, God *is* infinite numbers of attributes.

> God or substance consisting of infinite attributes, each one of
> which expresses eternal and infinite essence, necessarily exists.
> (I, Prop. XI)

The primary meaning of God's absolutely infinite nature is that he is
unlimited, unqualified, complete, in any and all ways (that is, every particular kind). What follows from such a qualitative sense of limits is a
quantitative corollary: the *number* of God's attributes is infinite, unlimited. God is, then, doubly infinite, numerically and qualitatively. He is
unlimited in every sense. It follows that God is inexhaustible in the specific sense that he can be thought or conceived, however perfectly, only
in inexhaustibly diverse ways. These different ways are the same but are
not one. Spinoza offers a profound if aporetic interpretation of inexhaustibility—that is, absolute infinity, quantitative and qualitative, divided by
infinite difference. It includes the dividedness essential to inexhaustibility in the multiplicity of attributes. What it lacks is a strong enough
sense of how the dividedness pertains to God and, in particular, of the
incompatibilities and incommensuratenesses that pertain to an infinite
multiplicity of ways under which all things fall. The fundamental aporia
is the oneness of God amidst the infinite multiplicity of his attributes.

The infinite intellect here is not equivalent with finite conception,
but with an ideal or perfect conception. It is closely related to the identity between the order and connection of things and the order and connection of ideas. The infinite intellect, ideas in God's mind, and the
order and connection of ideas and things are all closely related if not
identical notions.

> I say that although each thing is expressed in infinite ways
> in the infinite intellect of God, nevertheless, these infinite ideas
> by which it is expressed cannot constitute one and the same
> mind of a singular thing, but infinitely many minds. For each of
> the infinitely many ideas has no connection with any other, as I
> have explained in *Ethics*, II, Prop. VII, Scholium, and is obvi-
> ous from I, Prop. X. (Letter 66)

It follows that thought plays a singular role in Spinoza's theory,
expressed in the attributes that are the ways in which substance is to
be thought.

> Therefore the essence of the soul consists only in the exist-
> ence of an idea, or objective essence in the attribute of thought,
> originating from the essence of an object which in fact really
> exists in nature. I say "of an object which really exists" without

further specification in order to include here not only the modes of extension, but also the modes of all the infinite attributes, which have a soul just as extension does. (*Short Treatise*, Appendix)

If we think ahead to the criticisms of empiricism, classical and later, against a correspondence theory of truth, we may imagine that what is later rejected is Spinoza's sense of identity involving ideas and things. Yet insofar as ideas are human, derived from experience, they cannot be shown to correspond to things. This is no less true in Spinoza than in Hume. *Our* ideas, interpreted as modifications of our bodies and minds under the attribute of thought, qualified by other finite causes, can only be inadequate. (II, Props. XXX, XXXI) There is an adequate idea corresponding to every inadequate idea. (II, Prop. XXXII) There are then two kinds of "ideas" in Spinoza: one pertaining to human beings, regarded as modifications involving finite bodies and minds, the other pertaining to God and the infinite intellect. All ideas in God's intellect are adequate and true. All finite ideas, regarded as modifications involving other finite ideas and things, are inadequate. What is remarkable is the way Spinoza interrelates these two notions of ideas, in two important ways.

Every idea which in us is absolute, that is to say, adequate and perfect, is true. (II, Prop. XXXIV)

Falsity consists in the privation of knowledge, which inadequate, that is to say, mutilated and confused ideas involve. (II, Prop. XXXV)

In the one case, the order and connection of ideas *is* the order and connection of things. They are the same. Here knowledge and reality coincide: they do not simply correspond. Ideas *are* reality. On the onto-logical side, thought and extension are two attributes of God that entirely coincide. To say that "man is composed of mind and body, and that the human body exists as we perceive it," (II, Prop. XIII: Corollary) is not to *add* mind and body, thought and extension, together, but to see them as identical, conjointly relevant to human being. Because what we usually call ideas in the human mind are confused, mutilated, and inadequate, these ideas are not simply identical with things as thought in God. How-ever, and this is the second kind or sense of "idea," there is also an identity between the confused and inadequate ideas thought by human beings and adequate ideas in God. Moreover, human beings are able to think adequate as well as inadequate ideas.

The first kind of idea falls within the attribute of thought as it expresses God's essence under the attribute of extension. The two attributes are identical. (II, Prop. VII, Note) The mind that comprehends substance under these attributes is the infinite intellect: the mind of God. We are concerned here with the way in which ideas "objectively" express reality under an attribute. There is an attribute of extension under which extended things fall and an identical attribute of thought under which ideas of extended things fall, and, where adequate, these are the same. It follows that absolutely infinite substance falls under thought intrinsically. The absolutely infinite nature of God entails that God is thinkable (in being and in essence) in an infinite number of ways.

There are infinite numbers of infinite attributes, but human beings can know only two of them: thought and extension. We may suppose that this limitation follows from the finiteness of human being. Yet because all the attributes correspond, because they are all identical to God under some form of comprehension, why may not human beings think every one of them? If every attribute is an expression of God's essence and existence under some mode of thought, must they not all correspond to each other just as thought and extension do under human comprehension? Spinoza's only reply is no answer to the question posed:

> . . . the human mind can acquire knowledge only of those things which the idea of the actually existing body involves, or which can be inferred from this idea. . . . Now this idea of the body involves and expresses no other attributes of God than Extension and Thought. For its ideate (ideatum), to wit, body (II, Prop. VI), has God for its cause in so far as he is considered under the attribute of Extension, and not under any other attribute. (Letter 64)

He suggests that finiteness is restriction to one mode of being and thought— that of the human body, under extension. He does not consider that finiteness might itself be inexhaustible.

Human beings are, here, doubly finite: qualified by other finite modes and restricted to but two of infinite numbers of attributes. On the side of God, there are infinite numbers and kinds of attributes; there is also the fundamental importance of God's infinite intellect. One interpretation of the infinite numbers of attributes, then, after what Spinoza says in the Appendix to the *Short Treatise,* is that there is a "formal" attribute of thought corresponding to—or identical with—each particular "material" attribute, while all these attributes are themselves the same as expressions of the essence of God: an infinite number of identical ways in which God's inexhaustible essence is manifested. Thought here is not one of infinitely many attributes, but is one member of infinite numbers of identical pairs of attributes. Things are in an infinite number of ways, while each way is identical with a particular mode of thought in the infinite intellect. Such an interpretation[19] provides us with an important interpretation of the intelligibility of things amidst the inexhaustibility of God's absolutely infinite nature. It is the only interpretation that captures the sense in which ideas in God's infinite intellect permeate the theory: corresponding to every "material" attribute there is an attribute of thought identical with it.

Spinoza's argument for the restriction of human thought to ideas of bodies is unpersuasive. We might wish to abandon the restriction, adding the proviso that the finiteness of human experience makes thought of other attributes historically and contingently very difficult. Here the infinite numbers of attributes with their associated ideas would comprise the inexhaustible intelligibility of the universe under God, while human beings, capable in principle of thinking of things in infinite numbers of ways, find themselves restricted contingently to but one of those ways. On this interpretation, we find in Spinoza a powerful sense of the possibility of heresy conjoined with a severe sense of how difficult and unlikely it may be for human beings to achieve it.

This view of ideas in relation to the attributes depends on distinguishing three senses of thought: (1) thought in God's infinite intellect that produces infinite numbers of attributes; (2) thought that corresponds to extension as two of many attributes; and (3) human thought as typically confused, mutilated, and inadequate.

> But it is necessary to note that we are here speaking of the ideas which arise necessarily in God of the existence of things, together with their essences, not of the ideas which the things now actually present to us and produce in us. The two differ greatly. For in God the ideas do not arise as they do in us, from one or more of the senses, through which we are nearly always very imperfectly affected by the things, but from their existence and essence, that is, from all that they are. (*Short Treatise*, II, XX)

The first two senses are always adequate, and portray a sense of ideas "objectively" or "formally." Spinoza uses this language, following Descartes in part:

> The formal being of ideas recognizes God for its cause in so far as He is considered as a thinking thing, and not in so far as He is manifested by any other attribute; . . . . (II, Prop. V)

The formal being of ideas is the objective reality of ideas, understood in the double sense of being real and of expressing reality. These are ideas in God. There is the thought that expresses the inexhaustibility of God, his absolutely infinite nature in thinking infinite attributes, and there is the thought that expresses the inexhaustibility of extension, in thinking extension infinitely (in its kind) and inexhaustibly. We may refer again to the distinction Spinoza introduces between God's absolutely infinite nature and infiniteness in a kind. The kinds are particular attributes. There is, then, in God's infinite intellect, a fundamental doubling of thought: of God himself, in his infinite numbers of attributes (or kinds of being); and of any particular kind or attribute, to which a particular form of thought corresponds or with which it is identical.

This doubling of thought in relation to God's essence and his attributes is essential to the intelligibility of both God and nature. Here ideas formally and objectively *are* reality actually, to the extent that reality is intelligible. If God is absolutely infinite, then there must be some divine form of thought that comprehends his nature, divided over infinite numbers and kinds of attributes. To each of these infinite attributes there is an equivalent attribute of thought. Another way of putting this is that the finiteness of the human intellect, regarded as a finite modification, may include the infiniteness of both thought and extension, in their equivalence, but not the infiniteness of all the ways in which God can be conceived. God is inexhaustible in the sense that infinite numbers of infinite kinds pertain to him, each of which is intelligible and thinkable. What follows is an infinite number of attributes, each of which is infinite and each of which is divisible into a mode of being and a mode of thinking (with the qualification that the thinking is also a mode of being), where these two are the same but different. The identity cannot obscure the differences that divide the attributes relative to each other, differences fundamental to inexhaustibility.

Another doubling of thought takes place, in Spinoza, at the level of confused human ideas. There are actually two such doublings, a consequence of the epistemic nature of thought. For such a thought must allow infinite numbers of ways in which it may reflect on itself. First, corresponding to every idea, adequate or not, is some modification in the body, so that corresponding further, there must be an adequate idea completely expressing every inadequate idea. (V, Prop. IV) Second, every idea may be thought adequately. Therefore, there are adequate ideas corresponding to inadequate ideas, and adequate ideas *of* other ideas. (II, Prop. XXI: Note; II, Prop. XLIII: Note) These two may be identical. However, it is essential, if ideas are real, that there be ideas of ideas, and ideas of those ideas.

> ... the idea of the mind, that is to say, the idea of the idea, is nothing but the form of the idea in so far as this is considered as

a mode of thought and without relation to the object, just as a person who knows anything by that very fact knows that he knows, and knows that he knows that he knows, and so on *ad infinitum*. (II, Prop. XXI: Note)

The question is why Spinoza does not recognize that if there are ideas of ideas, there must be inadequate ideas of ideas of ideas *ad infinitum*. This is not an infinite regress—or not a destructive one—but an expression of the ability of thought to think itself at ever higher levels of reflexivity. Spinoza is more concerned with how an idea of an adequate idea can express its adequacy than with how we may form inadequate ideas of inadequate ideas of inadequate ideas. Thus, he terminates the levels of reflexiveness in adequacy and truth. Moreover, it is not clear how an infinite hierarchy of reflexiveness in ideas could be compatible with his identity between thought and extension (unless extension also participated in an infinite hierarchy of reflexiveness). This profoundly limits his capacity to include complex forms of mathematics, science, and art within his theory. Nevertheless, there is a profound sense of inexhaustibility in Spinoza's view of God, the infiniteness of every attributes under thought, and the infiniteness of finite modes under qualification.

The complex reflexive interconnections involving ideas in relation to other ideas as well as to extension explain what is probably the most obscure aspect of Spinoza's theory. This is his privative view of falsity.

Falsity consists in the privation of knowledge, which inadequate, that is to say, mutilated and confused ideas involve. (II, Prop. XXXV)

There are at least two fundamental senses of idea involved. One is pertinent to human beings as thinkers and knowers: every human thought is inadequate and confused. Carried to its extreme, justified by Spinoza's emphasis on the particular modality of finite human being, every human idea is inadequate, privative or not. Human beings think about their surroundings in confused, imagistic terms, mixing up one object with another, one event with another. How is this privative?

An answer is given by the principle that corresponding to every inadequate idea is an adequate idea that expresses its truth completely. To every proposition thought by a human being, there corresponds an idea in God that includes that proposition and truly explains its nature and essence. There is a true description of every human being that explains why he had a particular idea and why that particular idea is in error, and the latter is an incomplete or partial expression of the former. The adequate account might run as follows: Conditions $C_1 \ldots C_n$ hold, and under such conditions person P will confusedly think proposition *p*. The latter is a thought embedded in a complete and adequate or true idea of both the embedded thought and why it is incorrect. Every inadequate idea is an incomplete expression of the adequate idea that includes it. Only such a view can make sense of the complete causal intelligibility of the universe. An adequate idea is a complete expression of an inadequate idea that both corresponds to it and includes it. Both nature and our understanding of nature are comprised of infinite strands of infinite causal sequences, each of which comprises finiteness.

Two senses of finiteness are present here. One is that every finite mode with its associated idea follows from God qualified by other finite modes and falls under a particular attribute. These two qualifications—by other finite modes and by a particular attribute—constitute finiteness. The second, not clearly identical with the first, is that every finite idea thought by a finite being is mutilated and confused—that is, incomplete. What is required is emphasis upon the incompleteness of human thought in relation to infinite chains of modes and causes.

The view of thought as pertaining to reality directly, by identity, gives us a certain view of the way the intelligibility of things lies within them as part of their nature. It is, in Spinoza, taken to its most sublime extreme, because what pertains to every thing, including finite modes, is an adequate idea, in God, either qualified by or free from qualification by other finite modes. Yet this sense of intelligibility in things does not of itself give us a rationalist epistemology. Here the question is how a finite being can know infinite ideas, can have an idea of God or, more simply, can have an adequate idea of an inadequate idea. Here we come much closer to the orthodox view of Spinoza as a "rationalist": where he says, for example, that:

> He who has a true idea knows at the same time that he has a true idea, nor can he doubt the truth of the thing. (II, Prop. XLIII)

In the case of knowledge derived from individual things, or concerning knowledge that pertains to individual things, Spinoza agrees that no true ideas exist in human experience that must be thought truly. (II, Prop. XLII) Knowledge of the first kind is from individual things and from signs or words. Knowledge of the second kind consists of "common notions and adequate ideas of the properties of things." (II, Prop. XL: Note 2) Knowledge of the third kind is intuitive science and is extremely general or common. Thus, adequate knowlege, true ideas that can only be thought truly, is always universal and general.

Those things which are common to everything and which are equally in the part and in the whole, can only be adequately conceived. (II, Prop. XXXVIII)

The example is again mathematical. Those ideas that pertain to all things, within the same, can only be thought adequately and truly. What we would almost certainly respond today is that there is no such idea that is not refracted through the finiteness of human experience, so that what is thought common to everything, or believed to be thought truly, is always finite. If all human ideas are confused, whether or not there is a corresponding thought by an infinite intellect that would express what is true about such human ideas, then geometry is no absolute and unqualified paradigm. On the epistemological if not ontological side, Spinoza's theory of true ideas is inconsistent with the aporetic side of his ontology.

This can be seen in what may be the most extraordinary of his claims about the way to wisdom and fulfillment. The principle that common ideas are adequate and true falls on the side of what is formally or objectively intelligible: common ideas pertain to no finite individual essences and therefore follow from the essence of God. (II, Prop. XXXVII) This mathematical paradigm is one of the greatest prejudices in the history of philosophy and science, that universal ideas are not only *more* knowable, but *fully* knowable in a way that individual things are not. That this is a prejudice is acknowledged by Spinoza, if not as forcefully as by Hegel, in his recognition that individual things have powers and essences that go beyond mere passivity, that therefore go beyond the causes that lie outside them including God. (III, Prop. VII) No understanding of individual things can follow from universal or common ideas alone. Spinoza's greatness—and his heresy—consist in his far-reaching sense of how the individuality of finite modes cannot follow from God alone. It is manifested predominantly in the two principles that finite modes follow both from God and from each other, *ad infinitum* (I, Prop. XXVIII), and that finite, individual modes have essences and powers that cannot and do not follow directly from God. The *conatus* of finite things, their striving and desire, manifests the infiniteness of the finite, but in a way incompatible with the common ideas that follow directly from God. In this sense, even if common ideas can be adequately conceived, and even if they are the only ideas that can be adequately conceived, they do not constitute adequate knowledge of finite things. This is because the finiteness of such things lies in their individual desires.

Each thing, in so far as it is in itself, endeavors to persevere in its being. (III, Prop. VI)

> The effort by which each thing endeavors to persevere in its own being is nothing but the actual essence of the thing itself. (III, Prop. VII)

Being, here, is striving to endure. No theory of desire in the entire Western tradition is stronger than Spinoza's, with the remarkable aporia that (infinite) desire defines finite being teleologically in a deterministic universe.

Spinoza's heresy is to achieve an unsurpassed sense of an inexhaustible universe that is nevertheless one through God. It is an even more remarkable feature of his point of view that he does not deny, but in many ways affirms, the aporetic nature of this unity amid inexhaustible multiplicity: the role of God and his attributes among infinite numbers of finite modes. Nevertheless, there are places where his insights falter, where strains are evident between his sense of the intelligibility of the relation between finite and infinite. He does not consider the possibility that the only intelligibility is that which pertains to finite things.

Ontologically and logically, common, universal ideas are the only adequate and intelligible ideas. Even here, we must distinguish two different senses of intelligibility: formal or objective, and epistemic or human. What is common to all things, part and whole, constitutes what is intelligible within them. We may think of these commonalities as the universal side of finite things, based on a geometrical paradigm. Only universal truths are adequate and intelligible. It is a quite different question how finite human beings can achieve an adequate idea of such universal truths. It is one thing to say that natural laws and other universal principles constitute the intelligible basis of natural events and another to say that human beings are capable, from their finite experiences, of finitely discovering and understanding such principles. Spinoza so completely emphasizes the former of these two that he has no reply to make to empiricist arguments that all knowledge of matters of fact, specific or general, is a posteriori. A posteriori knowledge is of the first two kinds for Spinoza, and cannot be adequate. All he can say is that adequate ideas (in God) *pertain* to human beings as they pertain to every being. No explanation can be given of how finite thought can think such adequate ideas, how otherness can achieve the same.

There is, in this sense, a divided rationalism in Spinoza, as in most of the rationalists except perhaps for Descartes. Rationalism has an ontological and an epistemological side. The ontological side concerns the nature of intelligibility, for Spinoza based on adequate universal ideas on the one hand unified through God and on the other identical with natural things. The epistemological side concerns how such universal principles can be finitely knowable. Spinoza's answer is that adequate ideas are self-validating.

> He who has a true idea knows at the same time that he has a
> true idea, nor can he doubt the truth of the thing. (II, Prop. XLIII)

This side of rationalism is implausible and is subject to empiricism's most strenuous criticisms. The former view of intelligibility is shared by the empiricists. Yet it too has its aporetic aspects. If Spinoza gives us the most powerful and thoroughgoing theory available of a unified universe founded on universal and necessary principles, we must still avoid taking his view of intelligibility for granted without acknowledging its heretical excesses.

These are evident in the corollaries of his principle of intelligibility. For if what is common is more adequately and fully knowable than what is individual and specific, then every way in which a human being can increase the scope of his relationships should increase his powers and understandings. This is precisely what Spinoza claims, in a number of extraordinary propositions that reach culmination in the assertion that:

> He who possesses a body fit for many things possesses a mind of
> which the greater part is eternal. (V, Prop. XXXIX)

This incredible conclusion follows from the confluence of two strains of thought. One is that common ideas are adequate and true. The other is that the disposition of the body and mind in relation to many other things produces such common ideas. (II, Prop. XIV, Prop. XXXVII, Prop. XXXIX) Here Spinoza emphasizes the formal and objective sense of ideas that pertain to the human mind and body. There exist "in the human mind"—belonging to God and pertaining to the human mind and body—ideas common to both that body and other external bodies, especially those that influence the body. There are general ideas of all the bodies that influence the human body and its various parts.

However, what Spinoza says follows from such a formal sense of universal and adequate ideas is that:

> Hence it follows that the more things the body has in common
> with other bodies, the more things will the mind be adapted to
> perceive. (II, Prop. XXXIX: Corollary)

The implausibility here lies in the gradation between finite and infinite ideas, as if there were a middle term between individual essences and ideas in the mind of God. To the contrary, reiterating the mechanistic analogy, there is nothing between natural (universal) laws and individual bodies, nothing between the infinite same and finite other. Bodies that have a great deal in common with other bodies—say, elementary particles—

are neither more knowable nor more accessible to human thought than ordinary bodies.

When Spinoza claims that there are ideas that cannot but be true, he means primarily to refer to ideas that give the full causal essence of what they pertain to. But he includes the claim that we can tell, in thinking such an idea, that it is true. Indeed, we can only think it truly. Similarly, in claiming that common ideas are necessarily adequate and true, he is describing them formally and objectively. It is another thing to claim that we can dispose our bodies so as to produce such common ideas. That the ideas which are common to all bodies may be adequate and true does not entail that as our bodies come to have more in common with other bodies we will know their ideas more adequately. There is no middle term, and there is no gradation from finite to universal knowledge. It is the error in classical rationalism to make this transition a priori. To the contrary, classical ontological rationalism has a certain view of the intelligibility of things in relation to what is universal and necessary, while classical epistemological rationalism holds a quite distinct view that what we can know, a priori and innately, corresponds to what is intelligible in things.

Modern science appears to hold as a defining characteristic some version of ontological rationalism: what is intelligible in things is universal and, in some sense, potentially completable. There is, in principle, a general account of the natural world, through its general principles and forms, that provides a causal explanation of the essence and existence of each individual thing, regarded *sub species aeternitas*. There is, however, no corresponding epistemological rationalism in modern science, such that we may find in us, either innately or as a consequence of our wider experiences, universal principles that express the forms of intelligibility of the natural universe. Rather, what is needed is constant vigilance against deceptive intuitions and hasty conclusions, based on experimentation and observation. Sufficient vigilance of this kind, it must be added, will lead us to question every version of ontological rationalism, even the idea of rationalism.

There is the possibility that Spinoza's view that the body should be disposed so that it is "fit for many things" is an account of scientific method. The more things that a body has in common with other things, the more it is fit to perceive. Yet there is no empirical justification for such a claim, and implausibility on both sides. What a body has in common with other things corresponds to the universality of natural laws. It is not within our control to increase or decrease this. Moreover, there is no connection between such commonality and the range or accuracy of perception. To the contrary, natural laws in common to all bodies might entail so radical a difference in levels between ordinary and very small and large events that what is in common (in the small and large) produced error, illusion, and deception at the ordinary level. Indeed, modern science suggests that specialized, not generalized, experience produces the most reliable conclusions. The more fit for many things a body is with its associated ideas, the less may its ideas share in the precision and rigor that reliable scientific method requires.

There is a more plausible interpretation of Spinoza's claim, consonant with its spirit rather than with what he says explicitly. Because things fall under many attributes and are inexhaustible, adequacy and truth are the result of widely ranging, diverse experiences more than narrow, restricted, specialized experiences. Such a principle is incompatible with increasing specialization in science, and suggests that modern science is not the primary paradigm of truth. Far more important, however, is the possibility that amidst the inexhaustibility of finite things, there are incommensurate differences, that nothing is altogether common among them. Here diverse experience is necessary to understanding, but there are no common notions that may constitute adequate ideas.

The other side of Spinoza's claim that a body fit for many things possesses a mind that shares in eternity follows from his equation of what is common and adequate in all things with ideas in the mind of God. Adequate ideas are both necessary and eternal. Thus, to know what is common in all things is to know God, and such knowledge of God is the eternal side of the human mind. Again, what is implausible is the suggestion that being fit for many things is a variable state of the body. It is implausible that a theory founded on natural laws can provide an account of divided, finite practices. Rather, what Spinoza should have said, and what he must mean, is that in the ways in which bodies share common traits with other bodies, the ideas that correspond to, or are identical with, such common traits are eternal themselves and manifest the eternal side of the mind. Proposition VII, Part II is sufficient as it stands for this conclusion, given that universal truths pertain to the essence of God rather than to individual things. The identity of ideas and things gives us eternity in the ideas that are identical in their relations to the eternal and universal side of nature. To know what is eternal in things is to have a mind that on this side is eternal. What must be added is the aporia that such an eternity can have nothing at all to do with personal identity and action, not even with finite knowledge and truth, since each individual identity reflects its individual, modal essence, not its universal and common nature.

Spinoza carefully avoids too extreme a conclusion concerning the eternity of the human mind and its awareness, indicating that most of his discussions of God and the human mind are independent of its eternity.

> Even if we did not know that our mind is eternal, we should still consider as of primary importance piety and religion, and absolutely everything which in the Fourth Part we have shown to be related to strength of mind and generosity. (V, Prop. XLI)

Such a claim corresponds exactly to what Socrates says in *Phaedo* concerning the immortality of the soul, a claim I have interpreted as a counsel of reassurance more than a proof of everlastingness. Indeed, the arguments match so closely that we may consider the possibility that Spinoza also recognizes the implausibility in his own position, not so much that there is something eternal in the human mind, for that follows from his metaphysical principles, but that we can know, through ordinary experience, of the eternal nature of the mind. The implausibility is that what is eternal is not individual and personal but what a human being has in common with all other persons and things: the ideas that comprise God's infinite intellect.

We may again divide Spinoza's insight into an almost conventional rationalism in which finiteness is merely an aberration on the surface of eternity and a view in which finiteness holds the center of the stage—at least, the center of *our* stage. The linchpin that conjoins these two moments is the human mind, which is both locus of the adequate ideas that are identical with things under the attribute of thought and the repository of the confusions that attend the finite modality of human existence. Spinoza's answer to why the mind can know only of thought and extension among the attributes is thoroughly aporetic, profoundly doubling the finiteness of human being. His universe is one in which all things, finite and infinite, follow from one God, in that sense *one* universe comprised of inexhaustibly diverse things, finite and infinite. Nevertheless, although all things follow from God, there is a fundamental difference between how infinite things follow from God—"directly, absolutely"—and how they follow under qualification *ad infinitum* by other finite things.

There is a recurrent and repetitive doubling (sometimes tripling and quadrupling) in Spinoza's view of things that repeats itself in relation to every fundamental notion. There is the infinite that pertains to God, absolutely infinite, the infinite numbers of attributes, and the infinite relative to each attribute; and there are finite modes *ad infinitum*. There is the causal relation of modes to God and the causal relation to other modes. There is the eternity that pertains to ideas in God and the duration that pertains to human ideas (although they are themselves eternal). There is the commonality that pertains to all things, whole and part, and the commonality that pertains to bodies fit for many things.

These doublings may be regarded as weaknesses in Spinoza's world view. Such a reading presupposes that there is a form of reason—philosophic or divine—that is able to think being consistently and free from aporia. In a view like Spinoza's, where inexhaustibility is fundamental, expressed in God's absolutely infinite nature, it is difficult to imagine what such freedom from aporia might be. Even the infinite intellect cannot think God as one, but only under infinitely many attributes.

How do we provide a distinction between finite and infinite being without collapsing the former into triviality? Spinoza's answer is through the aporetic doubling that intermittently betrays some of the strains in his view of things, most obviously in his efforts to conjoin the finite and infinite in human conscious experience. I am suggesting that we regard these doubling and tripling moments as expressions of Spinoza's greatest insights, only occasionally collapsing under the pressures of aporia.

Thus, it is a great insight that two modes of causation pertain to finite and infinite things, particularly because the two modes are conjoined under a geometrical paradigm. Such a view manifests the strengths of mechanistic theory turned in Spinoza into an inexhaustible cosmology. It is a profound insight that thought and things do not "correspond" but constitute identity, including the (aporetic) identity of inadequate ideas and the adequate ideas that manifest their truth. What may be added is that there is no way to show that human beings can finitely think adequate ideas, and every reason to doubt that such thought is possible for a finite being. What may be added further is that such adequate ideas are by no means incompatible with aporia, which is unmistakably present in the impossibility of thinking absolutely infinite substance in a unified way.

Finally, we may add that there is no way for a finite being to think infinite being without aporia, therefore no way to eliminate the incommensuratenesses within ideas that are thinkable by a finite thing. To say that by training the body to become fit for many things we come closer to eternity and to God is as strange as to say that by training his body, a philosopher comes closer to knowing the good. There is no connection between eternal or infinite truth and a skillful and healthy body. There is no connection between eternal and adequate ideas and a trained and healthy body. This is true even if we share Spinoza's view that finite being requires an inexhaustible foundation. And it is true even if we share the Greek view that the way to wisdom requires that we develop the powers of the body. Rather, there is a form of reason that pertains to the body as there are forms of reason that pertain to the mind.

All of these points are manifested in Spinoza's theory of emotion, still one of the most profound views of emotion, but also one that, in his theory, serves as a fundamental linking term between finite and infinite human experience. The definition Spinoza offers of emotion is that:

> By emotion I understand the modifications of the body by which the power of acting of the body itself is increased, diminished, helped, or hindered, together with the ideas of these modifications. (III, Def. III)

One part of this definition is straightforward and follows from the identity of ideas and things that defines the relationship of thought and extension. Nevertheless, the aporias of human ideas, adequate and inadequate, play a central role here. For the ideas whose order and connection are identical with the order and connection of things are the ideas that comprise the human mind but not the ideas of which human beings are aware in thinking about themselves. More important, however, is the emphasis on the "power of acting of the body." Spinoza has to this point equated all power with God and the being of finite modes with passivity. Here we find the remarkable recognition, aporetic though it may be, that finite modes possess powers if they can be said to have being (or essence) in any way at all. Finite being is, after all, a mode of being, with essence and power. (III, Prop. VII)

Emotion, then, is the manifestation of the relation between finite and infinite being. On the one hand, it is a direct consequence of the identity of the attributes of thought and extension in relation to finite human being. On the other hand, it expresses the two sides of thought in relation to the finite human body: the ideas that are conjoined with the body and the ideas that are a confused result of the finite modifications of that body. These cannot be identical except in the sense in which there is an adequate idea of any inadequate idea. In this sense, there may be adequate ideas that pertain to the human body and mind for any of its modifications, but these may not be "thought" by any human being. Moreover, the fact that human thought may not explicitly coincide, except through God, with the adequate ideas that pertain to human being is not a consequence merely of the finite nature of human being, but of the inexhaustibility of being in relation to God. It is not merely that human beings cannot think adequate ideas about finite modifications, but that they can think only under one attribute rather than another, and these are not thinkable even by the infinite intellect as all together unified. Even adequate ideas are in this sense incomplete.

Such a view is inherent in Spinoza's understanding of the relations among substance, its attributes, and finite modes. And it is inherent in many explicitly indicated ways. It is, then, a mistake to ascribe to Spinoza only a uniform sense of intelligibility and to deny that he manifests an explicit awareness of the aporetic nature of being. What must be added is that he appears to wish to overcome at least the skeptical side of aporia. As expressed in his final words in the *Ethics*:

> If the way which, as I have shown, leads hither seem very difficult, it can nevertheless be found. It must indeed be difficult since it is so seldom discovered, for if salvation lay ready to hand and could be discovered without great labor, how could it be possible that it should be neglected almost by everybody? But all noble things are as difficult as they are rare. (V, Prop. XLII: Note)

If adequate ideas pertain to every human mind, if the order of the universe, including human events, is always necessary, then wisdom should be either universal and necessary or impossible. Even if there is an order to the universe that expresses its eternal side, and even if that order lies within us as well as God, human beings may not be able to think or feel it consciously, due to their causal antecedents and conditions. Nor may they plan or seek to achieve such an understanding.[20] Spinoza's final reservations, then, do not simply acknowledge the rarity of wisdom and salvation in human life, but indicate something deeper: that there is no *way* from finite human ideas to infinite ideas, human or divine, nor can any be sought. There is no way to cross from finite experience to infinite understanding. The reason is not that finite experience is limited relative to infinite ideas but that the two are aporetically related.

Emotion is the point where this relation is manifest. On the one hand, his definition of emotion as bodily modifications conjoined with the ideas of those modifications follows directly from his view of the attributes of thought and extension. Emotion is the bodily side of every idea, and there always is a bodily side. Conversely, there is an adequate idea conjoined with every bodily state. Emotions are human experience under the identity of thought and extension. Because this identity is aporetic, emotion is aporetic as well, although Spinoza never quite says so. It is sufficient for the aporia that individual things should have both power and essence beyond the power and immanence of God. It is sufficient that there should be a power of action in human beings that is not simply the power of God. This is aporetic enough, and corresponds to the distinction between finite and infinite ideas.

Given this distinction, however aporetic it may be, the consequence is that emotions may be distinguished by the kind of idea that pertains to them: adequate or inadequate. Where the ideas are inadequate, emotions are passive, reflecting the infinite causal chain of modes that influence any human action. Where the ideas are adequate, emotions are active. (III, Prop. III) On this active side, corresponding to adequate and necessary ideas, human life is powerful and effective insofar as it produces commonality. (IV, Prop. XXXVI) Given that personal identity is individual and variable, it is related here to passivity and bondage. Freedom is associated with universality, a repetition of the same. It is not, however, personal freedom and requires abandonment of individual personality through the eternal side of God. Moreover, Spinoza notes that activity is effectively impossible. (IV, Prop. IV: Corollary)

Human reality is always inevitably partial, divided, individualized, and passive, but also common, shared, universal, and active. Human beings are both active and passive because they are finite modes, and nothing can make them more or less such finite modes. What ought to follow, on the cosmological side of Spinoza's thought, is that every human life is both finite and limited and universal and common. No consequences whatever can follow from this recognition for salvation and wisdom. Similarly, there is no way from ordinary life to fulfillment.

In relation to emotion, however, Spinoza offers us a theory of how emotions can be rational as they may be irrational, as active as they may be passive. Emotions are one of the pervasive and inescapable forms of finite human experience. Moreover, they are identical with finite bodily modifications and the ideas that pertain to them. It follows that emotion is universal in human life, not opposed to reason or thought as the tradition has frequently understood it. It follows further that desire does not war with reason but pertains to it. Plato's suggestion that there is a desire for wisdom and the good carries over in Spinoza to the pervasiveness of desire and emotion throughout human life and thought. Emotion and desire are as rational as irrational, as free as constrained. Freedom is to be defined, not as reason over and against emotion, but as emotion in its active form. The active side of human emotion is the life lived thinking of things eternally through God.

Yet thinking of things eternally is not thinking of things *as they are*, not in all ways. Their finiteness and otherness remains unthought. And there is no escape from this deficiency if we are to think of things determinately. It follows that it is not only personal identity that escapes us in salvation, but the individual identity and essence of every thing that is thought under the aspect of eternity. If Spinoza held that there were no such identities and essences, that might not involve an infinite sacrifice. He claims instead that every individual thing has a finite essence, one that therefore must escape human thought when we attain salvation. That is an incredible conclusion. It is nevertheless impossible to attain such a thought, because we as finite modes are inescapably affected by other finite things. The aporia is a famous one: wisdom is not merely difficult, but impossible on Spinoza's own view of the relationship between finite being and infinite substance.

The impossibility is obscured at times behind what appear to be direct contradictions:

> . . . a man is necessarily always subject to passions, ... (IV, Prop. IV: Corollary)

> An emotion which is a passion ceases to be a passion as soon as we form a clear and distinct idea of it. (V, Prop. III)

The first quotation takes precedence, because human beings can think ideas clearly and distinctly only in virtue of their finite relations to other finite modes. An adequate idea and an active emotion are closer to infinity than to finiteness. But God acts on human beings only through other finite modes. We can therefore think God in relation to his ideas only through other finite modes. There is no alternative for Spinoza if he is to keep the finiteness intact.

The conclusion is that there is in Spinoza, amidst a sublime understanding of inexhaustibility—the absolutely infinite nature of substance—an equally profound understanding of finiteness. In this conjunction of same and other, there is aporia and displacement, doubling and redoubling. Moreover, there is nothing in Spinoza that indicates that he, like the rationalistic reader, would decry aporia as somehow unintelligible and irrational. To the contrary, if the infinite intellect cannot think God whole, without aporia and incommensurateness, then the finite intellect cannot do so either. Yet this is not a deficiency but a greater wisdom. Finiteness and inexhaustibility are inseparable but incommensurately related.

The most forceful aporia is of the eternity that pertains to finite human being. The greater part of every human mind is eternal. Yet we cannot finitely think that eternal side, either by enhancing our bodily powers or by withdrawing from them into thought itself. In both cases, bodily and mental powers are finite modifications. To increase our bodily powers is on the one hand to share more with other things, but it is also to come more under the influence of other finite modes and to influence them more. The order of nature, the face of the universe, the modal side of Spinoza's universe, are not something a mode can hope to escape from. It would be unintelligible to do so. Every activity, every enhancement of a human power, increases the ways in which finite things are involved. This is because finite determinateness is the only determinateness there is. Even God's power requires exemplification in modes if it is to be finitely determinate. Eternity does not resolve the aporias of finiteness, but, with inexhaustibility, expresses them with exceptional poignancy.

The heresy that is Spinoza's is to have understood the aporias of finite determinate being more completely perhaps than any other philosopher before Hegel, conjoined with a profound and far-reaching account of a unified, eternal order of the universe. Spinoza maintains a powerful and moving sense of the unified order of the universe amid an equally powerful and moving sense of the inexhaustible plurality of finitely determinate things.

6 LEIBNIZ: THE HERESY OF PERFECTION

A profound relationship between being and intelligibility lies at the heart of metaphysical thinking: between what a being is and how it may be thought, between metaphysical truth and metaphysical representation. The heresy in all important metaphysical thinking consists in how this relation itself is represented. What we take to be important in a metaphysical theory is what calls into question both what we take to be intelligible and what we take intelligibility to be. Intelligibility is always fundamentally in question along with and inseparable from the question of being. The latter question defines the course of metaphysical history. The former question defines the recurrence of heresy throughout that history.

These preliminaries lead to Leibniz, who at once expresses the most extreme rational possibilities of a metaphysics of the same, grounded in the strongest possible principles of reason, and the most heretical possibilities inherent within intelligible being. Part of the heresy consists in how far familiar principles can take us from ordinary experience and common sense. But the greatest heresy by far lies within Leibniz's view of intelligibility and reason. Crudely put, there is a form of heresy that consists in departure from traditional norms. In Leibniz, we find a form of heresy that consists in unblinking adherence to established principles. Taken to an extreme, what is familiar becomes strange: the alienness of perfection.

Manifold heresies can be found in Leibniz's cosmology, some of which have passed into other heretical cosmologies.[1] The most important by far, however, lies at the center of his theory, the combination of the principles of sufficient reason and perfection.[2] It is the point where, in comparison even with Spinoza, Leibniz closes off the last vestige of indeterminateness, eliminates what appears to be the last remnant of aporia (although aporia is retained at every level of his system, and he claims explicitly that contingency remains).[3] There is, in Leibniz's monadology, relative to God, no latitude whatever (although there is free will). Everything in the universe proceeds by necessity, and the universe is the only universe among infinitely many possible universes. This conclusion is the most famous consequence of the principle of perfection: ours is the best of all possible worlds, therefore the one and only actual world: the supreme embodiment of the same. What must be noted is the aporetic form in which this claim must be expressed, even in Leibniz, and even in contemporary interpretations of "possible worlds." There is no avoiding contingency and possibility in a system in which both are completely repudiated.

Leibniz's entire theory may be read as a formal consequence of but a few central principles:

a. the independence of (created) substances.
b. the principle of sufficient reason.
c. the principle of perfection.[4]

Like Descartes and Spinoza, Leibniz inherits Aristotle's view of substance and modifies it significantly. The definition of primary substance, in Aristotle, follows from the principle that the individual being and its essence are logically independent of its properties, qualifications, and states. Substances are in this sense independent, although not of each other, for individuals can be efficient causes of other substances. For Descartes, however, mind and body are independent of each other. Spinoza's and Leibniz's interpretations are natural extensions of such a redefinition of the independence of substance, the first that substance is *absolutely* independent, of anything else, the second that substances are independent of each other, and consequently, "windowless." Leibniz's view begins, by definition, with a plurality of individual things, each of which is independent of the others, although all are dependent on God. This latter dependence, of created substance on uncreated substance, is a fundamental aporia at the heart of all later substance theories, and leads to Hegel's and Whitehead's criticisms of the arbitrariness of God in most cosmologies. It is what Heidegger characterizes as "ontotheology." Being requires ultimacy for its intelligibility.

There are several other, less explicit principles that define Leibniz's understanding of monads, some of which have passed into philosophic orthodoxy. We may consider some of these briefly:

1. The *monad* of which we shall have to speak is merely a simple substance, which enters into composites; *simple*, that is to say, without parts.

2. And there must be simple substances, since there are composites; for the composite is only a collection or *aggregatum* of simple substances.

3. Now where there are no parts, neither extension, nor figure, nor divisibility is possible. And these monads are the true atoms of nature, and, in a word, the elements of all things. (*Monadology*)[5]

Monads—individual substances—are independent of each other, simple, and indivisible. Leibniz argues from indivisibility to independence, not conversely. Yet the "simplicity" that pertains to monads is not an absolute indivisibility, but deeply qualified. For pertaining to the individuality and singularity of a monad is an inexhaustible plurality.

13. This detail must involve a multitude in the unity or in that which is simple. . . . consequently, there must be in the simple substance a plurality of affections and of relations, although it has no parts. (*Monadology*)

Every monad is simple and indivisible but with a multiplicity of affections and relations.

The aporias of unity and multiplicity, sameness and difference, are prominent in Leibniz. His entire system may be read as an attempt to establish the sameness and identity of a substance in the strongest possible terms along with a multiplicity of different substances.[6] The aporias are inescapable. One and many, we may say, have no altogether satisfactory resolution, where what we mean is that we cannot dissipate their difference. To dissipate that difference, of course, would be to transform multiplicity into unity, otherness into sameness, or the reverse, precisely what can (and should) not be done. Therefore, the aporia exists at two different levels: that in which the ways in which a being is multiple it is not one and conversely; and that in which multiplicity and unity are not the same.

Monads are simple and indivisible, but they are also many. How are they not divided by their states, conditions, and relations? How are they not divided by each other to the extent that each mirrors the universe? How are they not divided through time and by extension? Like most of his major predecessors, Leibniz considers only the latter form of division pertinent. Or rather, he understands by indivisibility that substances cannot be divided into other substances, ignoring the ways in which substances are divided by their determinations and through time. His view of how predicates are included within each substance makes time unintelligible.[7] A monad has no monadic, substantial parts. Because substance here is individual, neither temporal nor spatial extension can pertain intrinsically to substances, for they would then be divisible. The assumption is that divisibility pertains to the essence of extension, that every extended thing can be divided into other extended things, *ad infinitum*.

A monad is an individual. Everything else is either predicable of an individual or composite. And where there are composites, Leibniz argues, there must be individuals. Yet why should we accept such a principle? As far as we know, as far as contemporary physics tells us, every particle is composite in certain respects. What reason is there for rejecting the view that everything is complex, composite, divisible? That is, simplicity and complexity are not absolute conditions, but relational and complementary. Every being is divisible in certain respects if not in others—into properties, attributes, states, and conditions, if not into other beings. But conversely, every being is unitary in certain respects—in location, in the conjunction of its properties or its singularity of reference—if not all respects. Indeed, recognition of such singularity is the basis of Leibniz's principle of the identity of indiscernibles, for there can be no two substances of exactly the same properties. This can be read as asserting that two different substances must differ in some of their properties or states. It can also be read as asserting that the many states and conditions of a substance, over which it is "divided," are present in it but not essential to its singularity.

A recurrent if aporetic theme in the metaphysical tradition is reference to an ontological priority defined in terms of independence, self-sufficiency, and indivisibility. In *Parmenides*, young Socrates claims that he finds nothing self-contradictory in ordinary things sharing in opposing qualities—changing in place and form, possessing different forms at different times, different measures and conditions—but denies that it would be intelligible for a single form to be itself contradictory.[8] Yet it is precisely the combinations and oppositions among forms that are shown to be necessary in the second half of *Parmenides* and in *Sophist*. We find in Plato specific reference to principles of metaphysical intelligibility requiring freedom from aporia and self-sufficiency conjoined with devastating arguments against such a view of intelligibility. The result is a deeper sense of aporia.

In this respect, Leibniz's view of metaphysical intelligibility, taken without qualification, is a major regression (but also heresy) when compared with Plato. Leibniz has no argument whatever to give as to why, if there are composites, there must be simples. A composite is an *aggregatum* indeed, but not necessarily of indivisible things. What is involved is the implicit principle of the same that a substance is intelligible only if it is not divisible into other substances, effectively that divisibility is dependence of a whole upon its parts, and that such dependence would undermine the intelligibility of a being. Thus, a corollary of (a) above is that:

> a[1]. Substances are simple and indivisible, for divisibility into other substances is dependence upon them.

In both Spinoza and Leibniz, independence is given an absolute interpretation. The difference between their understanding is particularly acute here, however, because the multiplicity in being is in Spinoza relegated to the infinite attributes and infinite modes that follow absolutely and directly from God on the one hand and to the infinite numbers of finite modes on the other. In Leibniz, however, there is an infinite number of independent and indivisible monads, each of which is absolutely singular.

I speak of "absolute" independence in relation to Spinoza and Leibniz: absolute and unqualified. Yet unqualified absoluteness can pertain to neither of them, because substance would then be powerless, while for both, the essence of substance is power and activity. Thus, modes must either be understood to qualify substance essentially, if not absolutely, or they could not together with substance comprise nature. Similarly, monads must either be in some sense extended and related or they could not possess powers and activities. The "absoluteness" is aporetic.

Analogously, the sense in which monads are "simple" must be qualified because they are multiple and divisible in many ways, if not into other substances. The rejection of extension as pertaining intrinsically to substances is based on the view that any extended thing can be divided into other extended things indefinitely, in that sense divisible into other beings of the same kind. But monads are not divisible into monads. What is suggested is the corollary that monads are not aggregatable into other monads either, a conclusion clearly present in Whitehead although by no means entirely clear in Leibniz.[9]

Simplicity and complexity, divisibility and indivisibility, independence and dependence, are among the great pairs of opposing notions of same and other around which a major part of the Western philosophic tradition has revolved. In every case, I am suggesting, we find in the great philosophers—as well as in many of their followers—a deep sensitivity to the aporias within these notions even while they magnify their applicability. Monads are simple, but also multiple. They are indivisible into other substances (in certain ways), but divisible indefinitely into their affections, conditions, and stages. They are independent of each other, but adjusted to each other; moreover, they are dependent on God.

We have returned to ontological priority. The notion that a particular form of being is ontologically prior is plausible only where accompanied by a claim as strong as Aristotle's, that individual substance is
primary *in all ways*. For if prior only in certain ways, a particular form of
being can be regarded as *ontologically* prior only arbitrarily.

This drama is played out in force in Leibniz's universe. Monads are
not prior in all respects, either to God or to their properties and conditions. They are said to be independent of other monads, in that sense
prior to the adjustments within them that correspond to preestablished
harmony. But that is absurd because their harmony is established prior
to their being, part of their essence. They are simple and indivisible, but
would not be at all without properties and conditions.[10]

These notions of simplicity, independence, and indivisibility are
the aporetic axes around which a major part of the metaphysical tradition revolves. The aporias show themselves in the restrictions that must
be imposed on any plausible interpretation of simples and units. Monads
are simple only in a particular respect, that they are not divisible into
other monads. They are indefinitely divisible in other respects. There is
no obvious escape from the regress argument that appears, following
Aristotle, to be implicit in Leibniz's position: a being that is indefinitely
divisible into other beings has no substantial independence. An extended
being is divisible, therefore, extension is not essential to substances. The
point is that substances are not absolutely indivisible and are not simple,
absolutely. There can be no absolute and unqualified rule of the same.

The claim that wherever there are composites there must be simples is plausible only in terms of a regress argument. Leibniz does not
even argue for the claim. Is it an indubitable a priori truth? A similar
assumption can be found in empiricism, that where there are complex
ideas there must be simple ideas. Leaving aside what simplicity means
in relation to ideas, the point is that the tradition assumes that certain
fundamental principles define intelligibility—in this case, the intelligibility of simples over composites; other examples are the intelligibility
of changelessness over becoming and of determinateness over indeterminateness. Yet subsequent works of both philosophy and science
bring every such principle of intelligibility into question, heretically
and aporetically.

A fundamental aporia in Leibniz lies in the two extremes of his
theory. On the one hand, it rests on the strongest formulations of a priori
intelligibility to be found in the tradition, based on sufficient reason,
perfection, and simplicity. On the other hand, these principles can be
plausible only under explicit qualification. The aporia of one and many,
for example, lies at the heart of the simplicity of monads. The consequence is that a monad is not absolutely simple or independent, but

under qualification: independent of other created substances, other monads; not divisible into other substances or monads.

What does divisibility mean here, given its recurrence throughout the tradition? In particular, given complexity, how do we distinguish composition from division? In relation to space and time, division pertains intrinsically and metrically. Every temporal interval is indefinitely divisible *numerically* into other intervals. Every spatial region is indefinitely divisible into *numerically* smaller regions. A metric is assigned to the divisibility of space and time. In relation to monads, there is no intrinsic metric, neither of the size of a monad nor of the components of division. To say that a monad is not divisible into other monads leaves open whether there can be a clear distinction between division and aggregation in the absence of an intrinsic metric.

Consider, for example, the assumption of mutual influence between social collectives and their members. The society is divisible into its members; may we not say that a member is divisible into the other members that together with it constitute the society, or is divisible into that member's different social roles? How can aggregation be different from division without a metric? Membership and influence are not intrinsically metrical notions, and do not distinguish division and aggregation. Only where we may say unequivocally that the group is *larger* than the individual, metrically, can we distinguish divisibility from composition. Space and time are the fundamental forms of measure that define division and aggregation. Where the metrical forms of extension are rejected, as in Leibniz and Whitehead, division and composition cease to be well-defined.

In Leibniz, monads are indivisible because they are independent of each other. Independence is the notion that separates divisibility from aggregation. But if there is independence, then there is no way in which a collective can "divide" a monad into the other members of that collective. Aggregation becomes unintelligible. This is the unintelligibility that Whitehead seeks to resolve by making actual entities essential to the constitutions of other actual entities.

Leibniz's view of divisibility and independence is aporetic in part because divisibility cannot be distinguished from composition and aggregation without a metric and he has rejected every such metric along with extension. Division and aggregation are inverse functions, like left and right, that have no intelligibility except together; moreover, they are identical except within this contrast, each inverted relative to the other. Thus, either a metric pertains to being intrinsically, traditionally through space and time, qualifying independence and rendering it aporetic, or simplicity is not an ontological notion.

How are we to interpret these aporias? As "problems" that Leibniz fails to resolve, presupposing that there are ways of resolving them; or as moments reflecting the aporetic nature of things? Either way, there are two heretical movements in Leibniz's thought: the heresy of a perfection that cannot be thought except aporetically; and the heresy of the aporias of same and other that pertain to metaphysical intelligibility. The only way to avoid such heresies is to presuppose a form of metaphysical thinking entirely free from aporia. Leibniz does not offer such a presupposition despite his emphasis on absolutes and perfection. It is to be found only in an orthodox reading of his theory.

Because monads are simple, they can neither begin nor end. Beginning and ending are regarded here as forms of composition. (*Monadology*, 4, 5) Such a view is plausible only to the extent that beginning and ending are interpreted in relation to other substances, divisibly by parts. Leibniz, however, treats monads as units that begin and end "all at once" and that cannot be changed by anything outside them. (*Monadology*, 6, 7) Moreover, although monads cannot begin or end gradually, and cannot be altered by any other substance, they undergo changes due to their own inner nature. (*Monadology*, 11, 13)

Every monad proceeds from an internal principle of the same that is intelligible only in relation to God. In this sense, Leibniz's theory is thoroughly ontotheological, even the supreme paradigm of ontotheology. What must be added is that the way in which God provides "sufficient reason" for the being of any monad is both arbitrary and aporetic despite Leibniz's explicit denial of arbitrariness.[11] There is a profound aporia at the heart of rationalistic thought: the unintelligibility of intelligibility itself. No rationalism has overcome this fundamental aporia or even sought to do so. It is evident in the contingency of Spinoza's finite modes, which all together cannot follow absolutely from God. It is evident in Leibniz's view of the independence and indivisibility of monads, because, to comprise aggregates, they must be dependent either on other monads or on God and must be divisible by their compositions. There is no way a monad can be composable into aggregates involving other monads without being divisible by this composition. There is no way every state of a monad can be included in it, preserving its independence, in a universe in which there are aggregates.

A fundamental aporia exists in Leibniz's view of substance, yet one unsatisfactory only relative to a view of natural order that would have no aporias within it. Why should we assume that being lends itself to such a possibility of order? And who, if not Leibniz, has ever maintained such a view of intelligibility? We are led to his view of sufficient reason, for it is within some form of this principle that we find manifested our deepest understanding of intelligibility. Nevertheless, metaphysically speaking, Leibniz's principle of sufficient reason comes *after* monads and substances have been conceived. They do not follow from that principle alone. No sense of intelligibility can be provided in a single principle, and for two reasons. One is that every principle must be interpreted, and what it entails pertains to how it is understood as well as how it is written. This is a condition of thought itself, essential to its heresy. The other is that every ontology must contain more than one kind of being, posing the question of how these are related. This is the inescapable question of same and other.

Among the deceptive features of the philosophic tradition, recurrently manifesting its aporetic side, is an excess in the rational principles that have been taken to comprise it. The deceptiveness lies in the fact that the principles explicitly espoused cannot be transparent to thought, but always if covertly impose more stringent conditions than they appear to require. It would be absurd to suppose that the greatest philosophers have been engaged in a conspiracy to fool their readers into accepting untenable first principles. We must posit instead that every principle transcends by far any reading that may be given of it. Every judgment transcends any of its interpretations (and conversely), a surplus in reason, as every being transcends any of its relationships, a surplus in being.

An example is Bradley's apparently innocuous criterion of reality:

> Ultimate reality is such that it does not contradict itself; here is an absolute criterion.[12]

Bradley's language betrays itself—and we are not here misled by any translated intermediary: to be plausible, the principle should be innocuous, a version of the law of noncontradiction.[13] How such a principle could define "ultimate" reality and become "absolute" is extraordinary. The transition to such extremes is expressed by Bradley later:

> Things are self-contrary when, and just so far as, they appear as bare conjunctions, when in order to think them you would have to predicate differences without an internal ground of connexion and distinction, when, in other words, you would have to unite diversities simply, and that means in the same point.[14]

He says outright that the absolute criterion is that ultimate reality cannot be aporetic in any respect whatever. In ultimate reality, all internal differences vanish. Into what, we must ask? A reality—Experience—beyond any knowing, Bradley answers. Does not God know himself, we might ask? And does God know himself aporetically or nonaporetically? But Bradley does not follow Hegel quite that far.

In Leibniz, we find a similar principle defining the nature of intelligible reality: *Nothing happens without a reason.* This principle of sufficient reason also appears innocuous as it stands. It becomes momentous depending on what kinds of reasons we are prepared to accept and how far we demand that they be taken. The very name of the principle, as expressed in English, betrays its arbitrariness: "sufficient" reason. Sufficient, we ask, for what? Sufficient to make being intelligible. But what, internal to this principle, rather than to being itself, would be sufficient other than whatever, of any kind, constituted intelligibility, including aporia and heresy? No principle that defines intelligibility can do so without aporias and heresies.

The consequences Leibniz claims for the principle of sufficient reason are anything but trivial.

> The consequences of this principle are that we must avoid unstable changes as much as possible, that between contraries the middle term should be selected, that we may add what we please to a term provided no other term is harmed by doing so; and there are still many other consequences which are important in political science. (*The Principle of Sufficient Reason*, p. 93)

It is by no means obvious why a principle of sufficient reason should entail gradualism and stability. Leibniz reformulates the principle in terms reminiscent of LaPlace:

> . . . nothing ever happens without the possibility that an omniscient mind could give some reason why it should have happened rather than not. (*The Principle of Sufficient Reason*, p. 95)

Such an interpretation presupposes that an undivided, perfect knowledge is in principle possible of all things. This notion is akin to Spinoza's "infinite intellect" but lacks his insight that even the infinite intellect cannot think absolutely infinite being except divided. Leibniz's principle presupposes that being is not ultimately in conflict. Only reasons of a certain kind, presupposing a certain undivided order of the universe, are acceptable.

The surplus inherent in such a principle is evident when we compare the formulations of the principle with the consequences that Leibniz claims to follow from it, involving mediation and graduation. A view is presupposed of the continuity of the universe as part of its intelligibility. Leibniz himself rejects a universal metric in repudiating extension as pertaining intrinsically to substance. Yet if there is no common measure, how do we avoid incommensurateness? Does not preestablished harmony entail a metrical equivalent of space and time? We find aporia even within Leibniz's strong view of sufficient reason.

The principle of sufficient reason is not, after all, without qualification absolute in Leibniz's system. It serves rather to define how monads are adjusted to each other so that they may comprise a single universe when they are not and cannot be related. The principle of sufficient reason is the basis of both the principle of preestablished harmony and the ultimate origin of the universe. Nevertheless, it far transcends any of these functions, and defines a canon of intelligibility that leads finally to the principle of perfection. The intelligibility required is that knowledge is perfectible and that the universe along with everything in it is perfectly knowable. Sufficiency of reason here is effectively absolute. Even so, Leibniz's principle of sufficient reason falls far short of Bradley's criterion of ultimate reality.

In his *Monadology*, as in his other works, Leibniz juxtaposes the principles of noncontradiction and sufficient reason. (*Monadology*, 31, 32) That reasoning must seek to avoid contradiction is plausible. That any formulated version of the principle of noncontradiction can be taken as both necessary and sufficient is less so. Every version of such a principle, insofar as it defines intelligibility substantively and usefully, goes beyond what is trivially acceptable to its own aporias. Contradiction and aporia can be related and distinguished only aporetically.

Our traversal of the heretical side of the tradition suggests that we may regard the development of that tradition, not as overcoming aporia and contradiction, as if they then might altogether vanish, but as incessantly pursuing alternatives for thinking aporias heretically in the name of intelligibility. Although the distinction between aporia and contradiction can never be made entirely explicit—among the major sources of heresy—the attempt to do so is inescapable, producing the dynamic nature of philosophic thought. No major philosopher we have considered, whatever he may say about intelligibility, avoids aporias, but institutes them, in varying guises, at the center of his views of the intelligibility of things. Not only is what is regarded as contradictory by one philosopher—Parmenides, for example, or the young Socrates—not regarded as contradictory by another: reason requires that contradictoriness be transformed into aporia.

Another way of putting this is that in metaphysics aporia is sometimes to be regarded as contradictory, sometimes not, but is unavoidable. A more precise formulation is that being and knowing are inexhaustible and that inexhaustibility is the aporia of same and other. The metaphysical tradition has been marked by its attempts to resolve indeterminateness into determinateness without acknowledging their reciprocity. It is for this reason that perfection, in both Spinoza and Leibniz, does not provide an adequate representation of inexhaustibility.

That contradiction is a mark of falsity and that noncontradiction is a mark of truth applies only to established forms of reasoning, and is irrelevant to any deeper understanding. Every important philosophic insight confronts multiple far-reaching aporias, and must effectively determine, based on its own principles of intelligibility, whether such aporias are contradictions or whether they belong to aporetic thought and being. That being must not be contradictory cannot entail that it is free from aporia: that is the point at issue. That being is rational cannot entail that it is not aporetic unless rationality is defined as freedom from aporia. Every defense of such a definition must beg the question because it must presuppose some (aporetic or nonaporetic) principles of intelligibility.

In Leibniz's case, the principle of noncontradiction is largely trivial: all its significance is carried by the principle of sufficient reason. The question is what sufficiency requires. One formulation of the principle is that every event requires a cause. As we have seen, that principle is at the heart of Spinoza's system in two respects: every finite mode is caused by other finite modes *ad infinitum*; every mode follows from God (qualified by other finite modes). Even so, there is an aporetic "contingency" that pertains to all finite modes taken together (if that is possible), because they cannot follow directly and absolutely from God, and cannot all together follow from each other. Shall we conclude that in Spinoza's world view, there is *something* that does not conform to sufficient reason, that does not have a cause? Every mode has a cause—a double causation. On the one hand, all modes taken together may not comprise a *something* to have a cause. On the other hand, this double causation is aporetic. The question is whether the principle of sufficient reason must be interpreted to entail that causation cannot be aporetic. For if so, then the double causation, of modes in relation to each other as well as in relation to God, would be aporetic, therefore irrational, even if we were able to eliminate the final contingency of the universe. Double causation— one of Spinoza's greatest insights—is aporetic because its two moments cannot be mediated: they *are* the relevant forms of mediation. There can be no *reason* why every finite reason must be double. There is no way to eliminate every form of indeterminateness.

Reason is *sufficient*, ontologically, in Leibniz only where there is no arbitrariness whatever, where there is *nothing* that has not been given its reason or cause. What we have not done, however, and cannot do, is to give the reason or cause of this *nothing*.[15] Everything has a reason, but nothing has no reason. We know, of course, that nothing is not something. The point is that unreason cannot be eliminated *altogether*: following Heidegger, because nothing has no reason; in *Parmenides*, because in addition to what is true there are endless alternatives that *are not*. Otherness is present in sufficient reason in a variety of forms, one of which is that no reason can be sufficient for more than what it explains while no reason can explain everything because it cannot explain itself.

This is clear in Spinoza, where in order that causation be intelligible among finite modes and in relation to God, finite modality itself, concretely, must be aporetically unexplainable.

Leibniz is the only major philosopher in the Western tradition to seek to close off this last vestige of contingency, transforming it into necessity, as if there could be a reason for everything and anything, including the dismissal of every alternative. In the final analysis, this closure requires the principle of perfection and the world of all possible worlds, among which only one is actual. Leibniz's argument is in effect that of all possible worlds, only one is possible, betraying the aporia of his entire project. Yet long before we reach the principle of perfection, the drama of cosmic reason is played out at another level, that of the universe itself.

For sufficient reason demands a reason for the universe, precisely what is lacking in Spinoza. Leibniz's most dramatic argument is as follows:

> Suppose a book on the elements of geometry to have been eternal and that others had been successively copied from it, it is evident that, although we might account for the present book by the book which was its model, we could nevertheless never, by assuming any number of books whatever, reach a perfect reason for them; for we may always wonder why such books have existed from all time; that is, why books exist at all and why they are thus written. What is true of books is also true of the different states of the world, for in spite of certain laws of change a succeeding state is in a certain way only a copy of the preceding, and to whatever anterior state you may go back you will never find there a complete reason why there is any world at all, and why this world rather than some other. . . . From which it follows that even by supposing the eternity of the world, an ultimate extramundane reason of things, or God, cannot be escaped. (*On the Ultimate Origin of Things*, pp. 345-46)[16]

What we feared in relation to the principle of sufficient reason is here true: no reason other than a final, eternal, and supreme reason can be sufficient. No reason can be sufficient other than a "perfect" one. This theme runs throughout Leibniz's discussions, presenting us with the following theses:

a. The sufficient reason for contingent beings must be necessary, making every being necessary (by the principle of perfection) if not logically necessary.
b. We may think the entire series of finite events together, and seek their sufficient reason, which must then lie outside all

of them. The universe here is both an object of thought and subject to the principle of sufficient reason, rather than the sphere of beings and conditions that conform to that principle.

c. The sufficient reason for all things is also the "final" reason for all things, as if finality were not incompatible with intelligibility and explanation.

a. We have noted the striking analogy between Leibniz's argument in relation to the principle of perfection that of all possible worlds, only one is possible, and his claim that contingent beings and truths require necessary reasons, making them also necessary (although not in the sense that every alternative is self-contradictory). There is no latitude; there are no degrees of freedom in Leibniz's universe, for they are incompatible with sufficient reason. There are no alternatives possible under the principle of sufficient reason. There is only one world compatible with the principles of sufficient reason and perfection; every event is equally necessary.

b. Leibniz's argument that being altogether requires a reason presupposes that being can be taken altogether. This is not an obvious consequence of the principle of sufficient reason, although it may be implicit there. It is another example of the surplus inherent in all representations of intelligibility. The universe requires a reason because it can be taken whole, and everything requires a reason. Yet an aporetic view of the universe entails that it cannot be taken as a whole, altogether, because of the aporias that constitute plural beings. Reason, to be sufficient, presupposes cosmology, presupposes a necessary cosmos in which every element is also necessary.

c. Similarly, there are not actually many alternative worlds, only the one world in which we are situated. Yet if there is only one possible world, it must be necessary. To say that by the principle of perfection, of the many possible worlds, only one is actual, is aporetic. The others were never possible.[17] One does not argue from contingency to necessity through sufficient reason nor from possibility to actuality through perfection. Ours is the only possible, necessary, and perfect world. Voltaire satirizes this "best of all possible worlds." The satire misses the aporias within Leibniz's sense of perfection. Nevertheless, Leibniz virtually claims to seek to overcome the aporias in any world, possible or actual, through what he calls "absolute or metaphysical necessity":

We must therefore pass from physical or hypothetical necessity, which determines the later states of the world by the prior, to something which is of absolute or metaphysical necessity, the reason for which cannot be given. For the present world is necessary, physically or hypothetically, but not absolutely or meta-physically. (*On the Ultimate Origin of Things*, p. 346)

The principle of sufficient reason, like all representations of intelligibility, cannot be both plausible and sufficient. Its sufficiency wars with its acceptability. This is another way of saying that intelligibility cannot be defined without violating its own canons, for it is always in question. Thus, that every event has a cause appears to be a modest principle asking us to seek explanations for everything that occurs. That every *thing* has a sufficient reason makes two far stronger claims: the aggregate of all events is a thing that also requires a reason, and a reason, to be sufficient, must be perfect—and, as perfect, does not itself require a reason. This demand for perfection is neither modest nor plausible, especially to the extent that it both derives from mundane experience and violates the principle of sufficient reason. What is finally at issue is whether finite, mundane being requires infinite, perfect being for its intelligibility, and whether such an unintelligible, infinite and perfect being can be the basis for any intelligibility whatever.

Similarly, the principle of perfection far exceeds either its plausibility or its effectiveness in transforming possible being into necessary being. Possible being is, at least in part, conceivable being. We can imagine alternatives to any actual reality. By the principle of perfection, no such alternative is possible, imaginable or not.[18] What follows is that what we imagine to be possible is impossible. It is therefore a limitation inherent in finite reason that we should imagine what is impossible to be possible. The role of imagination in presenting us with the alternatives that define the epistemological and ontological possibilities that knowledge requires is repudiated. Such a position is inapplicable to any thinking being. To be able to think otherwise is essential to thinking truly. The aporias here pertain to the notion of possibility itself. Without possibilities, knowledge is unintelligible. Leibniz explicitly rejects the principle, ascribed to Spinoza, that only actuality is possible, even while arguing that actuality is altogether necessary.

The idea that the universe is necessary and that an adequate thought of it would be necessary, if not "absolutely or metaphysically" necessary, is aporetic. It denies what is essential to its own intelligibility: the otherness within the perfection of the same. The principles of sufficient reason and perfection, which function intelligibly only in the context of differential alternatives, effectively repudiate the possibility of such alternatives. If there were a perfect, sufficient, and absolute reason for the world, it would transform that world into complete necessity, so that there would be no room for thought and reason to function differentially. We may say, colloquially, that there is no room for error in Leibniz's system. What we must mean to say is that there is no room for any but perfect ideas because this is a perfect universe. There is an intimate relation among error, possibility, and aporia. Similarly, that by the principle of perfection this universe might be perfect, in all its disconnections and confusions, is equally aporetic. That we should be able to imagine each part improved without improving the whole is aporetic and implausible.

What follows is among the greatest heresies claimed in the history of thought: what is is perfect, physically, metaphysically, and morally.

> ... although the world be not metaphysically necessary, in the sense that its contrary implies a contradiction or a logical absurdity, it is nevertheless physically necessary, or determined in such a way that its contrary implies imperfection or moral absurdity. (*On the Ultimate Origin of Things*, p. 349)

> And in order that no one should think that we confound here moral perfection or goodness with metaphysical perfection or greatness, and that the former is denied while the latter is granted, it must be known that it follows from what has been said that the world is most perfect, not only physically, or, if you prefer, metaphysically, because that series of things is produced in which there is actually the most of reality, but also that it is most perfect morally, because real moral perfection is physical perfection for souls themselves. (*On the Ultimate Origin of Things*, p. 351)

This is the best, morally and physically, of all possible worlds. And its perfection is necessary and absolute—a perfection compatible with conflict and tension, a consequence of the balancing of simplicity and variety.[19]

Voltaire satirizes this "best of all possible worlds" by showing that it is actually quite terrible. This confronts the perfection of all being with the problem of evil. Leibniz's reply is the same as Bradley's: only in the small is there the appearance of evil: perfection lies in the overall composition and balance. The foundation of order is neither logical nor moral, but aesthetic.[20]

> Let us look at a very beautiful picture, and let us cover it in such a way as to see only a very small part of it, what else will appear in it, however closely we may examine it and however near we may approach to it, except a certain confused mass of colors without choice and without art? And yet when we remove the

covering and regard it from the proper point of view we will see that what appeared thrown on the canvas haphazardly has been executed with the greatest art by the author of the work. (*On the Ultimate Origin of Things*, p. 352)

Morally speaking, as Ivan Karamazov argues, we cannot justify the suffering of the innocent few for the happiness of the many. Even in relation to a work of art, we may imagine that some part might be improved without interfering with the beauty of the whole. More important, there is no perfection comparable to sufficient reason in a work of art. Whatever perfection there may be is not sufficient to explain each part, however minor; the beauty of the whole does not "explain" the incoherence of the parts, but dismisses it as irrelevant. Perfection in art is the sense that the work *could not be improved*,[21] not that the work as a whole justifies inadequacy in the parts.

Morally speaking, every individual has absolute worth. In such a perspective, there can be no perfection of the whole to which the parts are subordinate. It follows that there is no such thing as moral perfection. This "best of all possible worlds" is not absurd because it includes suffering and evil, because it is filled with imperfections, but because even if it were the *only* possible world, it could not be morally perfect because morality is not perfectible. Like all intrinsically finite conditions, morality is imperfectible and aporetic. It exists amidst the conflicts that constitute it. Its sense of the ideal is not a sense of perfectibility, but of compromise and reconciliation. Similarly, knowledge and understanding are both imperfectible and aporetic. The fundamental aporia in sufficient reason is that no reason is entirely, perfectly sufficient because no knowledge is perfect, omniscient. Behind Leibniz's theory of knowledge and being lies the aporetic idea of a perfect being who knows all perfectly and who has established a morally perfect universe. What is neglected are the aporias inherent in the imperfection of both goodness and truth. Leibniz's is the heresy of perfection.

In the only perfect, necessary universe, there would be no alternatives, and this would not be the *best* of all possible worlds, but the *only one* possible. This best of universes is the only universe, and to deny its existence or its perfection is to deny its necessity. The principle of sufficient reason makes it absolutely necessary. Yet neither necessity nor morality nor perfection nor understanding is intelligible without alternatives, without actualizable possibilities. These are the others excluded from perfection. Necessity is unintelligible without contingency and possibility. Morality is imperfect because it involves difficult choices among alternatives that do not cease to be possible even when wrong. Perfection is aporetic if it does not involve actual imperfection. Omniscience is unintelligible where error is impossible, not because we know of no forms of understanding that are free from error, but because there are inexhaustibly manifold and diverse ways of being wrong while being right inescapably coexists among them, inseparable from them.

All these aporias can be found in Leibniz's own writings. He cannot avoid speaking of "possible worlds" although there is, on his argument, only one such world. He cannot avoid speaking of suffering and unhappiness in the small although, on his argument, there is the greatest happiness and fulfillment in this best of worlds. What must be entailed, however we may wish to deny it, is that error is not error, possibility is not possibility, alternatives are not alternatives, and unhappiness and evil are really happiness and goodness. These are the aporias at the center of his theory. They express the inescapable aporias that lie within the perfection of the same.

There remains the famous heresy of extension. Leibniz denies that extension pertains intrinsically to monads on the grounds that they would then be divisible, but also on the grounds that substances are active and exercise powers, while extended material beings are devoid of activity.

> For continuity in itself—extension is, namely, nothing but a continuum with the character of simultaneity—is not more capable of constituting a complete substance than plurality or number requires the presence necessarily of things counted, repeated and continued. Hence I believe that our thought of substance is perfectly satisfied in the conception of force and not in that of extension. (*On Substance as Active Force rather than Mere Extension*, p. 158)

Monads are *entelechies*: "sources of their internal activities." (*Monadology*, 18) Yet, like Spinoza, Leibniz cannot hold such a position free from aporia. For God is the only power.

> 43. It is also true that in God is the source not only of existence but also of essences, so far as they are real, . . .

> 48. In God is *Power*, which is the source of all; . . . .
> (*Monadology*)

There are, then, two difficulties with regarding extension as intrinsic to monads. One is its infinite divisibility, the other its passivity. Substance is not infinitely divisible into other substances, into beings of the same kind, because that would violate the independence of substances, which would then be dependent *ad infinitum* upon their parts. Substance is also active while extension is "mere location," a passive principle, "mere continuity." One of the inescapable aporias here, a consequence of the extremity with which sufficient reason is conceived, is that monads have power only through God, derivatively.

Similarly, and aporetically, while extension does not pertain intrinsically to monads, it pertains to them in some form. Leibniz by no means denies that the material universe is an extended universe:

> 61. ... For since the world is a *plenum*, rendering all matter connected, and since in a plenum every motion has some effect on distant bodies in proportion to their distance, so that each body is affected not only by those in contact with it, and feels in some way all that happens to them, but also by their means is affected by those which are in contact with the former, with which it itself is in immediate contact, it follows that this intercommunication extends to any distance whatever. (*Monadology*)

These notions of "distance" and "contact" are both extensive and metrical. There may be no nonaporetic description of a universe of nonextensive creatures that are somehow together in that universe. This can be seen in Leibniz's remarkable definition of matter in terms of memory—or the absence thereof: a momentary mind without history.[22] For such a mind, the only form of connection is extension. Matter and extension pertain not to (immaterial and nonextended) monads, but to their defective, material forms.[23]

What extension provides, and what the notion of a "plenum" repeats, is a strong principle of the same: the generic condition of togetherness of all material beings in one universe. If we reject the intrinsic reality and relevance of extension to every being, substantial or derivative, then we lack a principle determining the aggregation of all such beings in one universe. This incompleteness of the material universe is compounded by but not a consequence of the windowlessness of monads. For external causation cannot of itself provide a single system of order to the material universe. We find here the generic question of cosmology: what constitutes the cosmos to be a single cosmos. On one level, we repeat the question of the ultimate origin of things, leading to God. On another level, such an ultimate is unintelligible without a proximate principle of togetherness. Leibniz denies the intrinsic relevance of extension to the being of monads but asserts the togetherness of all monads in one universe. Some generic condition other than extension is required.

It might appear that Leibniz rejects extension as the condition of togetherness because it is aporetic: that is, a passive condition where an active principle is required; a condition extrinsic to the activities of monads although an intrinsic condition is required. Yet the result of his analysis suggests that no condition of the togetherness of all beings in the universe can be intelligible and free from aporia.

The result is Leibniz's denial that monads are intrinsically extensive although they are connected, comprise a plenum, and interact at a distance. The notion of a plenum, in which the universe is effectively "filled," presupposes a notion of extension, at least of place, in which every location is well-defined. The appeal to God to define such locations, perhaps through the principle of perfection, does not suffice. If God is successful in defining every location as both well-defined and filled in the plenum, then that plenum of places and locations must be available for thought. How can it be thought except in extensive terms or their equivalent?

The alternative that Leibniz proposes—if it is an alternative, and not extension once more—is through preestablished harmony and internal representation. Monads are independent. Therefore, any action of one upon another is really the result of God's action in adjusting them to each other, while they conform to their own internal principles.

> 56. Now this *connection*, or this adaptation, of all created things to each and of each to all, brings it about that each simple substance has relations which express all the others, and that, consequently, it is a perpetual living mirror of the universe. (*Monadology*)

Every monad is adapted to every other, through preestablished harmony. (*Monadology*, 78) There is no alternative to the principle that, for monads to belong to one universe, each must represent both that universe collectively and every other monad individually. These conditions are not identical.

> 60. ... Because God, in regulating all, has had regard to each part, and particularly to each monad, whose nature being representative, nothing can limit it to representing only a part of things; although it may be true that this representation is but confused as regards the detail of the whole universe, and can be distinct only in the case of a small part of things, that is to say, in the case of those which are nearest or greatest in relation to each of the monads; otherwise each monad would be a divinity. (*Monadology*)

Again, there is apparently no alternative to describing monads in terms of extensive, even metrical relations, in terms of near and far.

Far more important is the notion of internal representation regarded as essential to the nature of monads. Leaving aside for the moment the question of whether every form of representation is not effectively extensive—as in images and icons—there is the far more profound question of whether a being that is intrinsically representative of others can be independent of them. In what sense is causation incompatible with independence while representation is compatible with it? It is not as if monads were volitional, for every state and condition within them is necessary. They represent other monads according to their own internal principle, defined by God's preestablished harmony.

The condition that manifests the togetherness of monads in one cosmos is the representation within every monad of every other monad in the universe. Even this can not suffice. It is not merely that in each monad, by preestablished harmony, there is a representation of every other, but there must be a representation of every other together with every other: that is, of the cosmos *as a cosmos*.[24] What is required is the double representation of the same inherent in the "detail of the universe": the universe *and* its detail. The latter involves each and every monad. The former is not provided by the detail alone. The simplest indication of this is through Socrates' example of a mirror, which can represent or reflect everything in the universe but does not represent the universe all together except from a particular point of view. The notion of a point of view either presupposes the totality of which it is a perspectival component or succeeds in unifying what is not otherwise unified. There is no escaping the aporia that nothing can define a representation of a universe that is cosmically unified only through that form of representation. Within each monad there must be a representation of every other monad—already a remarkably powerful and even aporetic assumption, because no other condition establishes the totality except God—as well as a representation of every monad's representation of all of the others, unifying them. As a consequence, without an independent ground of the totality of the universe, the perspectivity in each monad engenders a multiplicity of standpoints without a totality of standpoints. Moreover, Leibniz's view of representation begins to effloresce reflexively into the circles of representation that characterize aporia.

The representation of the detail of the universe is manifested through each monad's perceptions. Whether we assume that each monad perceives other monads, or merely perceives images and internal representations as a consequence of its adjustments to other monads, the detail of the universe is manifested through the internal representations that constitute the inner life of a monad: its adequate and confused perceptions. The condition whereby monads are together in one universe, if it is not an extensive relation, is given by confused and adequate perceptions together. Moreover, Leibniz cannot avoid identifying confused perceptions with remoteness and clear perceptions with proximity — both extensive notions. Either extension is presupposed in such a view of internal representation — as well as in the very notion of "internality" — or it is defined by internal representation.

It is not that some notion of spatial extension is required independent of the beings that inhabit it. Leibniz's is a relational theory of extension. As a consequence, the extension that pertains to any possible universe of monads is defined by them and unique to it.[25] Rather, it is that there is no condition of cosmological togetherness that is not aporetically both equivalent with yet distinct from extension. Such a notion of a multiplicity of forms of extension reflects both aporia and inexhaustibility, with the qualification that for Leibniz, only one universe and one extensive system is actual. Even more important, extension itself must be aporetic because it contains the aporias of the oneness of the universe conjoined with the inexhaustibility of finite things that inhabit it.

> 62. Thus, although each created monad represents the entire universe, it represents more distinctly the body which is particularly attached to it, and of which it forms the entelechy; and as this body expresses the whole universe through the connection of all matter in a plenum, the soul also represents the whole universe in representing this body, which belongs to it in a particular way. (*Monadology*)

Such a view of representation cannot provide the basis of the notions presupposed within it, particularly of "the entire universe" and of the body "attached" to the monad itself. Both of these notions are extensive, although aporetically. The notion of a monad attached to a body is extensive; the notion of the entire universe presupposes a total system of locations while extension is effectively the only system of such locations.

We may imagine nonextensive systems of locations that might define a totality, analogous perhaps to the system of integers. The latter comprises a system of members each of whose place is well-defined. We may imagine, analogously, a system of members comprising a logical if not a topological space, defined by a set of axioms and all its theorems. Each integer, we may say, contains within its conception every other number, because the principles that generate each entail all the others. Yet every such system, if it is not itself extensive, is isomorphic to a geometrical representation, equivalent if not identical with an extensive system. Another way of putting this is that no such system can be effective without defining a metric. The specificity of a "location" within any such system is equivalent to the presence of a metric.

These observations lead us to Leibniz's remarkable theory of representation, because it provides his only alternative to extension, aporetic or not. Monads *represent* each other, infinitely, as well as representing their own togetherness. Such a representation is intrinsically mathematical.

> Number is therefore, so to speak, a fundamental metaphysical form, and arithmetic a sort of statics of the universe, in which the powers of things are revealed. (*Towards a Universal Characteristic*, p. 17)

There is in things a universal, numerical characteristic which expresses the true form of representation, metaphysically and epistemologically. This universal characteristic is representation itself, that which lies within monads as their unifying principle and that which lies within human beings as the form of their capacity to understand nature. Representation to Leibniz is numerical, and number is "a fundamental metaphysical form." In such a context, to deny extension to substance, where substance is actively numerical, is obstinately aporetic. If monads are not extensive, geometrical, they are numerical, mathematical, while geometry and arithmetic are isomorphic. The only intelligible basis of a distinction must lie in the further properties of extension, that it is passive rather than active. Yet number is no more active than shape and location.

The universal characteristic is an extreme version of the writings of the same in the Book of Nature, providing the universal characters in which that book has been written and in which it may be understood.

> ... no one should fear that the contemplation of signs will lead us away from the things in themselves; on the contrary, it leads us into the interior of things. We often have confused notions today because the signs are badly arranged, but then with the aid of signs we will easily have the most distinct notions, for we will have at hand a mechanical thread of mediation, as it were, with whose aid we can easily resolve any idea whatever into those of which it is composed.[26]

Yet it in no way follows from the presence of such a book—that is, the intelligibility of the universe, defined in terms of perfection and sufficient reason—that there might be a single intelligible form in which the universe might be thought. Indeed, Leibniz frequently tells us that sufficient reasons may not all be accessible to human thought.

It follows that reason understood as the intelligibility that lies within things and reason understood as the form of human understanding cannot be identical, must be related aporetically. Part of this is evident in traditional views of language, for if nature is thought in words and names, then these cannot be identical with natural things and their own relations. Even eternal forms do not traverse this gap, because by their means things are thought generically, never individually. The aporia is clearly evident in Aristotle's multiplicity of causes conjoined with a multiplicity of unmoved movers and in Spinoza's infinite multiplicity of ideas of ideas. Sufficient reason, in its perfect Leibnizian form, requires that the many be reduced to one, though that is possible only aporetically.

There are, then, to be found in Leibniz both the aporias of perfection, realized among sufficient reason, its corollaries, and preestablished harmony, and the aporias of representation, expressed as the others in the same of the universal characteristic. This arithmetization of the universe not only does not follow from any understanding of its perfection, from its sufficient reason, but as thoroughly violates the principle of monadic activity as does extension. Leibniz is faced, as is Spinoza, with the disparity between reason in things and the reason that may understand things, humanly. Intelligibility, metaphysical and epistemological, contains an irresistible aporia in relation to perfection: the intelligibility sufficient for reality to be intelligible is never sufficient for human understanding.

Similarly, both monads and human understanding must be mimetic, representational, the former required by Leibniz's cosmological principles, the latter required by his epistemology. Yet the capacity of language and thought, even in arithmetic terms, to represent and refer can only be aporetically related to the capacities of things to represent each other. The ways in which monads "mirror" other monads cannot be epistemic because there are no windows. The ways in which human ideas "mirror" things cannot be windowless if ideas are to be epistemic. With or without windows, thought and its representations must reflect the limitations of confused as well as adequate perceptions, the intrinsic fallibility of finite relationships to an inexhaustible cosmos.

Related to these aporetic doublings is a peculiarity of Leibniz's historical influence, another reflection of the aporias of his view of intelligibility. For on the one hand, reason is manifested in the arithmetical necessity of the universe, while on the other, reason is manifested within each monad due to its independence and windowlessness. What follows is that the story of the universe is to be found represented within each monad as part of its history and psychology. Within Leibniz's extreme mathematical model of the intelligibility of the universe is to be found an anthropomorphic picture of internal representation that foreshadows Vico and Kant. Here, the condition that knowledge is possible of any contingent conditions concerning any substance depends on the determinate representations to be found within the knower of that substance, historically and psychologically, because no knowledge can be acquired from without. Windowlessness entails the anthropomorphization of reason and understanding.

> 83. ... souls in general are the living mirrors or images of the universe of creatures, but minds or spirits are in addition images of the Divinity itself, or of the author of nature, able to know the system of the universe and to imitate something of it by architectonic samples, each mind being like a little divinity in its own department. (*Monadology*)

The result is that on the one hand, the divinity in each higher monad is mathematical, while, as expressed in Vico, the understanding of the universe in such a monad is an internal representation of its own historical development. In this aporetic sense, Leibniz expresses the most extreme metaphysical and rational view of the universe conjoined with a position that virtually requires Kant's critical turn.

Thus, there is, even in Leibniz's "perfect" cosmos, a double aporia that revolves within and around the limitations inherent in perfection. These limitations are, very simply, that the perfections inherent in the whole are incompatible with perfection in every part, *ad infinitum*. Sufficient reason demands perfection in the whole taken as a whole while it tolerates and even demands imperfection in the parts. Only in the cosmic balance can we speak of perfection and of the "best of all possible worlds." What follows is that in relation to every form of human life and thought in which local considerations are relevant, and these include both science and morality, there is no form of reason that can mediate between part and whole, same and other.

It is not merely that human experience, along with that of every monad, is finite while God and the universe are infinite. It is that the perfection and the sufficiency of reason pertain only generically and cannot pertain locally and concretely. There is perfection in the whole but not in the part. Even if what follows is that this is the only intelligible and perfect universe, it cannot entail that any finite creature, any monad, any human being, can know anything in that universe adequately or correctly. To the contrary, the form of argument inherent in perfection entails the most unwelcome skeptical conclusions locally. The universal characteristic, in all its perfection, is an arbitrary and even incompatible notion in relation to the perfections of sufficient reason.

This arbitrariness lies within sufficient reason itself as the aporia that pertains to metaphysical perfection. That ours might be a perfect universe, morally as well as metaphysically, requires a principle corresponding to the principle of confused perceptions, one that divides local from universal perfections, with the consequence that every individual perfection then becomes aporetic. Sufficient reason depends on the assumption of omniscience although every knowing is local, from a particular point of view. Put another way, knowledge always locally depends on the confusion inherent in perspectives, and entails heresy in the modification and transformation of local perspectives. Analogously, moral perfection, regarded as a property in which all the parts are adjusted to the whole, is compatible with the greatest local abuses and violations. The traditional problem of evil suffers from the assumption that an omniscient and perfect God might achieve a nonaporetic moral perfection. Leibniz resolves this problem by aporia at the center of his entire view of moral perfection. Between whole and part, regarded morally, goodness is always aporetic. The reason, metaphysically, is that one and many, unity and multiplicity, the universe locally and generically, are always related aporetically.

The fundamental aporias in Leibniz's cosmology are those of the cosmos itself as the rift of same and other. These aporias are magnified by the principles of sufficient reason and perfection. What Voltaire's satires indicate is that there are local perspectives in relation to which universal goodness and understanding are not simply absent, but unintelligible. That the universe as a whole might be or be perfect while local perspectives might be deficient and aporetic carries within itself the aporia of being regarded unitarily. Being cannot be both same and other without aporia. This insight lies at the center of Hegel's view of dialectic. In Leibniz, where perfection constitutes the nature of the cosmos, where every aporetic manifestation of imperfection is rejected, we nevertheless find the inescapable aporias of inexhaustible local beings, manifested in the differences within perfection divided over its different local spheres of application.

7 EMPIRICISM: THE HERESY OF EXPERIENCE

AMONG the ironies of Western philosophy is the fact that empiricism, which arose in reaction against received truth, should have become a form of orthodoxy. One reason is that the reactions of empiricism against authority were part of the emerging authority of science. A more generic reason is that heresy cannot be implemented without becoming orthodox, without falling under the rule of the same. What was heretical in Locke, Berkeley, and Hume became orthodox in the name of Empiricism. What is required, if we are to understand philosophy and participate in it, is to rethink the heresies that constitute its history and to define our own heresies in relation to them.

Locke, Berkeley, and Hume no more deserve to be discussed together, as "empiricists," than Leibniz and Spinoza deserve to be discussed together as "rationalists." The latter have been discussed here in terms of their singular metaphysical views, quite incompatible with taking them together as rationalists. Similarly, Locke and Hume are assimilable under the name of empiricism only by giving one of them, usually Hume, primary place. What permits us in the present context to treat them together is the historical relationship of empiricism to metaphysics. Empiricism arose in reaction against a view of metaphysical thought associated with theology and hostile to the development of science. It was not until after Kant and Hegel that the return to experience could be treated as the foundation of both a scientific and a metaphysical understanding.

In its beginnings, and throughout its classical period—beginning with Hobbes and ending with Mill—empiricism was motivated by a demand to be shown truth with one's own eyes. No truth was to be accepted on the basis of hearsay or authority. Such a demand, carried far enough, is one of the most far-reaching heresies in the development of thought. Here Hume's skepticism is of fundamental importance: the rejection of any source of error that rests on established authority. This skepticism followed one side of Descartes' method of hyperbolic doubt. Yet the other side of Descartes became the other side of empiricism: a foundational moment that sought to establish another orthodoxy, in Descartes that of clear and distinct ideas, in empiricism that of sensory experience. In both Cartesian rationalism and classical empiricism there is found a fundamental if ambivalent affirmation of heresy in the form of skepticism, leading nevertheless to the replacement of one established authority by another.

These conflicting moments express the heretical side of the Western epistemological tradition. They are a consequence of the profound aporia that knowledge demands heresy but establishes orthodoxy. The aporias in the tradition all too frequently represent only the skeptical side of heresy, lacking positive recognition of how every significant advance in understanding requires a heretical movement.

Many of these conflicts can be discerned in the central passages in Bacon and Hobbes. Bacon opens his *Novum Organum* with a strong rejection of apriorism. (Bacon, *Novum Organum*, Introduction, p. 24)[1] Both rationalism and divine authority close off inquiry and treat understanding as completed. Bacon rejects, quite as vociferously, any trace of skepticism. (Bacon, *Novum Organum*, Introduction, p. 24) Yet he must acknowledge kinship with it because the heart of empiricism and science lies in the demand to be shown rather than coerced. To avoid what he regards as a stultifying skepticism, he proposes a striking form of certainty.

> There remains but one course for the recovery of a sound and healthy condition, — namely, that the entire work of the understanding be commenced afresh, and the mind itself be from the very outset not let to take its own course, but guided at every step; and the business be done as if by machinery. (Bacon, *Novum Organum*, Introduction, p. 24)

This mechanical analogy lies at the center of empiricism, one of the fundamental poles that defines its movement, intimately entangled with the contrary movements that affirm the inseparability of heresy from truth. One pole recognizes, in both Bacon and Hume, the kinship of science with skepticism, not merely in rejecting too strong a principle of reason, but in the continuing movement in science in which every truth is to be unceasingly interrogated and eventually rejected. The other pole requires from science a certainty that entirely avoids skepticism. In the extreme, science provides not only a challenge to dogmatism, but its own orthodoxy, expressed in the image of a mechanical procedure for generating truth in the same. On this theme, Bacon and Leibniz coincide: truth is to be produced automatically as a result of sound, repeatable methods. The two movements together—skeptical and foundational—are aporetic. Within the aporias lie the heresies of reason.

> XXXVI: One method of delivery alone remains to us; which is simply this: we must lead men to the particulars themselves, and their series and order; .... (Bacon, *Novum Organum*, p. 33)

> XIX: There are and can be only two ways of searching into and discovering truth. The one flies from the senses and particulars to the most general axioms, ... The other derives axioms from the senses and particulars, rising by a gradual and unbroken ascent, so that it arrives at the most general axioms last of all. (Bacon, *Novum Organum*, p. 31)

The emphasis in the first pole is on the "particulars themselves." The emphasis in the second pole is on the "unbroken ascent" to truth. On the one hand, in resting all knowledge on particulars, in reaching general truths "last of all," we confront the heretical possibilities in a science based on divided experience. On the other hand, the progress of such a science must be gradual and unbroken. Bacon approaches the aporia of local truth and recoils. The possibility is that there is no form of understanding derivable from experience that can provide a principled reply to skepticism. There is no undivided way to truth. Inherent in empiricism is the possibility that every understanding realizable from experience is mixed inseparably with error. Skepticism has only a local resolution. Empirical knowledge is always heretical.

With this understanding of the skeptical side of empiricism, we can recognize the aporias inherent in its fundamental tenet that sense is the origin of all our knowledge, all our ideas.

> The original of them all is that which we call *sense*, for there is no conception in a man's mind which hath not at first, totally or by parts, been begotten upon the organs of sense. (Hobbes, *Leviathan*, Part I, Ch. I, p. 131)

This origination of all knowledge and ideas in sensation is the fundamental principle of classical empiricism. It is not simply, without justification, equivalent with the principle that all our knowledge comes from experience. Empiricism depends on the assumption that experience is to be equated with sensation. In Hobbes, this assumption rests on a mechanical-causal principle:

> The cause of sense is the external body, or object, which presseth the organ proper to each sense, either immediately, as in the taste and touch; or mediately, as in seeing, hearing, and smelling; which pressure, by the mediation of the nerves, and other strings and membranes of the body, continued inwards to the brain and heart, causeth there a resistance, or counter-pressure, or endeavor of the heart to deliver itself, which endeavor, because outward, seemeth to be some matter without. (Hobbes, *Leviathan*, Part I, Ch. I, p. 131)[2]

One questionable feature of Hobbes' position is his assumption that sensation is the causal manifestation within of external bodies. A far more questionable assumption, however, is that we may understand internal representations as causal consequences of external bodies and conditions. Hobbes does not consider the possibility that what "presseth the organ proper to each sense" is a physical object, while the internal, sensible representation, the idea, is very different.

The difficulty here is that ideas serve as both causal consequences of physical processes and signs of other things. However, no ordinary causal account of representation can provide an explanation of its epistemic nature. Similarly, no ordinary causal account of physical nature can provide an explanation of the codes of life—RNA and DNA—regarded as forms of representation. No causal account of the origin of a word can explain its function as a sign. The relationship of a signifier to its signified is always divided by arbitrariness.[3] Physical nature is filled with representations, signs, and information: codes and references. Following this path far enough, we would be led to Whitehead's and Leibniz's shared view that even physical nature must be regarded as psychical because only such a nature can be representational. Closely related is an emergent view of nature: natural processes are novel as epistemic processes are heretical. In both cases, what is rejected is the intelligibility of repetition as the basis of natural and epistemic processes. Similarity is unintelligible without difference. Both are required for being and knowing.

The epistemological side of empiricism requires both a theory of experience and a theory of ideas. These constitute the question of understanding at the center of Locke's *Essay*. The fundamental notion is that of *idea*:

... I must here in the entrance beg pardon of my reader for the frequent use of the word *idea*, which he will find in the following treatise. It being that term which, I think, serves best to stand for whatsoever is the *object* of the understanding when a man thinks, I have used it to express whatever is meant by *phantasm, notion, species*, or *whatever it is which the mind can be employed about in thinking*; and I could not avoid frequently using it. (Locke, *Essay*, I, I, I, p. 32)

What is suggested is that a theory of experience is a theory of ideas more than it is a theory of sensation. Yet the first question Locke poses is "how they come into the mind" (Locke, *Essay*, I, I, I, p. 33)—not the nature of ideas but why they cannot be innate. It is no minor matter that the first part of Locke's *Essay* is on innate ideas.

It is remarkable that neither Leibniz nor Spinoza (as contrasted with Descartes) offers an explicit doctrine of innate ideas.[4] There is rather, in both, emphasis upon the principle that certainty cannot be derived from sensory experience. What is at stake is less the empirical question of the origin of our ideas than the question of how our ideas might fall indubitably within the same. In this context, Descartes' method of systematic doubt is aporetic: doubt is posited so that it may be overcome apodeictically. The only ideas—principles and notions—that might achieve such apodeictic certainty are innate. What may be added is that innate ideas are not more certain than acquired ideas. Mathematical ideas are not free from error. They are not subject to the kinds of errors that pertain to sensory experience, but are subject to others. One of the central aporias of empiricism is that it repudiates innate ideas as if their existence would challenge the fundamental principles of empiricism—as if innate ideas were not themselves aporetic.

No plausible doctrine of human experience can avoid innate capacities; no plausible doctrine of experience can deny the acquisition of knowledge from sensory experience. Classical empiricism, in Locke and Hume, presupposes certain forms of association whereby complex ideas are formed from simple ideas. These associative forms must in some sense be innate because without them we could not experience complex things at all. There must be an internal mechanism whereby simple ideas are combined into complex ideas, and this mechanism cannot itself be acquired. The epistemological consequences of this recognition are by no means free from skepticism.

There is a fundamental aporia in all empiricist theories of knowledge: what is acquired from experience can never be sufficient for knowledge. This observation is the basis of Hume's critique of induction. But it has a longer history and deeper significance, going back to Plato's doctrine of recollection. For Plato, the issue is how knowledge can be acquired, given that without knowledge we cannot acquire further knowledge. It follows that there can be no totally nonepistemic state of an epistemic subject. It follows further, if we reject the innatism of recollection, that all understanding is caught up in the circle of positing what cannot be proven in order to prove something else. All understanding in this sense is aporetic. There is no form of knowledge that can escape heresy.

What is at stake between empiricism and rationalism is not so much whether knowledge is the result of sensory experience or possessed innately, but whether there is knowledge free from aporia, whether all knowledge rests on conflicting foundations. What the empiricists recognized is that this aporia pertains to innate knowlege intrinsically. If a truth is innate, it is unverified and unverifiable. That some such truths may be proven deductively only extends the aporia more widely. The question is Spinoza's, whether there are forms of knowledge that, however they are acquired, cannot be thought except as true.

Rationalism postulates not so much innateness as self-evidence, the same closed within itself. The question is whether there are ideas that are manifestly and self-validatingly true. The aporia of such self-evidence is that, once challenged, no answer can be given as to why a self-evident idea is to be taken as true. The history of mathematics is filled with the debris of postulated truths that were later shown to be false. Yet the paradigm of mathematics has traditionally suggested not strenuous and fallible proof but immediate self-evidence. No internal criterion of proof can satisfy the demand to be shown.

These are the issues that lie behind the fact that Locke begins his *Essay*, not with the nature of ideas and experience, but with innate ideas.

> It is an established opinion amongst some men, that there are in the understanding certain *innate principles*; some primary notions, koinai ennoiai, characters, as it were stamped upon the mind of man; which the soul receives in its very first being, and brings into the world with it. (*Essay*, I, I, I, p. 37)

His reply is to show that all our knowledge may be acquired through and from experience, and that we may thereby attain certainty. We may divide this reply into two: one is that there is no idea or principle that cannot be formed from experience, so that we need not posit innateness; the second is that the ideas or principles that are so constituted from experience may comprise indubitable knowledge. We do not need innateness to explain knowledge, whether certain or fallible. Unlike Hume, Locke does not appear willing to follow the skeptical side of epistemic experience as far as necessary.[5]

Moreover, Locke does not clearly identify the aporetic side of innateness, but accepts its own description of itself. We may, with the help of later developments, view innateness somewhat differently. Three principles define the aporias that pertain to it:

   a. *Something* is innate. Human experience would otherwise be unintelligible.
   b. *Something* is acquired from experience. Human experience would otherwise be unintelligible.
   c. What is innate cannot be *knowledge*, epistemic, however true or unquestionable it may be.

   a. That nothing might be innate in human experience, if only the shape and structure of the body, would be unintelligible. Being is always antecedently conditioned. In the case of human beings, among the antecedent conditions are the historical and cultural conditions of human bodily life as well as the causal powers that pertain to the body. The epistemological consequence is that knowledge acquired from experience must begin with established forms of knowledge, with complex structures and capacities—for example, a sensory-motor system that can respond to its own discriminations.

   Current neurological research suggests that the newborn infant possesses a complex set of neural pathways comprising 30,000 to 60,000 connections. These are innate, but they are neither unquestionable nor permanent, for in the first nine months of life, they may be replaced by a far more complex, acquired set of connections. Such a model gives us both innateness and the capacity of an epistemic subject to learn from experience. It gives us an epistemology based on a circle of meaning, a physical representation of a hermeneutic circle. The model need not be true. The point again is that knowledge cannot be acquired from experience without prior knowledge. Knowledge cannot be based on mechanical conditions. Similarly, no forms of bodily knowledge can be acquired except from prior epistemic bodily capacities involving skills and powers.

   That newborn human beings might possess innate capacities and powers is far less implausible than that they might conform to Locke's famous image of a void:

   Let us then suppose the mind to be, as we say, white paper,
   void of all characters, without any ideas. (*Essay*, I, II, I, p. 121)

Suppose we imagine the human body to be, as Locke says, devoid of all characters. A body without characters is unintelligible enough—entirely indeterminate. A body that inherits from its forebears while devoid of characters would be altogether unintelligible.

Why, then, does the emptiness of the newborn mind sound plausible? What is required is that the inherited, innate conditions of the newborn mind might constitute knowledge and truth. Yet how could something entirely free from influence by the experienced environment comprise knowledge of it? Either we must posit innate competences and skills that do not comprise knowledge and truth or we must imagine a mind into which truth enters only subsequently. Both suppositions are contradictory. The question is how truth can emerge from a nature that does not know itself or anything else.

b. Something is clearly innate, but it cannot constitute knowledge and truth without experience. There can be no plausible theory that holds that all our knowledge is innate,[6] but must allow for the possibility of acquiring knowledge. We must acquire knowledge of the number of our limbs, our fingers and toes, from experience because we could easily have had different numbers of them. The question is how such acquisition is possible. The answer cannot avoid heresy.

Something must be known in advance in every case in which knowledge is acquired: otherwise that knowledge would be unintelligible, based on no grounds or evidence. Innatism is the logical conclusion. Something must be acquired in every case in which knowledge is involved: otherwise the possession of knowledge would be unintelligible. These two conditions are not of themselves aporetic: they affirm the complementarity of inheritance and learning. They are aporetic in the context of the issues that characterize the innatist tradition. If any knowledge is innate, then that other knowledge is acquired does not make the former more intelligible. That any knowledge is innate does not make the acquisition of other knowledge from experience more intelligible. This is the greatest difficulty within Kant's apriorism. Generic a priori principles do not and cannot entail specific and determinate truths. That grammar might be innate does not make the acquisition of new forms of linguistic production more intelligible.[7] The fundamental aporia of innate ideas is that with or without such innatism, empirical knowledge is heretical and aporetic.

c. What is innate cannot be knowledge because it follows from material conditions, and these do not comprise knowledge. To be knowledge, neural connections must be constituted by understanding and be supported by evidence. Even in the case of mathematics, the model of innateness cannot hold. It is not enough to understand the Pythagorean theorem; what is required is to be able to prove it. Yet one can prove it without understanding it. The proof and the understanding do not coincide, either logically or chronologically. Moreover, there are always other applications that lie within the sphere of "understanding."

The aporia here is that there can be no knowledge that, of itself, in some canonical form, constitutes truth. If there were, then mathematical knowledge would comprise it independent of either known or stateable truths and their proofs. Rather, there is no canonical form and no particular condition that constitutes the finality of knowledge from experience, only subjection to and submergence within finite empirical conditions. Not only cannot finite empirical conditions constitute certainty: they cannot constitute knowledge. There is no escape from the aporia that empirical knowledge is based on unknown conditions. The fundamental aporia of innate knowledge is that what is innate can comprise neither knowledge nor understanding, in any form, while there is no form in which knowledge is acquired from experience that does not presuppose innate powers and conditions.

Here we see the emptiness of what many take to be the Kantian endeavor: the attempt to define the absolute, universal, and unconditioned innate conditions of all empirical knowledge. These must be unchanging and nonemergent, therefore absolutely nonheretical and universal. What is striking about such knowledge is that it must be altogether empty, without application in human experience. Generic and pervasive conditions are not and cannot be epistemic because they do not comprise determinateness and specificity. What is innate can at best be schematic while what is known must be densely determinate.

The opening salvo of classical empiricism is directed against innatism in understanding but not in materiality. The attack cannot succeed because there can be no knowledge that does not begin somewhere. Yet the attack is unnecessary because whatever might be innate cannot be knowledge: knowledge is always later and never complete. The fundamental truth in empiricism is that knowledge is indistinguishable in principle from error, from its other, epistemology from skepticism. We are led to the ideas that constitute the aporetic fabric of lived experience.

The fundamental concept in classical empiricism is that of *idea*. Locke's *Essay* is primarily a treatment of human ideas, where the latter are understood, at least in the Introduction, to include whatever the mind can be employed about in thinking. In this formulation, Locke makes no intrinsic separation between ideas and things or ideas and words. Whatever the mind can think about — its object — is an idea.

An important ambiguity is involved here in the distinction between what the mind can think about and what it employs in thinking. The ambiguity is not resolved in Locke's first explicit discussion of ideas.

> Every man being conscious to himself that he thinks; and that which is mind is applied about while thinking being the *ideas* that are there, it is past doubt that men have in their minds

> several ideas,—such as are those expressed by the words *white-*
> *ness, hardness, sweetness, thinking, motion, man, elephant, army,*
> *drunkenness*, and others; . . . . (Locke, *Essay*, I, II, I, p. 121)

Here, ideas may be either things thought—that is, things themselves as
they are thought, including elephants and armies—or internal representations. There are ideas *of* individual things—the things themselves as
they are thought—and internal representations whereby we think these
things—the sensory universals into which they may be divided. If both
are ideas, then the difficulty is not that we should have ideas of things—
they are perceived in sensory experience—but that we should have ideas
of sensory universals that we cannot encounter and have never witnessed.
Locke's famous image of the empty mind suggests that it is stocked only
by what we encounter in experience. However, what experience provides are not objects thought, but sensory perceptions.

> First, our Senses, conversant about particular sensible
> objects, do convey into the mind several distinct perceptions of
> things, according to those various ways wherein those objects
> do affect them. And thus we come by those *ideas* we have of
> *yellow, white, heat, cold, soft, hard, bitter, sweet*, and all those
> which we call sensible qualities. (Locke, *Essay*, I, II, I, pp. 122-23)

Locke resolves the ambiguity concerning ideas in favor of sensory universals. He does not follow the line of thought suggested by his earlier
language, that we are conversant with sensible objects and form ideas *of*
those objects—that is, think about things rather than their qualities.[8]
Whitehead later strongly supports this conclusion, arguing that the senses
give us, not general ideas or sensory universals, but the qualities in and
of those individual things: "the yellow of the ear of corn," "the heat of
the sun."[9] What must be added is that this identity of being and representation is profoundly aporetic.

Locke's view of what stocks the mind is Cartesian, ironic in a view
that repudiates Descartes' rationalism. Here we find the aporia of both
classical rationalism and empiricism: contingent experience is posited
as fundamentally inadequate, confronting us with the specter of skepticism. The skepticism is inherent within Descartes' method of systematic
doubt: *could* the world be altogether different from how we experience
it? The empiricist answer is that if the world were altogether different,
there would be nothing that we could think about, for thinking requires
ideas derived from sensory experience.

We have noted Aristotle's assumption that where thinking changes
its object, where *nous* imposes its character on its ideas, then knowledge

is impossible. We have replied that without a determinate nature of its own, *nous* could not think anything, certainly not itself. That ideas are things thought or known does not mean that they are not changed by the thinking or knowing. Conversely, that knowing changes its object does not mean that ideas are not of things themselves, that they cannot be true, only that they cannot be true without qualification.

It is essential to Locke's empiricism that ideas be things themselves as they are thought, for only then can knowledge have an object. It is essential to Locke's understanding of the nature of the forms of experience that ideas, internal and external, be restricted to sensory universals. This conflict finds explicit expression in the difference between Locke's account of simple and complex ideas and his account of primary qualities.

> And there is nothing can be plainer to a man than the clear and distinct perception he has of those simple ideas; which, being each in itself uncompounded, contains in it nothing but *one uniform appearance, or conception in the mind*, and is not distinguishable into different ideas. (Locke, *Essay*, I, II, II, p. 145)

Locke continues the Cartesian theme of the clear and distinct ideas that constitute the epistemological foundations of knowledge, adding that they are both transparent and self-validating. The question is how to avoid the aporetic circle that we are unable to experience clearly and distinctly what we call clear and distinct. Simple ideas in Locke serve not only as the materials of thought about things, but as the basis on which we know them, although Locke has no argument whatever to overcome the skeptical side of contingent experience. The notion of simple ideas is unwarranted both in terms of the testimony of experience, because we never experience a simple, undivided idea not conjoined with others, and as an epistemic foundation, because an idea can be veridical here only where entirely passive. Passivity can be mechanical but cannot be epistemic. Passively derived materials can be constituents of knowledge only where supplemented by active observations and experiments. Similarly, unchanging sensory forms are intelligible only as they are perceived in changing experience.[10] Identity cannot be thought except within a horizon of change.

Locke's distinction between primary and secondary qualities continues this theme:

> . . . the ideas of primary qualities of bodies are resemblances of them, and their patterns do really exist in the bodies themselves, but the ideas produced in us by these secondary qualities have no resemblance of them at all. There is nothing like our ideas,

existing in the bodies themselves. (Locke, *Essay*, I, II, VIII, p. 173)

His view of substance repeats the aporia because he must both claim that the idea of substance is simple and deny that that is all it is.[11]

The aporetic side of empiricism lies in its iconoclastic skepticism that claims that knowledge derived from experience can only be inadequate. Empirical knowledge is heretical and aporetic. This point of view can be seen even in the distinction between primary and secondary qualities. Where resembling, ideas are passive and mechanical, requiring supplementation by the creative imagination. Where the result of internal activities, ideas can be true only where they organize experiences into a coherent whole. Resemblance and passivity, simplicity and repetitiveness, are aporetic notions.

The manifest aporia in Locke's view of resemblance is the joint affirmation that no ideas should be accepted unless they come from and are checked by experience while things are indeed the way they appear to be, at least in relation to their primary qualities. Among the implications of emphasizing experience is avoidance of the restrictions imposed by innate ideas. Experience makes it possible for us to know and to think of things that we could not imagine innately. Conversely, however, the creative imagination, freed from a priori rational constraints, makes it possible for us to think of things that we could never encounter in any perceptual experience. The heresy, realized frequently in the natural sciences, is that many of these imaginative thoughts are true. Things are by no means as they appear to be, not in the skeptical sense that truth is hidden behind its manifestations, but in the heretical sense that what is true requires all the resources of the creative imagination.

There is a radical side in empiricism inseparable from the orthodoxy that only what ordinary experience tells us is true. Experience threatens us with disruption as much as it offers repetition. There is, in Locke's explicit emphasis on the radical side of experience in relation to established authorities, conjoined with his conservative sense of the resemblances inherent in primary qualities and the repetitions inherent in simple ideas, clear testimony to the recurrent heresy of knowledge: what is known must be heretical while what is heretical is unintelligible. Nevertheless, he cannot bring himself to accept explicitly the full plenitude of heresy that pertains to his general view of experience.

Although compared with Locke and Hume, Berkeley plays but a minor role in the empiricist tradition, he plays a central role in relation to the heresy that characterizes its radical side. None of the empiricists is as outspoken as he concerning the defects of abstract ideas, rejecting them altogether and conclusively. An abstract idea is nothing but a distorted concrete image. A major aporia that pertains to this position is that both philosophy and science, all important forms of knowledge, would be impossible without general ideas. The fundamental question, to which only an aporetic answer can be given, is how we are to understand general or abstract ideas, given that they are unavoidable. How are they acquired and how are they implemented?

The dubious psychological suggestion in Berkeley's position, which runs throughout classical empiricism, is that we cannot think a general idea except as a distorted image. Compared with Locke's view, that the abstract idea consists of but the name, Berkeley's view is implausible. However, it contains so profound a commonplace truth as to comprise heresy: ideas are empty except as they are determinate—in this case, through concrete experience. Determinateness is a pervasive aporia because it is always mixed with indeterminateness.

Locke rejects abstract ideas because of the arbitrariness of the relation of words to things. Berkeley rejects abstract ideas because of the indeterminateness of the internal representations associated with them. The heresy implicit here is that knowledge, like being, is indeterminate in certain respects and determinate in others. Beings are not determinate in all ways; neither are our forms of representation, internal and external. Berkeley's criticism of abstract ideas is based on an implicit contrast with a totally concrete idea that suffers from no indeterminateness whatever. Such a notion is unintelligible. The defect of classical empiricism is that it moderates its radical insight concerning the indeterminateness of knowing and being into a foundational presumption that certain immediate forms of experience are entirely determinate and concrete. That general ideas are indeterminate does not entail that singular ideas of individual things are entirely determinate. To the contrary, no idea of any thing, however individual, can represent that thing in its density and specificity.[12] That is part of what is meant by inexhaustibility.

Another major heresy is to be found in Berkeley: the idealism for which he is best known. One argument for it follows from his critique of abstract ideas: the idea of matter apart from thought has no concrete image corresponding to it. *To be is to be perceived* because perception is required for the concreteness an idea must have to be intelligible.

> Let us examine a little the description that is here given us of *matter*. It neither acts, nor perceives, nor is perceived; for this is all that is meant by saying that it is an inert, senseless, unknown substance: which is a definition entirely made up of negatives, excepting only the relative notion of it standing under or supporting. But then it must be observed that it supports nothing at all, and how nearly this comes to the description of a

nonentity I desire may be considered. (Berkeley, *Principles*, par. 68, p. 546)

Several other arguments are implicit in this passage. One, the traditional reading of Berkeley, is that we cannot know what matter is—"an inert, senseless, unknown substance"—because what we know comes only from experience, the sensory individuals present in perception. Such an argument wears an air of paradox, because it would appear that we unmistakably know of the existence of material things from perceptual experience. Second, already mentioned, is that *matter* here is an abstract substratum, made concrete only through perceptual qualities, and therefore entirely lacks determinateness. Third, then, closely related to this absence of determinateness, there can be no relation between an "inert, senseless, unknown substance" and the active ideas of our experience. Matter and mind can have no resemblance or relation. It follows that it is unintelligible for a mind to think of such a matter.

This conclusion is the major heresy in Berkeley's theory, and is what makes his view endure. He is irreplaceable in the history of metaphysics because of his argument that matter is unintelligible insofar as it is inactive and senseless. The difficulty matter posed for earlier neo-Platonists passes in Berkeley into a fundamental aporia. If matter is unintelligible, then there is only mind. However, unless there is something external to and independent of mind, mind is equally indeterminate: there is nothing to think *of*. Among the most striking of Berkeley's claims is that he is defending common sense against the philosophers, as if common sense suggests that matter is unintelligible except as perceived.[13] The plausibility of Berkeley's claim is offset by its equally manifest absurdity. Common-sense thought bears little resemblance to his technical analyses. Alternatively, however, we may recognize in his claim explicit affirmation of the aporias of common-sense experience. To deny the autonomous existence of matter is an aporia within the "natural attitude."[14]

Several replies have been given to Berkeley. Matter is to be thought of as active rather than as passive. Qualities inhere in both material things and the mind identically. All such replies are both aporetic and heretical—as are those found in Whitehead, for example. Berkeley poses the aporias of indeterminate matter so forcibly that only heretical replies are possible. Material reality and its aporias force us to adopt an unfamiliar view of reality in general.

We need not follow Berkeley's criticisms of matter quite so far to disclose its aporias. We may again foreshadow Hegel as we did in our discussion of *nous*. Our questioning of Aristotle's description of *nous* was based on the understanding that nothing could be knowable or intelligible if it did not possess a determinate nature. The Hegelian principle is that only what is determinate is intelligible, and it can be known only in determinate ways, but determinateness is inseparable from indeterminateness. General, abstract knowledge, though unavoidable, always suffers from indeterminateness. We must add the pervasive aporia that nothing is entirely determinate. Everything is indeterminate in certain ways, for example, relative to its future, its transformations and modifications, or its instances and applications. Determinateness and indeterminateness cohabit in all being and knowing.

It follows that we may not equate determinateness with individuality and indeterminateness with generality. General ideas may be abstract, vague, and imprecise; but they may also be felicitous, accurate, and distinct. Individual things may be in such a flux of change that we cannot entirely ascertain their limits. Limits are never altogether determinate, but permeable and transformable. Every limit has two sides, expressing the reciprocity of determinateness and indeterminateness. Inexhaustibility pertains to both generality and individuality.

The generic aporia in empiricism is that there is no being, in or out of experience, that can be altogether determinate or altogether indeterminate. What empiricism offers is a certain understanding of this aporia, based on its view of experience. Experience is pervaded by indeterminateness and indeterminateness. Orthodox empiricism suffers from the conviction that this aporia can be resolved in terms of finite elements of experience—simple ideas. Yet the heretical side of empiricism would be compelling without the slightest vestige of a theory of simple ideas. Such a theory seeks to tame the profound heresies inherent in the experience of finiteness and indeterminateness.

With this background, we may turn to Hume, whom many readers regard as the only complete embodiment of classical empiricism. The place to begin is with his first statements in the *Treatise* concerning simple ideas and impressions.[15] Hume's entire theory resides in these earliest passages, although their implications and significance are not spelled out until later. What is justly admired is the inexorability with which his theory of causation and human nature develops from his stated assumptions.[16] What is frequently overlooked is that this inexorability is suffused with aporia. Consistency can be heresy.

The first principle of empiricism is that all our knowledge of matters of fact comes from experience. Yet Hume offers a remarkably thin view of experience,[17] resting on memory and repetition. The singularity of individual impressions and things has no standing in such a view. The reason is that without repetition and memory, no knowledge of any kind would be possible. Yet even these principles, insofar as they transcend the immediacy of simple impressions, are arbitrary and aporetic.

The nature of experience, we may reply to Hume, corresponds to our general view of things. Our surroundings are comprised of whatever things there are, and are nothing beyond them; similarly, experience is comprised of everything human, whatever that may be, and is nothing more or less than that. Such accounts of experience and nature offer two important qualifications. One is that experience and nature are not altogether transcendent, above and beyond what comprises them. There is no total Universe or Experience, only the beings that there are. The second is that experience includes whatever is relevant to human life or is influenced by human activities. What remains for disclosure are the forms of relevance. For if we believe that knowledge comes from experience, we must believe two things: that there are fundamental limitations inherent in experience that pertain to all our knowledge, scientific and otherwise; and that new forms of knowledge may emerge from unforeseen kinds of experience. There is a remarkable aporia pertaining to the finiteness of experience that classical empiricism realizes only marginally: while the limits of experience impose limits on knowledge and understanding, experience like being is inexhaustible.

It appears easy enough to distinguish ideas from things, signifiers from signifieds, in the case of stones and trees and their names. Here we may again acknowledge Berkeley's importance: matter is perceivable only through its sensory manifestations. It follows, if we suppose that ideas are sharply distinguishable from their objects, that the latter are neither thinkable nor perceivable, leaving only their traces behind in the ideas that represent them in their perpetual absence. The difficulty for the idealisms that follow is that ideas arc significant of nothing, complete in themselves. Signifiers—words and ideas—thereby have no meaning.

The heresy of empiricism, largely obscured by its emphasis on simple and complex ideas and their resembling relation, is that representation is an aporia: signifiers and signifieds in relation. This aporia is expressed by Saussure in terms of the arbitrariness of the sign, but is expressed in classical empiricism in the denial that ideas always correspond to or resemble some object—that would make error unintelligible—conjoined with the principle that ideas are intelligible only through resemblance and repetition. Hume's solution is that ideas are copies of impressions although there is no intelligible difference between impressions and ideas. Both ideas and words are signifiers without signifieds. The alternative, rejected by Hume, is that ideas are signifiers aporetically related to their signifieds—to things internal and external. Representation is aporetic, a union of identity and difference.

The distinction between impressions and ideas is essential if ideas are to have epistemic significance. Yet there is no difference in kind between impressions and ideas, only a difference in "force and liveliness." This distinction is both crude and implausible, psychologically speaking, because human beings with vivid imaginations may conceive ideas whose vivacity far exceeds that of irresistible perceptions. Hume suggests that we generally can tell the difference between impressions and ideas. No doubt this is true, although equally plausibly we can generally tell the difference between ideas and things. Moreover, both distinctions are aporetic. Ideas cannot be like material things to the extent that the latter are characterized by a matter different from anything perceivable or experienceable. Ideas are identical with impressions except for an unperceivable difference in vivacity, a difference that becomes meaningless in relation to Hume's theory of custom and habit. The identity between ideas and impressions carries the entire force of his epistemology—an identity based on a hidden difference. We may consider the aporetic alternative that ideas are identical with things (*things thought*, as in Locke) along with their differences. What we must admire in the empiricists are profound insights into the aporias of experience, the identities as well as differences in perceptual experience. What we may regret in the empiricists is their refusal to carry these aporias through to the extent, for example, that ideas are understood to be of things, aporetically and dividedly. Yet Locke and Hume do not altogether avoid this aporia, because even if simple ideas are copies of simple impressions, complex ideas are not copies of complex impressions, but are built up out of simple ideas through principles of association. Complex ideas have no models.

That there are simple impressions is fundamental to empiricism but is implausible. We never knowingly experience a simple impression, only find among the complex ideas and impressions that constitute experience certain indivisible qualities. Indivisibility is aporetic because it on the one hand is a criterion of primary reality whose internal divisions would undermine its intelligibility, while on the other hand nothing can be intelligible and be indivisible. Indivisibility is not an absolute notion but pertains only to certain respects: substances not divisible into other substances; ideas not divisible into other ideas. In order to be effective, substances must be divided over their effects; ideas must be divisible over the aggregates in which they participate. Similarly, an atom, if indivisible into other atoms, is divisible relationally over the different compounds into which it enters. That a sensory quality such as green is perceived phenomenologically as unbroken does not mean that it is not divisible extensively or spectrally. To grant sensory experience authority over all forms of divisibility and analyzability is aporetic where we acknowledge the contingency of finite experience.

It follows that the identity between simple ideas and simple impressions is either contradictory, given the complex finiteness of ideas and impressions, or is an aporetic requisite in empiricism for the possibility of knowledge. Knowledge is defined in terms of a resemblance incompatible with the contingencies of epistemic experience. No idea can be a copy of a thing or impression because the effectiveness of ideas is as much a function of their transformations as their repetitions. Repetition requires thought, understanding, and imagination, all of which are transformative. The result is that there can be no form of knowledge that is systematically distinguishable from error, no form of meaning that is free from arbitrariness. Yet the other side of the aporia that repetition cannot be epistemic, that being cannot be altogether determinate, is that there is no repetition without modification, no same without its other. These aporias are the positive conditions of knowing and being. And they are explicit in classical empiricism. The arbitrariness of the sign, the fallibility of knowledge, the creativity of the imagination, all pertain to knowledge intrinsically, the aporias that pass for skepticism.

Hume's theory is based throughout on resemblance and repetition. Yet both are aporetic, epistemologically and generically. There is no resemblance that is not accompanied by difference, and there is no similarity that is not arbitrary or applicable only in certain respects. Similarity and difference are dimensions of all things, in and out of experience. They are both inseparable and unintelligible alone. Thus, even that an idea might resemble an impression is unintelligible if they do not also differ. Otherwise there would be identity. Hume's distinction in terms of force and liveliness only masks the aporia that if ideas differ in any respects, they may differ in any others.

Hume acknowledges many of these aporias, although frequently denying that they are aporetic. For example, he presents a famous "contradictory phenomenon" to his principle that all our simple ideas are copies of simple impressions.

> Suppose therefore a person to have enjoyed his sight for thirty years, and to have become perfectly well acquainted with colours of all kinds, excepting one particular shade of blue, for instance, which it never has been his fortune to meet with. ... Now I ask, whether 'tis possible for him, from his own imagination, to supply this deficiency, and raise up to himself the idea of that particular shade. (Hume, *Treatise*, I, I, I, p. 6)

He treats this as an aberrant example, "particular and singular." He does not recognize that it expresses heresy. No theory of knowledge can be intelligible where the only means available to it is repetition. Resemblance is not an epistemic notion.

Memory is, of course, the repetitive principle *par excellence*.

> 'Tis evident, that the memory preserves the original form, in which its objects were presented, and that whereever we depart from it in recollecting any thing, it proceeds from some defect or imperfection in that faculty. (Hume, *Treatise*, I, I, II, p. 9)

Yet, memory never functions epistemically through unvarying repetition, even in Hume's theory, because only simple ideas are exact copies of impressions, and simple ideas cannot be knowledge without relations. Complex ideas are not copies but the result of association and dissociation. Even in Hume there is the important insight that knowledge can be effective only where memory is not simply duplication. Unless we add to ideas through conjunction, amplification, aggregation, and dissociation, we cannot know anything through them.

In his later discussions, Hume must acknowledge that time as well as space pertain to memory forcefully and influentially. (Hume, *Treatise*, II, III, VII, p. 432) Yet the principle of repetition, ascribed to memory intrinsically, entirely lacks temporality. This atemporality is the object of Bergson's critique of the "spatialization of time." Moreover, space is, as Hume acknowledges, as much a feature of memory and experience as is time. The conclusion is that memory is influenced by space and time intrinsically: the passage of time in experience and the location of experienced events in space characterize memory. Hume does not go quite that far, but the aporia is evident in the impossibility for memory to rest entirely and stably on a principle of repetition.

Moreover, Hume's own principle of vivacity entails that where we have strong beliefs based on custom and habit there can be no sharp distinction between memory and imagination. Memory is not duplication as much as knowledge of past experience mediated by the activities of the imagination. It is epistemic only where it may be false, transforming what we remember in relation to what we have subsequently come to know. The aporia of memory is that it is a direct form of knowledge without which we could not possess any knowledge of events, but which is nevertheless frequently erroneous, requiring supplementation by other forms of knowledge. There is in Hume no form of knowledge, no form of repetition that does not lead to the skeptical contingencies of empirical knowledge.

Hume's skepticism is both famous and prominent. And it touches on many aporias deeply, if limitedly. The reason for the qualification is that Hume is unwilling to acknowledge the aporias inherent in sensory experience, that no impressions can be simple and no ideas can be copies of impressions or things. Ideas are partial copies of what we experience, transformed creatively in the activities of internal representation. Only because creative transformations occur is it possible to develop new theories of the natural world. Only because signs are arbitrary is it possible to develop new forms of thought.

Hume's explicit aporias are found in the principles of association and the methodological principles that define classical empiricism. He describes the conditions underlying his view of association as follows:

> Were ideas entirely loose and unconnected, chance alone wou'd join them; and 'tis impossible the same simple ideas should fall regularly into complex ones (as they commonly do) without some bond of union among them, some associating quality, by which one idea naturally introduces another. (*Treatise*, I, I, IV, p. 10)

Association here serves two irreconcilable purposes: the one to explain the regularity of experience, quite neglecting the fact that the regularity of experience is not entirely of psychological origin; the other to define the conditions of knowledge and understanding. Yet no possible account of psychological regularity can be a justificatory ground for knowledge: repetition cannot be epistemic. Knowledge and experience are heretical, and the principles of association that define regularity must also admit, not simply variation, but heresy.

The methodological principle at the center of Hume's empiricism is first stated as:

> Wherever the imagination perceives a difference among ideas, it can easily produce a separation. (Hume, *Treatise*, I, I, III, p. 10)

What it becomes in the course of the discussion is stated in the Appendix:

> ... *that all our distinct perceptions are distinct existences*, and *that the mind never perceives any real connexion among distinct existences*. (Hume, *Treatise*, Appendix, p. 636)

Simple ideas are distinct ideas; and distinct ideas cannot be connected in the mind except through principles of association extrinsic to them. Given that knowledge consists of real connections among real things or ideas; given, moreover, that what can be known must be thought to inhabit synthetic relations, it follows that the mind can never know anything whatever, not even its own internal contents, without imposing its own connective associations upon them.

One way to think of Hume's position is that his principle that distinguishability entails separation is incompatible with any constructive theory of knowledge, however modest, and any constructive theory of reality. There can be no epistemology or ontology that does not rest on relations of power. Here we confront Hume's skepticism directly.

> Let men be once fully perswaded of these two principles, *That there is nothing in any object, consider'd in itself, which can afford us a reason for drawing a conclusion beyond it*; and, *That even after the observation of the frequent or constant conjunction of objects, we have no reason to draw any inference concerning any object beyond those of which we have had experience*; . . . . (Hume, *Treatise*, I, I, XII, p. 139)

To the contrary, we must reply to the first principle that there is no object that can be considered in itself, for everything is related to other things and requires from us conclusions concerning them. Rather, every inference is aporetic, caught between an individual being and the inexhaustible relationships in which it participates. We must reply to the second principle that although we may have no conclusive basis on which to infer from experiences that we have had to those that we have not encountered, there is no way to live and learn without doing so. These principles are antiheretical, but we cannot avoid the aporias in the fact that we are forced to perform such inferences. We cannot think without going beyond what is available from experience. That is the source of all epistemic heresy. Even repetition and resemblance, insofar as they are effective at different times and places, are epistemic only by transcending their origins.

In particular, knowledge and being are impossible without principles of connection, but these are incompatible with simple impressions and ideas. Morever, there is nothing in the general principles of empiricism that requires simple ideas. In both Hume and Locke, simple ideas are copies of simple impressions, giving us a representational basis for knowledge of what we perceive. Yet the idea of separation, inherent in the idea of simplicity, makes any knowledge derived from such perception impossible.

This is aporetic, not contradictory. Hume's insight is that there can be no experience from which empirical knowlege is derived that is not itself divided. If experience is taken in its aporetic complexity, then there are no simple ideas or impressions, and knowledge cannot be repetitive or representational. It is constructive and complex, continually faced with more than can be known in relation to both knower and known. If experience is conceived in terms of simple ideas and principles of association, then both simplicity and the contributions of the empirical subject make knowledge impossible. In this sense, both empirical knowledge and empirical reality are inexhaustible, while inexhaustibility is aporetic.

The heretical insight in empiricism, especially in Hume's version of it, is that empirical reality and empirical knowledge are divided inexhaustibly. This is a far stronger version of the insight, stated earlier, that finite, contingent experience admits of only heretical knowledge. What makes it stronger is that the very principle upon which knowledge is accessible and intelligible in empiricism—that all our simple ideas are copies of simple impressions—is also the condition that makes knowledge impossible.

Hume largely follows Berkeley's account of abstract ideas, emphasizing that such ideas can be intelligible only to the extent that they are determinate.

> . . . the mind cannot form any notion of quantity or quality without forming a precise notion of degrees of each; . . . . (Hume, Treatise, I, I, VII, p. 18)

This emphasis upon the determinateness of ideas closely parallels the corresponding emphasis upon simple ideas and the generation of complex ideas from them. Empiricism is based on the premise that only determinate ideas can be intelligible. What is overlooked is that "wholly determinate" ideas are unintelligible. Even the principle that distinguishability entails separability, interpreted as defining what is determinate in simple ideas and perceptions, indirectly expresses the truth that wholly determinate—that is, distinct—ideas can have no epistemic status. Otherness is required both for acquiring knowledge and for knowledge itself.

Many of the other themes in Hume's Treatise manifest similar insights into the aporetic necessity in finite experience of indeterminateness to intelligibility and truth. He argues against the infinite divisibility of space and time, in the face of most other writers and the testimony of mathematics, on the basis that no determinate conception can be formed of infinitesimal subdivisions.[18] He grants that we may form determinate and distinct ideas of different small numbers, but not of the images that pertain to the things to which they apply—for example, grains of sand. We may choose to emphasize the role of images in his arguments; the more general point is that he is insisting, as fundamental to his empiricism, that an idea can be meaningful only if it is determinate, and an idea can be determinate only if it can be separated from other ideas. The aporia is that such separation makes knowledge impossible. Closely related is his argument that what is infinitely divisible is not unitary (Hume, Treatise, I, II, II: p. 30), reflecting his understanding of the aporias of one and many. Closely related also is his view of the finiteness of extension.[19]

The fundamental heresy in empiricism is the extraordinary view that only entirely determinate ideas can be intelligible; only entirely determinate things can be real; yet, indeterminate ideas and things are necessary to knowledge.[20] This heresy of same and other produces the central aporia in Hume's theory that total determinateness is inseparable from skepticism. Only where there is otherness can there be knowledge, although knowledge is ruled entirely by the same.

These aporias and heresies play their roles in Hume's analysis of causation. All we can find, he claims, where there are causal relations, is the contiguity of cause and effect and the temporal priority of the cause in relation to the effect. Leaving aside the later arguments directed against the inadequacy of his analysis as a positive view of causation, especially to the effect that we may infer the existence of a causal relation, rather than a contingent conjunction, only where there is something stable underlying a transition, it is worth emphasizing that Hume himself is unsatisfied with his view as a theory of causation.

> Shall we then rest contented with these two relations of contiguity and succession, as affording a compleat idea of causation? ... There is a NECESSARY CONNEXION to be taken into consideration; and that relation is of much greater importance, than any of the other two above-mentioned. (Hume, *Treatise*, I, III, II, p. 77)

No such connection is to be found in experience for the reason that cause and effect can be thought of as distinct, and distinctness entails separation. Again, Hume's argument is aporetic: causation is genuine only where there is a necessary connection, while there can be perceived no such connection, necessary or otherwise, because distinct ideas must be thought of as separate. He denies that we can have knowledge of the "ultimate springs" of nature, (Hume, *Enquiry*, p. 45) yet takes the reality of such an underlying causality very seriously.

Hume denies that we can have knowledge of natural necessity yet grounds his theory repeatedly on repetition: the resemblance of ideas and impressions; the constancy of habit and custom and of causal succession, and, most radically, the rejection of every form of deviance—chance, liberty, and miracles. Despite basing his empiricism on whatever experience brings, Hume repudiates any possibility of an event that does not conform to repetition. Although a theory that denies all knowledge from experience should take as true whatever experience brings forth, other as well as same, Hume's principles of intelligibility adhere to total domination by the same: repetition, conformation, and regularity. The conjunction of divided experience with the demand for regularity is a remarkable aporia.

We can think of Hume's position as contradictory: postulating as essential to causation what cannot be ascribed to it from within his theory of experience. Following this line of thought, we may reject one side of this contradiction, concluding that his analysis of causation, based on contiguity and succession, is a full and complete theory, and that it entails that there is no necessity to causation. This is the traditional view of causation in empiricism. It entirely neglects the skeptical side of Hume's position. For Hume is arguing, through the example of causation, not that we cannot know real connections from within a divided experience, but that such connections are always aporetic. Reality is aporetic; knowledge of such reality is heretical.

Recognition of these aporias gives us a very different reading of Hume's skepticism. In particular, the familiar problem of induction is that,

> there can be no *demonstrative* arguments to prove, *that these instances, of which we have had no experience, resemble those, of which we have had experience.* (Hume, *Treatise*, I, III, VI, p. 89)

Yet, knowledge of every kind goes beyond what has been experienced. The generic aporia of knowledge is that what we know cannot be restricted to the evidence upon which it rests or the origins from which it is derived. There is a pervasive indeterminateness in knowledge, underlying the need for heresy. Every being transcends its origins; everything known transcends its conditions.

Emphasizing induction, then, tends to obscure the otherness in all forms of knowledge by suggesting that inductive knowledge is uniquely indeterminate. There is, in Hume's empiricism, a presumption of the certainty knowledge requires to be intelligible conjoined with a view of experience from which no such certainty can be derived. He claims that certainty is possible through the four relations of resemblance, contrariety, degrees in quality, and proportions in number. (Hume, *Treatise*, I, III, I, p. 70) Yet no such certainty is possible in relation to any matter of fact. The conclusion is skeptical, but the skepticism is intelligible only in relation to the posited certainty. Skepticism is the underside of a wholly determinate epistemology founded on repetition. If knowledge must be certain and entirely determinate, then where we find aporia, skepticism is the only tenable conclusion. The alternative is that both knowledge and being are aporetic, including every science. An aporetic view of being and knowing is incompatible with skepticism, not because it answers the criticisms of the skeptic, but because it rejects the postulate that only a wholly determinate knowledge is legitimate.

These heresies recur throughout Hume's analysis. For example, he assumes it necessary to offer an explanation of why, if we cannot experience a necessary connection, we believe that we do. What is required is an account of belief.

... when any impression becomes present to us, it not only transports the mind to such ideas as are related to it, but likewise communicates to them a share of its force and vivacity. (Hume, *Treatise*, I, III, VIII, p. 98)

His definition of belief is explicit:

A LIVELY IDEA RELATED TO OR ASSOCIATED WITH A PRESENT IMPRESSION. (Hume, *Treatise*, I, III, VII, p. 96)

Force and vivacity, which could not provide an adequate distinction between impressions and ideas, return in the definition of belief. What is lacking, as was lacking in relation to impressions and ideas, is an account of the epistemic nature of belief. In both cases, Hume offers a causal account of the forceful feeling of assent inherent in belief. That ideas and beliefs might be epistemic cannot follow from such a feeling. That we might strongly believe something to be true does not entail that it is true. One question is what must be added to belief to make it epistemic. The traditional answer is adequate justification or proof. Yet Hume's critique of induction shows that no empirical justification can be adequate. Justification is aporetic.

Belief is aporetic, hovering between a psychological frame of mind with emotional force and an epistemic function independent of desire. The aporia is that on the one hand there is no epistemic frame of mind that can be independent of emotion: a principle conclusively established by Spinoza. Emotion pertains to every idea.[21] On the other hand, emotional force is antagonistic to objective truth. Belief must be both a psychological and an epistemic condition inseparably, but cannot be both without aporia. Hume acknowledges this aporia explicitly.

An idea assented to *feels* different from a fictitious idea, that the fancy alone presents to us: And this different feeling I endeavour to explain by calling it a superior *force*, or *vivacity*, or *solidity*, or *firmness*. (Hume, *Treatise*, Appendix, p. 629)

There is no difference in the way in which a belief is held that can distinguish it as true or false. Truth and error occupy the same terrain. Not only is the psychological criterion inadequate: it obscures the aporia that while assent is a form of emotion, truth is not, while there is no knowledge that is not truth assented to. Knowledge is enmired in aporia in a theory that requires that all knowledge originate in lived experience.

Similarly, in the famous passage in the Appendix concerning personal identity, Hume explicitly acknowledges his confusions.[22] There is nothing in distinct perceptions that can be experienced as the self that conjoins them while there is no idea that can conjoin perceptions. He recognizes the aporia in the idea of a thinking subject, that it must derive its ideas from distinct experiences and consequently can have no idea of itself.[23] Yet he cannot avoid acknowledging that the self is forcibly present to us, however aporetically. His theory requires the self's presence for the forcible presence of anything else.

> The idea of ourselves is always intimately present to us, and conveys a sensible degree of vivacity to the idea of any other object, to which we are related. (Hume, *Treatise*, II, II, IV, p. 354)

He concludes with the aporia of personal identity, one of the most striking heresies in the history of philosophy.

> . . . all the nice and subtle questions concerning personal identity can never possibly be decided, and are to be regarded rather as grammatical than as philosophical difficulties. (Hume, *Treatise*, I, IV, IV, p. 262)

The traditional reading is that grammatical questions are somehow defective. Grammatical difficulties are not "real." The heretical reading emphasizes the aporias within personal identity: they cannot be decided because they are caught somewhere between grammar and evidence. No difficulties are *more* "real" than grammatical ones, as Wittgenstein suggests throughout his later work. These aporias are not resolved by Kant, but made more explicit. Hume confesses to skepticism: what he might have confessed to instead is aporia. Only if we posit a completely nonaporetic theory of the material world does his analysis of the self appear contradictory. It is rather aporetic and heretical.

Hume resolves his skepticism through repetition: habit and custom. Yet skepticism in its more strident forms cannot be so resolved because neither custom nor habit provides certainty. Thus, subsequent forms of empiricism have rejected the relevance of custom and habit to the problems of scientific knowledge but not repetition. Later empiricists have tended to seek a different repetition based on rules. What is obscured in this transition is the aporetic side of Hume's skepticism and view of custom.

> . . . *all our reasonings concerning causes and effects are deriv'd from nothing but custom; and that belief is more properly an act of the sensitive, than of the cogitative part of our natures.* (Hume, *Treatise*, I, IV, I, p. 183)

What is aporetic here is the contrast between the sensitive and cogitative parts of thought and experience, between feeling and knowing. It is a contrast Hume cannot sustain, although his skeptical position requires it. His view is that empirical knowledge *is* the working of custom and habit. He therefore introduces into reason a historical element, emphasizing the importance of the past and of tradition to the nature of knowledge itself.[24] We may want to say that custom and habit are attenuated and oversimplified accounts of far more complex historical and cultural relationships, but agree that empirical knowledge cannot be separated from the lived individual and social activities that constitute the conditions under which epistemic practices transpire. Such a position is aporetic again in rejecting any systematic distinction between knowledge and belief. The heretical insight in Hume's position is that that distinction cannot be sustained in relation to empirical knowledge.

There is, here, a profound insight into the nature of skepticism and its relationship to aporia. Hume cannot even define his position as skeptical without a distinction between objective knowledge and subjective belief although his view of custom entirely undercuts that distinction. Therefore, he claims, in the famous passage concerning "scepticism with regard to the senses":

> Thus the sceptic still continues to reason and believe, even tho' he asserts, that he cannot defend his reason by reason; and by the same rule he must assent to the principle concerning the existence of body, tho' he cannot pretend by any arguments of philosophy to maintain its veracity. Nature has not left this to his choice, and has doubtless esteem'd it an affair of too great importance to be trusted to our uncertain reasonings and speculations. We may well ask, *What causes induce us to believe in the existence of body*? but 'tis in vain to ask, *Whether there be body or not*? That is a point, which we must take for granted in all our reasonings. (Hume, *Treatise*, I, IV, II, p. 187)

We cannot defend reason by reason because to do so would be to reason in a circle. But we also cannot defend reason by reason because reason is heretical and changes itself. There is a fundamental aporia at the heart of all forms of reason: that knowledge cannot be derived from causes but cannot be understood without them. Hume's explicit position is that no empirical proof of the existence of body is possible or intelligible. The conclusion is that there is something fundamentally misconceived about every empirical proof. This is as true for the sciences as for philosophy. What must be added is that such an aporetic view does not make science and philosophy any more "irrational" except on the assumption of a view of reason entirely free from aporia. If skepticism cannot be practically maintained, it also cannot be eliminated. What Hume shows us is the contradictory nature of our ordinary beliefs, especially that we must believe in matter but cannot justify that belief.[25] There are real powers that we must believe in but which are not accessible to our senses.

A striking expression of this aporia is to be found in Hume's distinction in the penultimate sentence of the passage above between what causes us to believe in something and whether that belief is true. This relationship between causes and evidence, between being and knowing, is among the fundamental aporias of thought and reason. If we cannot help but believe that a proposition is true, then surely we must also believe that we know it to be true. Reciprocally, what we know to be true must be supported by causal connections in human individual and social experience that enabled us to learn it. There is no way to separate causes and proofs within human epistemic experience, but their relationship is aporetic. Knowledge cannot follow from or be intelligible in terms of causal connections, although it cannot exist without them. The conclusion is not skepticism but heresy. Hume's "skepticism" is effectively a heretical view of knowledge. What obscures this truth is that he appears to accept a nonaporetic view of knowledge behind his skepticism. We may discern here an important, if aporetic, distinction between skepticism and heresy. The former rests on the assumption that there is (in some sense) a nonaporetic form of reason that is not realizable through finite experience. The latter denies that any form of reason is free from aporia; consequently, skepticism is itself aporetic.

Similarly, the contrast between custom and reason presupposes the intelligibility of a nonaporetic form of acquired reason independent of causes. Hume acknowledges the aporias in such empirical knowledge in relation to custom, which he claims provides transitions in ideas and belief that are not founded on reason. What is aporetic is the assumption that these ideas and beliefs, these empirical connections, are not rational because they are customary. To the contrary, there is no unqualified distinction possible between knowledge and true belief or reason and custom. Knowledge *is* custom and habit as much as it is logic and argument—they too are custom and habit—with the consequent aporias that custom and habit are forms of causation and cannot be epistemic, and that logic and argument are not the sole paradigmatic forms of reason. That Hume *says* that they are does not mean that we can accept his word even for what he believes, given the rest of his account of experience. The principle behind this qualification is again that what is known always surpasses any of its manifestations.

We come to the most famous of Hume's maxims, that moral distinctions are not derived from reason because they cannot influence action.[26] If we posit his distinction between reason and passion, then all motivations belong to emotion. We have noted that Spinoza does not accept this distinction, but associates all ideas with emotions, distinguishing the latter into actions and passions. There is, then, an important if heretical reply to Hume: emotion is as rational as proof and argument. Reason is not to be distinguished from emotion but from error, futility, and insensitivity. What is missing in this reply is acknowledgment of the aporia within the emotional side of reason. It is missing in Spinoza himself, who deeply acknowledged many of the aporias of being and knowing.

The aporia, heretically presented by Hume, is that reason as it stands, even including passions, cannot move us to action. Or rather, looking ahead to Kierkegaard, there is an "infinite" gap between deliberation and action, not to be crossed by any intelligible form of thought. Action bears its own rationality distinct from that of thought and deliberation, but also from that of emotion.

Hume's arguments are given in two forms. One is based on a correspondence view of reason; passions cannot be true or false because they are "compleat in themselves" and cannot agree or disagree with matters of fact. We have seen that agreement is not an epistemic condition. The fundamental aporia here, however, does not concern the deficiencies of a correspondence view of truth but the idea that emotions are complete in themselves while propositions or ideas are not. Emotions are *facts*; propositions refer. The aporia is that no sign can avoid being a fact, complete in itself.[27] This is as true of linguistic signs as of emotional, volitional, and active signs.[28] All signs belong to the natural and human world as much as they belong to the spheres of meaning. The aporia concerns how a natural being can be representational.

Hume's other argument is more famous:

> ... reason, in a strict and philosophical sense, can have an influence on our conduct only after two ways: Either when it excites a passion by informing us of the existence of something which is a proper object of it; or when it discovers the connexion of causes and effects, so as to afford us means of exerting any passion. (Hume, *Treatise*, III, I, I, p. 459)

What is aporetic is that reason *must* have an influence on our conduct, and must have this influence whether it is scientific or moral. A scientific reason that cannot influence desire cannot be effective in human experience. The alternative is a passive, mirroring, contemplative reason with no efficacy whatever, rather like a material substratum.

It follows on Hume's account that there can be no reason that is not constituted by desire, influencing it and influenced by it. There is therefore something profoundly incongruous about the distinction between facts and values: the facts that are allegedly distinct from values cannot function in human experience apart from value and desire. There is no room for values and desire in relation to objective truth, but there is no truth derivable from human experience that is not constituted by desire.

A traditional criticism of Hume is that he is confuses psychological with logical accounts of how belief and evidence function. What is overlooked in this criticism is that causal and logical accounts cannot be separated. The reason is again that knowledge must not only be effective, it must be acquired, and the acquisition of knowledge is always at once causal and logical. Because a logical analysis of any epistemic condition can never be intelligibly derived from or related to a causal analysis, the complex of factors is aporetic. Facts and values are both distinct and inseparable.

What we find in Hume is that the notion of an objective, independent reason uncontaminated by motives, emotions, volitions, and actions is always contaminated by the incompleteness of desire. Reason is always both influenced by desire and incomplete (or inexhaustible). Hume describes the result as skepticism, but does not reach a skeptical conclusion. Rather, the result is aporetic: reason is always pervaded by desire and error. Yet error and desire are not "contaminations," for without them there could be no reason whatever. They are necessary to the positive side of reason while sources of its limitations.

There are many other heresies and aporias in empiricism, especially in Hume's version of it. Some of these are so singular that they belie the suggestion that Hume is the more orthodox empiricist compared with Hobbes and Locke. Some are so important that they have deeply colored all subsequent understandings of experience.

Perhaps the most important and famous feature of Hume's empiricism is his rejection of metaphysics, which has laid the basis for all subsequent attacks on the metaphysical tradition and has become virtually equivalent with empiricism itself.[29] All forms of empiricism reject aprioristic forms of metaphysics as not based on evidence derived from experience. This conviction has played a part in the extreme adulation of the natural sciences that has marked much of post-Enlightenment thought. To the natural reply that there is nothing intrinsically unempirical about metaphysics, Hume offers a striking response (in Philo's words):

> I have still asserted that we have no *data* to establish any system of cosmogony. Our experience, so imperfect in itself and so limited both in extent and duration, can afford us no probable

conjecture concerning the whole of things. (Hume, *Dialogues Concerning Natural Religion*, VII, p. 726)

The irony is that no form of thought has since become more totalizing than science itself. There is also the aporia that every form of knowledge transcends the evidence upon which it may be said to rest.

Far more important to metaphysics, however, are Philo's subsequent remarks that concern the wild and untrammeled nature of the speculative imagination.

What you ascribe to the fertility of my invention, replied Philo, is entirely owing to the nature of the subject. . . . Without any great effort of thought, I believe that I could, in an instant, propose other systems of cosmogony which would have some faint appearance of truth, though it is a thousand, a million to one if either yours or any one of mine be the true system. (Hume, *Dialogues Concerning Natural Religion*, VIII, p. 729)

The key notion here is the ease with which we may produce, "without any great effort of thought," other plausible cosmological and metaphysical systems.

That the creative imagination is capable of producing great systems of fabulous design that have little resemblance to actual conditions is of fundamental importance, not only to art but to science. Two qualifications must be added; First, it is extraordinarily difficult to produce a compelling imaginative construction of great breadth and power. The testimony of art is that greatness, mating invention with compulsion, is very difficult to achieve. Second, without such an inventive, heretical capacity, science would have little power. The construction of extraordinary visions of great compass is required by any theoretical activity, from science to philosophy to art.

Philo's words express a major effort to curtail the heretical side of philosophy and science. They are closely related to the antiheretical impulse within the empiricistic principle that all our knowledge comes from experience in repetitive ways. That the greatest works of human thought are heretical entails that the creative side of human thought is fundamental, with the proviso that its fruits must be confirmed by the collection of evidence.

The first qualification above is the most radical, and it is the one most pertinent to metaphysics. It is extraordinarily difficult to present a grand vision of the natural and human world that is both heretical and plausible. The heresy emphasizes the importance of novelty and transformation. The plausibility pertains to all forms of validation. Hume's rejection of metaphysics rests on the conviction that it is easy to produce a plausible account of things free from the bonds of evidence. Analogously, it is easy to produce an imaginative work of art that compels our assent by its structure and forcefulness. Yet it is not easy at all to produce a compelling and plausible vision. Given the breadth and complexity of human experience, it is among the greatest of human achievements to develop a systematic theory that is both compelling and plausible. Truth here lies between the powers of the imagination and the bounds of evience. The space is filled by heresy.

Philo's words are presented in the context of natural theology. He argues that "A total suspense of judgment is here our only reasonable resource." (Hume, *Dialogues*, VIII, p. 733) Yet, he concludes that "no one has a deeper sense of religion impressed on his mind or pays more profound adoration to the Divine Being as he discovers himself to reason in the inexplicable contrivance and artifice of nature." (Hume, *Dialogues*, XII, p. 753) One view is that Hume is unwilling to carry his skeptical reasoning concerning natural religion to its rational conclusions. An alternative is that the *Dialogues* manifest the aporias of natural theology and of reason, which must be constrained by intelligible rules yet capable of heretical invention, breaking every rule. The importance of metaphysical speculation is to manifest the aporias inherent in inexhaustible being and the heresies inherent in all forms of understanding. The reason why all forms of thought, including science, lead to metaphysics, in its speculative heresies, is that metaphysical thought has historically manifested the aporetic side of human thought more profoundly than any other form of thought, including literature and art. What these have offered, in relation to metaphysics, is the explicit presence of those aporias that metaphysical heresies have hidden from themselves. Without art and practice, metaphysics tends to lose its aporetic convictions.

We find in Hume recurrent acknowledgment of the aporetic nature of experience and of the heretical nature of empirical knowledge. Such acknowledgments are to be found even in the midst of his most strident arguments against metaphysical speculation. In the context of his arguments against the necessity of causation, for example, he comes very close to Kant's antinomies concerning the beginning of the world.

> Whatever is produc'd without any cause, is produc'd by *nothing*; or in other words, has nothing for its cause. But nothing can never be a cause, no more than it can be something, or equal to two right angles. . . .
>   . . . 'Tis sufficient only to observe, that when we exclude all causes we really do exclude them, and neither suppose nothing nor the object itself to be the causes of the existence; and

> consequently can draw no argument from the absurdity of these
> suppositions to prove the absurdity of that exclusion. (Hume,
> *Treatise*, I, III, III: p. 81)

In the first place, there is no necessity to the presence of a cause, therefore no cause is required for the origin of things. Things may, we say, be
caused by nothing. In the second place, however, because there is no
necessity to a cause, nothing is not a cause either. The aporia in Hume's
arguments is that he excludes "nothing" as a cause, but cannot exclude
its relevance. Even if we deny a causal relationship between nothing and
something, nothing remains a possibility in the absence of causal necessity. We have seen the similar aporia in relation to the impossibility of
thinking of something as nonexistent—that is, thinking of nothing. That
we can only think of something as existing does not mean that nothing is
impossible. Nonbeing is aporetic regardless of our view on its intelligibility.

We may conclude our discussion of Hume's empiricism by considering more carefully the hypothesis that it is aporia that Hume has identified, explicitly if incompletely. What he has not done is to recognize
that aporias are sources of rather than obstacles to knowledge.

> But knowledge and probability are of such contrary and dis-
> agreeing natures, that they cannot well run insensibly into each
> other, and that because they will not divide, but must be either
> entirely present, or entirely absent. ... I had almost said, that
> this was certain; but I reflect, that it must reduce *itself*, as
> well as every other reasoning, and from knowledge degenerate
> into probability.
>
> Since therefore all knowledge resolves itself into probabil-
> ity, and becomes at last of the same nature with that evidence,
> which we employ in common life, ... (Hume, *Treatise*, I, IV, I:
> p. 181)

All knowledge degenerates into probability, including even the knowledge of this degeneration. This may be called skepticism, but it is aporia:
reason is constituted by unreason.[30] Although empiricism became dogmatic after Hume, its understanding of itself is aporetic because it can
affirm its own limitations only limitedly, probabilistically. The aporia is
that probability presupposes a nonprobable knowledge as the basis of
the argument that all knowledge degenerates into probability.

Hume recognizes, as few in the tradition before and after him
have, the ways in which finite knowledge pertains to itself aporetically.
What must be emphasized is the aporetic nature of both knowledge
and skepticism.

Reason first appears in possession of the throne, prescribing laws, and imposing maxims, with an absolute sway and authority. Her enemy, therefore, is oblig'd to take shelter under her protection, and by making use of rational arguments to prove the fallaciousness and imbecility of reason, produces, in a manner, a patent under her hand and seal. This patent has at first an authority, proprtion'd to the present and immediate authority of reason, from which it is deriv'd. But as it is suppos'd to be contradictory to reason, it gradually diminishes the force of that governing power, and its own at the same time; till at last they both vanish away into nothing, by a regular and just diminution. The sceptical and dogmatical reasons are of the same kind, tho' contrary in their operation and tendency; .... (Hume, *Treatise*, I, IV, I, pp. 186-87)

Skepticism argues from reason to probability, using the devices of reason to undermine her.[31] Hume recognizes here the similarity of rationalism and skepticism, postulating the certainty of reason and the self-referential nature of knowledge. The aporia is that there is no form of empirical knowledge that can assert the intrinsic limitations of knowledge without confronting its own limitations. What follows is not dogmatism and certainty, but an aporetic fallibility in which the grounds of knowledge are always in question, always disruptive.[32]

Hume comes close to describing the phenomenology of aporia when he describes the conclusion of his skepticism. It is a powerful description of heresy.

I am first affrighted and confounded with that forelorn solitude, in which I am plac'd in my philosophy, and fancy myself some strange uncouth monster, who not being able to mingle and unite in society, has been expell'd all human commerce, and left utterly abandon'd and disconsolate. ... (Hume, *Treatise*, I, IV, VII, p. 264)

Here then I find myself absolutely and necessarily determin'd to live, and talk, and act like other people in the common affairs of life. But notwithstanding that my natural propensity, and the course of my animal spirits and passions reduce me to this indolent belief in the general maxims of the world, I still feel such remains of my former disposition, that I am ready to throw all my books and papers into the fire, and resolve never more to renounce the pleasures of life for the sake of reasoning and philosophy. (Hume, *Treatise*, I, IV, VII, p. 269)

Hume describes these as the "sentiments of my spleen and indolence." (Hume, *Treatise*, I, IV, VII, p. 270) What they are is an explicit expression of philosophic heresy. Hume's position is both profoundly aporetic and aware of itself aporetically. For this reason, all subsequent philosophies, whatever their nature, must in one way or another be empiricistic, whatever their claims to be otherwise.

8 KANT: THE HERESY OF APORIA

WITH Kant, aporia becomes explicit in far-reaching ways. Yet we cannot say that aporia is more explicit in Kant than in Heraclitus or Hume. Nor can we say that aporia is expressed by Kant in a more thoroughgoing way. What we may say is that aporia is raised to a new level of explicitness and reflexiveness. It is the focus of the critical position. The fundamental aporia of Kant's metaphysical theory, that of the supersensible, is an explicit attempt both to resolve the aporias he finds at every other level of experience and to accommodate the apodeictic certainty that he takes to be required for the legitimacy of the cognitive faculties. The a priori certainty at the core of Kant's theory rests on an aporetic foundation.

Given our endeavor, the place to begin is with the antinomies, interpreted as aporias. Yet we cannot do them justice without prior discussion of the purity of reason that constitutes the basis of the first *Critique*. What Kant says at the very beginning of the *Critique* concerns the aporetic nature of reason:

> Human reason has this peculiar fate that in one species of its knowledge it is burdened by questions which, as prescribed by the very nature of reason itself, it is not able to ignore, but which, as transcending all its powers, it is also not able to answer. (CPR, Preface, First Edition, p. 7)[1]

This aporia, that reason is faced with questions that it cannot escape but cannot answer, is at the center of Kant's critical theory. The *Critiques* do not propose to resolve this aporia, but to establish its presence and to explain its nature. Kant takes it to be the foundation of the certainty that science requires for its intelligibility. For he accepts Hume's "skeptical" aporia that knowledge derived from the senses is contingent and therefore defective. What is required, according to Kant, is that empirical knowledge rest on a transcendental, a priori, and certain foundation although that foundation does not make scientific knowledge any more certain and although its apriority is aporetic.

For Kant concludes his first *Critique* by emphasizing that pure reason cannot be ignored, not because it is an irresistible human tendency, but because it is the foundation of the possibility of science. The result is a heretical view of metaphysics:

> For the same reason metaphysics is also the full and complete development of human reason. Quite apart from its influence, as science, in connection with certain specific ends, it is an indispensable discipline. For in dealing with reason it treats of those elements and highest maxims which must form the basis of the very *possibility* of some sciences, and of the *use* of all. That, as mere speculation, it serves rather to prevent errors than to extend knowledge, does not detract from its value. On the contrary this gives it dignity and authority, . . . preventing those who labour courageously and fruitfully on its behalf from losing sight of the supreme end, the happiness of all mankind. (CPR, p. 665)

The limits of pure speculative reason that define the antinomies and establish the dialectic of pure reason are essential to the possibility of both science and morality. The aporia that one and the same world is to be understood without contradiction as falling under both necessity and freedom is dependent on the same supersensible realm whose conditions constitute the foundations of science. Moreover, the certainty possible in relation to phenomena rests on the same aporetic foundation. A profound heresy in Kant is that apodeictic truth is a consequence of aporia.

We may consider the antinomies and paralogisms, not as "contradictions" that express the deficiencies of pure reason—defects it is the purpose of metaphysics to resolve—but as expressions of the aporias that make scientific knowledge possible. Such a heresy requires that the antinomies be regarded as profound expressions of the nature of reason and intelligibility.

First Antinomy:
    The world has a beginning in time, and is also limited as regards space.

> The world has no beginning, and no limits in space; it is
> infinite as regards both time and space. (CPR, p. 396)

"If we assume that the world has no beginning in time, then up to every given moment an eternity has elapsed, ..." If there was a beginning, then before it there was only "empty time. Now no coming to be of a thing is possible in an empty time, ..." (CPR, p. 397)

The arguments assume that the beginning of the world and its limitation in space are free from aporia. If the world cannot have begun then there must have been no beginning. The alternative is that the beginning is aporetic. Yet the aporia pertains not only to the beginning of the world, but to the world itself. One reply is that there is no world, simply the collection of all beings. Yet we cannot think of "all beings" except as an aggregate. We cannot think without aporia of either the totality of things or its absence.[2] To say that "the world" is not a determinate concept does not eliminate the aporia, any more than to say that the beginning of the world is indeterminate. Determinateness and indeterminateness are aporetic separately or together. The world is aporetic because it is both an inexhaustible manyness—all beings—and one—the totality of all things. Kant's arguments here pertain more deeply to the aporias of the world and its totality than to its beginning and end.

Kant is neither the first nor last to emphasize the aporias of time. We cannot think of time itself beginning because every beginning presupposes time. We cannot think of time unending because that would entail an actual infinite. Time cannot be thought except dividedly. McTaggart's arguments also make this point. We must think of time in terms of two successions of events: earlier and later; past, present, and future. The former is identical in structure with a nontemporal sequence based on geometric relations—for example, left and right; the latter presupposes time itself, for it assumes the intelligibility of the movement from past to future as well as the changing status of past events with the changing future. Time requires at least two conflicting modes of thought for its intelligibility.[3] What must be added is that time itself is aporetic, not merely our thinking of it.

There is no thought or understanding of time free from aporia. Included are not only Bergson's criticisms of the "spatialization" of time, but Heidegger's and Whitehead's critiques as well. The most felicitous interpretation of the position Bergson rejects is not that time is extensive, but that it is free from aporia. The true nature of time according to Bergson is that the present includes the past and future intrinsically, entailing that time is as indeterminate as it is determinate, a pervasive field of aporias.

Kant's antinomies are particularly striking in expressing aporia explicitly and directly. He does not intend that they be regarded as contradictions and explicitly rejects such an interpretation. It is not that we must assert that the world has a beginning but also no beginning, a limit in space and also no limit, contradictions without resolution. The aporia is resolved in terms of the unconditioned, a pervasive aporia.

> For a given conditioned, reason demands on the side of the conditions—to which as the conditions of synthetic unity the understanding subjects all appearances—absolute totality, and in so doing converts the category into a transcendental idea. . . . Reason makes this demand in accordance with the principle that if *the conditioned is given, the entire sum of conditions, and consequently the absolutely unconditioned* (through which alone the conditioned has been possible) *is also given.* (CPR, p. 386)

We cannot think what is finite and conditioned except in terms of its completion in what is unconditioned. But we cannot think of what is unconditioned except aporetically. Consequently, what is finite also must be aporetic. Kant does not explicitly take this final step. It would entail that science is as aporetic as art and philosophy. Yet apodeictic certainty is as aporetic as freedom from rules.

Although in his claims to certainty, Kant appears to deny it, there is no part of his system that is not suffused with aporia. The different parts contribute aporias to each other; more important, each is aporetic relative to the others—especially, freedom in relation to necessity, the supersensible in relation to phenomenal experience. This pervasive aporia, variously characterized as reality in relation to appearance, noumena in relation to phenomena, morality in relation to science, lies within every other fundamental notion. It is, however, disclosed only after pure speculative reason itself has been shown to be aporetic. What is left is the aporia of pure practical reason. It is as if practice does not demand freedom from aporia while speculative reason requires the absolute determinateness of the same.

Both the world and time are aporetic, in part because each contains the unconditioned as essential to its intelligibility. We might reply that there is nothing unconditioned, that being is always conditioned and finite. Yet finiteness is aporetic because finite being is inexhaustible, inseparably same and other. Time is both a series in the same of earlier and later and a series divided by the otherness of past, present, and future. The world is both the aggregate of all finite beings and the inexhaustible promise of novel beings. Each of the antinomies expresses a particular form of the aporia of same and other.

Second Antinomy:
>Every composite substance in the world is made up of sim-
>ple parts, and nothing anywhere exists save the simple or what is
>composed of the simple.

>No composite thing in the world is made up of simple parts,
>and there nowhere exists in the world anything simple. (CPR,
>p. 402)

If we imagine the elimination of all composition, all complexity,
and nothing is simple, then nothing would remain.

If we imagine that there are simples, then they cannot be combined in space, which is a complex manifold.

These arguments are less decisive than those for the first antinomy. Time and space cannot be thought without aporia: they contain
their own dividedness. Complexity and simplicity are aporetic together:
they comprise a complementary pair. Nothing can be simple and be
combined with other simples through composition. Nothing can be complex and composed of simples. We have seen, in discussing Leibniz (who
is clearly present here), the implausibility of the view that if there are
complexes there must be simples. There might be complexes only, and
complexes of complexes indefinitely. What is required to complete the
argument is the view that only what is simple or fully determinate in the
same can be real.

The aporia here is that of same and other. A single being, if simple,
cannot be combined with other beings since complexity is a form of
otherness. The complex being is both singular and many. The reply, that
we cannot think of any being except as both one and many, one being
composed of many parts, is aporetic because we cannot think of one
and many together.

Third Antinomy:
>Causality in accordance with laws of nature is not the only
>causality from which the appearances of the world can one and
>all be derived. To explain these appearances it is necessary to
>assume that there is another causality, that of freedom.

>There is no freedom; everything in the world takes place
>solely in accordance with laws of nature. (CPR, p. 409)

If there were nothing but natural causality, then there would be no
explanation of the sequence of all natural events.

If there were an extramundane cause of all beings, then its action
at the time it occurred would be inexplicable, arbitrary.

This is a central antinomy in Kant's theory. It becomes the focus of his view of both practical reason and natural teleology. We cannot think of nature except as falling under design. We must think of ourselves, agents and subjects, as falling under freedom. Yet the arguments given here do not speak to the central dialectics of the relevant issues. Rather, Kant's arguments (again with Leibniz in mind) are that natural causality is incomplete without an extramundane cause, while any such extramundane cause must be aporetic. Natural causality and the mundane world are aporetic together. If there were only natural causality, the question would remain of how such a relationship could be established. If there were extramundane causality, the question would remain of how it could act except through natural causality.[4] Each requires the other. The complementarity of same and other lies profoundly within Kant's own theory of the relation between noumena and phenomena, things in themselves and appearances, each indeterminate without the other, while their relation is aporetic.[5]

The aporia of freedom in relation to necessity is at the heart of Kant's theory from the first to the third *Critique*. To read the first *Critique* primarily in terms of its attempt to define the certainty he ascribes to the underlying a priori rules of the understanding overlooks the overall structure of that work, not to mention the entire system. For, as Kant describes in the Preface to the Second Edition,

> Thus it does indeed follow that all possible speculative knowledge of reason is limited to mere objects of *experience*. But our further contention must also be duly borne in mind, namely, that though we cannot *know* these objects as things in themselves, we must yet be in position at least to *think* them as things in themselves; otherwise we should be landed in the absurd conclusion that there can be appearance without anything that appears. (CPR, p. 27)

Taken out of context, what is suggested is merely that signs must have referents. The context, however, is quite different.

> So far, therefore, as our Critique limits speculative reason, it is indeed *negative*; but since it thereby removes an obstacle which stands in the way of the employment of practical reason, nay threatens to destroy it, it has in reality a *positive* and very important use. At least this is so, immediately we are convinced that there is an absolutely necessary *practical* employment of pure reason—the *moral*—in which it inevitably goes beyond the limits of sensibility. Though [practical] reason, in thus proceeding,

requires no assistance from speculative reason, it must yet be assured against its opposition, that reason may not be brought into conflict with itself. (CPR, p. 26-27)

There are two inseparable purposes to the first *Critique*: first, to ground the possibility of "knowledge *a priori*; and, in addition, to furnish satisfactory proofs of the laws which form the *a priori* basis of nature, regarded as the sum of the objects of experience . . . ." (CPR p. 23); second, to establish the possibility of practical—moral—reason, in particular, to show that the idea of freedom, however aporetic it may be, does not contradict itself. The limits imposed on speculation, conjoined with the possibility of freedom, transform pure reason into practical reason. The entire first *Critique* is the establishment of this transformation, resting on an aporetic but not contradictory foundation.

> For what necessarily forces us to transcend the limits of experience and of all appearances is the *unconditioned*, which reason, by necessity and by right, demands in things in themselves, as required to complete the series of conditions. If, then, on the supposition that our empirical knowledge conforms to objects as things in themselves, we find that the unconditioned *cannot be thought without contradiction*, and that when, on the other hand, we suppose that our representation of things, as they are given to us, does not conform to these things as they are in themselves, but that these objects, as appearances, conform to our mode of representation, *the contradiction vanishes*; . . . . (CPR, p. 24)

We cannot think finite, conditioned being without thinking infinite, unconditioned being. But we cannot think unconditioned being without aporia. And this aporia does not vanish, as the antinomies and paralogisms show. Kant's entire analysis is devoted to showing that the "contradiction" is an aporia in the sense that we are not thinking two contradictory properties of the same being in the same respects. The analysis is aporetic in the sense that the unresolvable tensions involved in the opposition of noumena and phenomena, unconditioned and conditioned, freedom and necessity are at the heart of the critical enterprise and remain there. The transcendental ideas that express the departure of pure speculative reason from possible experience—freedom, immortality, and God—are irresistible moments in the dialectic of scientific understanding.

> *Fourth Antinomy:*
>   There belongs to the world, either as its part or as its cause, a being that is absolutely necessary.

An absolutely necessary being nowhere exists in the world, nor does it exist outside the world as its cause.

Conditioned being presupposes unconditioned being as its cause.
Unconditioned being "conflicts with the dynamical law of the determination of all appearances in time; . . . ." (CPR, pp. 415-16)

This antinomy extends the application of pure speculative reason to the unconditioned, implicitly to God, and adds little cosmologically to the second and third antinomies. The argument is important, however, because it indicates the movement between the conditioned and unconditioned that characterizes pure speculative reason. The beginning of the world and its totality are aporetic because the world is reciprocally conditioned and unconditioned, finite and infinite. Even if we entirely reject the intelligibility of unconditionedness, finite being is still aporetic. The pervasive aporia of same and other is transformed into the unending aporias of inexhaustible finiteness.

The four antinomies all concern the movement from finite beings to the world in which such finite beings are situated. They all involve a cosmological movement whereby the universe is thought as a whole. It is a contradiction to think of the cosmos as a whole, except that we cannot, in Kant's view, avoid thinking of finite beings as a totality. The relevant aporias establish the foundation of freedom and practical reason.

I would argue against extending reason to the totality of the world, to being from finite beings.[6] The totality is unintelligible. However, it is not that the totality is contradictory while finite beings are free from contradiction. Finite beings are both aporetic and inexhaustible. Instead, if aporia is the result of thinking of the world as a whole, and if there is no such whole that can be an object of thought, then we are required to think *through* instead of *away from* the aporias of finite and inexhaustible beings. The infinite is a poor substitute for aporetic inexhaustibility. Freedom is to be found, not beyond possible experience but within it; among natural laws, not in contravention of their necessity. It is, however, to be found there only in aporetic form.

The antinomies directly express the aporetic nature of Kant's theory. Yet aporias are found at every level and in every one of the *Critiques*. What may be undertaken at this point is a review of the structure of the *Critiques* to examine the aporias inherent in the a priori principles that constitute their intelligibility.

The central issues in the Preface to the First Edition of the first *Critique* concern what Kant calls "metaphysics": "the battlefield of these endless controversies that 'transcend the limits of experience' and 'are no longer subject to any empirical test.' " (CPR, p. 7) The Preface, therefore, defines the aporias of metaphysics in relation to pure speculative reason's transcendence of the limits of experience. This transcendence is in Kant's view necessary to the very possibility of knowledge. Therefore, the movement of reason beyond the limits of experience, which generates the unending controversies that comprise metaphysics, is required for the possibility of science.[7]

Two aporias lie here at the center of the plan of the first *Critique*: (1) the basis of natural science is given to it, not from nature, but from reason apart from all possible experience; (2) this pure transcendental basis in reason makes natural science possible. Yet, how can what is given to knowledge by reason itself, transcendentally, when reason in its pure form is aporetic, produce apodeictic certainty? And how can anything involving the facts of nature follow from a pure reason entirely independent of experience?[8] It is an aporia in Kant's theory that there can be no logical relationship between possible experience and pure reason. Pure reason's aporias are the foundation of certain truth. This aporia is manifested in the striking fact that nothing whatever follows from the categories of the understanding for any empirical science. Kant does not hold—no major philosopher other than Leibniz holds—that the contingent truths of the natural sciences follow logically from the a priori truths of reason. Even if there were such truths—and they are, in Kant, typically aporetic—they could comprise no foundation for science.

Moreover, the aporias of pure speculative reason comprise the foundation, not merely of the certainty inherent in a natural science, but of moral freedom. Logical necessity is inherent in the a priori conditions of the understanding while freedom is inherent in the purity with which reason can divorce itself from phenomena. Kant's solution to this aporia, that necessity pertains to phenomena while freedom pertains to things in themselves, defines the aporia of the relationship of the supersensible to sensible experience. If these are interpreted as things and appearances, then there can be no intelligible relationship between them. Apodeictic certainty is possible only to the extent that what we know are not things themselves, but only appearances. Freedom is then possible through a return to the things themselves although it is impossible to know them. Kant claims that the result is the establishment of morality and religion on firm foundations.

> But, above all, there is the inestimable benefit, that all objections to morality and religion will be for ever silenced, ...
> (CPR, p. 30)

The first *Critique* begins, after the Preface in which the entire system is reviewed, with the question of how knowledge may be derived from possible experience. Kant distinguishes the claim that "all our knowledge begins with experience" from the claim "that it all arises out of experience," (CPR, p. 41) a distinction central to his view of synthetic a priori knowledge. The issue concerns the legitimacy of a reason transcendent of the limits of possible experience. That reason may supply certain aspects of our knowledge from itself does not entail that what is so supplied is knowledge.

We have considered in connection with empiricism the aporias of innate ideas, in particular that a knowledge that is in this sense pure, not originating in experience and subject to its confirmations, cannot be knowledge. What Kant means by a priori knowledge is knowledge absolutely independent of all experience, therefore absolutely independent of any tests lying outside itself, in this sense not knowledge at all. His primary example is that of mathematics, which he contrasts throughout with metaphysics. Yet mathematics is deeply aporetic on this view and perhaps on any other. It is true about the natural world, and holds in possible experience, although it is entirely self-sustaining. If mathematics is a priori true, based on deductive inferences, how can it apply to possible experience? If it is derived from or projected onto possible experience, how can it be apodeictically true, based entirely on deductive relationships? It is suspended forever between irrelevance and proof. Moreover, there remain within it two additional aporias. The first is how a creative imagination can have more fruitful empirical applications the more it frees itself from empirical constraints. This aporia of the free imagination applies to mathematics as well as art. The second is that of epistemic fallibility: however deductive and universal mathematical knowledge may be, it does not and cannot eliminate the possibility of error. It can only limit the kinds of errors that pertain to it.

Kant's famous distinction between analytic and synthetic judgments, the former where the predicate is entirely contained in the subject, the latter where it is not, is then also aporetic. For the distinction depends on the notion of being "contained in" or "belonging to" the subject, where such a notion embodies whatever we can know of that subject. Kant's example of an a priori mathematical judgment, $7+5=12$, makes the aporia explicit, though he denies it in this form. He claims that:

> ... the concept of the sum of 7 and 5 contains nothing save the union of the two numbers into one, and in this no thought is being taken as to what that single number may be which combines both. (CPR, pp. 52-53)

Yet it is far from clear what the "sum of 7 and 5" contains. What is in question are the limits of any concept, however mathematical, scientific, or empirical. In a heretical epistemology, no concept and nothing known, even a priori, can be entirely determinate, simply the same with itself. Whether the sum of any two numbers is entirely determinate, and from what it is derived, are precisely at issue. Analytic judgments are possible only to the extent that the relevant concepts are determinate, while because no concepts are altogether determinate, and there is indeterminateness complementary with determinateness in all knowledge and being, every judgment is synthetic. This mixture of analytic and synthetic judgment is what Kant calls synthetic a priori. It does not derive from pure reason, but from the otherness inherent in all knowledge, including contingent empirical knowledge. Any empirical truth can be made analytic. The disadvantages of doing so argue for a heretical view of empirical knowledge in which same and other wage unending struggle.

Kant's first topic after the Introduction concerns the nature of possible experience, defined in terms of *intuition* and *sensibility*:

> Objects are *given* to us by means of sensibility, and it alone yields us *intuitions*; they are *thought* through the understanding, and from the understanding arise *concepts*. (CPR, p. 65)

The form in which "we represent to ourselves objects as outside us" is that of space, outer sensibility. The form in which intuitions of ourselves are represented is that of time, "a pure form of sensible intuition," (CPR, p. 75) "the form of inner sense, that is, of the intuition of ourselves and of our inner sense." (CPR, p. 77) It follows that "time is the formal a priori condition of all appearances whatsoever." (CPR, p. 77) An explicit aporia is at the center of this view.

> Alterations are real, this being proved by change of our own representations—even if all outer appearances, together with their alterations be denied. (CPR, p. 79)

> This form [of time] is not to be looked for in the object in itself, but in the subject to which the object appears, nevertheless, it belongs really and necessarily to the appearance of this object. (CPR, p. 80)

Time is real, along with change, because internal representations change even if outer appearances do not. Indeed, only by the changing of our internal representations can the constancy of external objects be intelligible. The conclusion is that (internal) appearances are "real"—an aporia that pervades Kant's view of possible experience. For experiences are real even if they are not the only reality. But reality, then, along with time, is aporetic because we cannot conjoin inner and outer realities under a concept.

To this we add the aporia that the transcendental aesthetic, defining the conditions of sensible knowledge, "should have that certainty and freedom from doubt which is required of any theory that is to serve as an organon." (CPR, p. 85) Kant moves throughout his theory of the understanding from a heretical view of empirical knowledge—emphasizing its contingency—to requiring that it rest on an indubitable foundation. Two questions then arise: whether certain knowledge can survive the aporias of contingent knowledge; and whether contingent knowledge can be related to its certain and indubitable foundations in a way free from aporia. There is throughout Kant's theory the question of how, even if there were absolutely necessary and indubitable synthetic a priori truths, they could in the least influence contingent scientific laws that can be known only through empirical observation.

Time is aporetic because it inhabits the midworld that comprises the relationship of nature to experience. That time should pertain objectively to nature and be derived from it confronts us with the first antinomy of the beginning of the world. The aporia concerns the being of a time "in" which events transpire, because time "is nothing" without events. In this sense, alteration and change both belong to time and can be understood only through time, aporetically.

> Time is not something which exists of itself, or which inheres in things as an objective determination, and it does not, therefore, remain when abstraction is made of all subjective conditions of its intuition. (CPR, p. 76)

Although Kant interprets this aporia in terms of the determination of time apart from things in themselves, it is rather that time cannot be thought either to belong to things and events or to be independent of their reality. Time is unintelligible except as a divided condition of natural being and experience. Moreover, it is not even here an equal condition of all being and experience—for example, of mathematical structures and patterns or of works of art. These aporias are transformed by Kant into that of the form of inner intuition, which expresses the possibility of sensible intuition but cannot both express the multiplicity of indeterminateness that pertains to time and experience and provide a basis for the certainty that rests on the unified manifold. Another way of putting this, expressed by McTaggart in his divided view of time, is that time expresses both the determinateness of natural being and events, *in time*, and the indeterminateness that comprises the alternatives of a future "not yet determined."[9] Time is both the determinate historical condition of natural being and a plenitude of a not yet determinate future. Events are both earlier and later, forever the same, and past, present, and future, divided by an emergent history. Closely related is the single dimension of passage that pertains to time, because that one dimension makes unintelligible alternatives and variations *of time*, while we can think of the future only in terms of variations and alternatives *in time*.

The generic conditions of sensibility according to Kant are time (but not space) and the consciousness of self that determines the unity of the manifold. The latter aporia is perhaps the most striking of those that constitute his view of possible experience. The unity of experience for a given subject is an absolutely necessary condition, but cannot be derived from sensory intuition. Kant accepts Hume's argument that sensible experience gives rise to a divided and contingent object, making the notion of unified experience unintelligible. The self possesses a double status, both a (unified) condition of the unity of apperception and an objective (but divided) appearance under intuition. This status is doubly aporetic: of the self objectively, because it can be known empirically only as both contingent and divided into the multiplicity of intuitions that constitute it; and of the self transcendentally, because it is known to be a single constitutive condition of experience but cannot be known with any sensible determination.[10]

These transcendental notions, of time, space, and the self, constitute the aporetic conditions of possible experience, and inhabit the midworld of aporias of same and other to which Kant's system recurrently returns. The larger architectonic of the first *Critique* begins by defining the a priori conditions of the certainty required by natural science in terms of transcendental notions that are aporetic through and through, then moves from this foundational grounding of empirical knowledge to the paralogisms, antinomies, deductions, and dialectics that constitute the transcendental ideas. Empirical knowledge requires the foundation given by pure a priori knowledge, but the latter is thoroughly aporetic.

The pervasive aporia of Kant's system of pure reason concerns the relationship of the transcendental ideas to empirical truths. How can a transcendental and pure reason comprise a foundation for contingent judgments? The question parallels that in Spinoza of how finite modes can follow from absolutely infinite substance, where whatever follows directly from substance must be infinite.[11] Similarly, even if there were mathematical a priori truths, even if these were both innate and conditions of reason itself, nothing whatever could follow from them concerning empirical judgments. Even if we say that mathematical judgments constitute conditions for any empirical judgment, when we add the creativity of the imagination to mathematics and logic it is as if such judgments defined no constraints whatever upon the varied possibilities of empirical theories. Nothing follows directly from mathematics concerning contingent empirical judgments; nothing follows from empirical evidence that entails a given mathematical form of representation. There is no solution in a priori transcendental ideas or pure reason that enables us to avoid the indeterminatenesses of empirical knowledge. This is the aporia that the third *Critique* is required to resolve, by introducing still another range of aporias.

It follows that Kant's most famous dictum—"Thoughts without content are empty, intuitions without concepts are blind" (CPR, p. 93)— expresses a profound aporia: sensible intuitions and concepts, experience and thought, can only be aporetically related. Concepts and principles do not follow from any empirical evidence, while empirical evidence of itself is not knowledge at all. We have an insight into the heretical side of knowledge. Nothing in itself or that simply repeats something in itself can be knowledge. Knowledge always goes beyond whatever empirical foundation can be offered for it, transcends both its empirical sources and their meaning. The conjunction of concepts and principles with intuitions and evidence is irremediably heretical. Each adds to the other its own indeterminateness—that of the creative imagination on the side of concepts, that of the plenitude of an inexhaustible nature on the side of empirical data. What follows from Kant's principle is that empirical knowledge—the only knowledge there can be—is a complex and unending adjudication of the relation between concepts and principles, which escape from any definite limits we ascribe to them, and contingent facts, which are unintelligible only in terms of these transcending concepts, but equally escape their control. It follows further that there can be no "pure" reason, either in concepts independent of all empirical conditions or in a logic abstracted from them. Logic passes from an analytic to a dialectic, the critique of pure transcendental reason and explicit manifestation of its aporias.

The structure and scale of the first *Critique* tell us something of its aporetic nature. The transcendental aesthetic, which defines the general conditions of sensibility, is twenty-nine pages (in the English edition); the transcendental analytic, which defines the elements intrinsic to pure understanding, is 195 pages; the transcendental dialectic, which embodies the critique of pure reason and its aporias, is far longer, 274 pages. It is followed, moreover, by the transcendental doctrine of method, the most aporetic of Kant's writings, comprising another ninety-eight pages and the entire second part of the first *Critique*. If we add to the analytic the aporias of the deductions, very little can be found that constitutes a positive theory of knowledge. Such a positive theory would explain both how it is possible to arrive at knowledge from within the conditions of experience and how such knowledge is legitimate and determinate. Instead, although Kant recurrently claims such a positive theory, the result is pervasively aporetic.

If there is any question to which Kant cannot and does not give an answer, in his first *Critique*, it is how finite empirical knowledge is possible. At best he can hope to supply the conditions of the possibility of any experience, of any sensible intuition. But that such conditions obtain does not and cannot entail that the concrete universals (borrowing Hegel's expression) that constitute scientific knowledge are either determinable or knowable. There can be no answer whatever to skepticism from within the a priori conditions of pure understanding.[12] Rather, what Kant can at best hope to supply is an indeterminate relation between contingent scientific knowledge and the a priori conditions that constitute the possibility of a science.

Another way of putting this is that corresponding to the impossibility of determining the finite by any relation whatever to the infinite, for example, in Spinoza, there is the impossibility in Kant of determining the empirical by the transcendental. Finite and infinite, empirical and transcendental, are related through the aporia of other and the same. Generically, this insight is manifested by Kant in relation to the paralogisms and antinomies — the aporias within pure speculative reason. Specifically, however, the same aporias are manifested in the deductions. Every condition of the possibility of determination and freedom calls for a transcendental deduction in relation not only to pure reason and the understanding, but to practical reason and judgment, aesthetic and teleological. Every such deduction is an explicit aporia. In relation to the understanding, the aporia resides in "the transcendental faculty of imagination" (CPR, p. 133) whereby a synthesis of apprehension and reproduction is possible. The condition that makes this synthetic unity possible is that of the unified self. Yet no such self can be disclosed within empirical phenomena. "No fixed and abiding self can present itself in this flux of inner appearances." (CPR, p. 136) This aporia becomes the fundamental paralogism of pure reason: the difference between the a priori noumenal self that is a necessary condition of the possibility of unified experience and the contingently unified self that is an object within experience.

If conscious experience is relevant to things, then it must make a difference to them, although no such difference can be included within the system of natural laws. Kant offers two views of such differences, both aporetic. The first is the possibility of a freedom that constitutes the basis of morality though that freedom cannot contribute to the determinate effects of causal laws. The second is the unification that comprises experience, a unity that cannot come from experience itself.

The influence of Kant's aporia of the synthetic unity of apperception on subsequent philosophical thought has been overwhelming, from

Hegel and Schelling to Bergson, Whitehead, and Dewey, and present in most post-Heideggerian Continental thought. Most of Kant's successors sought to escape from the aporias of noumena and phenomena and of things in themselves. They did not so strenuously attempt to escape from the second and more pervasive aporia present in unity in relation not only to conscious experience but to being in general. Kant argues that there must be a transcendental ground of the unity whereby sensory intuitions comprise the objects of possible experience. It follows that the noumenal self is the transcendental ground of the being of things—their "Being." What this ground determines are the rules whereby objects fall under concepts. Yet if beings are inexhaustible and knowledge is heretical, then they do not fall under rules. Conversely, that objects of possible experience should derive their conditions of unity from the self that constitutes experience is aporetic because beings must be unified whether or not they fall within possible experience. *To be* is to be unified, experienced or not.

The consequence of the deduction is acknowledged by Kant to have "alarming evil consequences." Two aporias are present. One Kant acknowledges explicitly: that in order to restrict a priori knowledge to possible experience, we must be able to think without restrictions in the imagination. The other, closely related, is that a priori knowledge is derived from pure understanding, not from experience.

> We cannot think an object save through categories; we cannot *know* an object so thought save through intuitions corresponding to these concepts. Now all our intuitions are sensible; and this knowledge, in so far as its object is given, is empirical. But empirical knowledge is experience. *Consequently, there can be no* a priori *knowledge, except of objects of possible experience.* (CPR, p. 174)

Thus, we have an absolutely certain apodeictic knowledge of the conditions of the possibility of pure experience that is derived in no way whatever from experience. Moreover, this knowledge belongs to a faculty of subsuming under rules, so that we have a certain knowledge of rules and their conditions without the possibility of departing from them. One aporia here is that of freedom of thought: how freedom can pertain to practice without pertaining to understanding. The other aporia is how a priori knowledge of general rules can be relevant to empirical truths. What follows is Kant's schematism. With it we return to the aporias of time.

How are we able to derive particular scientific truths from the concepts of pure understanding? To this question Kant has no answer. He has, in this sense, no foundational theory whatever. Instead, he offers an explanation of how it is possible to subsume a representation of an object under a concept. In fact, he offers two such explanations, one in the first *Critique* in relation to the schematism, the other in the third in relation to determinant judgment. We may assume the latter eventually takes precedence over the former. Both explanations are aporetic. Moreover, as Kant defines it, the problem itself is one of aporia.

> In all subsumptions of an object under a concept the representation of the object must be *homogeneous* with the concept; . . . .
> But pure concepts of understanding being quite heterogeneous from empirical intuitions, and indeed from all sensible intuitions, can never be met with in any intuition. . . . How, then, is the *subsumption* of intuitions under pure concepts, the *application* of a category to appearances, possible? (CPR, p. 180)

The aporia lies between the pure concepts of understanding and sensible intuitions: they are too different to allow for mediation. The more generic aporia is never addressed by Kant: that difference is unresolvable into the same. Nor is the question of how factual knowledge may follow from pure understanding. He is faced with the aporia of the disjunction between pure and empirical concepts of the understanding. What he proposes is a mediation that he calls the *subsumption* of intuition under the general categories.

What allows this subsumption to occur is time.[13] Time is, here, both universal and a priori, therefore homogeneous with the categories and a generic condition of sensory intuition. Kant appears to overlook the fact that it cannot serve both roles at once. In the way it is homogeneous with the categories, it is unlike empirical intuitions. In the way in which it belongs to empirical intuitions, it may be a priori, but cannot be universal. As the transcendental schema, time is doubled like the self that constitutes the ground of the manifold. The time that is universal is not intuitable; the time that pertains to intuitions is not universal.

Far more important, however, is the role assigned to time as the transcendental schema, mediating between the universal and the intuitable. Time is the universal condition of inner experience although not everything that can be thought, not every experienceable being, is subject to time. If mathematics is synthetic a priori, then its objects are thinkable and experienceable without being temporal. Although we may be able to think and experience these mathematical objects only in (our) time, successively, they do not inhabit time generically and cannot do so and be known a priori. There is aporia in the very idea of a transcendental schema: that something might bridge the distinct worlds of pure and contingent concepts, analogous to whether something might bridge the worlds of freedom and necessity. Nothing intelligible could do so, yet the two must belong to one world.

Where these aporias are explicitly manifested is in Kant's expressions of how time, as the transcendental schema, defines the metaphysical concepts of reality, causality, community, possibility, actuality, and necessity.[14] Reality cannot pertain to time alone because there must also be a mathematical reality, not to mention the reality of God and the world. Not all intuitable beings are permanent in time, nor are any individual substances permanent and unchanging. Causality *in time* is successive, but there are other powers than efficient causes and their succession. Community and reciprocity pertain to any system of relationships, temporal or not. Possibilities in dramatic works are synthesized with the conditions of time only to the extent that they are available for physical intuition. Mathematical actualities may exist at no times and be necessary.

These qualifications are expressions of aporias inherent in time more than difficulties in Kant's view of time. Time is aporetic in addition to the aporias expressed in the transcendental aesthetic because it both pertains with necessity to all possible experience, therefore to all forms of understanding, and fails to pertain universally to all beings. It is aporetic both because it bridges two unbridgeable worlds and because it constitutes the basis of a science whose foundations serve no relevant purpose in any science.

Following the schematism, in the first *Critique*, is "The Transcendental Doctrine of Judgment (or Analytic of Principles)." It is entirely founded on the disjunction between sensible intuitions and pure principles of the understanding, continuing the aporia within the transcendental schema.

> Synthetic *a priori* judgments are thus possible when we relate the formal conditions of *a priori* intuition, the synthesis of imagination and the necessary unity of this synthesis in a transcendental apperception, to a possible empirical knowledge in general. We then assert that the conditions of the *possibility of experience* in general are likewise conditions of the *possibility of the objects of experience*, and that for this reason they have objective validity in a synthetic *à priori* judgment. (CPR, p. 194)

The aporia here is the result of the independence within each of the moments that comprise the synthesis. The pure concepts of the understanding are blind without intuitions, but they are also possible and thinkable without them. Similarly, the imagination must be free and creative independent of the pure concepts of the understanding (although Kant does not develop the ramifications of this truth until the third *Critique*). The freedom of the formal conditions of the understanding and of the creative imagination must be conjoined with sensible intuitions in a way that produces objective validity, while no form of necessity can conjoin the different moments without compromising their independence.

An example of this aporia can be found in the principle of the axioms of intuition: "All intuitions are extensive magnitudes." (CPR, p. 197) Kant defines this extensiveness in terms of the way the parts comprise the whole:

> I entitle a magnitude extensive when the representation of the parts makes possible, and therefore necessarily precedes, the representation of the whole. I cannot represent to myself a line, however small, without drawing it in thought, that is, generating from a point all its parts one after another. (CPR, p. 198)

Thousands of pages have been written after Kant—Bergson is a good example—arguing that the intuition of extension moves in the opposite direction, from whole to parts. The dispute is futile, masking the inherent aporias. For what is required is that there be an intuition simultaneously and indistinguishably of the whole, the parts, and how they are conjoined. Yet no single thought can include them all together. This aporia of same and other recurs throughout Kant's account of mathematical thinking.

> The mathematics of space (geometry) is based upon this successive synthesis of the productive imagination in the generation of figures.

> The assertion that $7+5$ is equal to 12 is not an analytic proposition. For neither in the representation of 7, or in that of 5, nor in the representation of the combination of both, do I think the number 12. (CPR, p. 190)

The first claim follows Hume in the suggestion that the composite figure is a synthesis of parts, just as composite extension arises from a synthesis of points. Yet there can be no such synthesis where the continuum is infinitely divisible. Wholes, although they comprise the field of experience, are not intelligible *as wholes*. The second claim is inconsistent with the first because the same synthetic operation entails that we traverse every number in thinking any—that is, 12 is intelligible only in an intuition involving seven and five. Kant does not consider the possibility that the synthesis involved in every a priori operation effectively makes each of them analytic. Nor does he consider that his view of *intensive* magnitudes, in which there is synthesis without parts, demands an entirely different sense of magnitude, requiring a different sense of synthesis.[15]

The aporia lies within the doubling that pertains to Kant's view of synthesis. It is on the one hand the field of pure concepts and a priori conditions of the understanding. In this form, there is no relation whatever between the elementary intuitions that comprise possible experience and the forms of pure understanding. The introduction of synthesis through the imagination brings these into relation but has the consequence that pure and a priori concepts are made dependent on a synthetic operation upon elementary intuitions. The point is again that the purity of a priori concepts and the contingency of empirical intuitions prevent their conjunction without aporia. All the axioms and analogies of pure understanding manifest the same aporia.

Far more striking are the sections that follow what Kant treats as the completion of the "territory of pure understanding." (CPR, p. 257)

> This domain is an island, enclosed by nature itself within unalterable limits. It is the land of truth—enchanting name!—surrounded by a wide and stormy ocean, the native home of illusion, where many a fog bank and many a swiftly melting iceberg give the deceptive appearance of farther shores, ... (CPR, p. 257)

This description cannot be passed over. The territory of pure understanding, although it comprises the conditions of possible experience, cannot be related in any intelligible way to actual experience. Moreover, its domain is an island, enclosed by nature itself—a nature both unthinkable and unknowable. Truth pertains to possible experience but not to nature, yet nature inevitably surrounds truth. This is a remarkable figure, entirely excluding any sense of how understanding may penetrate nature. Yet Kant must insist that nature surrounds truth. In addition, the illusions that we discern through the fog are themselves presences: appearances are real and true—*as appearances*. Kant must have it both ways: noumenal reality is outside truth; phenomenal reality is appearance but constitutes the island of truth. Not only is there an aporia *between* noumena and phenomena, that of the relation between experience and nature, but there are aporias pertaining to noumena themselves: they are both nature and beyond nature, things in themselves yet unknowable, metaphysical conditions of truth yet unintelligible.[16]

The section that follows Kant's discussion of the analytic of the pure concepts of the understanding is concerned with noumena and phenomena. What follows thereafter comprises a number of explicitly aporetic notions: first, in the appendix to the analytic, the amphiboly of concepts of reflection; second, in the transcendental dialectic, leading to the paralogisms and antinomies. Every one of these terms—amphiboly, dialectic, paralogism, and antinomy—explicitly expresses aporia.

The amphiboly arises, in Kant's words, "from the confusion of the empirical with the transcendental employment of understanding." (CPR, p. 276) And there is no avoiding this confusion. Kant's list of the transcendental concepts of reflection is a list of the aporias that have constituted the metaphysical tradition: identity and difference; agreement and opposition; inner and outer; matter and form. His answer to all these aporias lies within the equally aporetic relation of the sensible and supersensible as well as within the purity of reason itself.

The dialectic expresses this truth directly. Kant defines it as a *logic of illusion*. It is required by pure reason.

> All our knowledge starts with the senses, proceeds from thence to understanding, and ends with reason. (CPR, p. 300)

The aporia present in this beginning with the senses is that although all knowledge begins with experience, it does not all arise out of experience. (CPR, p. 41) Yet if knowledge may arise out of a faculty independent of experience, that very independence produces both the possibility of error and the actuality of illusion. In both the understanding and reason, then, there is the presence of transcendental illusions, an expression of the aporias that comprise the efforts of pure reason to go beyond possible experience, but which at another level is an expression of the irresistibility of error. The independence of the faculties of pure understanding and reason is at once the ground of the a priori categories and the source of the aporias that require a transcendental dialectic. The transcendental ideas are the origin inseparably of both apodeictic knowledge and of the paralogisms and antinomies.[17]

> A transcendental paralogism is one in which there is a transcendental ground, constraining us to draw a formally invalid conclusion. Such a fallacy is therefore grounded in the nature of human reason, and gives rise to an illusion which cannot be avoided, although it may, indeed, be rendered harmless. (CPR, pp. 328-29)

That pure reason *requires* us to draw a formally invalid conclusion is aporetic if it is not skeptical; but it is not skeptical because it can be rendered harmless. We should regard this as another aporia.

The paralogisms express an illusory understanding of the concepts that pertain to them, especially the soul as a simple, unitary substance that acts upon bodies in space. The antinomies are aporetic, and express the same understanding.[18] Because, for Kant, the movement of knowledge from the senses through the understanding to reason is not an irresistible impulse but is inherent in the intelligible conditions of any understanding, then again, that there is empirical knowledge inescapably manifests the aporias of reason. These express themselves in the four antinomies.

What we are forced to conclude, long before terminating our discussion of Kant, is that his system is to be understood, not as a foundational account of scientific knowledge free from aporia, but as an account of the aporetic transcendental conditions of a science. The entire system of the *Critiques* is an ongoing expression of the aporias that constitute knowledge. The final section of the first part of the first *Critique* concludes with "The Final Purpose of the Natural Dialectic of Human Reason," designed to show the limits of pure speculative reason so that we may find within its aporia the possibility of freedom. The limits of pure speculative reason constitute the aporetic basis of practical reason. To establish this conclusion is the purpose of part two of the first *Critique*, essentially to establish the need for a second.

Part two is the "Transcendental Doctrine of Method," divided into four parts: the *discipline, canon, architectonic,* and *history* of pure reason.[19] Part one emphasizes the understanding and its foundations in pure reason. The greater part by far of the work consists of the critique of pure reason and our relationship to it. Pure reason, however, is thoroughly aporetic, and its aporias are necessary to both the understanding and the possibility of freedom that lies within the second *Critique*.

Kant describes pure reason in an extraordinary image.

> We have found, indeed, that although we had contemplated building a tower which should reach to the heavens, the supply of materials suffices only for a dwelling-house, just sufficiently commodious for our business on the level of experience, and just sufficiently high to allow of our overlooking it. (CPR, p. 573)

What makes the image of the Tower of Babel so remarkable here is the representation of the heavens as a legitimate object, capable of being reached by a very high tower, although we do not have materials sufficient to build one high enough. Pure reason, however, defines objects as beyond our reach not because of our finite materials—the escape of the infinite from our finite grasp—but because they are illusory and defective. Noumena are not simply "beyond" our understanding: they can have no epistemic status whatever. The aporia of pure reason is that it defines concepts that cannot be thought without contradiction but that must be thought. Another way of putting this, in terms of the present image, is that if the heavens are not within possible experience, they cannot be thought at all, while if they are within possible experience, they can be known. Similarly, freedom, immortality, and God are either intelligible in relation to possible experience or they are altogether unintelligible. For Kant, however, they are neither intelligible nor unthinkable.

> I understand, therefore, by Transcendental Doctrine of Method the determination of the formal conditions of a complete system of pure reason. (CPR, p. 573)

From the standpoint of an empiricism that would reject the illegitimacies of pure reason, this passage, defining a "complete system of pure reason," is extraordinary. What it implies is that Kant does not *reject* pure reason, but seeks to define its limits. Not to do so is to leave the speculative notions that define it antinomical. What is required is to define *their* conditions of possibility apart from the conditions of possible experience. These include the foundations of morality and religion. The aporia of pure reason is the basis of all the cognitive faculties, ranging from the understanding and imagination through practical reason and teleological judgment. The system of pure reason plays the remarkable role of delimiting pure speculative reason systematically so that morality and art cannot be overcome by scientific understanding. There is, therefore, a profound aporia inherent in science: were it to be free from aporia, were it to possess no inherent divisions and limits, it would be unintelligible.

Science, however, does not know its own limits. The thinking of limits belongs to philosophy rather than science. "Indeed it is precisely in knowing its limits that philosophy consists; . . . . " (CPR, p. 585) The thinking of limits *is* the thinking of aporia. There are aporias throughout the faculties, but it is the province of philosophy to seek to delimit them, not of the faculties themselves. The special role that philosophy acquires, in Kant, is therefore not of establishing the faculties on an unimpugnable foundation, but of establishing the aporias that make knowledge possible. The transcendental argument that establishes the basis for any epistemic faculty also defines the absolute limits that pertain to reason. The aporia is that a form of argument with absolute limits undermines its own authority. The standpoint of the critic becomes inherently aporetic. Kant expresses this insight as the antecedent of an interrogative proposition:

> Since criticism of our reason has at last taught us that we cannot by means of its pure and speculative employment arrive at any knowledge whatsoever, ... (CPR, p. 612)

The conclusion of the discussion, to which the entire system of pure reason leads, is the limit of pure speculative reason:

> ... compelling pure reason to relinquish its exaggerated pretensions in the realm of speculation, and to withdraw within the limits of its proper territory—that of practical principles. (CPR, p. 628)

The limits of pure speculative reason are defined so as to establish the proper territory of pure practical reason. Science must possess intrinsic limits in order that morality be given an adequate foundation. This is again the aporia of nature and freedom. Yet to deny this aporia, to deny that nature and freedom are distinct, is equally aporetic. It is the aporia to which both parts of the third *Critique* are devoted.

The discipline of pure reason exists to define the limits of pure speculative reason. The canon of pure reason—the totality of the a priori principles that constitute it—cannot exist for speculative, only for practical reason.

> There is therefore no canon of its speculative employment; such employment is entirely dialectical. . . . Consequently, if there be any correct employment of pure reason, in which case there must be a canon of its employment, the canon will deal not with the speculative but with the *practical employment of reason.* (CPR, p. 630)

It follows that what we may regard as Kant's greatest achievement, to define the conditions of scientific understanding, turns out to delimit the aporetic conditions that pertain to practical reason. Indeed, we are given an explanation of why reason is impelled to transcend its ordinary scientific employment.

> Reason is impelled by a tendency of its nature to go out beyond the field of its empirical employment, and to venture in a pure employment, by means of ideas alone, to the utmost limits of all knowledge, ... Is this endeavour the outcome merely of the speculative interests of reason? Must we not rather regard it as having its source exclusively in the practical interests of reason? (CPR, p. 630)

Practical reason and morality lie, on this analysis, at the most aporetic point of Kant's view of reason.

> The ultimate aim to which the speculation of reason in its transcendental employment is directed concerns three objects:

the freedom of the will, the immortality of the soul, and the existence of God. In respect of all three the merely speculative interest of reason is very small; .... (CPR, p. 631)

Each of these notions is aporetic. Moreover, there is a generic reason why speculative reason must extend its attention beyond the limits of possible experience—to think the aporias within the nature of limits, including the limits of experience and nature. If we expect knowledge to resolve the aporias that it finds, if we expect science to be free from heresy, as Kant appears to suggest, then it must be restricted to possible experience. Yet in order to so restrict it, we must confront aporias everywhere. It follows that scientific knowledge as well as philosophy is heretical. It follows as well that it is the province of philosophy to confront aporia as such whereas science relates to its aporias obliquely. Here, pure speculative reason transcends the limits of possible experience *because* they are aporetic and because it is "beyond" those limits that it confronts its own aporias.

On Kant's view, the transcendence of speculative reason "beyond" possible experience is achieved only to return.

Reason, in its speculative employment, conducted us through the field of experience, and since it could not find complete satisfaction there, from thence to speculative ideas, which, however, in the end brought us back to experience....

All the interests of my reason, speculative as well as practical, combine in the three following questions:

1. What can I know?
2. What ought I to do?
3. What may I hope? (CPR, p. 635)

Yet, just as the return from pure speculative ideas to experience is unintelligible, so are the three practical questions that constitute the domain of its application. They presume a transcendence of the limits of possible experience that is at once impossible, unintelligible, and unavoidable. The answers to all of these questions, but especially the latter two, require that we be able to escape from the bounds of sensible experience, if only in the realm of thought. Moreover, the entire contribution of philosophy here offers nothing that is not part of ordinary common sense.

... in regard to the essential ends of human nature the highest philosophy cannot advance further than is possible under the

> guidance which nature has bestowed even upon the most ordi-
> nary understanding. (CPR, p. 652)

What, then, is the point of constructing a system of pure reason? What is the purpose of what Kant calls its *architectonic*? The answer lies within speculative reason itself. Indeed, this idea of a systematic whole that constitutes the metaphysical ideal brings us to a deeper aporia.

> The legislation of human reason (philosophy) has two
> objects, nature and freedom, and therefore contains not only
> the law of nature, but also the moral law, presenting them at
> first in two distinct systems, but ultimately in one single philo-
> sophical system. (CPR, pp. 658-59)

The ideal in Kant's architectonic is not to make a multiplicity one, for that would destroy the purpose of the system. It is, rather, to heighten the sense of aporia that constitutes the possibility of science on the one hand and of freedom on the other, of natural reality on the one hand and human reality on the other. Metaphysics becomes, not the resolution of its fundamental aporia, but its systematic articulation. In this extraordinary development of the aporias that pertain to being and to philosophy, Kant's own viewpoint is remarkably heretical. Despite all his claims to apodeictic certainty, suggesting closure in foundational thinking, he affirms a heretical view of metaphysics.

> ... we shall always return to metaphysics as to a beloved one
> with whom we have had a quarrel. For here we are concerned
> with essential ends—ends with which metaphysics must cease-
> lessly occupy itself, either in striving for genuine insight into
> them, or in refuting those who profess already to have attained
> it. (CPR, p. 665)

The second part of the first *Critique* is concerned with defining the systematic limits of speculative reason so that we may assign pure reason its practical role. Pure reason is practical reason; it is essential to Kant's entire theory that it be so. It is essential to a priori truths that they may be constituted independent of experience, precisely what is essential to morality; it is essential to the faculty of understanding that there be a realm independent of phenomena.[20] The strongest statement by far is in the Introduction to the *Critique of Judgment*.

> Understanding and reason exercise, therefore, two distinct
> legislations on one and the same territory of experience, with-

out prejudice to the other. The concept of freedom as little disturbs the legislation of nature as the natural concept influences the legislation through the former. (CJ, p. 11)

This is the most far-reaching aporia in all the *Critiques*, far exceeding the corresponding formulations in the first. Here freedom and natural necessity cohabit within the "same territory of experience" without contradiction, without even "disturbing" each other. On such a view, freedom is efficacious without in the least influencing the flow of natural events falling under natural laws.

Briefly leaving aside the third *Critique*, we find Kant claiming, in the second, that of the three speculative ideas, freedom, immortality, and God, we may know only of the possibility of freedom, through morality.[21] While the proximate basis of such knowledge is our sense of the moral law, it is more profoundly based on the conditions of reason itself. Kant calls this knowledge of noumenal freedom, inherent in the critical enterprise, an "enigma":

Here first is explained the enigma of the critical philosophy, viz. how we *deny objective reality* to the supersensible use of the *categories* in speculation, and yet *admit* this *reality* with respect to the objects of pure practical reason. (CPrR, p. 90)

He goes on to deny that it is an inconsistency or contradiction, although it may appear to be one, for the inconsistency disappears in relation to the supersensible. Moreover, through morality,

... practical reason itself, without any concert with the speculative, assures reality to a supersensible object of the category of causality, viz. *Freedom*, although (as becomes a practical concept) only for practical use; .... (CPrR, pp. 90-91)

Two independent but coextensive realms of law inhabit human experience, one natural law, under natural causality, the realm of natural science; the other moral law, under causality of the will, the realm of practical reason. Not only are two overlapping but independent spheres of law aporetic in their relations, but Kant explicitly acknowledges their aporia in the dialectic of supersensibility. The explicit and recurrent aporia in his system is that the foundation of natural necessity is the possibility of supersensible freedom.

A fundamental aporia of law pervades Kant's view of natural and moral necessity. It is apparent in the very idea of a moral law as the ground of freedom. Freedom of the will is conformity to law, if only to a law defined by reason itself. The aporia goes much further, however, lying in the nature of law as embodiment of the same. Universal laws are the a priori conditions of a cognitive faculty while a priori universality is incompatible with individual contingency and error. On the one hand, then, if universal principles are derived from sensory experience, the derivation is aporetic. On the other hand, if universal principles belong to the faculties themselves, then where those faculties are employed in their pure operation, there can be no contingency.

Thus, in science, where natural laws predominate there is the logical problem of individuals and their variations within those laws. The structure of this issue parallels that of how particular scientific truths are to be derived from a priori principles. The latter contribute nothing to the determination of the former. In ethics, where moral laws predominate, there is the corresponding logical problem of how individual practices are to be derived from universal laws, especially where they conflict. Contingent practices never conform exactly to universal laws. This aporia pertains, in Kant, to law itself: lawfulness, in natural or human spheres, stands in a relation of alterity to the individual cases that fall under it. The aporia may be expressed in terms of governance and power: laws cannot govern events without being independent of them, while without a notion of governance by necessity, causality is unintelligible. Similarly, if moral laws admit of any exceptions, or may conflict, then it is unintelligible that individual practices may be derived from them. What is required, absent in Kant, is recognition that power and sovereignty are representational, that the relation between governance and governed is a public representation within the rule of the same (and other).

The second *Critique* begins with the aporia of desire.

> All *material* practical rules place the determining principle of the will in the *lower desires*, and if there were no *purely formal* laws of the will adequate to determine it, then we could not admit *any higher desire* at all. (CPrR, p. 109)

As Schopenhauer perhaps more profoundly than any other philosopher shows, although there are traces in classical Stoicism, it is impossible to define happiness or morality in terms of desire alone. What is required is a distinction between lower and higher desires, and such a distinction cannot be defined from within desire. Yet desire cannot be intelligible without a higher form.[22] The aporia is that of higher desires where desire is the basis of practice. It is particularly evident in Mill, whose attempt to determine a rational empirical basis for higher desires notoriously fails, not because there are no higher desires, without which moral and artistic practices would be unintelligible, but because there is no basis within desire itself for their determination.

Kant, far more than Mill, recognizes the aporia and seeks to resolve it, at least at the level on which it first emerges, that of the intrinsic arbitrariness of any distinction among desires where desire is the determinant of practice. Desire must be supplemented by respect (for the law)—pure reason itself—which, despite its entirely nonempirical nature, must have empirical implications. Kant does not resolve this aporia but displaces it to other levels. For example, law cannot be added to desire without aporia; where unconditioned moral laws conflict, they are as unable to achieve resolution as where desires conflict without a higher principle, yet every such principle is arbitrary.

The fundamental aporia in Kant's view of practical reason is that of freedom, the incommensurateness of moral and natural necessity. Several others pertain to the moral law and the will. One concerns the relationship between the good will and happiness: the *summum bonum*. Happiness is the concrete goal of every finite being, but happiness is an empirical determination, and cannot be determined by pure practical reason. Indeed, there can be no connection between morality and happiness because there is no connection between will and desire. This denial is far too strong because without such a connection, morality would always be an infinite sacrifice. What is essential is that will and desire be related aporetically. There is only an arbitrary relationship between conformity to moral law and happiness. This aporia lies within the nature of Kant's understanding of law.

> A rational being cannot regard his maxims as practical universal laws, unless he conceives them as principles which determine the will, not by their matter, but by their form only. (CPrR, p. 114)

An a priori law cannot determine any empirical results because its only determinations are formal. In relation to the understanding, no formal conditions of natural law can determine its empirical results. In relation to practical reason, no formal conditions of moral law can entail concrete results. This is seen particularly where moral principles conflict, but it is evident in the arbitrariness of any rational proof of what Kant calls a material principle of the will.

The second aporia of practice finds particular expression in terms of the categorical imperative.

> Act so that the maxim of thy will can always at the same time hold good as a principle of universal legislation. (CPrR, p. 119)

Several aporias lie within this formulation. One again concerns the relationship between practice and law. Kant assumes that the determination of the will can be rational only where determined by an unconditioned maxim. It follows that no individual action can be moral or rational. Concrete consequences bear no intelligible relationship to any action that causes them.

A second aporia concerns the universality Kant takes to be essential to freedom. Freedom is conformity to law, acting as everyone else would or should act. There is no room in such a morality for complex and subtle determinations of one's actions, contingently, based on variations in individual empirical circumstances. There is, therefore, no room in Kant's view of morality for the most important empirical principle of practical morality, that the pathway to hell is paved with good intentions. A good will can produce horrible consequences, yet they are irrelevant to its goodness. Within this aporia is another: the relationship between righteous acts and practical success is always aporetic. Failure inhabits moral practices irresistibly.

Kant speaks of the *autonomy* and *heteronomy* of the will. The latter contains all material and empirical considerations. Yet only the former can be the basis of morality.

> The *autonomy* of the will is the sole principle of all moral laws, and of all duties which conform to them; on the other hand, *heteronomy* of the elective will not only cannot be the basis of any obligation, but is, on the contrary, opposed to the principle thereof, and to the morality of the will. (CPrR, p. 122)

The aporia here is that of duty, which cannot be derived from empirical considerations but which must determine empirical conditions if it is to be effective. Will must simultaneously belong to noumena and to phenomena, just as it must be capable of autonomy while heteronomously capable of producing happiness. The result is the mixture in all practice of both empirical and a priori determinants of the will, the aporia again of freedom and necessity. Its resolution, in terms of the supersensible, is a transcendental name for aporia itself.

> ... the concept of a causality free from empirical conditions, although empty (*i.e.* without any appropriate intuition), is yet theoretically possible and refers to an indeterminate object; but in compensation significance is given to it in the moral law, and consequently in a practical sense. (CPrR, p. 146)

This "indeterminate object" or "indeterminate concept" (in the third *Critique*) is aporetic, not simply because Kant denies its intelligibility in the first *Critique*, but generically, because of the aporia of indeterminateness.

The explicit aporias in Kant's *Critiques* are manifested in the antinomies that characterize each of the cognitive faculties. The antinomy of practical reason expresses the aporia inherent in the conjunction of happiness and virtue.[23] They must be joined although the latter pertains entirely to form, the former entirely to empirical desire. This disjunction of will and desire entails that there can be no intelligible relationship between virtue and happiness.[24] Facts cannot determine values nor values facts. The dichotomy, here, is aporetic, for although there can be no intelligible relationship between facts and values, they cannot be unrelated. More generally, the realm of nature under natural law is complete from the standpoint of scientific understanding, leaving no room whatever for moral determinations while no human point of view can be intelligible without desire.

Kant's "critical solution" to the antinomy is again in terms of the supersensible, leading to another aporia.

> The first of the two propositions—That the endeavour after happiness produces a virtuous mind, is *absolutely false*; but the second, That a virtuous mind necessarily produces happiness, is *not absolutely false*, but only in so far as virtue is considered as a form of causality in the sensible world. (CPrR, p. 210)

The contingency of a desire that leads to happiness cannot produce the universality required for virtue, but the universality and apodeicticity of the moral law *might* produce happiness transcendentally. The subjunctive is aporetic enough, as is the impossibility of either proof or understanding. Moreover, the causality postulated between morality and happiness defies the testimony of experience. The respect for moral law embodied in virtue demands that we be prepared to sacrifice ourselves and our empirical happiness for virtue. That we might nevertheless be happy, supersensibly, makes happiness aporetic. Kant cannot avoid the aporia, for it involves the relation between will and desire. Why, that is, should the form of the moral law take precedence in action over empirical considerations concerning desire? Without a conjunction between law and desire, the *summum bonum* is unintelligible.

Kant claims that the *summum bonum* not only requires freedom, but involves both immortality and God as conditions of its perfectibility.[25] His arguments make a transition from the *possibility* of a *summum bonum*, required as a concept essential to morality, to the *actuality* of, first, the perfection inherent in the realization of the highest good, then the production of that highest good in reality. These arguments are puzzling in relation to his rejection of a priori proofs of the existence of God. The latter, of course, is a speculative proof. The former, then, may be thought of as practical. The dichotomy between theory and practice is pervasive.[26]

Kant's argument is that practice must presuppose both that it could conceive the highest good perfectly and that such a perfect good is realizable. The former requires immortality (an infinite time) for its conception; the latter requires God for the realization of perfection. Because time is aporetic, especially infinitely, the former argument embodies an aporetic expression of the highest good and how we may conceive it. We cannot act without an ideal, but no ideal can be realized in time *as an ideal*—that is, unconditionedly. Similarly, we cannot act without an ideal, but no ideal can be realized in existence unconditionedly.

The latter part of the second *Critique* concerns what Kant calls the "methodology of pure practical reason." The entire discussion turns on the aporia of the possible purity of a reason that to be practical must be effective. What Kant has to say is notoriously incredible: imagine a person faced with horrible consequences—torture and death—for himself and his loved ones if he does not yield to injustice:

> Yet virtue is here worth so much only because it costs so much, not because it brings any profit. (CPrR, p. 254)

We are reminded of the antinomy of the *summum bonum*, that happiness and virtue must conjoin. Here the *purity* of the will is the highest good. Not only would few human beings agree: there is the aporia that a virtue that could achieve nothing whatever is to be considered the greatest human fulfillment.

> Even if it should happen that, owing to special disfavour of fortune, or the niggardly provision of a step-motherly nature, this will should wholly lack power to accomplish its purpose, if with its greatest efforts it whould yet achieve nothing, . . . then, like a jewel, it would still shine by its own light, as a thing which has its whole value in itself. (CPrR, p. 10)

Kant does not acknowledge that the impotence of a good will pertains to its goodness. Yet a will that can accomplish nothing is not good for achieving results. In this sense, a morally good will may not improve human life and may even find itself slipping along the pathway to hell.

This aporia belongs intrinsically to practice, not just to Kant's view of practical reason. He raises it to a central place in his theory as perhaps no one before or after has done, although there are important expressions of it in Kierkegaard and Sartre. It is prominent in rights-based criticisms of utilitarian theory. We apparently may, on a utilitarian view, legitimately sacrifice a minority of individuals to the benefit of the majority. It follows that no ethical theory can be grounded entirely on consequences, because principles sometimes war with results; yet no ethical theory can overlook consequences, as if morality has nothing to do with influencing events; and no theory can provide a rational conjunction of principles and outcomes, autonomy and heteronomy, purity of will and efficacy of results. It does not help matters that Kant recurrently speaks of the mixture of empirical and a priori principles. A faculty's purity is essential to its legitimacy.

Similar aporias pertain to other formulations of the categorical imperative. In particular, the third and fourth formulations speak of:

> ... the idea of the will of every rational being as a *universally legislating will*; (CPrR, p. 50)

and of:

> ... a kingdom which may be called a kingdom of ends, since what these laws have in view is just the relation of these beings to one another as ends and means. (CPrR, p. 52)

The aporias here are again of a freedom that is conformity to law and of a kingdom of ends that have nothing to do with results. Far more important, however, is the sacrifice in this notion of a kingdom of ends of all individuality. Human beings are to be treated as ends entirely in terms of what they share in common—their legislative rationality—and not in terms of the ways they differ. Morality pertains to human beings entirely indifferent to their individual variations. It is as if any human being could be exchanged with, substituted for any other, from the standpoint of the good. The achievement of a concrete, tangible community—a kingdom of ends—is the highest goal of practical experience, a community to be achieved although its reality can never be demonstrated[27] and although it is at the expense of the individuals who comprise it. On the empirical side, community under practical law is aporetic. On the formal side, the universal side of thought sacrifices to its purposes all individuality and specificity. These aporias are unresolvable in the context of the first two *Critiques*. The resolution, in the third, is no less aporetic.

If the first and second *Critiques* are pervaded by aporia, the mere existence of the third is aporetic. Moreover, it is assigned the function, not so much of resolving the aporias that initiate philosophic thought as of reconstituting them at another level. This aporetic movement of thought is philosophy, expressed through heresy.

We have noted the supreme aporia in Kant, expressive of his view of experience. Freedom and necessity pertain together to the same territory of experience, but they do not constitute one realm.[28] (CJ, p. 11) They limit each other in the world of sense, but not in reality. Kant cannot even describe this relation without confronting the aporia that two forms of law pertain to sensible experience, each complete in itself, each limiting the other without interfering with it.

The solution is no less aporetic.

> There is, then, an unbounded but also inaccessible field for our whole cognitive faculty—the field of the supersensible— wherein we find no territory and therefore can have in it, for theoretical cognition, no realm either for concepts of understanding or reason. (CJ, p. 11)

The supersensible field is both inaccessible yet required for thought; is an unbounded field but not a territory; cannot be known but must be thought. Freedom and natural law meet in phenomenal experience but are divided in supersensible reality, although we can understand neither their togetherness nor their separateness.

Into this profound disjunction that is the foundation of his speculative philosophy, Kant introduces a third term, although his system appears to admit of only two: "*natural concepts* and the *concept of freedom*." (CJ, p. 7)

> ... in the family of the supreme cognitive faculties there is a middle term between the understanding and the reason. This is the *judgment*, of which we have cause for supposing according to analogy that it may contain in itself, if not a special legislation, yet a special principle of its own to be sought according to laws, though merely subjective *a priori*. (CJ, p. 13)

He does not claim that judgment eliminates the aporia, for it is aporetic itself.[29] The four moments of the analytic of the beautiful are explicit aporias.[30] Satisfaction and dissatisfaction, pleasure and displeasure, delight and revulsion, pertain to all practice and desire. Moreover, desire is universal yet beauty requires a satisfaction independent of desire. Universality in the first two *Critiques* is achieved in terms of concepts of natural law or morality. Yet there is a universal pleasure independent of a concept while beauty involves necessity apart from concepts.

All these notions are explained by Kant in terms of the subjective necessity that pertains to judgment. The fundamental aporia, however, that results in these subordinate aporetic moments, is that freedom and necessity exhaust his systematic universe. Beauty can be realized in such a universe only aporetically. Yet without the judgment that, on its subjective side results in beauty, freedom and necessity would lack mediation. This aporia, between universal and particular, infinite and finite, pure reason and contingent experience, has only aporetic resolution. The presence and absence of mediation are both aporetic. For this reason no empirical science can be determined by pure a priori principles and no practical undertaking can be determined by a pure formulation of the moral law.

It is the role of judgment to resolve the aporia of the disjunction of universality and particularity, autonomy and heteronomy.

> Judgment in general is the faculty of thinking the particular as contained under the universal. (CJ, p. 15)

This is what Aristotle calls *phronēsis*, and if it is a cognitive faculty, it is one without rules. Such a faculty follows from the singular role played by judgment in Kant's theory because the spheres of application of rules are exhausted between theory and practice. He explicitly acknowledges the departures of rules required by art in his theory of genius. What he does not explicitly acknowledge is that judgment as such cannot be rule-governed. The indications of this absence of rules in his theory of art lie: (1) in the dialectical nature of the concepts defining taste;[31] (2) in the conjunction of taste and genius;[32] (3) in the notion of *aesthetical ideas*;[33] all moments in the conflict between reason and imagination that constitutes the sublime.[34]

1. Kant's view of genius is explicitly aporetic: genius is the capacity to break rules while giving rules to others as if nature determined them. Genius is therefore rule-breaking while rule-determining. Kant distinguishes between following rules and establishing exemplars from which subsequent geniuses may depart, a description of heresy.[35] He restricts it to art although the model of rules he proposes pertains to all understanding, moral, philosophic, or scientific.

2. Genius is the result of unbridled imagination, and may result in disproportion. Taste is required to make genius beautiful. Yet this addition, like judgment in general and genius in particular, cannot be governed by rules, not only because the heretical nature of genius forbids, but because the conjunction of genius and taste is aporetic. Taste must curb a heretical, original impulse. Yet unless taste can be as heretical, if only responsively, it must be a conservative impulse that would demolish the originality of genius. Taste is the aporetic moment in genius whereby defective products of the heretical imagination may be recognized. Taste is then no less heretical, if less inspired, than genius itself.

3. Aesthetical ideas are indeterminate ideas. This theme, of an inde-terminate concept or idea, is the major positive expression of the aporias that pervade Kant's system.

Kant must find that beauty bears a fundamental relationship to the good although his system forbids it. The fundamental relationship is that art, especially through genius, manifests the freedom inherent in the cognitive faculties. Without morality, without practical reason and the good, there would be no possibility of freedom. Yet art is not practical reason, and its freedom is not practical freedom, not merely because art does not conform to law, but because it can be moral without morality, can be truthful without asserting truths. There is an aporia to the moral side of art: that art can be moral as art only by holding morality and the good at a distance. This aporia recurs in the closing words of the first part of the third *Critique*:

> Hence it appears plain that the true propaedeutic for the foun-dation of taste is the development of moral ideas and the cul-ture of the moral feeling, because it is only when sensibility is brought into agreement with this that genuine taste can assume a definite invariable form. (CJ, p. 202)

In the end, Kant must claim that morality is the means to artistic sensi-bility, the reversed image of Tolstoi's view that art can be great only insofar as it raises the moral sensibility of humanity.

The aporia that judgment is introduced to resolve is that there is no meeting ground between noumena and phenomena, unconditioned principles and contingent empirical intuitions. The fundamental aporia within judgment is that it cannot mediate intelligibly between the finite and the infinite. What is required, even to suggest such a mediation, is a notion of natural order contrasted with purpose or intention. Kant begins the third *Critique* with beauty rather than natural teleology to establish the distinction between disinterested purposiveness and interested pur-pose. However, what follows from such a distinction is that the media-tion between pure a priori principles of the understanding and contingent empirical generalizations is aesthetic. What must be added is a distinc-tion between a disinterested delight in the free play of the cognitive faculties and ascribing design objectively to nature. In both cases, we must assume a purposive harmony between the free play of the imagina-tion and the contingent events of phenomenal experience. The assump-tion is arbitrary in the twin senses that no proof is available and that natural order always falls short of perfection.

The arbitrariness is aporia. But it is also testimony to the heresies in Kant's epistemology. These appear primarily in the third *Critique*, where artistic judgment requires a genius for which heresy is normal, but also where the finality ascribed teleologically to nature must include the freedom of the imagination. What is important is that the first two *Critiques* are incomplete, even in relation to science. What is necessary in science, then, cannot give us science itself.

> ... that the things of nature serve one another as means to purposes and that their possibility is only completely intelligible through this kind of causality—for this we have absolutely no ground in the universal idea of nature, as the complex of the objects of sense. (CJ, p. 205)

Similar views are expressed in the closing sections of the first part of the first *Critique*. What is new in the third is the explicitness of the aporias that pertain to natural design. Kant speaks in the first *Critique*, in his third antinomy, of a second causality, that of freedom. What is required in the third *Critique* is a third causality, that of design. Two are aporetic together and incomplete. Not only is their mediation aporetic—the aporia of the first two *Critiques*—but they do not suffice even in conjunction.

The second half of the third *Critique* presents an objective design to nature distinct from purpose[36] and natural causality.[37] Kant's conclusion is an extraordinary departure from efficient causation in natural events.

> ... a thing exists as a natural purpose if it is both *cause and effect of itself.* (CJ, p. 217)

A tree engenders another tree according to natural law, but its offspring are like itself: it perpetuates itself generically. Moreover, it perpetuates itself, through growth, as an individual. Finally, a congruence of whole and parts is required for such perpetuation.

> ... each part of a tree generates itself in such a way that the maintenance of any one part depends reciprocally on the maintenance of the rest. (CJ, p. 218)

The organization of natural events into natural kinds requires an order independent of natural laws though compatible with them. It is as compatible with natural laws that there might be instability and fluctuation as that there might be complex aggregates with stable forms of order. Our surroundings are populated by complex objects with complex forms of structure and order, compatible with natural laws, but these laws do not demand such structures. Our surroundings are populated by enduring objects of complex natural kinds, but natural laws would be compatible with very different kinds of natural beings.

There is present here what has been called an *anthropic principle*: natural events are to be explained by reference to the presence of human beings and their understanding of natural kinds.[38] The principle suggests that the universe be understood *so as to* bring about human life and culture. That is too strong a conclusion. Rather, efficient causation and natural laws do not require, and in that sense do not explain, the development of enduring structures and recurrent patterns in natural beings that reproduce themselves. In Kant, this generation and reproduction is essential to the effective functioning of the cognitive faculties: the harmony between scientific understanding *of* nature and scientific understanding *in* nature. These must be harmonious in order for science to be possible and intelligible, but the harmony cannot lie within either science or nature alone. There is a profound aporia inherent in any system of multiple causation: more than one mode of causality generates aporetic moments at the junctures between the modes.[39] Nevertheless, on the other side is the aporia that no single mode of causality can be adequate to the complexity of a nature that can be understood by what belongs to it.

Reason and understanding demand that they be understood as purposive (if not purposeful, a function of desire). It follows that whatever is intelligible and reasonable must be both cause and effect together, again purposively.

> *An organized product of nature is one in which every part is reciprocally purpose* [*end*] *and means*. In it nothing is vain, without purpose, or to be ascribed to a blind mechanism of nature. (CJ, p. 222)

The blindness here is irrationality. Science thus aporetically both requires a mechanistic view of natural things and is incompatible with that view. Every natural thing is both means and end, containing within itself whatever follows from it, but possessing an intrinsic order. Nothing can be means only, or it could neither be understood nor function causally.

The aporia here, between two rational imperatives, leads to the antinomy of teleological judgment. One side reflects a scientific view of rationality. The other is demanded by nature insofar as she transcends scientific or technical rationality.

> *Proposition*: All production of material things is possible according to merely mechanical laws. *Counterproposition*: Some production of material things is not possible according to merely mechanical laws. (CJ, p. 234)

The contradiction is avoided, as always in Kant, by dividing the domains of application between freedom and necessity.

> All appearance of an antinomy between the maxims of the proper physical (mechanical) and the teleological (technical) methods of explanation rests therefore on this that we confuse a fundamental proposition of the reflective with one of the determinant judgment, and the *autonomy* of the first (which has mere subjective validity for our use of reason in respect of particular empirical laws) with the *heteronomy* of the second, which must regulate itself according to laws (universal or particular) given to it by the understanding. (CJ, p. 236)

Science must view events as conforming to mechanical laws yet cannot find its proper objects intelligible in terms of such laws alone. To this Kant adds the summary, expressed as headings of two consecutive chapters:

> THE REASON THAT WE CANNOT TREAT THE CONCEPT OF A TECHNIQUE OF NATURE DOGMATICALLY IS THE FACT THAT A NATURAL PURPOSE IS INEXPLICABLE (CJ, p. 243)

> THE CONCEPT OF AN OBJECTIVE PURPOSIVENESS OF NATURE IS A CRITICAL PRINCIPLE OF REASON FOR THE REFLECTIVE JUDGMENT (CJ, p. 245)

Natural purposiveness is both necessary (for reflection) and inexplicable. Natural design is essential to any rational understanding, even in science, but is unintelligible from a rational point of view, while the forms in which we attempt to represent it—in terms of God or preestablished harmony—are both unintelligible and aporetic. (CJ, p. 272)

Kant concludes the third *Critique*, paralleling the others, with "the methodology of the teleological judgment": a discussion of the role of judgment in the critical system. He formulates it in terms of an anthropic principle:

> If now things of the world, as beings dependent in their existence, need a supreme cause acting according to purposes, man is the final purpose of creation, since without him the chain of mutually subordinated purposes would not be complete as regards its ground. Only in man, and only in him as subject of morality, do we meet with unconditioned legislation in respect

of purposes, which therefore alone renders him capable of being a final purpose, to which the whole of nature is teleologically subordinated. (CJ, p. 286)

This proof, as Kant acknowledges, is aporetic because the moral freedom upon which it is based is not susceptible to proof. What he is emphasizing here, in relation to both morality and God, is that human reason cannot apply itself to natural events without imposing its own values upon them. Teleology follows from the freedom that establishes the basis of reason itself, although it cannot lend itself to proof.

We may return to our opening words on Kant to consider a fundamental principle of metaphysical heresy. Kant's views are not *more* aporetic than those of his predecessors. They are, however, explicitly and reflexively aporetic. In Kant, aporia becomes doubled, tripled, and more. Aporias at one level are resolved into aporias at other levels. Proximate aporias are resolved into generic aporias. Universal aporias are mediated by proximate aporias. Kant closely follows what we have taken to be the dialectical method, in *Parmenides* and *Philebus*, in which reason incessantly and aporetically pursues the aporias of one and many, limit and unlimit, same and other, and equally incessantly pursues their resolution, still aporetically. He forcibly presents us with the recognition that aporias engender other aporias, at different levels of generality, specificity, and reflexiveness, that aporias pertain to each other reflexively. In this sense aporia both contains and manifests inexhaustibility. The implication is that reason is the inexhaustible thinking of aporia, unendingly, in terms of both the recurrent indeterminatenesses that it finds and the recurrent determinatenesses that allow it local, but still aporetic resolution.

We may add another principle, suggested in Kant by the pervasiveness of aporias throughout his system, conjoined with his attempt to resolve them aporetically in terms of the supersensible. The resolution of many aporias into one, the relegation of aporia to a single place in a systematic view of things, effectively denies the pervasiveness of local aporias. To think that all such aporias reflect the one aporia of the unconditioned effectively closes the circle of aporia. The principle that aporia is everywhere is incompatible with the view that there is a most profound or generic source of aporia.

9   HEGEL: THE HERESY OF DIFFERENCE

APORIA is explicit in Kant in relation to a strident pursuit of apo-deictic certainty. The result has been for many of Kant's readers, to obscure the manifest presence of aporia. Similarly, aporia pervades Hegel's writings in far-reaching and explicit ways, while surrounded, no less aporetically, by the absolute certainty with which Spirit knows itself. The result again, among those who write on Hegel, although all acknowledge the presence of aporia at some level, has been that many represent Spirit as the resolution of all aporia,[1] the closure of a system for which openness is the moving impulse.[2] It is as if the restlessness that pertains to self-consciousness, and therefore to being, might profoundly cease, leaving us with no fundamental principle of variation. This singular aporia is supplemented by the aporias of absolute Spirit and absolute knowledge. What must be added is that absolute Spirit and absolute knowledge in Hegel are deeply and thoroughly aporetic. For them to cease to be aporetic would be for them to transcend history and experience. Scientific necessity struggles endlessly with the emergence of history.[3]

The certainty of Spirit in its overcoming is among Hegel's most striking aporias. For he never understands sublation or supersession as overcoming without preservation.[4] " . . . to supersede (*aufheben*) is at once to negate and to preserve." (PM pp. 163-164)[5] Aporia is at the center of Hegel's theory, from sublation to absolute Spirit. The dialectical process is a restless aporia that can neither resolve itself into freedom from aporia nor remain contented with any particular form. Absolute Spirit is aporia both in sublating concrete events and as concrete universal.[6] If we believe that Hegel's treatment of aporia is incomplete, it cannot be because it is unemphatic. Rather, it emphasizes beyond all others the aporias of the infinite in relation to historical experience.

Even so, the tragic side of Hegel's writings, especially in his Jena period, but also in his discussion of *Sittlichkeit*, in connection with *Antigone* in the *Phenomenology*, profoundly expresses the aporetic side of Spirit's absolute knowledge of its own aporetic nature. Absolute knowledge is knowledge of the aporia that comprises Spirit. The Absolute is the identity of identity and contradiction, aporia itself.[7] The highest achievement of Spirit is to think itself as aporia.

Both sublation and the universality that encloses the particular within it are explicit aporias. The oppositions within them are the source of both the movement of the dialectic and the completeness of Spirit. Indeed, the idea of completeness in a dialectical universe is deeply aporetic, as is the universality attained by finite Spirit.[8] Neither the Idea nor history can be the complete fact, only the two together, although they can be united only in aporia.

The notions of sublation and of universality in concreteness are explicit aporias. It is as if Hegel finds in self-consciousness and its self-knowledge both generic aporia and its concrete results, realized as heresy. Aporia is both the moving impulse and the fulfillment. Absolute Spirit and absolute Knowledge are at once and inseparably themselves aporetic (because there is no escape from aporia or from finiteness), the resolution of aporia, and a combination of aporia and its resolution. The last aporia marks the recurrent strain of return within sublation that constitutes the central movement of Spirit. It also manifests the unending movement of a thought that thinks aporia more and more aporetically, of a consciousness that finds the fulfillment in every desire to be its impossibility of fulfillment.

A fundamental aporia in Hegel lies in his view of finiteness as history, manifested in time and expressed in sublation. The dialectic is aporia made both explicit and efficacious: the moving force of a Spirit for whom being is power. The dialectic of history, in which negation belongs to every moment intrinsically, also belongs to Spirit intrinsically in the double sense that it can come to be only through the process that realizes it and that it is the unending repetition of its own becoming. Absolute Spirit, the negation of the negation that constitutes its own determinateness, includes negation within itself in infinite recollection.

> ... this substance, which is spirit, is the development of itself explicitly to what it is inherently and implicitly; and only as this process of reflecting itself into itself is it essentially and in truth spirit. ... This transforming process is a cycle that returns into itself, a cycle that presupposes its beginning, and reaches its beginning only at the end. (PM, p. 801)

This resolution in negation negated is the aporia of aporia.

Two great images express the themes of movement and repetition in Hegel. One is that of circles, found in the famous passage defining his understanding of systematic philosophy.

> Each of the parts of philosophy is a philosophical whole, a circle rounded and complete in itself. In each of these parts, however, the philosophical Idea is found in a particular specificality or medium. The single circle, because it is a real totality, bursts through the limits imposed by its special medium, and gives rise to a wider circle. The whole of philosophy in this way resembles a circle of circles. The Idea appears in each single circle, but, at the same time, the whole Idea is constituted by the system of these peculiar phases, and each is a necessary member of the organisation. (LL, pp. 24-25)

The other is that of the infinite, good and bad, in which the image of a circle is repeated.[9] The bad infinite corresponds to the image of a straight line. The image of the good infinite corresponds to the image of a circle.

> The image of the progress to infinity is the *straight line*, at the two limits of which alone the infinite is, and always only is where the line—which is determinate being—is not, and which goes *out beyond* to this negation of its determinate being, that is, to the indeterminate; the image of true infinity, bent back into itself, becomes the *circle*, the line which has reached itself, which is closed and wholly present, without *beginning* and *end*. (L, p. 149)

What must be added to this static image is the theme of movement and becoming that is central within Hegel's view of determinateness.

> This determination of the true infinite cannot be expressed in the *formula*, already criticized, of a *unity* of the finite and infinite; *unity* is abstract, inert self-sameness, and the moments are similarly only in the form of inert, simply affirmative being. The infinite, however, like its two moments, is essentially only as a *becoming*, but a becoming now *further determined* in its moments. (L, p. 148)

The circle traditionally suggests a figure so perfect as to contain no impulse to movement and transformation. It contains no imbalance. Yet Hegel's entire system is filled with dynamic movements, negations, oppositions. Moreover, he rejects a static circle as empty, mere formalism.[10] What is missing is what he calls the "inner activity and self-movement" of the actual life of Spirit: the heretical events of history.

When he claims that each part of philosophy is a circle, what may be suggested in this isolated image is a perfect, autonomous faculty whereby some part of reflective thought—say logic or ethics—so completes itself as to require no further development. Yet philosophy is a circle of many circles, and there remains the aporia of how many different parts, however perfect, can be joined into a greater perfection. There is also the aporia of the circle itself, understood to include a return to its beginning from its difference. The circle is at once always the same and never identical: same and other in conjunction.

The image of circles of circles can, apart from the rest of Hegel's system, be taken in several ways. One is as a system of concentric circles, suggesting that each of the spheres of philosophic reflection, each faculty, is included in another, all together included in the greater circle that constitutes philosophy. Several difficulties for such an interpretation present themselves in relation to Hegel: he does not seek to show that, say, ethics is included within epistemology, aesthetics within ontology, but rather that each in its own sphere contains the Idea. The image of a circle always includes the notion of repetition. But it also includes the notion of negation. The circle is at once repetition and departure, same and other, aporia in their identity.

A more serious difficulty lies in the way in which a circle of circles is understood concentrically, not as the line that returns to its beginning but the area within. The area bounded by a circle has a within and without. In this sense, no circle can be complete or all-inclusive, and the process of concentricity is without end—as much a bad infinite as a straight line. All hierarchies, including the image of a spiral, either terminate arbitrarily or are expressions of a bad infinite because they can include their origins but cannot return to them. We must reject both a hierarchical structure to Spirit and a concentricity of circles to the good infinite.

The aporetic repetition of the Idea in each circle is closer to the good infinite than is the concentricity of circles. Each circle includes the Idea which is both its beginning and end. Each Idea, as the result of the movement within each circle, is both the outcome and present from the beginning. The good infinite is a circle that finds its end present at its beginning and repeats its beginning infinitely at its end. The image of aporia is clearly present in this unity of end and beginning. More extremely, it is aporia itself that is the beginning and end that comprise the circle. The image of a circle may express the perfection of a total resolution, but it also expresses aporia in the simultaneous departure and return. The circle is at once same and other, difference and closure.

Without aporia it would be fixed. It follows that a moving circle can be a dynamic expression of both aporia and its resolution. Each aporia that constitutes the dynamic movement of finiteness is a circle sublated in a higher circle; each such higher circle is doubly aporetic in sublating many subordinate aporias as its moments without eliminating their aporia. Sublation, here, is the intensification of aporia without cancellation. Here, the circle of circles is as aporetic as any of the subordinate circles but realizes itself in the more reflexive levels of aporia to which it aspires.

Several other models of circles come to mind. One is a system of circles strung like beads around a larger circle. A second is a system of partly overlapping circles around which a larger circle is passed. The latter again faces the difficulty of the inner and outer regions of a boundary. The former, if we emphasize that each smaller circle is to be understood not spatially but dynamically, repeating an infinite sublating movement, does not suggest an inner and outer, but includes all the phases of each within each movement, while each represents the form of the others and all are repeated again in the circle that is philosophical reflection in general. There is an infinite repetition present here: a hall of mirrors pervaded by an infinite same.

A brief moment may be taken to consider other alternatives that do not suffer from the break between inner and outer. One preserves circularity in a system of partly overlapping circles without an all-inclusive circle. In relation to philosophy, or to the diverse forms of knowledge, we have overlapping but no comprehensive form that includes all the others. There are only partial movements, finite forms without the possibility of an inclusive infinite, good or bad, because while each is a negation of the others, each also includes some of the others. There is no unyielding alternation because there is no unqualified externality. An example is the view that the future both (partially) includes the past and transforms it. In this sense, history would be neither a good or bad infinite, but aporetically inexhaustible.

Another image, equally finite but inexhaustible, that avoids both of Hegel's infinites, bad and good, is of each form of knowledge and experience as a tangle of threads, each turning back on itself, knotted with others, neither its negation nor its repetition, unqualifiedly. What might be said about both these images is that they do not allow for the kind of knowledge that Hegel calls science (although they are compatible with a modest view of science as one of many incomplete forms of knowledge): there is no total system, only locality. There is no escape within either from a finite to the (bad) infinite, but neither is there the infinite movement that knowledge requires to be complete.

This notion of completeness in Hegel is very difficult. That absolute Spirit might complete the circle of its own development to return to its beginning suggests that time will be abolished in this movement, and either history will cease or it will become entirely circular. Neither of these possibilities is plausible. What Hegel claims is that with the notion, transition is to be understood, not as alteration but as *development*.[11] With the notion, with its culmination through history, there is no longer the passage from one form of determinateness to another, but simply unfolding. The heresy that constitutes the concrete embodiment of thought in history is replaced by entirely internal principles of development. The cunning of reason (*List der Vernunft*) becomes entirely manifest.[12]

Are we to take this as suggesting that, for Hegel (and for us),[13] the possibility of heresy has come to an end? Such an interpretation is found in so remarkable a reader as Kojève.

> The Hegelian solution,. . . is that . . . the enunciation of the universal, rational principles of the rights of man in the French Revolution marked the beginning of the end of history . . . . In this perspective Kojève interprets our situation; he paints a powerful picture of our problems as those of post-historical man with none of the classic tasks of history to perform, living in a universal, homogeneous state where there is virtual agreement on all the fundamental principles of science, politics, and religion. He characterizes the life of the man who is free, who has no work, who has no worlds to conquer, states to found, gods to revere, or truths to discover.[14]

The suggestion is that reason has *already happened*, that there are no fundamental discoveries remaining for human life—science, politics, religion, freedom, or practice: no remaining heresies. Such a view of closure virtually demands the end of reason (and philosophy) in the name of heresy. Yet we may reply at two levels, one that the fundamental principles of moral and practical reason today include controversies as violent as before, the other that revolutions continue, if in altered form. Heresy continues unabated even in the most scientific of the sciences. Without heresy there would be no effective thought at all.

To Kojève's view of things, the suggestion that even science continues to undergo revolutionary change is devastating. Even science is heretical. The issue is one of difference: heresy and aporia. Yet aporia pertains to difference itself, and what is altogether different is and must be unintelligible. There is no difference that is not, however aporetically, conjoined with sameness. There is, then, in the idea of development a fundamental qualification: what *has* no common measure may, through heresy, *come to have* a common measure. Incommensurateness must be distinguished from incommensurability. The aporia is that what has and what has not a common measure are not different but cannot be the same.

We may explore what Hegel means by development by imagining to be true what he claims is true. We may also consider Marx's similar view of the transformation that will be wrought when alienated labor is abolished. In both cases, what cannot be concluded is that the changing nature of human experience will be abolished as well. Alienated labor will end, but human beings will engage in productive and efficacious activities. Alienated consciousness will end, but an effective consciousness, aware of its own powers, will surely continue. Carrying the image further, suppose that all human beings lived in a free, lawful, and rational society. Suppose that the fundamental principles of natural science had been established. One possibility is that, as some scientists recurrently claim, we will soon know everything fundamental about the nature of the universe. The difficulty is that such a knowledge cannot include itself. When it does, it must find that the universe that includes itself has moved beyond its own knowledge, risen (or declined) to another level. It cannot be knowledge without sublating itself heretically. An alternative is that despite universal agreement concerning the credibility of natural science, what remains is an inexhaustible, heretical project of scientific activity. It is philosophy that is said to end with Hegel, not physics, mathematics, chemistry, or history. It ends because it is always too late.

> One word more about giving instruction as to what the world ought to be. Philosophy in any case always comes on the scene too late to give it. As the thought of the world, it appears only when actuality is already there cut and dried after its process of formation has been completed. ... The owl of Minerva spreads its wings only with the falling of the dusk. (PR, pp. 12-13)

We can think the thought of the world only after the world is done. Yet the doing of the world cannot be completed. The dusk of the world precedes the dawn. Every (too-late) philosophy is in and for its time, facing an unknown and undetermined future.[15] For philosophy, and therefore for reason, the future remains an absolute abyss. That there is *one* philosophy, *one* science, and *one* history amidst *many* futures is an aporetic rift in Hegel's view of history.

The other theme of this passage concerns the relationship between philosophy and human life. The latter must continue after the death of God. Political practice must continue in the complex, unending activities that shape the course of human life even though certain fundamental principles of political reason may have been determined. The conclusion is Kantian despite the difference of dialectic: only the most general principles of rational activities may be so determined. Moreover, these rational principles function aporetically in Hegel as they do in Kant. They cannot determine concrete practices. The notion of development here is profoundly aporetic. It is both end and beginning where thought can only think retrospectively. Every consciousness is blind to its own meaning and development, of which it is the task of philosophy—too late—to be aware. Even philosophy, however, must be blind to its own meaning before the future.

Arendt notes that there is something remarkably paradoxical—she does not think of it as aporia—about conceiving of the active principle of history as coming to an end in a theory in which history cannot end.[16] Either time and the universe end or a new principle of activity emerges. Yet the emergence of such a principle, be it absolute Spirit or development, is but a larger repetition of the principle of dialectic at every subordinate level. Aporia is rational only if it fulfills itself in a novel production that includes its different movements. There is, then, the aporia of aporia that to the extent that the novel form of thought or practice entirely and without negation includes the different movements, the aporia was only apparent, while if the aporia preserves its aporetic character, the resolution must itself be aporetic.[17]

What is at stake in Hegel is the possibility of emergent self-consciousness or heresy. The proviso is that an emergent form of consciousness can never know itself to be final. The truth of dialectic is truth itself; there is no being without aporia.

> . . . the life of the mind is not one that shuns death, and keeps clear of destruction; it endures death and in death maintains its being. It only wins to its truth when it finds itself utterly torn asunder. (PM, p. 93)

What Hegel calls development—where nothing happens that is not already implicitly present—is a manifest denial of historical emergence. Such a view of history can never be prospective. It can only be too late. If absolute Spirit is the form history must take to be rational, no such history can ever be total, because it cannot include its own future. Heresy can be rational only retrospectively—only by being turned into orthodoxy.

There is a view of history in which all the principles of explanation have become manifest, in which the future is merely the working of forms already present. With such a view, we recover the platonism of the theory of Ideas (but not Plato's dialectic), with the difference that in platonism these forms were always present, while in Hegel they are emergent with the notion. But once established, through history, there would be no future to which they did not apply. There would be no historical future in the sense that anything could make a fundamental difference. Heresy would be abolished although it is the only form in which thought can be effective.

By implication, here, such a theory of the notion exists, in Hegel, as the resolution of aporia. Aporia is the central force in history, with the proviso that aporia has been resolved in relation to any history that could make a difference to the future. What follows is that the future—many futures—cannot be significant to the past. Moreover, Hegel accepts neither stasis nor mere repetition; that would be the bad infinite, abstract universality. Development must include novelty. Heresy cannot be abolished because dialectical knowledge is heresy itself. If there is no other to absolute Spirit, it is not because heresy ends with it, because it finally resolves all aporia, but because it includes heresy and aporia within itself. Absolute Spirit *is* aporia.

There is another side to heresy present in Hegel's view of absolute knowledge. The side emphasized so far here is the negative moment in the dialectic, the departure of thought from itself to realize its development. This is the side in which heresy departs from rules. The other side is that heresy must become orthodox. It cannot follow that no further heresies will transpire, invading orthodoxy with their disruptions. Rather, subsequent heresies will disrupt a different orthodoxy, take place in a different world. Heretical knowledge makes a fundamental difference, marked by the difference between external and internal principles of development. What Hegel calls development reveals the power of heresy itself, in which further change works from within, a consequence of its own productive emergence. Heresy remains in the aporia of this development, that it cannot be truth without being sublated.

The most we might be able to say is that certain forms of self-consciousness and reason may have become orthodox in nineteenth-century Germany, just as we may want to say that certain forms of musical thought and of literature have come to an end with Beethoven or Wagner, Shakespeare or Borges. All forms of Spirit, philosophy, science, and art, belong to history and cannot belong to every time equally. Orthodoxy here is neither stasis nor repetition but the transformation and sedimentation of the forms that define the art or genre in question: the classical symphony or opera. Such a transformation indicates the two sides of creative emergence, expressed in Kant's view of genius: both the breaking and establishing of rules; heresy conjoined with orthodoxy. Self-consciousness comes to know itself as this aporia. It is contradictory to this deepest insight to suppose that absolute Spirit might establish rules that cannot be broken. At best, it might establish a new regime in which different rules functioned in different ways. More likely, it would establish rules that demanded their own overthrow from within their aporetic orthodoxy.

It is extraordinary that Hegel does not explicitly consider the future of absolute Spirit. Even to suppose that with it time comes to an end is unintelligible, while we want more than anything else to know how Spirit will be able to know its future. Instead, Hegel repeatedly gives us an image of absolute Spirit as *memory*, repetition of the same, required because without embodiment—another fundamental aporia—Spirit is empty and abstract. Spirit is memory because it must think the world only afterward. Thus, the final passages of the *Phenomenology of Spirit* restore the abstract self-identity of Spirit as the pure notion to its history.

> Knowledge is aware not only of itself, but also of the negative of itself, or its limit. Knowing its limit means knowing how to sacrifice itself. This sacrifice is the self-abandonment, in which Spirit sets forth, the form of free fortuitous happening, its process of becoming Spirit, intuitively apprehending outside it its pure self as Time, and likewise its existence as Space. (PM, pp. 806-07)

The fundamental images here involve the repeated rejection of the abstractness of Spirit, thereby the rejection of an autonomous, self-caused God. God belongs to the concrete historical embodiment of a self-conscious human spirit. This is not an unlimited God, but one that knows both its limit and how to sacrifice itself. The two pervasive forms of this sacrifice are time and space, history and nature, although the theme of sacrifice repeats itself throughout, in particular in the thesis that self-consciousness entails a willingness to risk (and lose) one's life. The first form in which Spirit establishes its concreteness is history; the second is nature:[18] the Absolute's past.[19] Absolute Spirit must negate itself into nature so that it may be understood as the embodiment of Spirit's rationality. Nature of itself is unknown and unintelligible, meaningless. That it should be known and intelligible, rational, demands that it issue into knowing subject or spirit. The image is again of sacrifice, first into the externality of a nature without self that issues in knowledge of itself, second into history (inverting the order just mentioned), the concrete embodiment of self-knowledge. Nature knows itself as history. No other possibility can be rational or intelligible. Nevertheless, this natural self-knowledge is disruption and sacrifice.

For the first concrete aspect of Spirit is that of history, manifested as repeated memory of the shapes (*Begriffen*) of consciousness.

> This way of becoming presents a slow procession and succession of spiritual shapes, a gallery of pictures, each of which is endowed with the entire wealth of Spirit, ... Since its accomplishment consists in Spirit knowing what it is, in fully compre-

hending its substance, this knowledge means its concentrating itself on itself, a state in which Spirit leaves its external existence behind and gives its embodiment over to Recollection (*Erinnerung*). (PM, p. 807)

Spirit remembers and recapitulates its own development: therein lies its concreteness. Yet in this restriction to past history, Hegel offers his only image of the future: a new beginning.

In thus concentrating itself on itself, Spirit is engulfed in the night of its own self-consciousness; its vanished existence is, however, conserved therein; and this superseded existence—the previous state, but born anew from the womb of knowledge—is the new state of existence, a new world, and a new embodiment of mode of Spirit. Here it has to begin all over again at its immediacy, as freshly as before, and thence rise once more to the measure of its stature, as if, for it, all that preceded were lost, and as if it had learned nothing from the experience of the spirits that preceded. (PM p. 807)

This is clearly recollection in the sense that Spirit closes the circle, leaving the future unintelligible. Even the "new world" is to be understood as a repetition.

While, then, this phase of Spirit begins all over again its formative development, apparently starting solely from itself, yet at the same time it commences at a higher level. The realm of spirits developed in this way, and assuming definite shape in existence, constitutes a succession where one detaches and sets loose the other, and each takes over from its predecessor the empire of the spiritual world. (PM, p. 808)

The succession can be neither mere repetition nor mere alternation. History, to be rational, must constitute a progression, one that knows itself through its own development, thereby initiating a new form of development at a higher level. A new beginning that includes itself in repetition is the conjunction of heresy with orthodoxy.

What is essential, amid the complexities of Hegel's view of Spirit, is the idea of progress, embodied in a dialectic in which past aporias are sublated. Yet the idea of progress is no less aporetic than that of time, and the sublation cannot escape the contingencies of the events that constitute it. Here the image of sacrifice is all-important. For what progress has meant in too much Enlightenment thought is overcoming without sacrifice. Such a view of progress is suggested in the famous lines from the *Philosophy of Right*, repeated in the *Encyclopaedia*:

> What is reasonable is actual;
> and, What is actual is reasonable. (PR, p. 10; LL, p. 10)

These lines are aporetic. What they are not is an apologetic for a view of progress without loss. Part of the aporia lies in the notion of actuality.

> Actuality is the unity, become immediate, of essence with existence, or of inward with outward. The utterance of the actual is the actual itself: so that in this utterance it remains just as essential, and only is essential, in so far as it is in immediate external existence. (LL, p. 257)

The unities of essence and existence, inwardness with outwardness, possibility and actuality (LL, p. 259) are all aporias. But there is also the aporia of universal reason in the contingent events of history.

The lines above contain a fundamental ambiguity. If only what is reasonable is actual, then what is irrational is not actual. However, if whatever is actual is reasonable, then reason must include not only the forms of being that triumph in the march of history toward its fulfillments, but marginal voices and suppressed forms of human being and thought. Hegel speaks directly to this point:

> The actuality of the rational stands opposed by the popular fancy that Ideas and ideals are nothing but chimeras, and philosophy a mere system of such phantasms. It is also opposed by the very different fancy that Ideas and ideals are something far too excellent to have actuality, or something too important to procure it for themselves. (LL, p. 11)

Part of what is involved, then, is a concrete historical understanding of Ideas and ideals, of reason, as exemplified in events.

Hegel appears to ignore the contingencies and accidents, the marginalizations, in historical development. Where the density and specificity of historical events and beings pass into mere moments in the development of a later fulfillment, only what can be used by Spirit can be actual and reasonable. Alternatively, no understanding of Spirit can be anything but abstract that does not include history.

Suppose, however, that within the specific events of history are incommensuratenesses. Suppose no fulfillment can include the density of past events without loss. Hegel speaks explicitly to this sacrifice.

... as regards the logical bearings of the question, that existence is in part mere appearance, and only in part actuality. ...
But even our ordinary feelings are enough to forbid a casual
(fortuitous) existence getting the emphatic name of an actual;
for by fortuitous we mean an existence which has no greater
value than that of something possible, which may as well not be
as be. (LL, p. 11)

What is reasonable is simultaneously and aporetically both affirmation
of the concrete details of history, including its marginalizations and sup-
pressions, where these contribute to the future that they portend, and a
denial of the efficacy of all of history, much of which issues in irrelevance and waste.

Such an understanding speaks directly to both heresy and history.
If there are no external ideals against which events are to be measured,
then they work through power and determine the future. If desire
(*Begierde*) is the form in which self-consciousness is realized,[20] relating
to itself through another, through risk and practice, however incompletely,
then there can be no form of self-consciousness, no form of knowledge,
that is not the result of power and desire.[21] The question is how the
imbalances of power and desire can be resolved in absolute Spirit, when the
I realizes its collectivity. Alternatively, the aporetic truth in Hegel is that
mastery is impossible because of the inescapable dividedness in desire.[22]

The idea of progress demands that we understand the future in its
ideality to be the sole measure of what contributes to it. Yet even without such a notion, there is no view of reason in history that can avoid the
judgment of the past by the future as intrinsic to the determination of
the past. Two considerations may be added that are not explicit in Hegel
(though they are frequently implicit): that there are many futures for
any past, so that what has been relevant for one future may be irrelevant
to another; and that consequently there is no total history in relation to
the moments that contribute to it, so that the different determinations of
the past may not comprise a single intelligible story.

It follows that every view of progress, including Hegel's, must
include waste, the sacrifices that are paid in any history's realization of
its development. A better world in any future is realizable only through
the outright loss of some of the moments of the past, which become
mere appearances, possibilities and not actualities, irrational in relation
to the progression of history. This highly selective sense of progress pertains as much to Marx as to Hegel. Nevertheless, for both, although
more explicit in Hegel than in Marx, there is no one future that constitutes the rational principle for the past. We may go further, for while
Hegel cannot avoid the presence of many futures for any past, succeeding

each other heretically, he does not pursue the implication that as these different futures emerge, they may divide each other. No one future can constitute the rationality of its past. Every present is in this way inexhaustibly divided. Moreover, these divisions war with each other agonistically, and the war constitutes the heresies essential to history. Freedom lies within the war of power and desire.

It follows further that the relationship between actuality and rationality must be reformulated. Only what is actual can be reasonable: reason emerges within history. Reciprocally, what belongs to history is intelligible, and nothing can be excluded at the price of rationality. Nevertheless, there is no rational view of finite events that does not exclude, for selection pertains intrinsically to reason. It follows that no view of finite events, however rich and inclusive, can constitute reason of itself. There is no totality of things and events that can constitute intelligibility, only "many totalities." This is one of the fundamental consequences of heresy and aporia. It is the negative moment that constitutes the way in which absolute knowledge externalizes itself, realized in the irresistible presence of power and desire.

This notion of externalization pertains to the most important ideas to be found in Hegel, in every case aporetically. Some of these ideas are worth explicit consideration.

The idea of dialectic contains two aporias together: that of becoming and that of sublation.[23] Both are retained at every level of the system, including that of absolute knowledge, which negates itself into finite events. Attainment of the Idea, which provides the measure of all its moments, is entirely abstract without its infinite repetition in concrete events. Sublation therefore never ceases, even for absolute Spirit, which cannot preserve itself without negation. It follows that the time that pertains to the external movement of sublation is itself sublated: cancelled and preserved. It follows, as well, that absolute Spirit embodies within itself an unceasing movement toward its future in virtue of its sublation of its past.

Sublation is virtually aporia itself. What is added to it that constitutes its dialectic is movement. What it requires that constitutes its life is history. For Hegel rejects mere circularity along with mere contradiction and mere difference, although each is essential to the dialectic of Spirit. Indeed, the recurrence of this "only" in philosophic thinking is perhaps the greatest weakness to which Hegel's own view of Spirit is a response. Formal circularity, logical contradiction, differences that are not themselves negated, are empty abstractions. Concreteness pertains to history, and the dialectic is the necessary movement within the specific events of history.

Dialectic is the movement of sublation; sublation is the aporia in the historical succession. Where, in aporia, do we find necessity? For

Hegel repeatedly claims that the march of Spirit is necessary and that science is the understanding of this necessity. If we think of dialectic as the movement of heresy, how can heresy be understood in terms of necessity? How can necessity be compatible with historical contingencies? Four answers come to mind.[24] Two are that the necessity is either efficient or teleological and largely of a familiar kind. The former is clearly rejected by Hegel, because Spirit is the fulfillment of historical necessity. The latter, teleology, is traditionally qualified by the requirement of fortuitous circumstances. An acorn will grow into an oak tree only if not eaten by a squirrel. Yet such qualifications are relevant only prospectively. Retrospectively, after the oak has grown, the acorn grew into it with necessity and in the absence of contradictory conditions. (Even this account is implausible because there are many cases where the result is a triumph over adversity.)

Similarly, the third answer—where our view of progress is epochal and of knowledge is heretical—suggests an important sense in which retrospective review of even revolutionary events displays necessity inherent in them *after the fact*. Heretical knowledge belongs to its antecedents in the sense that they are included in it as completely as in more orthodox forms of knowledge. This is the sense in which we may think of the future as the result of the past even where there has been emergence.

Yet, there is no inclusiveness without sacrifice. Such an inclusiveness would be unintelligible for any understanding of the negation required for Spirit to be concrete, but is also unintelligible where time and history are retained. History is the determinateness in the Idea without which it would be empty. Movement is the determinateness in the dialectic without which it would be abstract and formal. With both, sacrifice and loss pertain intrinsically to teleology. There is then the aporia in Spirit that its necessity is belied by its own determinateness.

The dialectic within history that constitutes both its movement and its determinateness is not the sublation that Spirit requires once it has been realized. Sublation is the generic term of which dialectic is a species. The knowledge that constitutes Spirit is both concretely of the finite events that constitute history and of the Idea or notion that constitutes reason in history. Analogously, knowledge of dialectic is both itself a dialectical succession in history and a universal. Here—the fourth answer—the necessity pertains to sublation generically and aporetically. What follows is that Spirit cannot know itself without sublating itself. "It only wins to its truth when it finds itself utterly torn asunder." (PM, p. 93) Such sundering pertains no less to absolute Spirit than to any of its manifestations. And the sundering is aporetic, at once opposition and unity, the alterity of alterity as the same. "... in other words, absolute opposites are immediately posited as one and the same reality." (PM,

p. 181) The reality is both same and different, opposing and identical. Even in its absolute form, Spirit must sublate itself, and must then sublate its sublation without end. The generic externalization of Spirit is nature; the primary forms of externality are time and space.

> Space is that kind of existence wherein the concrete notion inscribes the diversity it contains, as in an empty, lifeless element in which its differences likewise subsist in passive, lifeless form. (PM, p. 103)

We are to understand nature, first, as empty, passive, lifeless—pure extension.

> The first or immediate determination of Nature is *Space*: the abstract *universality of Nature's self-externality*, self-externality's mediationless indifference. It is a wholly ideal *side-by-sideness* because it is self-externality; and it is absolutely *continuous*, because this asunderness is still quite *abstract*, and contains no specific difference within itself. (PN, p. 28)

Nature here is Spirit's other, lifeless rather than alive, abstract rather than concrete, continuous rather than differentiated, material rather than self-conscious. Here, nature possesses all the properties ascribed to it by a materialist science, absolutely other to a nature that includes its own capacity to be known. Such a nature cannot be known and cannot be intelligible. A lifeless, passive nature—pure extension—is unthinkable. Because of nature's passivity, we cannot think of it as engendering life from within. Therefore, Spirit must externalize itself into nature in order to establish its own intelligibility—thereby conferring intelligibility on nature. Here both Spinoza's and Berkeley's, not to say Aristotle's, criticisms of material nature are pertinent. Pure space is empty space; material, extended nature is empty and lifeless with no principle of movement or alteration. Its continuity and homogeneity are incompatible with movement requiring time. Empty, homogeneous space requires time for its determination.

There are two fundamental senses of time in Hegel, the time of Spirit's becoming, history, and the time of nature, alteration. The first meaning of time is history, irrelevant to material nature. The second is the time of nature, essential to the determinateness of Spirit.

> Time is just the notion definitely existent, and presented to consciousness in the form of empty intuition. Hence spirit necessarily appears in time, and it appears in time so long as it

does not grasp its pure notion, i.e. so long as it does not annul time .... Time therefore appears as spirit's destiny and necessity, where spirit is not yet complete within itself. (PM, p. 800)

The aporia within this notion is the abolition of time when Spirit is completed. For the completion requires its own sublation, involving the remembering of history. (PM, p. 807) Moreover, the sacrifice that Spirit undertakes to be determinate requires emptying itself into time and space to reveal itself spatially and temporally.

The goal of the process is the revelation of the depth of spiritual life, and this is the absolute Notion. This revelation consequently means superseding its "depth," is its "extension" or *spatial* embodiment, the negation of this inwardly self-centred ego—a negativity which is its self-relinquishment, its externalization, or its substance: and this revelation is also its *temporal* embodiment, in that this externalization in its very nature relinquishes (externalizes) itself, and so exists at once in its spatial "extension" as well as in its "depth" or the self. (PM, p. 808)

Spirit must overcome time and space only to sacrifice itself to them from within itself. Anything less would be pure abstraction. Time and space are purely abstract moments in a process that requires them to be concrete. Put another way, the time of nature, understood as the negative externalization of Spirit's life, cannot sustain it.[25] Space lacks all differentiation; time is fundamentally differentiated. Space and time here are nature's, not Spirit's—that is, the externalization of Spirit, to be overcome in its becoming.

Both space and time, then, with regard to nature, are antitheses of Spirit, the sacrifices it makes to become determinate. With regard to Spirit in its historical development, such space and time are both necessary and overcome, transformed into the concreteness of historical events and the dialectical development of history. Time, in particular, is aporetic in its double meaning, pertaining both to nature and history. Only in relation to nature is time momentary—Hegel defines it as directly self-sublating.[26] Therefore, even moments are not pure and undivided, but are sublated and sublating. This is particularly clear at the beginning of the *Phenomenology*: there is no *Now* that is not other to every *Then*, no *Here* that is not other to every *There*.

Far more important is the division of time into past, present, and future.[27] As a consequence of this division, Hegel concludes that there can be no science of time and no intrinsic measure. A measure of time would be an abstraction reflecting the emptiness of Spirit's self-externalization. Time itself, in producing Spirit, is becoming, past, present, and future together, and only together intelligible in Spirit's recollection.

The time of nature is, therefore, the empty externalization of the concrete life of Spirit.[28] Similarly, the absolute Idea is without process or transition, and is abstract, because only the whole is determinate, including contingency and process.[29] The end is the Idea, but the Idea must be sacrificed into its opposite, recapitulating the historic moments in which it is exemplified. Without that sacrifice, there can be no concreteness. We return to the circularity of the movement that is the process of history. The good infinite returns infinitely to its origin, recapitulating at higher and higher levels the process whereby it reached its own self-knowledge. The circularity of Hegel's time is aporetic because natural time cannot be circular, because there always remains the terror of an unknown future. What may be said, without reservation, is that this terror of a heretical future haunts Hegel's system absolutely.

We may come back to the distinction between the lifelessness of space and the vitality of time. Relative to nature understood as the emptying of Spirit out of itself, both space and time are lifeless. However, the sublation of the lifelessness that Spirit requires is both historical and temporal, so that time must betray itself and its own emptiness. For some reason, although he is not alone in this, Hegel does not recognize that space is as differentiated as time, that Spirit not only must occupy history—different times—in order to realize itself, but different places. Or rather, he understands different places as the joint but opposing workings of time and space.

> Place, as this *posited* identity of space and time is equally, at first, the posited *contradiction* which space and time are each in themselves. (PN, p. 41)

In this sense, just as time is uniquely essential to experience in Kant, the pure form of intuition and the schematism, time is uniquely essential in Hegel, the source of the dividedness that Spirit requires in order to undertake development. It is as if space were divided only by a consciousness that can occupy different positions at different times. Yet the different places pertain to space itself. Put another way, homogeneous space is externally aporetic in having no inward divisions that could constitute its determinateness, while space divided into places is inwardly aporetic in being divided while always everywhere the same.[30]

The fundamental question for Hegel in relation to nature is how it is to be understood as external to consciousness while not sacrificing all possibility of understanding how consciousness might develop from it and be related to it—how, for example, it may be known. In this sense, a "positive" science accepts the externalities without question, leaving both the nature and origin of consciousness and its own intelligibility obscure. Nature must be understood to issue in Spirit, therefore to contain the divisions that constitute the reality of Spirit. Nevertheless, nature is external to Spirit, its self-sacrifice. The result is that time and space are the origin of Spirit in the sense that they are both the final stage *after* absolute Spirit and the beginning. For it is only as Spirit can establish the negation of itself that it can possess the limits it requires to be determinate. The limit here is the externality in nature represented by time and space, with the proviso that these are not identical to the time and space of Spirit's development as history.

The distinction between the time of history and the time of nature carries over into the science of spirit and the science of nature. Hegel seeks to fulfill Kant's goal, to establish the possibility of a unified science based on dialectical rather than apodeictic principles. The major difference is that timeless a priori conditions establish the possibility of an empirical science in Kant—his aporia—while the conditions belong to time in Hegel—his aporia. Two things follow from Hegel's view: that the possibility of a science is emergent—a doubly heretical view—and that as emergent, historical science has not yet been (and may never be) fully determined by its establishment.

> A building is not finished when its foundation is laid; and just as little is the attainment of a general notion of a whole the whole itself . . . . In the same way science, the crowning glory of a spiritual world, is not found complete in its initial stages . . . . it is a whole which, after running its course and laying bare all its content, returns again to itself; it is the resultant abstract notion of the whole. (PM, pp. 75-76)

What is suggested is that the science that is the goal of Hegel's system does not exist fully realized in that system—that is, in Hegel's writings—but only in its initial stages. In his own terms, Hegel can only be understood, historically, as the incipient moment in a new form of understanding that must thereafter bring itself to fruition through time. Thus, the *Phenomenology of Spirit* is at once the story of the becoming of science and the expression of its limits, because this becoming cannot be more than the production of its initial stages.

> It is this process by which science in general comes about, this gradual development of knowing, that is set forth here in the *Phenomenology of Mind* . . . . To reach the stage of genuine knowledge, or produce the element where science is found—the

> pure conception of science itself—a long and laborious journey
> must be undertaken. (PM, p. 88)

The journey of Spirit to science is not the end of Spirit's journey, because
science exists at the end only in its initial stages.

> . . . science, in the very fact that it comes on the scene, is itself a
> phenomenon; its "coming on the scene" is not yet *itself* carried
> out in all the length and breadth of its truth. (PM, p. 134)

These remarks are made in the Preface, written after the story of Spirit
has been told. But we have seen as well at the very end, in absolute
knowledge, that Spirit opens a "new world" in its realization. More
succinctly, absolute Spirit is "History (intellectually) comprehended,"
the unity of particular historical events and universal science. What the
Phenomenology never expresses, and cannot express, is the living presence of the self-knowledge that constitutes science. Nor can the *Encyclopaedia*. Science is always "coming on the scene" and never "there."
This follows from the fact that science "belongs to its time." Absolute
Spirit is another stage in the circle of history. This is as true for development as for becoming, for fulfilled Spirit as for alienated spirit. As soon
as Spirit *succeeds* in becoming, as soon as it *has become*, it can no
longer be anything but a lifeless universal. Knowledge is always "coming
on the scene" and always too late.

Exactly the same aporia pertains to truth. For the "diversity of
philosophic systems" Hegel refers to is not only "the progressive evolution of truth" (PM, p. 67): it is truth itself in its concreteness.

> The truth is the whole. The whole, however, is merely the
> essential nature reaching its completeness through the process
> of its own development. Of the Absolute it must be said that it is
> essentially a result, that only at the end is it what it is in very
> truth; and just in that consists its nature, which is to be actual,
> subject, or self-becoming, self-development. (PM, p. 83)

Truth is both the result and the development. The Absolute is the truth
at the end and in its becoming, together. It is culmination *with* development. Truth *is* aporia. It is the whole together with the moments that
divide it. The temptation to take the Absolute as the reconciliation of all
the opposing moments—the resolution and dissipation of aporia—must
be resisted. It leads away from Hegel to Bradley and McTaggart. For the
latter, appearance is contradictory but reality is absolutely not (although
it is absolutely unintelligible). To Hegel, neither appearance nor reality

is contradictory, but aporetic. Appearance is *thought* contradictory, but its overcoming leads to aporia. Falsity, contingency, aporia, difference, all belong intrinsically to truth and knowledge.

> It is, in fact, out of this active distinction that its harmonious unity arises, and this identity, when arrived at, is truth. But it is not truth in a sense which would involve the rejection of the discordance, the diversity, like dross from pure metal; nor, again, does truth remain detached from diversity, like a finished article from the instrument that shapes it. Difference itself continues to be an immediate element within truth as such, in the form of the principle of negation, in the form of the activity of Self. (PM, p. 99)

Hegel goes on to say that we cannot claim that falsity either is or belongs to truth, for they cannot be mixed. What we must conclude is that falsity *is* truth only after having been cancelled or sublated. Difference lies coiled within truth as both its other and its essence. Hegel's truth is not aporia overcome, but aporia *as sublation*. (Metaphysical) truth is aporia negating (and resolving) itself aporetically.

Nevertheless, Spirit's truth is not aporia as such, but aporia as process. Time pertains to Spirit in a fundamental way. "Thus, then, it is the very nature of understanding to be a process; and being a process it is Rationality." (PM, p. 115)[31] Understanding is a process, and with difference coiled within it is heretical. Reason is not merely heretical: it is heresy fulfilled, become orthodox, provided that orthodoxy preserves heresy within it. The trouble with orthodoxy is that it does not know that it is heresy. Truth is heresy, and heresy can be realized as reason only through time.

Time is not the only aporia, nor its fundamental form. There is an excessiveness in Hegel's view of history that constitutes another aporia. Reason is a process of sublating heresy heretically because truth and being are aporias. Put another way, with Hegel the discovery is made that *truth is aporia*. What remains are the further discoveries that Hegel's discovery is aporetic and that the aporia of aporia—same and other—is inexhaustible.

The notion that carries the force of this recognition is the concrete universal. If Hegel's view of concreteness is restricted by his emphasis on historicity, his affirmation of the contingency of historical events and what comprises them is unqualified. Concrete, particular beings are rational only insofar as they are to be thought in universal terms while mere universality is empty.

Hegel seldom addresses bare individuality without universality; he does so, however, at the beginning of the *Phenomenology*:

> If nothing is said of a thing except that it is an actual thing, an external object, this only makes it the most universal of all possible things, and thereby we express its likeness, its identity, with everything, rather than its difference from everything else. (PM, p. 160)

In the *Encyclopaedia* he requires that individuality and universality be conjoined.

> The Notion as Notion contains the three following "moments" or functional parts. (1) The first is Universality—meaning that it is in free equality with itself in its specific character. (2) The second is Particularity—that is, the specific character, in which the universal continues serenely equal to itself. (3) The third is Individuality—meaning the reflection-into-self of the specific characters of universality and particularity; . . . . (LL, p. 291)

And he recurrently denies that universality is reality.[32] He insists that the Absolute not only organize the whole of determinate and complete knowledge—all contingent and finite events—but that it *be* the whole. This aporia is the essence of the completeness Hegel's system requires to be rational.

> . . . a so-called fundamental proposition or first principle of philosophy, even if it is true, is yet none the less false just because and in so far as it is merely a fundamental proposition, merely a first principle. It is for that reason easily refuted. The refutation consists in bringing out its defective character; and it is defective because it is merely the universal, merely a principle, the beginning. (PM, p. 85)

Yet, it is not merely at the beginning, but also at the end, that the abstract universal is both defective and lifeless where torn from the contingent particulars that comprise its process of realization. This is why religion, which presents the Idea of Spirit in its greatest purity, is not the stage in which Spirit is present absolutely.[33]

Particularity and concreteness belong to history in the form of individual and distinct events—the "density and specificity" of material human reality. There is in this sense nothing "idealistic" about Hegel's understanding of the nature of concreteness. For Hegel as well as Marx, praxis is the fundamental form of human activity with theory following "always too late."[34] Spirit is intrinsically *embodied*, incorporating nature within itself.[35] Praxis, especially *work*, is the sublation of desire,[36] the truth of consciousness, transcending knowledge of the other by its transformation.[37] The fulfillment of the movement of consciousness is the unity of thought and practice. What is missing in Hegel is not the unity of philosophy and praxis but explicit expression of their surplus relative to each other, the contingency and waste of history that is explicitly if incompletely manifested in Kant.

There is a reductiveness (or overemphasis) in Marx that is absent from Hegel, but reciprocally, there is a certain diffusion (through lack of emphasis) in Hegel of the forms of material power that constitute human reality. How they conceive of concrete universality displays these different movements in Marx and Hegel transparently. For Hegel, the universal becomes concrete in history through praxis but is fulfilled by being thought historically. For Marx, the universal becomes concrete in history by being embodied in material productive structures and is fulfilled there. If we take Marx seriously, yet wish to avoid the restriction of human reality to only one of its facets, however major, we must consider the possibility that the concrete may become universal and conversely, not so much — or only — by being thought, philosophically and scientifically, but entirely practically. Philosophy is not the only form that practice must take to be rational. Practice can be rational insofar as it is both concrete and generic, but there is no form of practice that embodies universality. Thought and practice, philosophy and praxis, are interrelated in inexhaustibly manifold ways, but are neither identical nor mere moments in a synthesis. Their reciprocal surplus comprises one facet of the aporia of same and other at the center of determinate historical experience.

In Hegel's *Logic* and *Phenomenology*, the movement of the dialectic is from indeterminateness to determinateness, and the entire movement of history to Spirit can be understood as the concrete knowledge of determinateness.[38] On the side of individual things, determinateness is the universal whereby what is different may be identified. On the side of universality, determinateness is particularity. Thus, determinateness is the unity of universal and particular: same and other. It is aporetic not only in this union, but in the dialectic that inhabits it intrinsically. What is determinate is so because it includes alterity within it. What is determinate is so because it is indeterminate.

> Essence is mere Identity and reflection in itself only as it is self-relating negativity, and in that way self-repulsion. It contains therefore essentially the characteristic of Difference. (LL, p. 215)

Two notions repeat themselves in Hegel's view of determinateness. One is difference, the indeterminateness that determinateness requires for its distinctiveness. The other is limit.

> If we take a closer look at what a limit implies, we see it
> involving a contradiction in itself, and thus evincing its dialecti-
> cal nature. On the one side the limit makes the reality of a thing;
> on the other it is its negation. (LL [*Zusatz*], p. 173)

Determinateness is finiteness, limit, and difference, all involving not
merely a unity of opposites, but opposites of opposites, negations of
negations. There is here, in Hegel's view of determinateness as negation
of negation, a strong suggestion of the complementarity of same and
other that comprises limit and finiteness. What offsets the clarity of this
complementarity is his emphasis on the temporality of the dialectic in
which determinateness works itself through to Spirit. Complementarity
is a certain view of aporia, as is dialectic. The latter suggests that supersession is required historically and temporally, that the sublation involved
is the development of Spirit. Alternatively, to emphasize sublation as
complementarity, as the reciprocity of same and other, is to regard
time not as the primary form of determination but as but one of its
major forms.

Hegel appears to suppose that being is at least intelligible independent of nonbeing, albeit an abstract, empty universal, that the Idea is
intelligible independent of its history as the whole, albeit requiring recu-
peration of its own historic development. Complementarity entails that
being is unintelligible without distinction and differentiation, that the
Idea is intelligible only insofar as it carries within it the manifestation of
concrete events. A limit always has two sides, on one side bounding
what is within, on the other side opening to other limits. The circle,
taken as the limit circumscribing an area, is surrounded by two areas,
within and without. The circle taken as the inscription of the line that
returns to its beginning is no limit in that respect, but is a limit in other
respects. The circle of history, which Spirit recollects in its fulfillment,
constituting its meaning, is not the only limit, not the only relevant determination. If being determinate is being limited, then even being universal is being limited in certain ways—*that* universal and no other.

The notion of determinateness as limit (including difference), understood to involve its alternates complementarily is, then, antagonistic to
all totalities. There is a certain plausibility, albeit a dubious one, to a
closure in history: that in which all heresies have taken place. It is more
plausible that the closure of history is but a temporary expedient, ignoring its future. There can be no closure to the inexhaustibility of diverse
determinate beings, each limited and, in virtue of this limitation, open to
what lies beyond it, in other determinations. Complementarity entails
the unending opening of one limit of being and truth to what lies on its
other side only to establish there new limits. There is no totality except

within a circumscribed limit, never more than this partiality among inexhaustible and diverse beings.

This theme, of the totality of being that comprises absolute Spirit and its absolute knowing, is the aporetic movement to be found throughout Hegel's system. The idea of a system comprises the totality. Both the *Phenomenology* and *Logic* express the unity of being and *logos* that is Hegel's sense of ontology. In some passages, Hegel is explicit that the "completeness" and "totality" constitute the negation of the absolute Idea:

> To speak of the absolute idea may suggest the conception that we are at length reaching the right thing and the sum of the whole matter. It is certainly possible to indulge in a vast amount of senseless declamation about the idea absolute. But its true content is only the whole system of which we have been hitherto studying the development. (LL [*Zusatz*], pp. 374-75)

Here the primary emphasis is upon rejecting the abstractness of the Idea apart from the whole. Absolute Spirit requires, not an infinite in which what succeeds does so without recollection of what entered into its development; the "whole" here is the history with its moments and its outcomes. What makes the system "complete" is that it includes its past in its sublation. Here the future, with its yet-to-be-determined remains an utter mystery. The aporia of the circle that constitutes the whole is that it can never include its future.

There are other passages which are not so clear that the issue is concreteness, that suggest a totality in which the circle becomes entirely self-enclosed.

> This specific character, or the content, leads itself with the form back to the idea; and thus the idea is presented as a systematic totality which is only one idea, of which the several elements are each implicitly the idea, whilst they equally by the dialectic of the notion produce the simple independent of the idea. The science in this manner concludes by apprehending the notion of itself, as of the pure idea for which the idea is. (LL, pp. 378-79)

Even here, however, the totality is represented by two factors: the one Idea and the circle which it takes into other forms to realize itself. The *Logic* ends with the return to Being in the form of nature. The *Phenomenology* ends with the recollection of history, including its newly found significance.

The fundamental image here is of the great return—an image that passes in Nietzsche's hands into the eternal return. If the only significance the past can have is in terms of a future that forever rethinks it, then the future of that future must be an eternal reconstitution of that past. Totality is aporetic in relation to whatever future remains for it. Hegel presents us with a knowledge that is absolute because it encloses its own past in infinite memory, in ever deepening circles, but that cannot have a future of its own. It is the aporia here of the end of the world—a view of history that, ultimately, can be realized only when history is ended. It is the aporia of an absolute that cannot be absolute in time.

The world of Spirit will come to an end, and to a consciousness that knows its history, at that moment—if such a consciousness has a moment in its annihilation to reflect—its historical reflection will be absolute in a way that no predictive reflection could ever be. In this respect, Hegel's is the "final" theory of the universe—except that such "finality" is aporetic. The deepest aporia in Hegel's system is that the totality that constitutes the absoluteness of Spirit can never be unqualified and complete in history. It is always a local totality, inclusive of whatever Spirit can remember, in any present, faced with the terror of a new world that cannot be remembered because it has not occurred. The twilight in which the owl of Minerva spreads its wings must be the end of a universe that cannot end in grey, only in unbroken black.

If Hegel's system is based on aporia, and, moreover, aporetically in the sense that the relation of the totality to its aporetic moments and its dialectical structure is another unending aporia, then perhaps it is true indeed, as he says, that he marks the end of traditional philosophy and the beginning of something new. What comes to an end, however, is neither affirmation of aporia nor the denial of heresy, but their marginalization in the name of orthodoxy. And the orthodoxy pertains not to the major works that constitute the tradition, but to their reading, sometimes by later heretical philosophers. The fact is that Hegel, whose work is based on aporia through and through, has become doubly orthodox. Even Kierkegaard and Heidegger could not see through the aporetic veil of Hegel's absolute knowledge to the aporias that constitute it.

The double orthodoxy that pertains to Hegel tells us something about heresy and its transformation into orthodoxy. One form of orthodoxy is the taming of heresy. The aporia that pertains to absolute Spirit is dissipated into the completeness and perfection that express only one of its moments. Absolute Spirit is seen, not as a more complex aporia in which each aporetic moment plays multiple historical and metaphysical roles, but as transforming each dialectical aporia into a no longer aporetic moment. While it cannot be denied that Hegel's own language is responsible for much of this reading, it must be denied that such a reading pays full attention to the aporias that constitute Spirit's realization of its future. Absolute Spirit is aporia at inexhaustibly more complex levels of reflexivity insofar as it infinitely recollects each aporia that constitutes its development. It is not, however, except aporetically, the supreme expression of such aporia because there is no such perfectibility. That it may be thought so is the movement of heresy into orthodoxy, the centering of aporia (logically and theologically) where it is understood to be inescapable.

With the contemporary movement of aporia to the center of Hegel's theory, there has arisen another orthodoxy, one that perhaps cannot be altogether resisted. Whether Hegel is properly credited with its achievement or seen as its major opponent, aporia as difference has become the focus of all important philosophic writing after him. We are still in the shadow of Hegel's understanding of both heresy and aporia, manifested both in the ideas in which they are expressed—difference, nothing, and time—and the prominence of historicism. If this is so, and if all discussions after Hegel of the end of philosophy circle around his aporias, domesticated to the extent that they lack the supreme aporia of absolute Spirit's "totalization," then the claim may be correct that with Hegel philosophy has come to an end—or, at least, must be granted to be so until another heretical understanding of philosophy's relation to aporia can be established.

After Hegel, the movement of aporia in philosophy becomes *Hegelian*, in the double sense indicated and in the additional sense that no philosophy can be "more" aporetic than Hegel's. Nevertheless, no philosophy can be "more aporetic" than Heraclitus' or, for that matter, Plato's. Aporia is not a matter of degree. The question is what we are to do to make aporia central (but not absolute) after it has become orthodox; what we are to do to think heretically after heresy has become orthodox. Are we to deny all orthodoxy? Hegel is a good example of how difficult that would be. Are we to bring aporia more to the center of the philosophic stage? How could one do so more than Hegel or Kant? Are we to repudiate the totalizing movement that characterizes Hegel's system—perhaps the most striking of his aporias—replacing it by building aporia upon itself inexhaustibly?

These are the questions that constitute post-Hegelian philosophy. Given the inescapability of aporia, how are we to think it? Given its positive importance for truth and knowledge, how are we to establish heresy? As another orthodoxy? How would we avoid doing so? As heresy and aporia take the center of the stage, another orthodoxy raises itself, this time to reject all views that are not sufficiently aporetic, that do not present heresy heretically enough.

There is a paradox in heresy and aporia—call it the aporia of heresy: that even the thought of aporia can become orthodox, can become a vehicle whereby power is exercised and desire is manifested. Because both power and desire work by exclusion, what is involved is a recollection of the past in which only what has been certified as orthodox is acceptable. Here Hegel's insistence that whatever is actual is rational—and aporia here is actual—forces us to oppose even the orthodoxy of heresy. The tradition is as divided by aporia and heresy as it is unified by orthodox reactions.

Hegel must be salvaged from the second orthodoxy while the first is acknowledged—that all understanding of aporia after him is post-Hegelian. What must be added is that there is no escape from effective history—that is Hegel's primary lesson—but every effective history must be resisted in the name of its heretical movements.

No writer can be more aporetic than Hegel. Moreover, every present writing on aporia exists in Hegel's shadow—that of limit, finiteness, and otherness. What heresy demands is that we come to recognize contrary movements even within this shadow—contrary not in being less aporetic, but in bearing inexhaustible manifestations of aporia. Heresy suggests that the restless movement of aporia is the movement of effective metaphysical history, making progress while achieving nothing—or, conversely, developing without progress. What is required is to understand within the aporia of heresy that heresy *is* reason, and conversely, that within the rational affirmation of heresy itself there resides the importance of other heresies; within the rational affirmation of aporia there are the aporias that constitute its own denial. Orthodoxy here not only is the foil for heresy through which history becomes effective, but is an aporetic moment within which heresy can know itself as heretical—its other—and through which aporia manifests its own nature as the same.

10 THE HERESY OF THE END

AMONG the striking developments in post-Hegelian thought is the suggestion that philosophy has come to an end.

> We are asking:
> 1. What does it mean that philosophy in the present age has entered its final stage?
> 2. What task is reserved for thinking at the end of philosophy?[1]

> This difference already suggests a mode of writing without presence and absence—without history, cause, *archē*, or *telos*—which would overturn all dialectic, theology, teleology, and ontology. This mode of writing would exceed everything that the history of metaphysics has conceived in the form of the Aristotelian *grammē*: the point, the line, the circle, as well as time and space themselves.[2]

This apocalyptic motif is repeated within the arts and sciences. It is the contemporary form in which nostalgia for heresy manifests itself, a protest against the pressures of historical materiality. The novel has exhausted all its possibilities. Soon we will know all the fundamental truths about the natural world. Because natural and imaginative worlds are inexhaustible, such claims are incredible. They presuppose that philosophy, art, and science are enough the same to be exhausted.

281

>The end of philosophy proves to be the triumph of the
>manipulable arrangement of a scientific-technological world and
>of the social order proper to this world. The end of philosophy
>means the beginning of the world civilization based upon Western
>European thinking.[3]

>We are thinking of the possibility that the world civiliza-
>tion which is just now beginning might one day overcome the
>technological-scientific-industrial character as the sole criterion
>of man's world sojourn.[4]

The end of philosophy of which Heidegger speaks has already taken
place.

>According to this view, then, once philosophy is purified
>of all unscientific elements, only the logic of science remains.
>. . . We prefer to say: *the logic of science takes the place of the
>inextricable tangle of problems which is known as philosophy.*[5]

The end of philosophy here is closely related to the adulation of science
as the arbiter of truth. Such a view cannot explain the persistence
of similar themes of exhaustion found in science and art. What is involved is the denial that judgment requires heresy and that philosophy
requires aporia.

>As a completion, an end is the gathering into the most
>extreme possibilities. We think in too limited a fashion as long
>as we expect only a development of recent philosophies of the
>previous style.[6]

These "extreme possibilities" and the rejection of "recent philosophies
of the previous style" are affirmations of heresy. What is presupposed,
nevertheless, is the uniformity of the "previous style." Equally important
is the suggestion of a gathering into the *most* extreme possibilities, an
emphasis incompatible with continuing heresy.

A central assumption in such an understanding is that the philosophic tradition is sufficiently coherent that it may be characterized as a
whole, to be supplanted by another form of thought that forbids totality.
Because the "metaphysical tradition" is a creation of orthodoxy, because
being is aporetic and metaphysics is heretical, no totality is intelligible.
Metaphysics is heretical, deeply and inexhaustibly pervaded by aporia,
in its most systematic works as thoroughly as in those that iconoclastically
call for its end. Writers who would claim heresy for themselves too fre-

quently neglect its presence in the tradition. This blindness is intrinsic to the millenial movement, which must conceive its past comprehensively and must therefore deny its heresies. It is a withdrawal before the force of heresy in a future yet to be determined in which our understanding of the past will be transformed. There is, moreover, the recurrent irony that the discourse in which heresy is claimed denies its existence in those who preceded. The tradition is denied its heresies in an act of appropriation in which no thought of the past remains unthought.

Such a view of heresy betrays a deficient view of time, rejection of a major aporia of history. This latter claim may appear astonishing in relation to Heidegger and his successors, who criticize the tradition for rejecting the dividedness of temporality. Yet to claim an undivided past orthodoxy and to emphasize a particular present heresy is to reject the aporia of past and future. The present heresy is made absolute. Even to claim the certainty of death in every future is to acknowledge its absoluteness. Rather, every present heresy is qualified by future heresies. The heresy of the present will pass into the orthodoxy of the past and conversely. The aporia of time is that every sense of history is divided and heretical, including heresy and aporia themselves. The alternative is a monolithic sense of heretical movement.

A striking theme in modern philosophy is this sense of closure, the expression of one's own heresics by denying them to others. Beginning with the empiricists, closely related to the rise of modern science, the philosophical tradition has repeatedly rejected its past. Philosophy will end by rejecting dogma, replacing it by reliance on hard evidence, culminating in science. That fallibility becomes dogmatic skepticism and that evidence provides its own dogmas are only a few of the relevant aporias.

In relation to the millenial spirit, the importance of the rise of science — "true" science — cannot be overstated. What is rejected is dogmatic, mistaken, unscientific philosophy. What must replace it is a philosophy that knows itself to be science. Here the irony is empiricism's rejection of the certainty that characterizes science, based on a certainty that characterizes experience.

Among the prominent themes in the modern repudiation of the tradition is a sense of the dogmatic inadequacies of prior standpoints. The contemporary repudiation of the tradition shares this sense of inadequacy, but has become suspicious of every proposed alternative as equally dogmatic. We may think of this suspicion as a sense of self-criticism raised to a higher level: rejection not merely of the dogmas of prior philosophers, but of the tradition itself. What remains is a different sense of the possibility of philosophy, avoiding the premises in terms of which closure is intelligible. Here the heresy is that the certainty with which philosophy has proposed to understand itself is called into question as unfounded.

Yet even this relatively sophisticated sense of self-awareness rests on an undivided characterization of the tradition. The heresy in which the certainty inherent in the tradition is called into question presupposes both that the tradition is undivided and that the new heresy will not conform to similar orthodoxies. The heresy of the end of philosophy must think of the philosophy whose end is at hand in undivided terms. The heresies that repeatedly characterize the tradition must be denied in thinking of that tradition as at its close. For that the tradition might continue, heretically, entails that its orthodoxies may be evanescent, that what is at one time taken as settled will at another time be disrupted. Thus, a heretical view of philosophy and of knowledge in general entails that any uniform characterization of its tradition, however involuted, is an orthodoxy, denying its heresies, and that any sense of its closure repudiates the heretical possibilities within it.

A vivid presentation of this aporia is found in Hegel's sense of dialectic. A dialectical progression is profoundly heretical in each moment while the totality that makes such moments intelligible must repudiate their heresy. If the understanding that Spirit attains of its own development is scientific, then it must be the only possible understanding. In this achievement, the dialectical progression comes to an end by denying any further heresy. If the understanding that Spirit attains of its own development is still dialectical, then its future will heretically transform that understanding into passing moments. Even the limited resolution attained by absolute Spirit cannot be compatible with a dialectic in which heresy retains its disruptive relevance.

One possible conclusion is that no view of science is compatible with heresy, that heresy pertains only to philosophy and art. An alternative is that science is as heretical as philosophy and art. Such a view is rarely maintained,[7] yet it is inescapable. Moreover, it is present in a powerful, if covert, form in Hume and Kant, whose views have largely established the orthodox view of scientific certainty. Again, the orthodox view is not the only acceptable standpoint. Indeed, the historical breaks in natural science, from classical mechanics to relativity theory, quantum mechanics, and even superstring theory, suggest that it is the heresies in the physical sciences that determine their reliability and precision. The doctrine that a science achieves certainty and stability is belied both by the history of science and the importance of heresy in every major discovery. Heresy is truth, even in science; repetition cannot be knowledge, certainly not then truth.

A contemporary form in which the end of philosophy has been proclaimed is in relation to the certainty that is claimed traditionally for philosophy. For Dewey, all knowledge must be recognized to be fallible. For Rorty, philosophy and science must understand the possibility of knowledge without mirrors. For both, this recognition runs against the tradition, interpreted in the one case as seeking complete certainty,[8] in the other, as seeking a truth that mirrors reality.[9] For both, the tradition seeks unquestionable foundations; for both, knowledge and being are without foundations.

Dewey and Rorty, along with Heidegger, Nietzsche, and Wittgenstein, present an unorthodox reading of what they take to be an orthodox tradition that repudiates heresy. Each, then, would assert his own heresies in defiance of a tradition that rejects heresy. They all fail to take sufficiently into account the fact that they belong to that tradition along with the other heretics. We have only to think of Locke and Hume, whose heretical repudiations of the dogmas of scholasticism and rationalism have passed into the supreme authority of empirical science, and Hegel and Whitehead, whose heretical repudiations of a static temporality have passed into an orthodoxy in which both knowledge and truth partake of eternity.

To Rorty, systematic philosophers are orthodox and foundational; heretical philosophers are iconoclastic.[10] There is, then, a close relationship between repudiating the philosophic tradition and engaging in philosophic heresy.

> If one takes "our time" to be "our view of previous times," so that, in Hegelian fashion, each age of the world recapitulates all the earlier ones, then a post-Philosophical culture would agree with Hegel that philosophy is "its own time apprehended in thoughts."
>
> In a post-Philosophical culture it would be clear that that is *all* that philosophy can be.... The modern Western "culture critic" feels free to comment on anything at all. He is a prefiguration of the all-purpose intellectual of a post-Philosophical culture, the philosopher who has abandoned pretensions to Philosophy. ... He is the person who tells you how all the ways of making things hang together hang together. But, since he does not tell you about how all *possible* ways of making things hang together *must* hang together—since he has no extra-historical Archimedean point of this sort—he is doomed to become outdated.[11]

The "post-philosophical" philosopher is doomed to become outdated and also aware of that reality. It colors his picture of how things hang together. It follows that he regards both himself and other philosophers as engaged in heresy (Rorty calls it "abnormal discourse.") The major heresy consists in repudiating the tradition's attempt to define an Archimedean standpoint.

Rorty fails to acknowledge the heresy within such an Archimedean point: its unyielding aporias. But Rorty fails in general to acknowledge aporia, and can therefore accommodate only an attenuated sense of heresy. A forceful manifestation of this limitation lies in his denial that systematic philosophy can be heretical. The contrary point of view is powerfully expressed by Nietzsche:

> *Historia abscondita.* Every great human being has a retro-active force: all history is again placed in the scales for his sake, and a thousand secrets of the past crawl out of their hideouts— into *his* sun. There is no way of telling what may yet become history some day. Perhaps the past is still essentially undiscovered! So many retroactive forces are still required![12]

Santayana's is a similar view.

Nietzsche's incredible heresy is that future heresies transform the past because the orthodoxies that define the future have been overcome by heresy. Thus, if Rorty is correct, the postmodern philosopher will redefine the nature of modernity, thereby redefining both past ortho-doxies and his own heresies. Heresy is always directed at itself, and simultaneously redefines its own nature and the orthodoxies in relation to which it can be heretical.

Philosophy is both aporetic and heretical; metaphysics is among the great historical stages upon which this drama is played out. Rorty regards the systematic side of philosophy as hostile to its iconoclastic heresies, as if a critical and heretical philosophy could not be system-atic. He finds a similar strain in Dewey, although such a claim cannot withstand detailed scrutiny.

> When it is acknowledged that under disguise of dealing with ultimate reality, philosophy has been occupied with the precious values embedded in social traditions, that it has sprung from a clash of social ends and from a conflict of inherited institutions with incompatible contemporary tendencies, it will be seen that the task of future philosophy is to clarify men's ideas as to the social and moral strifes of their own day.[13]

All that is lacking is Dewey's acknowledgment that these "strifes" are aporias. For there is little doubt that the great systematic works of the tradition share the concern of human beings with their most pre-cious values.

> Thus philosophy marks a change of culture. In forming patterns not to be conformed to in future thought and action, it is additive and transforming in its rôle in the history of civ-

ilization. Man states anything at his peril; once stated, it occupies a place in a new perspective; it attains a permanence which does not belong to its existence; it enters provokingly into want and use; it points in a troubling way to need of new endeavors.[14]

This passage is an explicit affirmation of philosophic heresy and its place in history. What must be added is that the works that play the most provoking roles are frequently the most systematic. There is a pervasive aporia in the fact that the works that seek to exhaust the possibilities they confront are those that most unleash new and unexpected possibilities.

I have referred to Rorty's attenuated sense of aporia and the heretical possibilities in systematic philosophy and have suggested that it is related to the conviction that the philosophic tradition is stable enough to be overthrown. This last motif pervades all discussions of the end of philosophy, neglecting the aporias that inhabit the tradition. We have noted the striking aporia that those who would continue the tradition largely would continue its orthodoxy, while those who would end it assume, similarly, a uniform understanding of its variety. It is as if orthodoxy provides the only terms in which we can understand a tradition while the most striking property of a tradition is that it is able to include within itself the most heretical possibilities.

This last recognition is hermeneutic—I take it to be definitive of hermeneutic thought. In principle, hermeneutic thinking includes heresy as the otherness that understanding requires. What may be questionable is whether hermeneutics equally includes aporia. For without aporia, heresy is merely otherness. It lacks a strong enough sense of inexhaustibility, transforming its complementarities into negations.

The elements of a hermeneutic epistemology are finiteness, circularity, otherness, and mediation. The first, finiteness, is the defining characteristic of which the others are expressions. A hermeneutic knower is a finite knower, and what he knows cannot escape its finiteness. Yet there can be no knowledge without universality. It follows that universality must also be local. This aporia is fundamental within pragmatism. It is not so clear that it is present in a hermeneutic epistemology. What is more clearly present is the circularity of understanding.

> Schleiermacher . . . regards as an essential ingredient of understanding that the meaning of the part is always discovered only from the context, i.e. ultimately from the whole. . . .
>
> It was always clear that this was logically a circular argument, in as far as the whole, in terms of which the individual element is to be understood, is not given before the individual element, ...

> ... Fundamentally, understanding is always a movement in this kind of circle, which is why the repeated return from the whole to the parts, and vice versa, is essential. Moreover, this cycle is constantly expanding, in that the concept of the whole is relative, and when it is placed in ever larger contexts the understanding of the individual element is always affected.[15]

In Hegel, the circle is the image at once of infinite repetition and aporia. Here too, the repetitiveness of the circularity of understanding is belied by the new circles in which understanding finds itself.

The hermeneutic circle has two sides. In their interrelation—essential to any understanding—heresy and aporia are manifest. What is not equally manifest is that these sides must be interrelated, therefore, that any hermeneutic understanding must be both aporetic and heretical. The force of heresy to this extent is blunted in Gadamer's sense of hermeneutics. This is evident where he refers to Heidegger for the notion of the hermeneutic circle.

> Heidegger writes: "It is not to be reduced to the level of a vicious circle, or even of a circle which is merely tolerated. In the circle is hidden a positive possibility of the most primordial kind of knowing. To be sure, we genuinely take hold of this possibility only when, in our interpretation, we have understood that our first, last and constant task is never to allow our fore-having, fore-sight, and fore-conception to be presented to us by fancies and popular conceptions, but rather to make the scientific theme secure by working out these fore-structures in terms of the things themselves."[16]

If (in Gadamer's language) we compare Heidegger's sense of the circularity with Schleiermacher's, we must be struck by how the latter's image of part and whole passes into the image of forestructure. The whole that constitutes the movement of the circle in relation to the parts has a double existence.

> A person who is trying to understand a text is always performing an act of projecting. He projects before himself a meaning for the text as a whole as soon as some initial meaning emerges in the text. Again, the latter emerges only because he is reading the text with particular expectations in regard to a certain meaning. The working out of this fore-project, which is constantly revised in terms of what emerges as he penetrates into the meaning, is understanding what is there.[17]

There is a prior meaning—forestructure, prejudgment—that understanding requires; and there is a subsequent meaning that understanding produces. These are inseparable. The unity of meaning that is projected prior to an understanding that makes it possible is projected as the synthetic outcome of the act of understanding. This is the circularity of hermeneutic understanding. What may be asked is whether the image of circularity here is not effectively antiheretical, despite the fact that it is aporetic.

For the projected totality of meaning plays a double role. The forestructure and projected structure are totalities that understanding requires. Yet, because they are divided by time and circumstance—in some cases, by great intervals of historical time—they cannot be identical; and if they are not, then the circle is aporetic. The projected universality both denies its locality and must affirm it. This aporia loses its heresy as it is replaced by otherness. While otherness is essential to the hermeneutic act of understanding, it is an otherness that obscures its own aporia. The aporia is that the projected totality of meaning is *never* any given or resultant meaning, *cannot be* any given or resultant meaning. It is not merely that totality is unavailable in any local experience, but that the totality is aporetic and can be manifested only through heresy.

This is the truth within the hermeneutic circle as Heidegger conceives it. In Gadamer's words again:

> The point of Heidegger's hermeneutical thinking is not so much
> to prove that there is a circle as to show that this circle possesses
> an ontologically positive significance.[18]

The heresy here is that this positive significance is the revelation of aporia, undermining itself in its positivity. Gadamer recognizes this limitation, but does not resolve it.

> The idea of the whole is itself to be understood only relatively.
> The totality of meaning that has to be understood in history or
> tradition is never the meaning of the totality of history.[19]

Universality is still fundamental for his view of understanding—a universality projected within every set of finite horizons that functions like a totality:

> Not only is an immanent unity of meaning guiding the reader
> assumed, but his understanding is likewise guided by the con-

stant transcendent expectations of meaning which proceed from the relation to the truth of what is being said.[20]

He discusses the apparent conflict directly:

> Does not the universality of understanding involve a onesideness in its contents, inasmuch as it lacks a critical principle in relation to tradition and, as it were, espouses a universal optimism?[21]

His modest answer is that:

> It seems to me, however, that the onesidedness of hermeneutic universalism has the truth of a corrective. . . .
> What man needs is not only a persistent asking of ultimate questions, but the sense of what is feasible, what is possible, what is correct, here and now. The philosopher, of all people, must, I think, be aware of the tension between what he claims to achieve and the reality in which he finds himself.[22]

The irony is that a modesty that comes from avoiding ultimate questions, with their aporias, might lead to universality. For the universality is an aporia, the projection of the infinite from the finite in such a way that both heresy and aporia are denied. The modesty is incompatible with the universal optimism.

Yet even this way of putting the matter is inappropriate, as if only mediation and universality were optimistic. To the contrary, the significance of the heretical side of understanding is that heresy and aporia are as positive achievements as are commonality and universality. There is a positive side to heresy and aporia even in the absence of universality. Heidegger expresses this in the closing words of the lectures on "The Nature of Language": "This breaking up of the word is the true step back on the way of thinking."[23]

A characteristic feature of the Western epistemological and metaphysical traditions, in their orthodox manifestations, is the assumption that knowledge is consensus, that agreement is closer to reason than is difference. An aporetic ontology must hold that there is nothing upon which all can agree unequivocally; a heretical epistemology must hold that heretical differences are as positive achievements as are consensual agreements. Knowledge is not simply a movement from difference to agreement, but a reciprocity involving differences that require mediation and the emergence of differences within mediation. Conformity is as oppressive as it is productive. Heresy realizes not simply failure in understanding but the inexhaustible differences that cannot be assimilated under any conformation. An undivided truth is no truth at all; an undivided freedom is no freedom at all. In short, freedom and truth are local, as are same and other.

Gadamer assumes the Kantian image of a successful understanding amid a profound sensitivity to the aporias of finiteness. The result is that the projected ideal, deeply aporetic in its relationship to finiteness, has no explicit room for heresy.[24] A hermeneutic epistemology, in Gadamer's terms, is one that moves through the aporias of finiteness without finding any of them an overwhelming obstacle. Heresy here is the mark of the deadendedness of aporia, with the qualification that the cul-de-sac is no less aporetic than the opening. There is finiteness in Gadamer, but not otherness; difference but not aporia; circularity but not heresy; unity but not rupture.

> Our task is to extend in concentric circles the unity of the understood meaning. The harmony of all the details with the whole is the criterion of correct understanding. The failure to achieve this harmony means that understanding has failed.[25]

The key words here are "unity" and "harmony." The disruptions, differentiations, divisions, and incommensuratenesses in heretical understanding are ignored. Similarly, in relation to language:

> In reality, language is the single word whose virtuality opens up the infinity of discourse, of discourse with others, and of the freedom of "speaking oneself" and of "allowing oneself to be spoken."[26]

This "infinity" of discourse is a unifying discourse although what it unifies is neither whole nor subject to a common measure. What is missing in this otherwise striking sense of the inexhaustibility of discourse and understanding are the local aporias and heresies that constitute finite inexhaustibility, the local disruptions that constitute any tradition, the unthought that constitutes thought.

The images of circles and of circles of circles that comprise the aporia whereby we are able to conceive of finiteness is found not only in Hegel, Heidegger, and Gadamer, but in American pragmatism as well—in all the views that make finiteness the foreground of philosophic thought. Dewey argues, for example, that all thought emerges from and depends on its context, and that the fundamental fallacy consists in neglect of context.[27] Two such fallacies are *unlimited extension or universalization* and the *analytic fallacy*: "found wherever the distinctions or elements that are discriminated are treated as if they were final and self-sufficient."[28]

The result of thinking contextually is practically indistinguishable from hermeneutic understanding:

> Philosophy is criticism: criticism of the influential beliefs that underlie culture; a criticism which traces the beliefs to their generating conditions as far as may be, which tracks them to their results, which considers the mutual compatibility of the elements of the total structure of beliefs. Such an examination terminates, whether so intended or not, in a projection of them into a new perspective which leads to new surveys of possibilities.[29]

The termination is in a new context—"forestructure"—that establishes the terms for subsequent thought. Here the novelty suggests heresy. Even so, the circular images persist, concentrically:

> Examination discloses three deepening levels or three expanding spheres of context. The narrowest and most superficial is that of the immediate scene, the competitive race. The next deeper and wider one is that of the culture of the people in question. The widest and deepest is found in recourse to the need of general understanding of the workings of human nature.[30]

Two suggestions here must be rejected: that there is a widest and deepest sphere of context; and that contexts comprise a hierarchy. Heresy forces us to deny that any context can be most comprehensive. Aporia forces us to deny that contexts and understandings comprise a hierarchy. To the contrary, the role played by universality serves us only to the extent that it promotes heresies. Even in Dewey, where finiteness is most prominent, there is an incomplete affirmation of aporia.

Much more of a sense of aporia can be found in Heidegger, though even there not unmixed. The ontological difference is aporia itself, with the qualification that aporia may not have a self. Heidegger surely recognizes this chameleon-like, inexhaustible nature of aporia, because the ontological difference is never simply *one* difference. It is *the* difference while also *many* differences: between being and nothing, language and being, being and human being, all equally equiprimordial. This is aporetic enough. Yet Heidegger fails to acknowledge the extent to which the metaphysical tradition revels in aporia.

> Philosophy is metaphysics. Metaphysics thinks beings as a whole—the world, man, God—with respect to Being, with respect to the belonging together of beings in Being. Metaphys-

ics thinks beings as being in the manner of representational thinking which gives reasons. . . .

What characterizes metaphysical thinking which grounds
the ground for beings is the fact that metaphysical thinking,
starting from what is present, represents it in its presence and
thus exhibits it as grounded by its ground.[31]

Metaphysical thinking represents what is present in its presence—but
not its absence. It thinks of the belonging together of beings in being—
but not of their incompatibilities and incommensuratenesses. Yet Heidegger never speaks overtly of incommensurateness. To the contrary, he
emphasizes the ways in which beings and being, *Dasein* and *Sein*, language and being, are together rather than incommensurate. More accurately, he emphasizes both their togetherness and their opacity.

If we are to think through the nature of language, language must
first promise itself to us, or must already have done so. Language must, in its own way, avow to us itself—its nature. . . . The
essential nature of language makes itself known to us as what is
spoken, the language of its nature. But we cannot quite hear this
primal knowledge, let alone "read" it. It runs: the being of
language—the language of being.[32]

We speak our language. How else can we be close to language except by speaking? Even so, our relation to language is
vague, obscure, almost speechless.[33]

Being is together with language and language with being: yet the relation cannot be spoken. In speaking our own language, our relation is
obscure, almost speechless. The relations of language and being, of language and thought, are unspeakable aporias. Similarly, the relations of
beings and being, of identity and difference, are aporias. When Heidegger
rejects metaphysical thinking, he rejects a thinking that does not think
its own aporias, that does not think its other as disruption. Such a metaphysical thinking is ontotheological. It thinks of beings totalistically in
terms of reasons: beings, totality, logic.

The essential constitution of metaphysics is based on the
unity of beings as such in the universal and that which is highest.[34]

It is true that metaphysics has, historically, frequently concerned
itself with the universal and supreme ground of reality. Yet the discussions of the preceding chapters show how profoundly such a claim must

be qualified. Just as being cannot be thought without qualification—manifesting its finiteness and inexhaustibility—neither human being nor its fundamental modes of expression can be thought without qualification. In this respect, there is no "human being" that universally must remain the same, no human history, no tradition, no science, and no metaphysics.

Metaphysics is heretical for many reasons, not least because being is aporetic. Science and technology cannot escape the aporias of being and experience, but they render them recessive, while aporia is dominant in metaphysics. Yet although aporia is dominant in metaphysics, because being is inexhaustible, aporia is not and cannot be the essence of metaphysics, because there is no essence to a heretical episteme, not even heresy itself, which can be no essence. An ironic contemporary expression of this finite universality is in terms of a groundless ground, an essenceless essence. If aporia and heresy are universal metaphysical conditions, then they speak against any essence but themselves, but cannot be essences like any others. It appears to follow that heresy, aporia, finiteness, and inexhaustibility are atypical, universal essences nevertheless.

This conclusion is opposed by the entire argument presented here. To say that universality is finite is not to say that finiteness is universal, *everywhere*, but that wherever universality is found, finiteness is found as well. What follows is that there is no unqualified universality, only local universality; no unqualified totality, only local inclusiveness, but also, that qualifications are themselves qualified, that locality is local, not absolute. A striking expression of this insight can be found in Gadamer, although he still denies aporia.

> ... historicism that takes itself seriously will allow for the fact that one day its thesis will no longer be considered true, i.e. that people will think "unhistorically." And yet not because the unconditional assertion of the conditioned character of all knowledge is not meaningful, containing a logical contradiction.[35]

Aporia is not the essence of metaphysics because many of the important works in the metaphysical tradition have been ontotheological. Nevertheless, they have been so both aporetically and heretically. There is a coexistence of heresy and orthodoxy that, while aporia, resists their universality disruptively.

"The Onto-Theo-Logical Constitution of Metaphysics" addresses Hegel's view of Being, and for that reason may suggest that generalization to the entire metaphysical tradition is inappropriate. Even so, however, only one side of Hegel appears in the essay:

(... Being is the absolute self-thinking of thinking. Absolute thinking alone is the truth of Being, "is" Being. Truth here means always that the knowable as such is known with a knowledge absolutely certain of itself.)[36]

What is lacking is the aporia that comprises "absolute certainty." To the contrary, because the absolute self-thinking of being is the nonabsolute, aporetic thinking of nothing, absolute certainty is absolute same and other.

For Hegel, the matter of thinking is: Being with respect to beings having been thought in absolute thinking, and as absolute thinking. For us, the matter of thinking is the Same, and thus is Being—but Being with respect to the difference from beings. Put more precisely: for Hegel, the matter of thinking is the idea as the absolute concept. For us, formulated in a preliminary fashion, the matter of thinking is the difference as difference.[37]

What is implied is that difference is not fundamental in absolute Spirit, especially difference as difference. Yet the truth in absolute thinking is that it is the thinking of the difference, recapitulated endlessly. The point is that absolute Spirit is the culmination of its own process, and in the thinking of this process, is thought absolutely and unendingly as both sameness and difference.

There is, of course, a fundamental difference between Hegel and Heidegger despite their affinities. The difficulty is to find a way to express it. Heidegger comes close to a compelling distinction, except that his general nostalgia works against it.

For us, the criterion for the conversation with historical tradition is the same [as Hegel's], insofar as it is a question of entering into the force of earlier thinking. We, however, do not seek that force in what has already been thought: we seek it in something that has not been thought, and from which what has been thought receives its essential space. But only what has already been thought prepares what has not yet been thought, which enters ever anew into its abundance.[38]

He appears to assume that absolute Spirit is the infinite recapitulation of its own development, devoid of newness, while in this infinite recapitulation, Spirit must continually produce its own otherness. Hegel's is a theory of heresy and aporia, with the qualification that what is achieved in finite experience must be able (aporetically and heretically) to know itself absolutely. Now thinking what has not been thought, prepared by what has already been thought, is heresy. The qualification is that after having been thought, even the heretical thought becomes "already thought," that is, orthodox.

This is the aporia of heresy: that heresy cannot be found within what precedes it, but cannot be dissociated from it either. The heretical thought is, as such, unthinkable; it is thinkable only as it becomes orthodox. Put another way, heresy is thinkable only insofar as it is the same, but it is heresy only insofar as it is other. What must be added is that same and other comprise aporia. By accepting it as the center of a metaphysical theory, we make heresy central to the metaphysical tradition.

If so, then to say that that tradition is ontotheological is either deficient or aporetic. In both cases, it is equivocal because "the tradition" is always divided, uniform and orthodox, heretical and aporetic. However determinate a tradition, it is both divided within itself inexhaustibly insofar as its future will also be that tradition and divided inexhaustibly by its many futures. The metaphysical tradition is ontotheological; yet once known to be so, may cease to be so. This is what Heidegger calls the "step back," and it is profoundly aporetic.

> The difference between beings and Being is the area within which metaphysics, Western thinking in its entire nature, can be what it is. The step back thus moves out of metaphysics into the essential nature of metaphysics.[39]

The step back leaves metaphysics (the "end of philosophy") and returns to it (its essential nature). The same aporia is found in other discussions of the end of philosophy.

> The end of philosophy is the place, that place in which the whole of philosophy's history is gathered in its most extreme possibility. End as completion means this gathering.[40]

> The end of philosophy means the beginning of the world civilization based upon Western European thinking.[41]

The end of philosophy is at once, ambiguously and aporetically, both the *completion* of philosophy (in the scientific-technological world) and the *beginning* of thinking (in a different way). It is appropriate to recall Dewey's related comment:

> To insist that nature is an affair of beginnings is to assert that there is no one single and all-at-once beginning of everything.

> ... And since wherever one thing begins something else ends, what is true of beginnings is true of endings.[42]

Setting aside the far from trivial point that things may begin *in media res*, where nothing else ends, that beginnings and endings far more often overlap than connect in orderly fashion, Dewey's relevant point is that beginning and ending within philosophy are inseparable, even indistinguishable. They require their future and comprise part of the aporia of any tradition. The end of philosophy is not the cessation of philosophy, but its transformation. The beginning of a new philosophy always belongs to the tradition from which it emerges. That is what it means to understand that heresy belongs to every tradition.[43]

Metaphysics is ontology because it thinks beings. It is theology because it thinks beings in totality.

> The wholeness of this whole is the unity of all beings that unifies as the generative ground. To those who can read, this means: metaphysics is onto-theo-logy.[44]

The question is how (and why) the deity enters metaphysics. The answer leads again to totality.

> Metaphysics thinks of beings as such, that is, in general. Metaphysics thinks of beings as such, as a whole. Metaphysics thinks of the Being of beings both in the ground-giving unity of what is most general, what is indifferently valid everywhere, and also in the unity of the all that accounts for the ground, that is, of the All-Highest. The Being of beings is thus thought of in advance as the grounding ground. Therefore all metaphysics is at bottom, and from the ground up, what grounds, what gives account of the ground, what is called to account by the ground, and finally what calls the ground to account.[45]

Metaphysics is foundational thinking, where being is the ultimate and highest foundation.

How true is this claim about "all metaphysics at bottom and from the ground up"? How true can any such claim be about an aporetic and heretical tradition? The metaphysical tradition is divided within itself by heresies and aporias. It has no bottom and rests on no ground, although among its deepest aporias is that of the ground, the finality of the origin. Heresy is an expression of the aporias of inexhaustibility. However unified it appears to be at different times in the Western tradition, philosophy must be deeply heretical if it is to reflect the aporias that it finds within itself. In the recurrent aporias that comprise the tradition, and in the heresies whereby these aporias find expression, there is the profound realization of inexhaustibility.

We find here, in the midst of the heretical side of the metaphysical tradition, among the aporetic features of experience and being that it both influences and reflects (but frequently does not reflect deeply upon), not merely the contingent history of a particular tradition, but an example of something more pervasive than any metaphysics can contain. It is not merely the historical fact that the metaphysical tradition, however unitary it may be in certain ways, constituting its orthodoxy, is divided deeply in other ways, constituting its heresies. It is not merely that at the limits of thought or experience there lies the unthought.[46] It is that no tradition, no society, no political order, no form of human life, judgment, or reason, can be the same without being divided by otherness, by differences and oppositions.

However aporetic its major works may have been, the metaphysical tradition has not known its own aporias. It has been aporetic without knowing that it is constituted by aporia. It is heretical while always resisting heresy. On the one hand, this resistance comprises another aporia: heresy requires orthodoxy; aporia cannot be accepted without overcoming itself. On the other hand, the metaphysical tradition always fails in some profound ways to know itself, comprising another aporia: that what a metaphysical theory tells us is true is never true about itself. It is as totalizing for metaphysics to claim to be aporetic and heretical as to deny it, as if aporia might be thought without further aporia, as if there might be an "ultimate" thinking of aporia. It is as inadequate to deny that there is an essence of truth as to seek to know it, and in the same totalizing respects. One of the consequences of the continuing presence of heresy and aporia is that aporia is always plural, dissolving into other aporias, heretically. This continuing heresy is philosophy, except that a philosophy that claimed to be know this without aporia would be aporetic. Philosophy is an infinite play of aporia and heresy, including the heresy of its own self-denial.

There is something profoundly misguided yet true in the claim that philosophy has somehow come to an end. It has come to an end because philosophy is always ending in heresy only to emerge again, phoenix-like, in the same heresy; because the dream of a completed philosophy is a dream of no philosophy at all. What is not true is that the metaphysical tradition may now know itself to be more heretical and divided than it could have known itself to be in the past. Nietzsche is a salutary example: the most profoundly critical philosopher of metaphysical thinking, who understood the inseparability of the death of metaphysics from the death of God, was himself irremediably metaphysical in his view of the will to power. There is no heresy that does not become orthodoxy, including the end of both God and philosophy.

It behooves us, therefore, to consider what lies beyond the official claim that the end of philosophy is at hand. Here we may include those who have proposed other fundamental forms of thinking than philosophy. For Heidegger, philosophy will end not only with another form of thought, but with the thinking of itself. This is the Hegelian aporia, still throwing its shadow over us:

> Perhaps there is a thinking outside of the distinction of rational and irrational, more sober-minded than scientific technology, more sober-minded and hence removed, without effect, yet having its own necessity. When we ask about the task of this thinking, then not only this thinking but also the question concerning it is first made questionable.[47]

> The task of thinking would then be the surrender of previous thinking to the determination of the matter for thinking.[48]

Philosophy can reach its fruition or end only in a culmination in which it is entirely re-thought. Here history constitutes the only legitimate philosophic viewpoint, and philosophy is the unending project of re-thinking its history. A similar view is found in Derrida, for whom the thought of the limits of philosophy marks its close.[49]

An alternative, ironically perhaps found in Foucault, where history is re-thought but metaphysics is rejected, is to escape from a philosophy that denies its own materiality and a history that imposes unity upon itself under a principle of the same.

> From one end of experience to the other, finitude answers itself; it is the identity and difference of the positivities, and of their foundation, within the figure of the *Same*.[50]

This principle (of the human sciences) is metaphysical, with the proviso that modernity rejects metaphysics.

> Modern thought, then, will contest even its own metaphysical impulses, and show that reflections upon life, labour, and language, in so far as they have value as analytics of finitude, express the end of metaphysics: the philosophy of life denounces metaphysics as a veil of illusion, that of labour denounces it as an alienated form of thought and an ideology, that of language as a cultural episode.[51]

History falls under a principle of disruption:

> . . . the notion of discontinuity assumes a major role in the historical disciplines.[52]

> . . . the theme and the possibility of a *total history* begin to disappear, and we see the emergence of something very different that might be called a *general history*.[53]

> We must renounce all those themes whose function is to ensure the infinite continuity of discourse and its secret presence to itself in the interplay of a constantly recurring absence.[54]

History is to be re-thought, in genealogical and archaeological terms, but without an overarching project. Foucault would escape from the aporia that there is no history that is not a unified history into the aporia that there is no such history. Even so, that there is history implies both stability and variation. Whatever history there is contains the possibility of coming to an end.

> . . . what political status can you give to discourse if you see in it merely a thin transparency that shines for an instant at the limit of things and thoughts? Has not the practice of revolutionary discourse and scientific discourse in Europe over the past two hundred years freed you from this idea that words are wind, an external whisper, a beating of wings that one has difficulty in hearing in the serious matter of history?[55]

In this end, we discover the aporia of aporia, that:

> . . . we are difference, that our reason is the difference of discourses, our history the difference of times, our selves the difference of masks. That difference, far from being the forgotten and recovered origin, is this dispersion that we are and make.[56]

Whether orthodoxy or heresy wins, it can triumph only if discourse possesses materiality. But materiality is heresy. Here, modern science is the most material and influential form of modern discourse—even the most heretical and aporetic. That is something Heidegger cannot accept.

> . . . science is not an original happening of truth, but always the cultivation of a domain of truth already opened, specifically by apprehending and confirming that which shows itself to be pos-

sibly and necessarily correct within that field. When and insofar as science passes beyond correctness and goes on to a truth, which means that it arrives at the essential disclosure of what is as such, it is philosophy.[57]

Here, science is the essence of the metaphysical tradition that will come to an end out of which a new philosophy will emerge. Despite the irony, Heidegger denies that science is heretical and originary. Yet if it is to be true it must be both; if it is to be efficacious amidst inexhaustibility it must be both. Science both defines orthodoxy and establishes the terms of heresy. Foucault's apocalyptic vision is more striking:

> Since man was constituted at a time when language was doomed to dispersion, will he not be dispersed when language regains its unity?

> As the archaeology of our thought easily shows, man is an invention of recent date. And one perhaps nearing its end.[58]

This is another view of the "end" of the modern episteme—or merely its "closure." In either case we are speaking of heresy if not aporia.

> The future can only be anticipated in the form of an absolute danger. It is that which breaks absolutely with constituted normality and can only be proclaimed, *presented* as a sort of monstrosity.[59]

Is this danger heresy itself? If so, then, it is found everywhere and we are surrounded by monstrosity even within orthodoxy. The heresy is that orthodoxy is heresy. What we cannot say is that it is absolute or that any break is more absolute than any other. Our historical moment's break with normality has been given the non-name of "postmodernism," as if we might attain a new epoch, heretically, simply by wishing it. Here we may consider Lyotard's two definitions of postmodernism:

> Simplifying to the extreme, I define *postmodern* as incredulity toward metanarratives.[60]

Such metanarratives constitute an overarching legitimation of an epistemic discourse.

> There are many different language games—a heterogeneity of elements. They only give rise to institutions in patches—local determinism.[61]

This notion of locality is essential to any adequate theory of heresy and aporia. Yet we should not overlook Lyotard's other definition of post-modernism, not obviously equivalent to the first.

> The postmodern would be that which, in the modern, puts forward the unpresentable in presentation itself; that which denies itself the solace of good forms, the consensus of a taste which would make it possible to share collectively the nostalgia for the unattainable; that which searches for new presentations, not in order to enjoy them but in order to impart a stronger sense of the unpresentable.[62]

What is required is to understand how we are to think what is unpresentable and unattainable: certainly not as a "what," not even that of aporia. This aporia returns to claim us. What is unpresentable pertains to every being, singly and totally, its inexhaustibility. Yet this is not to say that there *is* something—an element or moment—in any being that escapes presentation, but rather, that a local being is never simply the same but is inescapably other, even to itself. The heretical truth of locality is that same and other are inseparable yet divided.

"Postmodernism"—ultramodernity—cannot be the end of philosophy and metaphysics, of linear writing and logical reason, of the hegemony of science over other forms of thought, of technology over nature.[63] Yet to say this is not to deny, nor is it to claim, that we may be on the verge of a new and far-reaching heresy, of a radical change in how reason and truth are to be understood and how they function. Philosophy and metaphysics have always been heretical and aporetic. That thought is always heretical, however, does not entail that it has been and will continue to be the same, even as heresy. Heresy is never the same, not only because it is always different, but because it is comprised of aporia.

11 LOCALITY AND APORIA

METAPHYSICS is aporetic because being is aporetic; philosophy is heretical because truth is heretical. Several tasks remain: to show the aporias of any being and the heresies of any truth; more important, to understand the aporias of aporia; the heresies of heresy. For we have not grasped what is aporetic about the aporia of metaphysics and the heresy of philosophy.

What is required is a theory of metaphysical aporia and epistemological heresy, a theory no less aporetic than what it would explain and no less heretical than the heresies it would uncover. Now an "aporetic theory" may sound more contradictory than aporetic, except that the contradiction may be resolved by rejecting too orthodox a view of theory. To the contrary, the aporia of our theory must belong to it in virtue of its rationality. That philosophy is heretical is not a defect. That metaphysics is aporetic does not diminish its capabilities but is the origin of its formidable achievements. Here the contrast is with a view of science—not science itself—for which aporia and heresy are defective, a view that would abolish all aporia and avoid all heresy in the clear illumination of a present and undivided truth. This view of science—I call it scientolatry—is an expression of its orthodoxy. What is called for are a science and a philosophy of science that affirm their own heresies. The question is whether science can think its own disruption.

To claim heresy for oneself is always to define a double orthodoxy: that in relation to which one's own views are heretical; and that into which one's own heresies will be resolved. In this sense there is no avoiding orthodoxy. What can be avoided is an orthodoxy that does not acknowledge the heresies that comprise it, that fails to acknowledge aporia. What is required is a theory in which orthodoxy does not dispel heresy, even if orthodoxy cannot be avoided and must attempt to tame heresy. What is needed in both cases is positive recognition that aporia belongs to both being and truth.

Aporia is the form in which reason realizes its own inexhaustibility along with that of any being. Two explicit aporias are present: of what thought finds to be its object, the relationship between thought and being; and of being in relation to beings. Whatever thought thinks is aporetic: reason finds aporia wherever it engages itself. Yet to claim that therefore being is pervaded by aporia, where being is not being-thought but being-itself, is aporetic. For there is no being-itself that can be realized to be aporetic without being thought. There is no non-aporetic resolution of the question of whether being is itself aporetic or aporetic merely as thought. The relation between thought and being is aporetic where thought is understood to exercise power.

Similarly, there is no being that is beyond or other than beings, especially the being of beings. Being is inexhaustible because beings are a union as well as disjunction of same and other. The relation between being and beings is aporetic to the extent that there "is" no being other than beings, different from them: there is "nothing but" beings. Yet beings are inexhaustible, and there is always "more than" any being's determinateness within it.

These two aporias, although different, are the same: thought cannot think anything without exceeding it; more generally, there cannot *be* anything that does not exceed itself. Excess is part of limitation. Otherness belongs to beings insofar as they are determinate, and there is no being without both determinateness and indeterminateness. To say that each being is inexhaustible is to say that it transcends itself, a plenitude exceeding thought; to think of the inexhaustibility of a being is to think of it in inexhaustibly manifold ways.

To be is to be local, qualified and qualifying: located and locating. A being is located in and among other beings. A being is a sphere of locations for other beings. This multiple locality is the basis of both inexhaustibility and aporia. More accurately, it is because locality is equivalent with inexhaustibility that reason is aporetic.

In *A Pluralistic Universe*, James explains what pluralism means in a passage that suggests inexhaustibility.

> Everything you can think of, however vast or inclusive, has on the pluralistic view a genuinely "external" environment of some sort or amount. Things are "with" one another in many ways, but nothing includes everything, or dominates over everything. The word "and" trails along after every sentence. Something always escapes. "Ever not quite" has to be said of the best attempts made anywhere in the universe at attaining all-inclusiveness.[1]

Two notions in this passage are important. One is that everything has an environment that includes it but is other to it. It is worth adding that what belongs to an environment of a being includes that being in its own environment. Locality and otherness are reciprocal. The other important notion is that something always escapes. James employs the image of a surplus in being to capture inexhaustibility. The difficulty is that his notion of a surplus is not explicitly aporetic. Indeed, aporia is quite hidden in the passage, although it could be argued that it is present latently. The "and" that always escapes is not manifest aporia.

Pluralism suggests that there is no system of thought or being that can include everything or dominate over everything. This is a strong rejection of the movement to totality. Nothing is *all*-inclusive. Yet James speaks without qualification of "the universe." Dewey is more sensitive to the deceptiveness of language.

> It is often said that pragmatism, unless it is content to be a contribution to mere methodology, must develop a theory of Reality. But the chief characteristic trait of the pragmatic notion of reality is precisely that no theory of Reality in general, *überhaupt*, is possible or needed. ... It finds that "reality" is a *denotative* term, a word used to designate indifferently everything that happens.[2]

He agrees with James that no theory of reality in general is possible or intelligible. But he acknowledges that there are in our language terms that "designate indifferently everything that happens." What must be added is that such terms produce aporia because all-inclusiveness is unintelligible. All-inclusiveness is unintelligible but we cannot avoid thinking inclusively. This aporia pertains to metaphysics because of its pervasive generality. It also pertains to other forms of reason, to science no less than to philosophy.

The alternative is that inclusiveness is always local (the aporia that locality is "everywhere"). It is local yet universal. What it is not is unqualified. Similarly, *all* knowledge is heretical; *every* being and every thought of being is aporetic. The aporias of locality are that it is universal without ceasing to be local and is "everywhere" without being universal.

Can one claim that everything is finite without appeal to the infinite? It is necessary to do so. What is not possible is to insist that the claim be free from aporia. It may, however, be free from contradiction, because the "everywhere" that finiteness is and the "everything" that is finite are not unqualified. Finiteness is qualification, including its own qualifications. To be is to be located and locating. More accurately, *each* being is local, but there is no totality of beings, prospective or retrospective, that can be local. Not *all* beings are local, because there is no totality.

Locality is not *everywhere* because there is no such location or collection of locations. Whatever infinite pertains to local being is qualified.

Two analogies may be helpful. To say that there is no totality of knowledge may be to say that we cannot know everything about everything. A totality is implied that is unavailable to us. Alternatively, there may be no totality because to know one thing is incompatible with knowing others. If all knowledge is from a point of view, there may be no point of view that includes every other. This would be true despite the imperative within any form of reason that any limit be transgressed.

A second analogy follows the idea of location. That any being is located somewhere in space and time cannot entail that there is a "being" to "everywhere" and "everywhen." While the orthodox homogeneity of space may suggest a plenum of all spatial locations, whether or not occupied by material things, there is no similar homogeneity of temporal locations. The question of the totality and homogeneity of historical time is the question of human locality. If there are diverse and local spatial regions divided by singularities—black holes, discontinuously curved gravitational fields—then spatial relations are both external and local. Similarly, if time marks the loss of some features of the past, permits only some of its features to pass with influence into the future, then temporal events are both relational and local. There is the "everywhere" of spatiality, but no point of view can be taken in relation to all spatial locations. There is the "everywhen" of temporality but there is no comprehensive historical point of view. Analogously, there is no totality of beings within any region—no totality of "things in a room," for example— and no totality of locations, precisely because to "be" is to define a limited sphere of locations and relations. Totality is aporetic because it is always local.

There are only local points of view, and every being is local along with every point of view. That this should be so, and intelligible, does not mean that it is free from aporia. Locality and inexhaustibility are aporias, the one that locality is "everywhere" without ceasing to be local, the other that every being is both local and inexhaustible.

That indeterminateness is complementary with determinateness, and conversely, the endless play of same and other, is the aporia of aporias (but not the "ultimate aporia") in the metaphysical tradition. The tradition may be interpreted as an ongoing struggle with this aporia, too frequently demanding the elimination of all indeterminateness, the transformation of all otherness into the same. The continuing irony, manifested in the impossibility of the task, is that the resolution is aporetic. A local being is inexhaustible *because* it has limits, and every limit defines its otherness. Every limit has its limits.

To be is to be local: located and locating. This multiple locality is the origin of aporia and heresy. A locus is multiply located: located in other locales, themselves loci, and a locale for its own constituents. Locality here is relevance or influence—that is, power: to be located in a locale is to constitute it; to be a locale is to constitute conditions for other loci and their constituents. The identities of loci are therefore functions of the locales in which they are located and the locales they constitute for other loci. Locality is limitation.

Fundamental to locality is that locating and being located are inseparable and complementary. The constituents of a locus comprise it in a particular location in virtue of the locale in which it is located. To be located in a given locale, a locus must be constituted in certain ways, defining its relationship to its constituents. Because a locus is multiply located, its constituents vary with its locations, as do its diverse identities and relations. This multiplicity and diversity constitute inexhaustibility. Inexhaustibility is the unending trio of same and other.

Locality is equivalent with limitation. Multiple locatedness is equivalent with inexhaustibility. The relationship may be described in many ways: for example, inexhaustibility is the limitation of every limit, the complementarity of every generic relation. Because every limit is limited, it cannot limit absolutely. It follows that every limit has two sides corresponding to locality and multiple locality. The two inseparable sides of every limit manifest the inexhaustibility in finiteness and the complementarity in locality. On the one side of its limitation, a locus is determinate because it is limited. On the other side of its limitation, inseparable from the first, a locus is indeterminate in the local transcendences that pertain to it inexhaustibly.

Inexhaustibility is multiple locality, equivalent with the reciprocity of same and other. This reciprocity is aporia, with the qualification that every aporia is different from every other: always the same and always different. The complementarity that pervades locality, antitheses that are neither antagonists nor contradictory, identities that are not the same, are aporias. The Western metaphysical tradition has recurrently attempted to resolve otherness into the same, although the proposed resolutions have never escaped alterity. In this important sense, there has been no "quest for certainty" or "mirror of nature" that escaped the aporias of uncertainty and distortion. To the greatest philosophers, indeterminateness cried out for determinateness, but not for freedom from aporia.

The theory of locality is an expression of the aporia of same and other. This aporetic reciprocity is neither of Hegel's infinites: good or bad. There is no inclusion of all oppositions into an absolute that contains them all, only recognition that each requires the other within itself: sameness complementary with difference; difference inclusive of similarity. There is no alternation of oppositions, each nullifying the other.

Each includes the other without cancelling their differences. Determinateness and indeterminateness are, together and complementarily, the determination of aporia. The complementarity is equivalent with both locality and inexhaustibility.

Every being is local: locating and located. Every being is a locus, multiply located in diverse locales and locating many diverse constituents. Moreover, the nature and identity of a locus are functions of its constituents and its locales, complementarily. A locus is a function of its constituents and the locale in which it is located; but it is located in inexhaustibly many locales. Moreover, its constituents and its locales are constituted by it as well. This tightly coiled knot of identity and constitution, divided by multiplicity, is the complementarity of similarity and difference, unity and multiplicity, that is local aporia. To be is to be both one and many, unified and divided, similar to other beings and different from them, complementarily, inseparably, and locally. What is unified in certain respects or locations is divided in others; what is similar to other beings in certain locales is different from them in others; what is one in a given location is many in others.

In a local theory, difference is as much part of being as is identity. Every locus is different from every other in certain respects and locations—even different from itself (in different locations). Every locus is similar to every other in certain locations and respects—even similar to what is different from it. Similarity and difference are local, in that sense functional, notions. A local ontology regards the generic traits of loci as functions of locations. There are no properties that are not functional; all functions are reciprocities of determinateness and indeterminateness.

Determinateness and indeterminateness are functional notions, so that what is determinate in one location is indeterminate in another, the basis of their complementarity. In the pairs of generic notions functionally characteristic of local being, one may be locally regarded as representing determinateness, the other indeterminateness. A locus is one in a location, the same, but divided over many locations. A locus is unified insofar as it has *a* location, but multiple insofar as it has many locations. What is determinate in it is a function of a given location, its unity; what is indeterminate is a function of its multiple locations. A locus is functionally the same as itself but also different in different locations. Each of these relations is a function of location, entangling it with aporia.

A locus is both locale and constituent, inseparably and complementarily. A locus is a locale for its constituents; it is a constituent of the locales in which it is located. Two things follow. One is that constituency is always reciprocal—"the same"—without obliterating difference. If a locus, A, is a constituent of another locus B, then B is a constituent of

A—in both cases, in some location. Each is "what it is" in virtue of the other. Nevertheless, in any location, to the extent that one is a locale for the other, the other is a constituent of, not a locale for the first. There is reciprocity with difference.

The second implication is that to be a locus is to be both locale and constituent, complementarily. It follows that being is always functionally divided. There is no univocal sense of being, because to be is to be both a locale and a constituent, unitary and divided, same and other. A local ontology preserves the complementarity of same and other in the dividedness that characterizes every generic way of being. In this way, there are many senses of being—being is inexhaustible—and no univocal, comprehensive sense of being. Inexhaustibility and locality are not "ways of being," as are the local categories, but manifest the aporias of different ways of being.

To be is to be a locus—both locale and constituent, a function of multiple locations. This pair, locale-constituent, comprises one "way of being." Its divided complementarity is aporia. To be is also to be one locus in a given location, although a locus is divided over many locations and divided even in a single location because that location is itself divided. The respects in which a locus is unitary in a given location—"the same" in that location, "one" constituent of that locale—comprise its *unison*. A locus possesses a unison in any location comprising the constituents that constitute its unitariness. A locus also possesses diverse and plural *ramifications* in any of its locations, comprising its other constituents to which it is relevant that do not comprise its unitariness. Unison and ramification are categorial expressions of same and other.

This pair of categories expresses "what" a locus is in a location, unitarily, and the wider sphere of powers that it exercises in that location. And there is no location in which a locus does not possess both unison and ramifications. Moreover, a locus is multiply located and possesses a different unison in each location. To be is to be both one and many, constituted unitarily and exercising diverse powers. This complementary dividedness is the aporia of inexhaustibility.

The reciprocity of constitution and relevance may be expressed in terms of unison and ramification. Wherever two loci are relevant to each other, they must be constituents together in a common locale. There is no other intelligible sense of being relevant. It follows that each must be among the ramifications of the other—to be relevant to it—but each may be among the constituents comprising the other's unison. Thus, relevance is either unisonal or ramificational. This is a difference that pervades the mutuality and reciprocity of local relevance and power. Where two loci, A and B, are relevant to each other in a given location, then three alternatives are possible:

A and B are each constituents of the other's unison.

A is a constituent of B's unison, but B is a constituent of A's
    ramifications.

A and B are each constituents of the other's ramifications.

The last is the minimal condition of relevance.

Being is power. To be is to exercise power, to be relevant, to influence other beings and to be influenced by them. Power is divided, over many locations and within a given location. To be relevant in a location is to be unitary in that location, to possess a unison, but also to exercise diverse powers over other locations and over other constituents in that location.

Unison and ramification together express the aporia of power, that power is everywhere and divided. Power is relevance and is indeed "everywhere." The first truth of locality is relevance. The second truth, inseparable from the first, is that relevance is always divided. A locus is constituted by a given location but inhabits other locations that also constitute it. Similarly, the ways in which a locus is constituted by its unison are different from the ways in which it is constituted by its ramifications. A being is constituted in part by what it exercises power upon, its "sphere of influence." A ruler imposes his authority on his subjects, but they constitute the sphere in which his power may be exercised. They constitute the very possibility of his being ruler. The latter is a unisonal relationship; the former is ramificational.

Power is everywhere because influence is everywhere. Being is relevance and relation. But among the relationships of power are those divided by unisons and ramifications. Even more important, locales in which power is exercised are divided by other relations of power. In this sense, not only is power everywhere, but so is resistance—that is, reciprocal, dividing, and antagonistic relations.[3] The dividedness of every locale has the consequence that no society, government, ruler, class, or tradition can impose undivided authority on its subjects. This is not simply a social, historical, or political condition. It is an ontological consequence of the aporias that pertain to local being.

To be is to be multiply located in diverse locations. Yet to be a locus is also to be "the same" over many different locations. The category of unison expresses unitariness within a location, complemented by a multiplicity of locations. There is "identity" in this sense expressed as unison within a location. There is another sense of identity: "gross identity" over many locations—through time and space, for example. Yet there is no other sense of unitariness and identity that than of unison, and none that is not divided by multiple location.

A locus is "the same" over many locations when there is a locale, inclusive of the relevant locations, in which the locus has a unison—a "gross unison" and "gross identity." Because unison is complementary with ramifications, wherever a locus is the same, identical over many different locations, it possesses diverse ramifications not included within its gross identity. A locus belongs to many locations and possesses a gross unison over these different locations while there can be no totality of all locations, for all beings taken together and for any being taken separately. This is the surplus of inexhaustibility in any local being. Thus, a locus possesses a gross unison over many locations but inhabits other locations not included within that unison. A locus then "belongs" to a subaltern location relative to an inclusive locale in which it possesses a stable gross unison that includes the locus's subaltern unison, and "departs" from a subaltern location relevant to which its unison is not included in that gross unison. Departing is the generic form of desire, the surpassing within every local being corresponding to the generic form of power that is equivalent with relevance. Local being is constituted by desire and power, by surplus and relevance. Each is both same and other: center and excess.

Identity over different locations is a function of a gross unison over many subaltern unisons, defined by an inclusive locale over many subaltern locales. Yet every gross unison, defining where a locus belongs, is incomplete, replete with otherness—a manifestation of inexhaustibility— and every locus departs from certain subaltern locations in any given location. Furthermore, every unison is a gross unison over certain subaltern locations, and every gross unison is a particular unison, with ramifications and departures.

Sameness here is local and aporetic. The aporias are multifarious, but generically, to be—a locus—is always functionally divided. The different categories express different "senses of being," different ways of being a locus, and there is no all-inclusive sense of local being. In the immediate context, identity over different locations is always partial and incomplete, divided by departures and ramifications. The history of theories of time has been a recurrent struggle over whether there is an overarching sense of location within which temporal beings possess univocal identities, or whether time is divided into multiple locations, dividing the identities of temporal beings. The answer here is that time is both same and other, that it is divided into multiple locations and divides temporal beings into multiple identities.

Several of the locative categories are threefold functions of locales and constituents. To be a locus is to be located in a particular locale and to be a locale of constituents; moreover, these different relations comprise a single relation because the constituents of a locus both constitute it and are functions of its locale.

Identity and gross unison are fourfold functions of locales and constituents. A locus is located in locales L_j with constituents C_{ij} for each locale. Its unison is comprised of constituents C_{km} of its locus in each locale, L_m, while its ramifications are comprised of constituents C_{lm} in each locale, L_m, where $k+l=i$. However, a locus belongs to a locale L_j in virtue of its gross unison over many subaltern unisons, U_{kj}, each comprising constituents C_{jkm} in different subaltern locales L_m. Belonging and identity are fourfold functions of constituents, unisons, superaltern locale, and subaltern locales. Moreover, each term of this relation is a function of the others. This functional inseparability is equivalent with locality and inexhaustibility. Local being is functionally divided as well as unitary, complementarily and inseparably, divided by the inexhaustible multiplicity of locations, by other local beings comprising more and less inclusive locales, and there is no locale inclusive of all others nor any total system of locations for any locus.

The locative categories are the ways in which loci "are," and there is no more generic sense of being.[4] There is no more fundamental sense of being than being a locus, and in virtue of the complementarity of indeterminateness and otherness in relation to loci, to be a locus is not to be another locus—*other* to it. Nothingness and nonbeing are difference and otherness, with the qualification that, locally, nonbeing is both inexhaustible itself and inexhaustible within every being. The locative categories are the generic senses of being, and there is no more total or general, more complete or universal, more determinate or inclusive sense of being than expressed in these categories. This may be the most intimidating of all aporias, that there is no (one) sense of being, but always many: being a locus, being a constituent, being a locale, being a unison, being a ramification, belonging, departing, being the same as, being different from. There are many divided senses of being and no generic sense inclusive of them all; moreover, each is divided by its complement. That being is local and inexhaustible is not a way of expressing a certain determinate totality of being, but rather, expresses the complementarity of same and other that divides loci.

The categories of locus and constituent and unison and ramification, express the locality of beings in relation to their constituents and locations. Belonging and departing express relations among the unisons of a locus in relation to its other unisons. In addition, in any locale, a locus's constituents conform to certain relations among themselves. These are important for understanding material experience and powers, and are expressed in another pair of categories.

Among the constituents of a locus in a particular location—a threefold relation—are relations that define kinds and degrees of latitude. Given certain constituents, others are "settled" in certain respects in that location. Yet also, given certain constituents, others are "unsettled"; open in certain respects. The traditional terms for designating this relation, neglecting locality, have been "actuality;" and "possibility." Given certain features of a locale, certain other constituents are actual, without relevant alternatives, others coexist with relevant alternatives: these are possibilities. Alternatives are a consequence of multiple locality and inexhaustibility. At the level of constituents and their interrelations they comprise what may be called "situalities" and "availabilities." Given certain constituents in a locale, others are settled, situated, without alternatives, while still others comprise available alternatives, and coexist among them.

Situalities and availabilities, like belonging and departing, comprise a fourfold relation among constituents and their subaltern constituents. The former express the stability of a gross unison over subaltern unisons. The latter express the stability and variability of constituents in relation to other constituents. Given the law of gravitation, an object that falls from a high window must fall, without relevant alternatives. Even so, a person who falls may scream, fall silently, limply or waving his arms.

Situality and availability are complementary categories in relation to a locus in its locations. Given certain features, others are settled; still others, however, are available as alternatives among other alternatives. Moreover, what is situal in one location is available in another, and conversely. This inversion with location is a fundamental trait of the complementarity that defines inexhaustibility. What is a locale relative to its constituents is a constituent relative to another locale, and each of those constituents is a locale for the first. A constituent of a unison of a locus in one location is a constituent of its ramifications in another, and conversely. What belongs to a locus in one location departs from it in another. What is possible in one location is actual in another, and conversely.

Inexhaustibility is multiple locality. A locus and its constituents, a category and its complement, are functions of its location, and vary with different locations. There is no comprehensive sense of "being a locus," only an inexhaustibly divided sense of being. There is no all-inclusive locale—the world—relative to which any being may be entirely determinate; no comprehensive or generic sense of being that is not divided within itself—for example, into differential categories; no "identity" of a locus that is not divided over many incongruous unisons. This absence of a total identity for every being is the most compelling of all the aporias that confront us. Identity is as local as is being, so that "what" a being is is a function of its locations, varying with its locations, and there is no all-inclusive identity. In this sense, inexhaustibility entails that being transcends any local identity, any local understanding, not merely in that there is something "more" to be known, but that what is unknown pertains as deeply to every being as what is and can be known.

There are two compelling sides to the aporia of local being that constitutes inexhaustibility. One is that beings always escape us, both in understanding and practice. We are always exceeded by the things that surround us, as we exceed both them and ourselves, despite the compelling need to understand and to act, and even worse, despite the powers that other beings exercise upon us. The other side is that every being, in its inexhaustibility, exceeds any form we impose upon it or within which we comprehend or use it. Inexhaustibility, in practice, confronts us with the condition that while we cannot avoid using and imposing ourselves on beings, what we force to conform to our control is inexhaustible. This inexhaustibility in beings from the standpoint of power and control I call "valor." The sense of valor, of beings' inexhaustibility, I call "charity."[5] What inexhaustibility requires from us in practice is a charity pervaded by awareness of the unending sacrifices that local being requires.

This is the aporia within practical judgment, recognized intermittently throughout the Western tradition, especially in the greatest works of literature—Antigone, Philoctetes, Lear—but also in Plato, Kierkegaard, and Nietzsche. There is no practice without its sacrifices, and what is sacrificed is inexhaustible. There is no avoiding infinite sacrifice, yet finite practice must be undertaken. There is a validation that resides within the acceptance of the aporia of sacrifice, just as there is a validation that resides within the acceptance of the aporias of truth. With these recognitions, we turn from aporia to heresy.

We have an ontology in which aporia is the immediate ramification of locality and inexhaustibility and in which the generic form of aporia is the reciprocity of same and other that manifests the dividedness of being. What is required is a theory of heresy, the implications of aporia for reason. We require a local epistemology consonant with our local ontology. This epistemology is based on a theory of local judgment divided into multiple modes. Heresy is constituted by the locality of reason.

To say that reason is local is less to deny universality than to assert that universality is local—located and locating. That reason is located entails that judgment is qualified and conditioned, including the qualification of every qualification corresponding to the limit of every limit. In this insight into the locality of locality we find the difference between aporia and contradiction, heresy and paradox, fallibility and skepticism. In the extreme, skepticism asserts what it is in no position to claim: that knowledge is impossible because no judgment may constitute unconditioned knowledge. Because judgment is local, knowledge and reason must also be local. What must be added is that locality is also local. From this we may conclude that a local theory of aporia must be aporetic and a local theory of heresy must be heretical.

A young man cannot be old; a strong man cannot be weak; a woman who bears children cannot be childless. These predicates are contraries. Yet with the appropriate qualifications, both apply to the same person at different times and places. This phrase, "at different times and places," expresses the locality of predication and truth. That judgments are local includes the locality of locality. That judgments are qualified includes qualifications of qualifications. Logical principles are uttered in a timeless, unqualified voice. But they are true only locally, with unknown qualifications. One important conclusion is that the distinction between aporia and contradiction is always local, manifested in the continuing aporia after Heraclitus of the relation between contradiction and aporia, between unintelligibility and heresy.

To be is to be located and locating, multiply, where different locations confer different and sometimes opposing properties and constituents, even identities, on the "same" beings. Multiple locality imposes difference upon the "same" beings, but also sameness upon different beings, in different inclusive locations. What is rejected is any entirely determinate, all-inclusive, unconditioned location whereby any being possesses an entirely determinate nature. Also rejected is any location whereby an entirely determinate distinction between sameness and otherness may be established. Aporia is inexhaustibly multiple locality, where difference coexists with sameness and conversely, determinateness with indeterminateness. Skepticism, paradox, contradiction—all are local, qualified notions that frequently defy locality. It is as mistaken to deny locality by asserting multiplicity without qualification as to deny multiple locality without qualification, asserting the presence of a totally inclusive locale.

It follows that just as being is divided by multiple locations, judgment and reason are divided by multiple perspectives. What this means, primarily, is that there are many, even conflicting judgments that pertain to any being validly, but also many modes or kinds of judgment and many modes and kinds of validation and reason. This is effectively heresy itself: that judgment is divided into local modes with different and incommensurate modes of validation. It is important here to distinguish again between incommensurateness and incommensurability, the latter denying the limitation of limitation relevant to different modes of judgment. Different modes of judgment are incommensurate in that in any location, there cannot be found a common measure between them, mediating them, but any difference is mediatable in some location. The locality of measure is essential. The relevant aporia is that judgment inexhaustibly demands escape from locality even while its demands are local. It is manifested in the impossibility of specifying the difference between incommensurability and incommensurateness.

There are many different modes of judgment, three of which have been recognized traditionally, characterized by Aristotle as saying, doing, and making: assertive, practical, and fabricative judgment. I would add a fourth mode characteristic of philosophy, especially metaphysics: comprehending or conjoining—syndetic judgment—including distinctions relevant to such conjunctions. In addition, there may emerge, through heresy, in the future, other modes of judgment, as there have emerged in the past, through heresy, novel modes of reason.

Judgment is characterized by selection and validation. Wherever there is selection that aims at validation there is judgment. Kant emphasizes that there are diverse modes of cognition and that each possesses a singular mode of validation which is unintelligible as a mode of validation from the standpoint of the others. This is what incommensurateness means in judgment. It does not follow that each mode of judgment is simply unintelligible from the standpoint of the others. Each mode is pervasive throughout judgment and experience and is interpretable from the standpoint of any of the others. Science is a form of practice; politics is a form of behavior. Each mode of validation is unintelligible *as validation* from the standpoint of the others, but intelligible *as human* from every judgmental standpoint. Here we see the importance of such human sciences as sociology and psychology of art, moral and political psychology, and political science, each inclusive of the others though incompatible with the judgments that comprise their subject matters. This conflict among modes of validation demands continuing heresy. The space between the modes of judgment is filled by aporia and heresy. It is the region in which truth and meaning emerge. The space between the modes of judgment is filled with aporia and heresy. It is the region in which truth and meaning are disruptive.

There are many and diverse modes of judgment. There are many and diverse modes of reason. Reason here is local, to be associated with the activities and processes that comprise validation. Crudely, we may associate science with assertive judgment, morality and politics with practical judgment, art with fabricative judgment, and philosophy with syndetic judgment. What is omitted from such associations are the multimodality and intermodality that characterize reason. The locality of reason has the two sides of any limit: the limitations of a particular mode of judgment, imposing a diversity of modes of reason, and the transcendence of any mode, imposing intermodality and multimodality.

In relation to science, traditionally, inquiry has been the name of the activities whereby assertive judgments are interrogated and validated. Yet it is misleading to think of morality and art as forms of inquiry, not least because of the incommensuratenesses among the different modes of validation. We may, therefore, introduce another term, *query*, to express the genus of which inquiry is the species: unending interrogation and reinterrogation, critically and self-critically, seeking validation and revalidation. Reason *is* query. A local reason is never done, because it constantly enters new locations, because it engenders new locations for itself in its own activities. A local reason, then, must be divided into a multiplicity of local modes of query without which no form could deeply interrogate itself.

There are diverse modes of judgment and diverse modes of reason associated with each of them. Science, here, is query typified by the conditions of assertive judgment—seeking propositional truth above all. Other modes of reason are associated with assertive judgment—courts of law, fact-finding bodies—and assertive judgments that are not query, whose interrogations are brought under closure. Nevertheless, science is the contemporary form in which assertive query may be realized, in which unending, inexhaustible interrogation culminates in propositional truth. Here we may understand the prominent emphasis on scientific method to be an expression of the quest for methods whereby assertive query—science—may produce propositional truth. And we may understand the prominent emphasis on the superiority of science over other forms of judgment and reason as the implicit claim that there is but one legitimate mode of reason. It is effectively a denial of heresy.

Some writers critical of such a view have characterized their position as a rejection of Method in science.[6] What can not be denied is that there are scientific methods, for reason is always methodic. Method is stability of judgment conjoined with stability of outcome and need not be incompatible with heresy where both method and stability are local. A rigid interpretation of method imposes repetition where there is variation and is incompatible with both heresy and discovery. In this sense, there is no Method for scientific discovery, no single way of producing novel results, but there are many methods that demand and enhance the prospects of discovery. Among these methods are those that include heresy: incommensurate differences among methods and submethods.

Science includes heresy among its methods, and must do so if it is to be successful. More important, however, science includes heresy within its forms of interrogation: it must utilize other modes of judgment than assertive judgment, other modes of reason than science, frequently in novel ways. Science cannot be merely assertive judgment, but must include practice and design, comprehensiveness and order, as part of itself, necessary to its interrogations. This requirement follows, first, from the multiplicity of modes of judgment and reason, which are incommensurate but inseparable. Each mode of judgment is pervasive throughout experience in the sense that any judgment may be interpreted to possess any modality. Any judgment may be interpreted as an implicit claim, something done, judged by its results, the design of order, or expressing relations of same and other. In this sense, science is practice as well as assertion, but also and equally, fabrication and synthesis.

Second, however, and far more important, the multiplicity of modes of judgment relevant to science follows from the requirement that reason be unendingly interrogative and self-critical, however aporetically. These interrogations lead to intermodality and multimodality. From within any given mode of judgment and reason, only certain questions are intelligible, and it is irrational to limit interrogation to them, irrational and impossible. Thus, it is essential to be able to ask of science how beneficial it is to human beings and to the natural environment, how effective it may be for improving human experience, how beautiful and authentic it may be, how comprehensive a view of nature can be expressed in scientific terms, and what kind of thought, what kinds of aporias, comprise the rationality of science. Some of these questions may appear "external" to science, in the sense that we do not think of them as part of its rationality. Some of them are incompatible with scientific reason and propositional assertion. Yet limitation and its limitation pertain to reason and science as they do to being, and no single mode of validation—in this case, propositional truth—can represent the entire range of validation requisite within any mode of reason. Questions of why certain scientific principles are accepted and others rejected lead to modes of validation other than propositional truth: to comprehensiveness and orderliness, to practical effectiveness and social influence, to elegance and symmetry. To the extent that other forms of validation are external to science, to assertive query, such otherness is required as part of the unending interrogations of query.

What makes science rational is not its progressive march toward agreement, although that is certainly a factor in its public influence, nor its authority as the predominant form of epistemic legitimacy. The latter is more the mark of the orthodoxy that science has been granted in the modern world. What makes science rational is its incessant refusal to accept any truth without evidence, its recurrent demand to be shown and shown again, its constant struggle against prejudice and error. It is not alone in exhibiting such unstinting interrogation: politics, philosophy, and art have traditionally shared in wealth and depth of interrogation, although they have not always been regarded as equally rational. Indeed, the claim to rational superiority that has finally cloaked science with legitimacy threatens to undermine both its superiority and rationality. Where science becomes orthodox it is because certain forms that represent its superiority have become canonical: certain methods or principles. Yet a canonical epistemic form is no longer rational despite having become canonical in virtue of its rationality. It has lost the sense of its own locality in the dominion of the same.

It follows that no form of reason can be entirely stable and well-defined. Stability is as local as variation. It is the nature of reason to interrogate and transform itself, sometimes radically, heretically, sometimes dissolving aporetically. It is the nature of reason to be heretical, science no less than philosophy or art. Moreover, the transformations reason imposes are a result of interrogations from within and without, intermodally and multimodally. What is essential to reason is the unceasing interrogation of judgment, an interrogation that manifests itself in heresy.

What characterizes assertive judgment, propositional truth, and science typically, what in this sense "belongs" to science, is a compulsion of evidence that presses toward the same. In the extreme, to say that science rests on empirical evidence is to say that among a variety of alternative natural laws and theories, all but one may be rejected on the basis of evidence. This compulsion is the ideal of science. Unfortunately, its formulation here is far too strong. One of the most unsettling recognitions concerning science is that empirical evidence cannot conclusively settle a theoretical conflict. What makes such a recognition heretical is that it challenges the implied superiority of science to other modes of query.

If science is more determinate than other forms of reason, it is in this respect alone: the adjudication of competing alternatives rests entirely on a law of the same. Closely related to this assumption is another: it is in principle possible to eliminate all indeterminateness from propositional expression. In the extreme, the assumption is that two theories that have the same empirical consequences are, however different they may be in other respects, propositionally or scientifically equivalent. Here, the presence of other modes of reason and validation is deeply unsettling, because competing theories that may be empirically the same—a marginal possibility for complex theories—are different structurally, practically, or formally. It follows that structural, practical, and formal considerations must be regarded as irrelevant to science. It is part of the legitimation of science that its superiority be established on the basis of empirical determinants that exclude other modes of reason. It is part of the practice of modern science that its legitimation be exclusive, that it impose upon otherness the law of the same.

If it is impossible, due to locality and inexhaustibility, to adjudicate conclusively among competing scientific claims on the basis of evidence; if it is impossible to eliminate intermodality from science; if science is intermodal and multimodal as a result of its own rationality, however much it strives for purity; if indeterminateness pertains to science as much as does determinateness, fragmenting its inexorable progressive march: nevertheless, science is among the prominent forms of reason, not despite these limitations, but in virtue of them. They are essential to its rationality. They are incompatible only with a narrow and deficient view of reason that cannot recognize its own heresies.

What is required is to recognize the aporia within the notion of progress. There is no progress without loss. There is no knowledge whose advance is without sacrifice. This is clear in relation to science as practice because its marvellous contributions to the benefit of human life frequently produce the most terrible consequences. Far less obvious is that the advance of science has been achieved at the expense of other forms of truth. Such exclusion is not unique to science, but is the basis of orthodoxy of any kind.

There is an association between the idealized authority of science and the rejection of more explicitly aporetic forms of reason. The goal of science is to achieve unambiguous propositional truth under the dominion of the same. This goal, which can be achieved only locally, passes into a mythology where progress is measured by solutions to problems succeeded indefinitely by other problems and their solutions. Inexhaustibility in science unfolds through history successively, no less heretical than any other form of reason. The difference is that the inexhaustibility of modern science is realized successively, its aporia unfolded rather than compressed. In philosophy above all, but also in practice, inexhaustibility and locality move in tightly woven coils of aporia, realizing constant heresies.

Science is no less aporetic than metaphysics or poetry. However, its particular form of validation—propositional truth, dependence on evidence, governance by the same—opens up its aporias over time, requiring a strong historical sense in an activity that repudiates its history. On the revolutionary model, a scientific paradigm functions regardless of anomalous evidence until the structure collapses. These anomalies are unmistakable aporias. What may be less obvious is that the resolution of such anomalies is also aporetic, a consequence of inexhaustibility, awaiting future anomalies for expression.

By way of contrast, although science achieves a local rule of the same in relation to evidence, known or unknown, practice—morality and politics in particular—finds itself confronted by constant variations in norms and principles, achieving consensus locally and by force. Desire and power are recurrent aporias that are not resolved through time but present us with conflicts that will not go away. They are not problems and have no solutions. Similarly, the presence of art amid assertive and practical judgment is a constant challenge and disruption, not so much because art is revolutionary as because any mode of validation that pertains to it is unintelligible from the standpoint of the two predominant forms of reason in our tradition. Neither practice nor art admits of idealization, although they would be unintelligible without local ideals.

Science seeks a validation in the same but always fails in some respects to achieve it—fails *because* it is rational, not despite its rationality. Morality and politics have no comparable evidence or proofs to determine their first principles, but are caught up constantly in arbitrariness and variation. Their aporias are manifested in continuing conflicts among their principles—especially in politics where violence is both unavoidable and proscribed. Art is based on no principles or proofs, yet without stability and recurrence can have no values. Philosophy inhabits a world in part its own, in part divided among these other three, demanding the kind of compulsion characteristic of science but always failing to achieve it, confronted constantly by conflicts among its fundamental tenets, knowing itself to have no principles that cannot be rejected. Its demand for comprehensiveness requires it to borrow from other forms of reason and judgment whatever can serve its purposes.

These local limitations that express inexhaustibility are manifested in aporias and demand heresies. Yet they are not irrationalities within reason, but reason itself. They appear irrational only insofar as a transparent view of evidence and proof is taken to be the paradigm of reason—a paradigm to which even science cannot conform. Reason requires these disruptions because they manifest the inexhaustibility without which reason could not unceasingly interrogate itself. Such incessant interrogation is founded on aporia and requires heresy.

From this point of view, science includes those forms of query—therefore, of reason—that emphasize propositional truth, that pursue the same through evidence but which confront heresy in an unending succession of theories and interpretations. Practical query—morality and politics—includes those forms of reason that emphasize control in the context of desire and power, but which are dominated by a lack of control that pervades life and practice. Resistances are present within any established power, desire is divided by other desires, and there is sacrifice within any achievement. Nevertheless, practical query, especially politics, is rational despite the inescapable presence of failure. This fundamental aporia of practice is expressed in the intense complementarity of practical judgment for which no achievement escapes loss. Art is the rational manifestation of inexhaustibility through the interplay of similarities and differences, "contrasts," raised to higher and higher levels through time, including the aporia that some "higher" contrasts revert to "lower" levels. Art, here, is the revelation of inexhaustibility and aporia, demanding incessant heresy. Philosophy includes those forms of reason for which all other forms of reason and being are materials, seeking forms of thought of utmost generality. Here, inexhaustibility and aporia penetrate every generalization, and philosophy—especially in its metaphysical forms—expresses aporia recurrently in the heresies that constitute its major works.

All of these major forms of reason are aporetic because being and reason are inexhaustible and aporetic, divided by difference and united by similarity. Thought seeks unification only to be divided by difference, seeks differentiation only to be overwhelmed by similarity. Time marks fundamental changes in the nature of thought and reason—heresy itself—manifesting their aporias.

To these fundamental forms of reason we must add the heretical results of intermodality and multimodality. The interrogations within any mode of reason, required for it to be query, lead to other modes of query. In this intermodality, new forms of interrogation and validation are engendered, therefore, new forms of reason. In art, such novel forms are considered typical, part of the inventiveness of art. In other modes of query, science and, at times, philosophy, the invention of new forms appears more revolutionary. Yet it is the nature of reason to broach whatever boundaries are imposed upon it, whatever boundaries consti-tute its rationality. Thus, there are in addition to our fundamental forms of reason many other forms, characterized by unique intermodal types of validation: psychoanalysis, structuralism, and technology. Here the question of whether psychoanalysis is a science, although it may once have been important, passes into irrelevance. Psychoanalysis has become a prominent form of human expression, an organizing framework whereby to locate the other forms of human thought and practice, a form of thought that stands face to face with its other.

More recent forms of reason share in this intermodality, opposing the restriction of reason to any particular modality. A feature of what some call "postmodernism"—I consider it our time's heretical modern-ity—is the challenge to legitimacy of any disciplinary form of reason: a challenge to science as the predominant contemporary form of reason, but also to the disciplinary structure of art and philosophy as well as practice. What postmodern writers understand is that the heretical side of reason has no intrinsic structure, that the most striking heresies are directed against the forms whereby reason represents itself to itself. They frequently fail to realize that such heresies have pervaded reason from the beginning of human experience. The development of science was one of the greatest and most radical of heresies, as was the romanticiza-tion of the individual artist.

One of the important implications of locality and inexhaustibility, then, realized in aporia and heresy, is that the forms of reason are no more determinate than what they determine, that indeterminateness and determinateness complementarily characterize query. In this sense, there is constant heresy not only within any form of reason, but among the different forms, confronting us with the recurrent question of whether any particular form is able to interrogate itself satisfactorily. Here the complementarity of heresy and orthodoxy presents itself anew in the realization that heresy requires orthodoxy for its very nature, requires that reason be reason just as power must be power—both manifested in the unending constellation of forms and practices that comprise the interplay of orthodoxy and heresy.

There are many ways of being and no generic way that includes them all. This multiplicity, including sameness as well as otherness, constitutes aporia. Here being is aporetic as it is local and inexhaustible. There is no being, generically or individually, universally or specifically, that is not limited. The fundamental aporia here is that limitation is openness, finiteness is transcendence, locality is inexhaustibility, sameness is otherness. To this we may add the aporia fundamental within a local metaphysics: it cannot allow itself to become orthodox and must facilitate its overthrow by other theories. A local ontology cannot claim superiority over other ontologies, as if it might become the new orthodoxy, but must maintain an ongoing heretical relationship to them. The pursuit of disruptive aporias within the tradition is essential to any local theory.

There are many ways and forms of knowing, and no generic way that includes them all. This multiplicity comprises reason and requires heresy. It constitutes reason, as query, intrinsically in the sense that no one form of judgment, no single form of validation, can provide the standpoints that are required for it to call itself into question unendingly. The incommensurateness that makes reason heretical is required for it to be rational. Conversely, the rationality inherent in a form of query includes many methods, but no method for producing rationality, and among these methods are the disruptions of heresy. Heresy, then, is not a cloak that reason wears because finite beings employ it, as if there might be an undivided reason possessed by an infinite being, but pertains to reason itself. The aporia here is that reason can be rational only by overthrowing itself.

In this respect, query can be query, reason can be reason, only insofar as it is heretical, where heresy is the shape judgment wears to manifest the inexhaustibility of local being. One of the most pernicious of contemporary forms of rational authority, in science but also in morality and politics, is the self-proclaimed legitimacy of established forms to the point where heresy is excluded and opposition is regarded as illegitimate. Politically as well as epistemically, the result is the use of reason to enclose itself. In this sense, the passage of heresy into orthodoxy all too frequently, although aporetically, demands the exclusion of further heresy, manifested in the recurrent claim that we are a truly civilized and rational people when compared to our forebears.

If such a claim is true, it is only as a result of the heresies that comprise our views of civilization and reason. For us to deny heresy—so radical a heresy that would interrogate reason itself—is neither rational nor civilized, but simply a form of imposed authority. Without heresy, there can be no authority—including the aporia that heresy throws every authority into disarray. The fundamental aporia of orthodoxy is that, like heresy, it requires its opposite to be intelligible. The exclusion of heresy from reason makes the latter irrational.

We may, then, both understand and reject the iconoclastic sense that the Western metaphysical tradition contains within it a monstrous deceit that must somehow be overcome: the claim that philosophy or science possesses the only legitimate authority possible over every other form of human life and reason. This claim is recurrent within the metaphysical tradition. Yet the iconoclastic response ignores the heresies that divide that tradition inexhaustibly, including the divisions and heresies that iconoclastic criticism requires. It ignores the aporias that divide the metaphysical tradition as thoroughly as they divide being and knowing, divisions without which knowledge would long ago have ceased to have significance and truth, degenerating into the infinite repetition of unyielding orthodoxy.

It follows that the metaphysical tradition is, like every local being, at once and inseparably one and many: one tradition divided into many heresies, many points of view that together comprise a tradition. The heretical rejection of the metaphysical tradition is but an assertion of heresy, dogmatically ignoring its own origins. The skeptical rejection of the metaphysical tradition is but an assertion of locality, dogmatically denying the aporias of locality. The iconoclastic rejection of the metaphysical tradition is similarly mistaken: it suggests that we may depart from a tradition that does not comprise an undivided unity. It follows that within every departure, echoes will be found of that tradition, infinite repetitions, grounded in the causes that made such departures possible, including the divisions in the tradition that support them.

We come to the truth that as the metaphysical tradition is divided within itself by the aporias that constitute it and the heresies that comprise it, every metaphysical theory is both aporetic and divided, including a local theory. Inexhaustibility is not something that, once named, no longer transcends itself. Aporia is not something that, once understood, ceases to be aporetic or can be understood without heresy. There is no "true" understanding of aporia and heresy that can replace all other understandings: that would eliminate both aporia and heresy. There is no "seat" of aporia that is its origin. There is no "true" understanding of locality and inexhaustibility that would comprise a reconstruction of philosophy against the metaphysical tradition, a thinking that would no longer either belong to that tradition or continue its aporias. Nor can we say that with the collapse of disciplinary authority philosophy might become more aporetic. It has always been aporetic and cannot become more so.

However, it has not always explicitly understood itself along with being and judgment to be local and inexhaustible. Locality and inexhaustibility are the basis of aporia and heresy, but they constitute a different understanding of aporia and manifest a different heresy. A systematic expression of locality and inexhaustibility may be inclusive without being *all*-inclusive, general without being universal, true without being altogether determinate. Locality is not less aporetic than aporia, but is itself aporia: limitation and the limitation of limitation. Inexhaustibility is not a ground of aporia, but its aporetic origin, including the aporia that it cannot be any kind of origin because it is found in both beginning and end. Locality and inexhaustibility pertain to themselves and to any theory that acknowledges them. This constitutes their primary aporia, with the qualification that unqualified primacy is unintelligible and arbitrary. There is no essence to being, but many; no one fundamental way of being, but many: many generic ways of local being.

12   METAPHYSICAL HERESY

 ${\bf B}$ EING is aporia and reason is heresy. As a result, metaphysics is both aporetic and heretical. Yet this conjunction is not unique to metaphysics, but pertains to every form of query: science as well as art. The presence and absence of aporia and heresy are not the ways in which the different modes of query are distinguished, not the ways in which they realize their multiplicity. Rather, each mode defines itself uniquely in relation to aporia through its own forms of heresy. Moreover, multimodality engenders aporias "between" the modes—for example, between the metaphysics of science and the science of metaphysics, between the language of metaphysics and the metaphysics of language. Intermodality brings the aporias from every other mode of reason into any particular mode.

The burden of the previous discussions is that heresy and aporia pervade metaphysical thinking. Two questions now arise: one concerning the presence of aporia and heresy in other forms of query, notably in science; the other concerning the relation of a heretical metaphysics to itself. We may begin with the first.

From the beginning, the Western tradition has interpreted epistemic orthodoxy in terms of science despite the fact that both science and our understanding of it have undergone heretical transformations. A recurrent motif in the tradition is that some form of science may resolve the aporias of both ordinary and metaphysical thought—an idea itself pervasively aporetic. Not only is the idea of a whole and undivided science aporetic, but science is as heretical as any other form of knowledge. *Theōria* is no freer from aporia than is *phronēsis*. Present in both is the "quest for certainty" and the "mirroring of nature," mistaken views of the possibility of science. It is not that philosophy is unscientific in contrast with physics and biology, or that philosophy might be transformed into a science. It is that science itself, including physics and biology, mathematics and history, is aporetic, always incomplete, always exceeding itself. One of the important characteristics of the classical empiricist tradition, in contrast with its more orthodox successors, is its acknowledgment of the aporias of any empirical science. Science exhibits its own forms of aporia and heresy.

One of these comprises the motif that has reappeared throughout our discussions of the metaphysical tradition: the aporia of an orthodoxy in which science is free from every aporia. The aporia is the unconditioned nature of scientific truth in relation to the divided experience that constitutes the basis of science. On the side of empirical evidence, the presence of universal natural laws is aporetic; on the side of universal principles, divided experience is aporetic. On both sides, science is a supreme embodiment of the aporia of same and other.

Another aporia in science manifests itself in recurrent heresy. The most widely discussed book on science of the past half century speaks directly to this point. Science undergoes repeated revolutions.[1] The idea of a revolutionary science has engendered strenuous controversy, not least because it suggests that science is heretical, no less so than religion, philosophy, and art.

That science is heretical is itself heretical within the Western tradition. In this sense, science presents itself as aporetic in relation to every other form of thought, unqualifiedly other. The form in which its otherness is defined is that of orthodoxy: science as reason, opposed to dogma. It is conceived within a contrast with other forms of thought, as exclusive without sacrifice. Modernity contains the suggestion of the possibility of a science that would triumph finally over its competitors. Yet such a view goes back to long before Descartes. Rather, modernity arose when science gained the authority to claim its triumphs. In this sense, the antagonisms between science and its others, philosophy and art, are essential to the historical supremacy of modern scientific method. Ultramodernity is based upon the possibility that science may no longer possess its traditional supremacy, challenged both by the dividedness of reason and the material influences of historical events that cannot be brought under the dominion of science.

Modern science claims (or has claimed for it) exclusive authority over the territories of truth and reality. The primary form in which such authority has been claimed is that science is free from aporia and heresy. Yet the claim that science is free from heresy suggests a closure upon judgment and truth, not in the sense that science will, in fact, ever give us knowledge of everything, but a totalizing point of view that, in its general structure if not its details, would be entirely determinate if attained. Such a point of view is inherent in the nature of a scientific reason that assumes that consensus is the measure of truth, that reason can escape from the circle of its own representations.

Why has science appeared free from aporia? One answer lies within the general nature of orthodoxy: to define itself in contrast with heresy. In the modern tradition, science is the name of orthodoxy, contrasted with both heresy and aporia. The lesson of classical empiricism, that any empirical science is aporetic through and through, has been supplanted by the Kantian suggestion that there are unconditioned principles that constitute the ground of empirical knowledge. The irony is that Kant's views are deeply aporetic while they are the basis of all subsequent rejections of aporia. It is part of the nature of modern science to claim orthodoxy—a consequence of the assumption that reason produces agreement. In the Western tradition, such an orthodoxy is a repudiation of both aporia and heresy.

Another answer concerns the nature of science itself. Even if we grant without reservation the picture of a heretical science, is there not an important difference between science and other forms of reason? If this difference is not sufficient to claim freedom from aporia and heresy, is it sufficient to claim unique authority? If it is impossible to claim with reason that philosophy might be a science, does it follow that philosophy then has no claim to truth? What lies within these questions and their intelligibility are the assumptions again that truth requires universality and that it is traduced by aporia.

The basis for the authority of modern science lies in its reliance on empirical evidence. The aporia is that evidence is finite while the conclusions derived from it are doubly infinite: in relation to both universality and authority. The first form of the infinite is the universality in experience transformed into apriorism. The second is more striking. Local and contingent experience can never be the basis for the authority of science over its competitors. To the contrary, it is a basis instead for asserting the illegitimacy of any inflated claim to epistemic authority. An empirical science does not gain greater authority, based on its incomplete and local efforts, than religion, theology, or metaphysics, but diminishes all strident claims to epistemic authority as illegitimate, including its own. Hume's skepticism here is fundamental, not a marginal aberration.

An expression of this realization can be found in Peirce's notion of *fixing belief*.[2] He suggests that there have traditionally been four methods of fixing belief: tenacity (holding on to a belief willfully and obstinately); authority (maintaining the forcefulness of a belief through social and institutional pressures); apriorism (based on arbitrary and dogmatic premises); and inquiry. All but the last impose epistemic authority without self-criticism. The last is the only form capable of criticizing itself. What follows is that science derives its authority from a refusal to impose any authority free from disruptive self-criticism. The authority of science lies in the fact that it is never in a position to claim authority.

The aporia is that the inquiry that must disdain all established forms of authority is assigned orthodox authority. Science is superior because it disdains every form of authority that does not undermine itself. This powerful form of criticism is transformed into a superiority that does not criticize its own authority. Even in Peirce, we find the authority of inquiry to rest on a unanimity that it cannot succeed in establishing.

> The opinion which is fated to be ultimately agreed to by all who investigate is what we mean by the truth, and the objected represented in this opinion is the real.[3]

The inquiry that depends on unending criticism produces ultimate agreement, although its nature is precisely to refuse to accept such agreement. The image of the gadfly is admired in Socrates' person and in the iconoclastic side of Humian empiricism, but it is largely impotent in the orthodox tradition, diminished into vacuity by the consensual authority that reason claims for itself. The characteristic that is the basis of the authority of science—unending self-criticism and disagreement, including heresy—passes into orthodoxy. This aporia lies within orthodoxy itself, and is inescapable. To accept unending self-criticism as the basis of epistemic authority is effectively, where the authority is claimed, to set at least that authority beyond self-criticism. The only alternative is that an epistemic authority based on unending criticism and self-criticism must insist that it is not the sole authority because it must not reject the possibility of its own rejection. It must recurrently find within itself seeds of its own disruption, divisions of consensus and authority, if it is to be a form of reason.

Here we see the dangers in the transformation of a heretical view of science—found in classical empiricism—into orthodoxy: a blindness to the divisions that pertain to any claim to authority. There can be no knowledge that does not rest on claims to authority, and no such claim that does not abrogate itself. This is particularly striking where such authority is based on evidence and self-criticism.

Some of the other characteristics of modern science play their role in these aporias. In particular, where the role of empirical evidence is to define the form of self-criticism science requires, the systematization and generality claimed for science compete strenuously with the disruptiveness of evidence. The insistence that a legitimate form of science must advance inexorably toward truth and reality competes with the fits and starts that a highly critical form of reason imposes on those who participate in it. The most obvious role of the orthodox Kantianization of our understanding of science, overlooking the pervasive aporias in Kant's own writings, is to transform the incessant demand for criticism, based on evidence, into an unchanging method that would encompass all human reason. A manifestation of the deficiencies of this development is the alleged superiority of general laws and principles over local determinations. At the local level, details produce differences and disagreements—for example, in practical affairs. Disagreement may be as truthful as consensus.

One goal of modern science is to pay attention to the facts in all their stubbornness and variety. Another goal is to achieve a structure inclusive of the resistant details that inhabit local experience. That science might achieve the second, especially by adherence to "the scientific method," is aporetic because the only method in empirical science is that of unremitting interrogation. In this respect, following Hume, science is the form in which dogmatic metaphysics is to be challenged. The irony is that today science is no longer the name of the challenger, but of the orthodoxy, and metaphysics takes on the role of heretic. It does so by imposing demands for generality that force the demand for evidence into aporia. The ways in which science achieves its other proximate goals, of progress, systematization, and generality, effectively blind it to the aporias that constitute whatever local methods human beings can employ.

Two notions are fundamental to science: reliance on evidence and proof, and an irresistible advance toward universality. Neither of these is incompatible with heresy and aporia nor with locality and inexhaustibility. To the contrary, the march of science demands inexhaustibility and can be interpreted only in terms of locality. Science is inexorably heretical, and a heretical reason can establish only local legitimacy. The inexorability of science is no more than its inexhaustibility. The locality of science is the source of its inescapable heresies.

If science is no more to be understood as progressing to an undivided view of reality, without heresy and aporia, than metaphysics and art, then in what lies its uniqueness? Is there not something irresistible in the demand of science for conclusive empirical justification? An answer is that the demand for conclusiveness is not fundamental to truth in science, its *raison d'être*, but is the particular form in which modern science has established its authority. To fulfill its own rational imperatives, science must refuse every dogma in the name of empirical evidence. And there is an unruliness to evidence, to facts, that imposes a wildness to the empirical side of science, an expression of a more generic rejection of orthodoxy. Where Hume went wrong was in subsuming science entirely under a principle of repetition and regularity. Where Kant went wrong, after Hume, was in suggesting that the empirical side of experience could be tamed.

There is, nevertheless, something to the view that science progresses toward enduring truth. It is not that science is progressive or stable, because it is heretical and revolutionary. It is not that science is more systematic and inclusive than metaphysics or art, because the demand for evidence constantly imposes unexpected demands derived from the richness of local experience. It is not that science is more legitimate than other forms of reason and judgment, because legitimacy is conferred by judgment itself, in any mode, though always local and aporetic. Legitimacy is aporetic.

The image of science as univocal and determinate where poetry and metaphysics are ambiguous and indeterminate obscures an important truth. The claim of science to progress is unjustifiable where agreement and consensus are the ultimate goals. Nevertheless, where the aporias of metaphysics are manifested in intense and compelling form, the aporias of science manifest themselves through time in the incompleteness of its activities and the impossibility of stabilizing truth. Metaphysics does not progress toward a stable truth because its aporias are intense, recurrent, and unavoidable. Science does not progress toward a stable truth because its truth is inexhaustible. The aporias of metaphysics are tightly coiled knots and tangles while the aporias of science are coiled so loosely that they present themselves locally as linear in form. Nevertheless, the linearity is local and in a general enough perspective betrays itself as repetition, leading to heretical revolutions.

The aporias of philosophy and art manifest themselves in the unending if heretical repetition of same and other. Contemporary philosophy is no less concerned with issues of reality and intelligibility than were the Greeks, however differently. The aporias of science manifest themselves in the continual emergence of new problems and solutions. The aporias of science in a sense conform to what Hegel called the "bad infinite" while the aporias of metaphysics conform to the "good infinite," in both cases aporetically. The infinite in both cases is inexhaustibility. Good and bad infinites are equally aporetic.

We may be tempted to think of tightly coiled aporias as the only aporias there are. A consequence would be to accept the orthodox view of science as free from aporia. The more plausible alternative is that aporia emerges in inexhaustibly diverse forms expressive of the inexhaustibility of query. Science, here, manifests one of the pervasive forms of judgment and being, the possibility that "problems" may be "solved," if not permanently and with total agreement. These problems and solutions, however, are artifacts of the way in which modern science establishes its authority and in no way manifest the absence of aporia. To the contrary, it is because thought and being are aporetic that the distinction between science and its competitors can be defined. Moreover, to establish the distinction is to undermine it. Anything less is to accept orthodoxy for aporia and authority for heresy.

Aristotle claims that metaphysics is the science of being *qua* being. He rejects a science of doing or making: *phronēsis* and *technē* are not *theōria*. Writers today suggest that even art and literature—at least, their criticism—must be science, not to mention economic and political praxis. These views neglect the inherent multiplicity of modes of validation and query, but they cannot be dismissed without further attention. For *between* metaphysics and science lie heresy and aporia as well as between science and practice. Among the greatest aporias of science is that it cannot escape from the human world of power and desire but is caught by them in both directions: a creature of desire and power but also an inescapable form in which power and desire are implemented.

There are important aporias among the modes of query as well as within any of the modes. Intermodality and multimodality comprise the aporetic play of same and other that defines reason. Yet there is something important and unique about metaphysical aporias. One of the striking features of logical positivism was that it rejected metaphysics as unintelligible —as not science—in a *metaphysical* way. The sense of metaphysics here is not that of the positivists, but it is not alien. By "metaphysical," they meant transcending the bounds of possible experience. Yet their thesis that all empirical truths can be reduced to truths of physics was equally transcendent. This step, from the pervasiveness of physical conditions throughout experience to the claim that all conditions are intelligible only in terms of physical processes cannot be justified by empirical evidence. It is "metaphysical"—not in the sense that it is unintelligible, but in the sense that it strives for a generality that transcends any locality.

Aristotle defines metaphysics as a science of being *qua* being. Leaving aside the question of the relation between science and metaphysics, what is implied is that metaphysics is the most general form of reason, concerned with *being in general*. What is not implied is that metaphysics is the science of sciences from which every special science may be derived. The extreme generality of metaphysics and, similarly, of a science of sciences, does not establish a total mode of knowledge from which all special knowledges can be derived. It is in this sense neither foundational nor prior to other modes; yet it includes them within its purview. The relationship of metaphysics and its generality to any other mode of knowledge is never precisely determinable. It retains the play of same and other.

That there cannot be a science of sciences that establishes the principles of every science, a mode of validation in relation to which every other mode is but a specification, follows from the multiplicity of modes of reason. The irreducibility here is an expression of locality. The multiplicity, which entails incommensurate limits among the different modes, is not incompatible with intermodality, but requires it. The presence of limits requires the transcendence of limits. Every being is local, limited; every limit is itself limited. The presence of diverse modes and limits entails otherness, but otherness demands reconciliation with the same. A limit that allowed for no transgression would be absolute, not limited. A limit that can be dissolved into the same is no limit at all. Limitation and aporia are the same, requiring heresy for their expression.

There cannot be a science of sciences—either physics or metaphysics—into which every other science dissolves as specification of its generality. There must, however, be a form of reason whose province is science in general. More accurately, there must be a mode of query for which the forms of knowledge relevant to each special mode are subject matters seeking greater generalization. Such a mode of reason may not be a science; it cannot, however, be entirely other to science.

There is no science of being nor is there a science of human being. Instead, there is a multiplicity of human sciences. In part, this dividedness is artificial, the historical efflorescence of disciplines with dispersed authority. In further part, however, the division reflects the locality and inexhaustibility of human being, demanding manifestation in a multiplicity of forms of knowledge each of which expresses not so much a *part* of human being—a divisible essence—as its transformation. Here the reciprocity of same and other is inescapable. There are only arbitrary differences—no difference at all—dividing the human sciences, for example, between sociology and anthropology. There are methodological, historical, technical differences indeed, but they do not comprise a natural division. Each human science may both enter another and be substituted for its methods. There is every reason to think that the differences between and among the human sciences are arbitrary. What they reflect, however, amidst their arbitrariness, is the impossibility of a single human science—a science of sciences—and the unintelligibiltiy of a single human nature. The differences among the human sciences, then, are both nothing and everything.

Similarly, there is no science of being in general, but many sciences as well as many other modes of query. Being and knowing are local and inexhaustible. Any science of being must be aporetic and heretical both within and without. From within, the natural way in science to achieve univocity is to reject the aporias that constitute reason. The result is that the aporias of being are dispersed among the many sciences and throughout the course of development of any particular science.

Traditionally, metaphysics has taken systematic form. To iconoclastic writers, the very idea of system suggests totalization and closure. Regarded as the story of the cosmos, a philosophic system would leave no room for locality and inexhaustibility. Three qualifications must be added. First, totalization can be effective only in the absence of aporia. Second, it can be plausible only where a philosophic system is able to establish itself as sovereign over competing systems. Third, a system based on locality and inexhaustibility, on aporia and heresy, may succeed in overcoming its own limits aporetically.

Every metaphysics is aporetic, divided by differences that it both must and cannot resolve, overcoming certain aporias only to present them in other forms. Instead of "overcoming" aporia, the greatest philosophers have deepened and enriched it, made it more prominent and inescapable. In this respect, the claims within a metaphysical theory to attain closure are among its greatest aporias. Rather than thinking of it as totalizing and orthodox, we should think of it as heretical, presenting totalization as aporia. In this sense, explicitly iconoclastic philosophers—Nietzsche, Kierkegaard, Heidegger, Derrida—are not more heretical than systematic philosophers.

Similarly, that many systematic metaphysical works—of Spinoza, Kant, and Hegel, for example—claim to be the truth, in some cases, to be undeniable truth, does not overcome the divisions that constitute their heresies. Every such claim to truth is aporetic; moreover, several such claims are heretical in relation to each other. To suppose that in the claim to general truth, a metaphysics seeks to establish sovereignty over all others presupposes a view of reason that is incompatible with aporia and heresy. The view is mistaken even in relation to science, given its own heresies. It is the view that some form of truth takes unqualified precedence over all others, and that, once attained, would dissolve all aporias and eliminate all heresies.

There remains the question of the truth of a local metaphysics based on heresy and aporia. Shall we suppose that even to propose such a metaphysics is to destroy oneself? The presumption is that aporia is destruction. It presupposes the notion of a truth, grounded in science, against which our entire understanding of metaphysical aporia is directed. To the contrary, the understanding of metaphysics here—that it is aporetic and heretical—is not different from the metaphysics itself, based on locality and inexhaustibility. That we must find, in such an understanding, aporias that reflect the limitations of that theory, despite the fact that, as metaphysical, it seeks utmost generality, is itself an expression of the metaphysical aporia of same and other.

It has been useful to compare metaphysical query with science to portray the difference between propositional and syndetic validation. It will be useful, if not quite as traditional, to compare metaphysics with politics and art. Yet another comparison may be even more revealing, comparing metaphysics with language. What makes the comparison fruitful is the importance of language to metaphysics: metaphysics is always in language. What makes it important is the generality of language, manifested in the principle that anything that can be meant can be expressed in language. Analogously, anything that is or may be can be brought within the purview of metaphysics.

It is possible to say whatever we want to say, possible to express whatever we can know or mean, in any language, natural or artificial, because the resources of language are inexhaustible.[4] We may extend, enrich, and develop any language so as to make it express what we require. A language is not inexhaustibly expressive simply as it stands, in terms of its established structure and lexicon, not even in terms of infinite numbers of strings of morphemes or phonemes. The fundamental principle of the expressibility of language is that we may find a way, *somehow*, to say whatever we mean or know. Within this "somehow" lie the heresies of language. It is manifested, typically, in the myriad languages, in the relations among them, but especially in the capacity of language to be changed, enriched, in the development of new forms of human life and activity. Above all, there is the aporia present in the differences that inhabit public forms of expression and there is the aporia of representation itself—the differences that comprise meaning. There are always different publics, at different times and places, involving us in different codes and structures, invading common meanings with differentiations. Every public expression, in this sense, both cries out for different interpretations relating to different futures, and must itself be interpretive of what constitutes its meaning. Within this interpretivity of all expression, translation always manifests aporia.

Translation is irresistibly aporetic, inhabiting the regions between languages within the play of same and other. Success in translation is always local, although economic and social factors may make a local practice predominant over long periods of time. In this midworld of expressibility, translation works amid inescapable differences in linguistic expression, achieving sameness nevertheless—local sameness. Like every language, and every expression—including painting and music—translation achieves its aims "somehow," by breaking rules, violating expectations. That many translations are tame reflections of their originals speaks of our aporetic relationship to heresy and aporia. That a very few are thought to surpass their originals is the other side of this aporia.

Inexhaustibility pertains to language, first, relative to any language, in its capacity for the development of new resources for expressing anything meant or known; then, second, relative to the multiplicity of languages, wherein we discover the limits of any particular language; also, third, among the multiplicity of expressive forms other than language wherein we discover the limits of language. This sense of limit is a striking aporia because anything whatever can be expressed in any language, in language in general, and in any symbolic form. Yet that anything that can be meant can be expressed does not entail that every such expression is either equivalent to every other or as successful in particular ways. Same and other return to haunt us with their aporia. There are differences between languages that invade every translation, typically and forcefully manifested in poetry, but also in other literary and philosophic forms. Anything can be translated from one language to any other, but there will always be losses as well as gains—transformations—in virtue of the limits that define any particular language. Similarly, anything expressed in linguistic form may be expressed in nonlinguistic form—painting or gesture—sometimes better, sometimes worse, always differently.

The aporia is that of same and other, entailed by the limits of language amidst its inexhaustibility. Anything can be expressed in any language—a consequence of its inexhaustibility—but every such expression is determinate only in relation to the limits of that language—its locality. There are limits to every language, but also limits to those limits, entailing inexhaustibility.

Metaphysical generality is in many ways the same as the generality of linguistic expressibility. For both, the task is to achieve "utmost" generality where there are no measures of degree. It follows that the generality metaphysics can attain is self-defined and belongs to a process of embodiment more than to a measurable fulfillment. There is no definitive realization of metaphysical generality, only the condition that whatever is, in whatever way, can achieve metaphysical expression, including the representation of what surpasses representation. Analogous with the principle of expressibility in language, anything whatever may be included in a metaphysical theory, but not without profound limits; anything whatever may be expressed in different theories that, in contrast, manifest each other's limits; finally, even all together, metaphysical systems cannot express whatever there is to express, cannot include all beings in all ways, because there is no aggregate of *all* such ways.

There is this fundamental, even "ultimate" aporia at the center of metaphysical thinking, that its task, to achieve utmost generality, is both constantly successful and constantly confronts its own limits. Metaphysical thinking achieves the generality that defines it in Aristotle and Spinoza, Hegel and Kant. Yet, each achievement requires the other, in part because the generality attained cannot define its own limits, in part because the generality attained is always torn asunder by aporia. It is not merely that every effort to attain generality is partial, as Santayana claims in his view of philosophic heresy, but that it is a requirement of metaphysical thinking to know itself and its generality as well as to attain it, and no thought can include itself generically without disruption. There is an "outside" to the thought of utmost generality, to metaphysics, realized in a multiplicity of metaphysical works, in a multiplicity of other forms of reason besides metaphysics, and in the heresies in every form of reason. The works that define the contemporary challenge to metaphysical reason, in Heidegger, Derrida, and Dewey, are in this way inescapably metaphysical, thinking at the limits of the generality metaphysics requires to know itself.

The aporias that lie between metaphysics and science may now be interpreted as moments in the life of metaphysics that it requires to interrogate itself—moments in a process without culmination. Where science is sufficiently general, it becomes metaphysical, sometimes indistinguishable from metaphysics, only to lose the capacity to know itself as such along with its own aporias. Where metaphysics seeks definiteness and specificity, it becomes scientific, with the same self-blindness to its aporias. This reconciliation of science and metaphysics is essential to the life of reason, except that it obscures the aporias that fall between them. Thus, science and metaphysics must be reconciled through the imperatives of metaphysical query, but they must be divided through the imperatives of diversity in query.

Similarly, the presence of other modes of query defines both metaphysics and other forms of reason. Even where pursued "for its own sake," metaphysics is not airy, intangible thinking, independent of power and desire, but is inescapably a form of practice. Nevertheless, power and desire do not simply contaminate the generality of its thinking, but also render it definite and effective. Conversely, practical query—politics and ethics—is not independent of metaphysical query, but requires it for legitimacy and pervasiveness. Generality is required in ethics and politics as well as language, if in very different ways, and leads inescapably to metaphysics.

The generality ethics seeks has traditionally been realized either within a universality of principles and rules or over a multitude of competing interests. This description is heavily indebted to the traditional distinction between a morality of duty and a morality of well being. In both cases, there is no avoiding the need for generality, even universality, despite the inescapable presence of local divisions. The universal principles that define the freedom of the will for Kant are either empty or result in indeterminable conflicts. The generic calculations among competing interests in any utilitarian theory either presuppose a universal metric or dissolve in local differences in perspective.

The greatest defect of such movements to generality is that they are not required by the conditions of practical validation and are frequently antagonistic to them. Agreement is only one side of reason, complemented by difference. Even in science, reason contains an inescapable movement toward specificity: the inexhaustible determination of details. Otherness breaks into the rule of the same. The result is an aporia central to the nature of propositional truth. The movement of reason opposes itself. To Hegel's ultimate aporia of absolute Spirit we reply with the inexhaustible aporia of reason. The dialectic does not culminate, even in a greater aporia, but remains within aporia itself—the same although always different. Reason requires not so much the alternation of same and other—Hegel's "bad infinite"—but their unending interplay through time.

Practical query seeks generality on the side of either principle or application, but can never attain it, and seeks specificity on the side of the circumstances of practical affairs, only to be mired in inexhaustible conflicts. There is no unqualifiedly good will, only a will good in virtue of specific conditions, and no principle that represents the universality of freedom. Against the unqualifiedly good will, the pathway to hell is paved with good intentions. Against the universality of moral principles, each situation requires sensitive responsiveness to its details. The conflict between morality and politics is to be regarded, not as a conflict between principle and expediency, but between universality of principle and generality of purview. Difference divides these aporetically.

Metaphysics seeks utmost generality; practice seeks maximal generality within the requirements imposed by power and desire. Metaphysics is inevitably practice insofar as it issues from historical conditions and has results. Reciprocally, practice is metaphysical insofar as its own generality transcends that inherent in origins and consequences. Thus, the search for general principles of practice is always deficient and in vain, but necessary nevertheless, a metaphysical movement in the quest of practice to realize itself in more than the passing moment. Aristotle's view of *phronēsis* tells us that virtuous practice may be achieved without rules or generalization, nevertheless transcending any situation in the life of virtue.

In its ongoing process of heretical development, metaphysical query is more like art and practice than science—more concerned to invent a new system of categories whereby a different mode of being is explicated or to transform life and experience than to illuminate either the laws determining events or the differentiae that characterize individual beings, more present at the limits of thought than at any center. Here we can go no further than Spinoza, in his infinite numbers and kinds of attributes, each a way in which the essence of things is manifested, with the qualification that each essence is aporetic within the totality.

Here the plenitude in art is analogous to the plenitude in metaphysics, with two major qualifications. One is that not all art is of so great a generality, for art revels as much in its details as its generalities. In this respect, the inexhaustibility of art lies in individuation, singularity, and specificity while the inexhaustibility of metaphysics lies in the generality of its categories and systematic interrelations. However, what is found in art is that the most individualized works achieve the greatest generality. Similarly, the generality of metaphysical thinking is tested, not simply in the formality of its systematic relations, but within local human experience, individual states of affairs.

The emphasis in art is upon differences and differences in differences, similar to the limits of limits that characterize locality. What follows in art is an inexhaustible interplay of other in the same. In metaphysics, the same relationship is found with a different emphasis: generality replaces specificity. If we call the play of other in the same "contrast," then contrasts in art are the manifestation of inexhaustibility while metaphysics is aporetic, emphasizing the play of the same in the other. The difference here is both everything and nothing. Metaphysics cannot be distinguished except at a time and place from any of its rational collaborators.

Aporia pertains to being generically because being is local and inexhaustible. Aporia pertains to metaphysics specifically because being is aporetic and metaphysics speaks of being. Yet the language of being is not the only form in which metaphysics may speak—and this is Spinoza's heresy again: the infinite ways in which being may be thought or expressed. Yet, the generality of being cannot be denied, for within it lies its aporia. Metaphysics is aporetic because being is aporetic, but more specifically, because of the generality that defines metaphysical query. The generality of metaphysics invades every subject it addresses, rendering it intensely aporetic.

Aporia is the power within metaphysics, the source of its rationality. If aporia were contradiction, this would entail the unintelligibility of metaphysical thinking. Yet, intelligibility does not lie outside metaphysics, but within. The intelligibility of being and the intelligibility of metaphysics are inseparable. Two things follow. One is that the distinction between aporia and unintelligibility is a recurrent aporia that defines metaphysics. The tradition that rejects metaphysics and other forms of aporetic thinking as unintelligible is but one of the forms of aporia within the tradition.

What also follows is that aporia is the manifestation of metaphysical thinking itself, that it cannot then be the purpose of metaphysics to eliminate aporia, but rather to think it as deeply, if aporetically, as possible. Here we must again acknowledge Hegel's fundamental importance, with three qualifications. One is that subsequent moments do not achieve a more profoundly reflexive sense of aporia than is found in earlier moments. Plato is as aporetic, in his dialogues, as any later philosopher. The second qualification is that the sense of deepening and widening aporia, at more complex levels of reflexivity, is not progressive and produces no culmination. There is no supreme thought of aporia, however aporetic: aporia is always local. Third, the thinking of aporia is itself aporetic. There can be no theory of aporia free from aporia and no theory of heresy free from heresy. To think at the limits of thought and representation is to think aporia, aporetically and heretically.

On the one hand, metaphysics is confronted inexhaustibly with aporia, but on the other, aporia is not contradiction, although the two are aporetically related. Contradiction is a mark of unintelligibility, but aporia marks the relation of intelligibility to unintelligibility. This aporia of aporia, in relation to intelligibility, constitutes the movement of thought into heresy. Metaphysics requires heresy generically because beings are local and inexhaustible, but also, more specifically, because intelligibility is always in question. Within this aporia lies the most general understanding we can achieve of beings and truth themselves.

A consequence of this pervasive aporia is that metaphysics finds itself constantly pervaded by unintelligibility, although its own thinking is essential in the achievement of intelligibility. Thus, metaphysics strives for generality only to find that what is general is empty and aporetic. Metaphysics responds by seeking to turn itself into a science, only to find that its relationship to science is aporetic. Moreover, in these aporias, metaphysical thinking constitutes a tradition essential to future metaphysical thinking in the doubly aporetic sense that the tradition must be constituted by orthodoxy while metaphysical thinking must be heretical.

What follows is that metaphysics is one form of thought, constituting a single tradition, divided in four fundamental ways: (1) into a multiplicity of systematic works that together constitute metaphysical truth, although their togetherness does not comprise a single system; (2) into a multiplicity of interpretations for any metaphysical system, given its indeterminate future, especially a future in which new heretical works will be developed; (3) in the aporetic relationship of metaphysical reason to other forms of reason; (4) in the aporia of metaphysical reason's relationship to itself.

1. Where truth is conceived as freedom from aporia, or where there is a truth of aporia itself, then one metaphysical system may be imagined to constitute metaphysical truth, whether we have yet conceived it or not. Where metaphysical truth is aporetic, what follows is

either that metaphysics is unintelligible, identifying aporia with contradiction, or metaphysical truth is aporetically constituted by a multiplicity of systematic works, including those still to be invented. Systematic philosophy is inescapably orthodox only where a single system is taken to constitute truth. The inexhaustibility and locality of things can be realized in no single system of thought, but, following Spinoza's insight, requires inexhaustible (numbers of) systems for its conception. Metaphysical truth is found within the interrelations among different metaphysical systems. Metaphysical truth is heresy.

2. No knowledge can be entirely adequate but, especially, no metaphysics can know itself adequately; no understanding can be an adequate self-understanding because knowledge requires externality. A consequence is that insofar as any metaphysical work enters a public world, it is subject to conflicting interpretations, realized not only in future works, in other philosophical interpretations, but also in judgments lying outside philosophy. The "meaning" of a metaphysical system is always partly indeterminate, facing an indeterminate future. Yet this indeterminateness is not simply a defect, but contains the possibility of future heresies. The positivity that pertains to metaphysical aporia is in the interrelationship of same and other that on the one hand constitutes intelligibility and on the other constitutes heresy as the form in which intelligibility can be realized.

3. The truth of metaphysics is a divided truth. There is no generic truth that can be realized in any one form of reason. Metaphysical truth is neither identical with other forms of truth nor clearly distinguishable from them. It is divided over time and location into different systems, where no one, overarching system takes precedence except locally. It is also divided over other forms of query in the sense that truth in science and in metaphysics are neither separable nor unifiable, but remain together in aporia.

4. The aporia of metaphysical thought is both intrinsic and divided inexhaustibly. There is no final truth of aporia, however aporetic, and no thought of the limits of metaphysical thinking, at the limits of representation, that is free from the aporias that continue to divide it.

Metaphysics is not a science to the extent that it is concerned with utmost generality, but science is also concerned with generality. Metaphysics is not art insofar as aporia is distinct from contrast; yet that distinction is overcome by both metaphysics and art. Metaphysics is not a form of practice insofar as it is not defined by its consequences, yet metaphysics is constituted by power and desire. Moreover, practice seeks authority and control over all walks of human life, including metaphysical thought. Here there is the profound aporia inherent in the materiality of metaphysical thinking: it seeks to influence a future that would be free from its influence. Yet a thinking that does not influence the future, that does not constitute a material "discourse," is empty.

One of the striking suggestions of "postmodernism" is that in its time the metaphysical tradition will come to an end. The implication is that the metaphysical tradition is somehow constituted unitarily by "modernity." Yet not only is that tradition heretical, but modernity constitutes one of its heretical moments. There is, however, within this millenial suggestion, a certain materiality. "Postmodernism" hopes to see the beginning of a new mode of discourse founded on aporia itself. Even more important, there is the promise claimed in postmetaphysical thinking of a new way of being human.[5]

What is important about "ultramodernity" is not its understanding of itself as a new heretical form of thought, but its possibility as a heretical form of practice. Here, following Foucault, we must understand metaphysics itself to be a form of discourse, of practice, with density and materiality, giving up any thought of its transparency. In this understanding, we see a greater importance to metaphysical heresy: participating in the discourse that, in its materiality, will comprise some future. Metaphysical heresy, here, is not simply the discovery of limits in a human understanding of things, but the establishment of limits in the nature of humanity itself and of the limits of those limits. Metaphysical thinking here, especially in its great systematic works, is both constituted by human practices and constitutes them. This interrelation falls between metaphysical thinking, apparently without any human purpose at all, and politics, responsible for the most important events in human life.

With this affirmation of the materiality of systematic thinking, we may bring our discussion to a close by considering a final question. If being is local and inexhaustible, if metaphysics along with all other forms of reason is both aporetic and heretical, then what is the status of a metaphysical theory of locality and inexhaustibility? And what may be expected of the aporetic readings of the metaphysical tradition that constitute the major part of the discussion here?

The only conclusion is that such a reading is but one of many readings; that even this metaphysical understanding, however significant, will be supplanted by other understandings. Yet there is something unsatisfying about such a conclusion, and in two respects. One is that it is easier to posit an understanding that is able to displace itself than to achieve one. The form of discourse present here, as in all systematic forms of discourse, professes truth. Such a truth is incompatible with self-effacement.

The second way in which self-effacement has been expressed returns us to the aporias of metaphysical truth and resolves the difficulty just stated. The "truth" inherent in the reading of the tradition given here is multiply aporetic. Locality and inexhaustibility are aporetic, but so is the relationship between a local theory and any other. Metaphysical truth is local and inexhaustible, realized in an inexhaustible multiplicity of local metaphysical works, some affirming inexhaustibility, some denying it. What remains is to be able to say, somehow, if only aporetically, what the truth of aporia amounts to. This, however, is a task of metaphysics itself. In the metaphysical theory here, aporia is locality and inexhaustibility. Like happiness, which can be achieved only when not sought, aporia can not be thought "itself," but be thought only through other inexhaustible local beings.

NOTES

PREFACE

1. I follow the genealogical strain in Foucault, entertaining:

> ... the claims to attention of local, discontinuous, disqualified, illegitimate knowledges against the claims of a unitary body of theory which would filter, hierarchise and order them in the name of some true knowledge and some arbitrary idea of what constitutes a science and its objects, (Michel Foucault, *Power/Knowledge*, C. Gordon ed., A. Fontana and P. Pasquino trs., New York, Pantheon, 1980, p. 83)

but challenging the principle of sameness in the author:

> ... I think that, for some time, at least, the individual who sits down to write a text, at the edge of which lurks a possible *oeuvre*, resumes the functions of the author. (Michel Foucault, *The Discourse on Language* (*L'ordre du discours*), Appendix to *Archaeology of Knowledge*, New York, Pantheon, 1972, p. 222)

The author and the text may instead be read heretically, as local and discontinuous, subjugated knowledges, disrupting both the *oeuvre* and the canon.

CHAPTER 1

1. George Santayana, "Philosophical Heresy," *Obiter Scripta*, J. Buchler and B. Schwartz eds., New York, Scribners, 1936, p. 94.

2. Martin Heidegger, "The End of Philosophy and the Task of Thinking," *Basic Writings*, D. Krell ed., New York, Harper & Row, 1977, p. 373.

3. Metaphysical philosophy tries to go beyond the empirical scientific questions of a domain of science and to ask questions concerning the nature of the objects of the domain. These questions we hold to be pseudo-questions. (Rudolf Carnap, *The Logical Syntax of Language*, Paterson, New Jersey, Littlefield, Adams, 1959, p. 331)

345

... is there a *first* possibility for thinking apart from the *last* possibility which we characterized (the dissolution of philosophy in the technologized sciences), a possibility from which the thinking of philosophy would have to start, but which as philosophy it could nevertheless not experience and adopt?

If this were the case, then a task would still have to be reserved for thinking in a concealed way in the history of philosophy from its beginning to its end, a task accessible neither to philosophy as metaphysics nor, and even less so, to the sciences stemming from philosophy. (Heidegger, "The End of Philosophy and the Task of Thinking," pp. 377-78)

The urge to make philosophy into Philosophy is to make it the search for some final vocabulary, which can somehow be known in advance to be the common core, the truth of, all the other vocabularies which might be advanced in its place. This is the urge which the pragmatist thinks should be repressed, and which a post-Philosophical culture would have succeeded in repressing. (Richard Rorty, *Consequences of Pragmatism*, Minneapolis, University of Minnesota Press, 1982, p. xlii)

4. Heidegger, "The End of Philosophy and the Task of Thinking", p. 377.

5. Martin Heidegger, "The Onto-Theo-Logical Constitution of Metaphysics," in *Identity and Difference*, J. Stambaugh tr., New York, Harper & Row, 1969.

6. Jacques Derrida, *On Grammatology*, G. Spivak tr., Baltimore, Maryland, Johns Hopkins University Press, 1982, p. 43.

7. Richard Rorty, *Philosophy and the Mirror of Nature*, Princeton, New Jersey, Princeton University Press, 1979, p. 389.

8. Michael Polanyi, *Knowing and Being*, Chicago, University of Chicago Press, 1969, p. 133:

To hold a natural law to be true is to believe that its presence may reveal itself in yet unknown and perhaps yet unthinkable consequences; it is to believe that natural laws are features of a realitiy which as such will continue to bear consequences inexhaustibly.

9. Martin Heidegger, *On the Way to Language*, P. D. Hertz tr., New York, Harper & Row, 1971, p. 111.

10. See Rorty, *Consequences of Pragmatism*, chs. 3 and 5.

11. See Michel Foucault, *The Discourse on Language*.

12. The fundamental principle of the following discussions is that aporia constitutes the positive as well as negative core of metaphysical thinking, and that it may not be dismissed as violating the law of noncontradiction because the

question of whether an aporia is "contradictory" is itself aporetic. What aporia demands is heresy.

13. Hans-Georg Gadamer, *Truth and Method*, New York, Seabury, 1975. This understanding of tradition constitutes the nature of hermeneutic understanding, qualified by Foucault's emphasis on disruption and exclusion.

14. Michel Foucault, *History of Sexuality, Volume I*, R. Hurley tr., New York, Random House, 1980; also *Archaeology of Knowledge* and *The Discourse on Language*.

15. T. S. Kuhn, *The Structure of Scientific Revolutions*, Chicago, University of Chicago Press, 1962.

16. Harold Bloom, *The Anxiety of Influence: A Theory of Poetry*, New York, Oxford University Press, 1973.

17. John Dewey, *Quest for Certainty*, New York, Minton, Balch, 1928.

18. Rorty, *Philosophy and the Mirror of Nature*.

CHAPTER 2

1. See Arnold Ehrhardt, *The Beginning: A Study in the Greek Philosophical Approach to the Concept of Creation from Anaximander to St. John*, Manchester, Manchester University Press, 1968.

2. Apparently Anaximander was the first to use the word *archē*. See Michael C. Stokes, *One and Many in Presocratic Philosophy*, Washington, D.C., Center for Hellenic Studies, 1971.

3. Ehrhardt, *The Beginning*, ch. 7.

4. The fragments referred to in this chapter are drawn from the translations in John Mansley Robinson, *An Introduction to Early Greek Philosophy*, Boston, Houghton, Mifflin, 1968, and Milton C. Nahm, *Selections to Early Greek Philosophy*, New York, Appleton-Century-Crofts, 1964, as indicated. All citations also indicate references where appropriate to Diels-Kranz, *Die Fragmente der VorSokratiker* (DK). In the different readings of the fragments, we find both acknowledgment and rejection of heresy. I generally emphasize the translation that calls the heretical side of the fragments more clearly to our attention. I do not mean by this to ignore the raging controversies.

5. As Aristotle puts it, capturing the aporia precisely:

> But it is not possible that infinite matter is one and simple; either, as some say, that it is something different from the elements, from which they are generated, or that it is absolutely one. For there are some who make the infinite of this character, but they do not consider it to be air or water, in order that other things may not be destroyed

by the infinite; for these are mutually antagonistic to one another, inasmuch as air is cold, water is moist, and fire hot; if one of these were infinite, the rest would be at once destroyed. Accordingly, they say that the infinite is something different from these elements, namely, that from which they come. (Nahm, p. 40)

6. Alfred North Whitehead, *Process and Reality*, Corrected ed., D. R. Griffin and D. W. Sherburne eds., New York, Macmillan, 1979, p. 39.

7.   Opposition is good; the fairest harmony comes out of differents; everything originates in strife. (Nahm, p. 71; DK 22 B 8)

It is necessary to understand that war is universal and justice is strife, and that all things take place in accordance with strife and necessity. (Robinson, p. 93; DK 22 B 80)

8.   Thinking and the thought that it is are the same; for you will not find thought apart from what is, in relation to which it is uttered. (Robinson, p. 110; 28 B 8)

For thought and being are the same. (Robinson, p. 110; DK 28 B 3; rendered by Nahm as, "For the same thing can be thought as can be," p. 93)

9.   It is necessary to speak and to think what is; for being is, but nothing is not; for being is, but nothing is not. (Robinson, p. 111; DK 28 B 6)

For never shall this prevail: that things that are not, are. (Robinson, p. 111; DK 28 B 7)

One way remains to be spoken of; the way how it is. Along this road there are very many indications that what is is unbegotten and imperishable; for it is whole and immovable and complete. Nor was it at any time, nor will it be, since it is now, all at once, one and continuous.
For what beginning of it would you search for? How and whence did it grow? I shall not let you say or think "from what is not"; for it is not possible either to say or think how it is not .... (Robinson, p. 113; DK 28 B 8)

10. See F. H. Bradley, *Appearance and Reality*, London, Clarendon, 1893.

11. Bradley, *Appearance and Reality*, pp. 120, 123.

12. Plato, *Parmenides*, 136. See herein ch. 2, note 1.

13. J. M. E. McTaggart, *The Nature of Existence, Vol. II*, Cambridge, Cambridge University Press, 1927, ch. 33.

14. See R. E. Allen and D. J. Furley eds., *Studies in Presocratic Philosophy*, London, Routledge & Kegan Paul, 1975, especially: F. M. Cornford,

"Anaxagoras' Theory of Matter"; Gregory Vlastos, "The Physical Theory of Anaxagoras"; Gregory Vlastos, "One World or Many in Anaxagoras"; Colin Strang, "The Physical Theory of Anaxagoras."

CHAPTER 3

1. Whitehead, *Process and Reality*, p. 39.

2. Ibid.

3. His personal endowments, his wide opportunities for experience at a great period of civilization, his inheritance of an intellectual tradition not yet stiffened by excessive systematization, have made his writings an inexhaustible mine of suggestions. (Ibid.)

4. Ibid., p. 40.

5. Søren Kierkegaard, *The Concept of Irony*, Bloomington, Indiana University Press, 1965.

> But what is the relationship between the Platonic Socrates and the actual Socrates? This is a question which cannot be dismissed. Socrates completely pervades the fruitful domain of the Platonic philosophy, in fact, he is omnipresent in Plato. (p. 67)

> Socrates, like Samson, seizes the columns bearing the edifice of knowledge and plunges everything down into the nothingness of ignorance. That this is authentically Socratic will certainly be admitted by all—Platonic, on the other hand, it will never be. (p. 77)

6. Leo Strauss, *The City and Man*, Chicago, University of Chicago Press, 1983.

7. See John Findlay, *Plato The Written and Unwritten Doctrines*, New York, Humanities Press, 1974; Kenneth M. Sayre, *Plato's Late Ontology: a Riddle Resolved*, Princeton, New Jersey, Princeton University Press, 1983.

8. In Sallis' words, "The contrast between *logos* and *mythos* is not a contrast between a perfected and an imperfect discourse." (John Sallis, *Being and Logos: The Way of Platonic Dialogue*, Pittsburgh, Dusquesne University Press, 1975, p. 16)

9. See the Introduction, note 14.

10. Neglecting the ironies of his own position, Crombie emphasizes that even if Plato had no doctrine, he spawned Platonism. Such a view, if historically correct, capitulates to orthodoxy.

> It can be argued that there is no such thing as Platonism. . . . To identify Plato's work with the philosophical theories which from time

to time Socrates or some other leading speaker appears to sponsor in the dialogues is to misrepresent him entirely; . . . .

This is a half-truth that should not be lost sight of. But common sense will protest that after all there is an attitude to the world which is, and has been since the itme of Aristotle, regarded as Platonism; . . . . (I. M. Crombie, *An Examination of Plato's Doctrines*, London, Routledge & Kegan Paul, 1962, vol. 1, p. 31)

11. Quotations from the dialogues are from *The Collected Dialogues of Plato*, Edith Hamilton and Huntington Cairns eds., Princeton, New Jersey, Princeton University Press, 1969.

12. As Gadamer points out, "It is not just at a particular hour in the history of Athens that the shadow of sophism accompanies philosophy, but always." It is not the *threat* of unreason so much as its inseparability from reason. (Hans-Georg Gadamer, *Dialogue and Dialectic*, New Haven, Connecticut, Yale University Press, 1980, p. 3)

13. Crombie notes the genuineness and importance of certain aporias in the dialogues, although he does not recognize how pervasive aporia is within them. (Crombie, *An Examination of Plato's Doctrines*, pp. 21-22)

14. The crudeness of these formulations is due in part to recognition that significant variations in Platonic interpretation arise with changes in the metaphysical tradition. Thus, in contemporary terms, it might be important to interpret 1 and 2 above in terms of reference and predication: we can predicate opposing terms to any sensible reality, but only to the extent that the predicates themselves are well-defined, intelligible, and noncontradictory and that reference to individuals is unambiguous. Similarly, the absolute intelligibility of the ideas may place them utterly beyond empirical understanding.

15. See Charles B. Bigger's references to Jacob Klein in *Participation: a Platonic Inquiry*, Baton Rouge, Louisiana State University Press, 1968, pp. 16-20; Jacob Klein, *A Commentary on Plato's* Meno, Chapel Hill, University of North Carolina Press, 1965.

16. Victorino Tejera, *Plato's Dialogues One by One*, New York, Irvington Publishers, 1983, p. 32.

17. Do you suppose that somebody entirely ignorant who Meno is could say whether he is handsome and rich and wellborn or the reverse? (*Meno*, 71b)

18. Alfred North Whitehead, *Modes of Thought*, New York, Capricorn, 1938, p. 66.

19. In Heidegger's language, there is concealment in every unconcealment. Unfortunately, Heidegger seems never to have acknowledged how deeply such a principle pervades the Platonic dialogues.

20. Ludwig Wittgenstein, *The Blue and Brown Books*, Oxford, Blackwell, pp. 81, 87.

21. The passage continues with a discussion of "limit," a concept that is repeatedly at the focus of the dialogues.

22. See Jacqueline de Romilly, "Plato and Conjurers," in Keith V. Erickson, ed., *Plato: True and Sophistic Rhetoric*, Amsterdam, Rodopi, 1979, pp. 160-61. Plato also uses the word *pharmatteis*: see note 23.

23. See Jacques Derrida, *Plato's Pharmacy*, in *Disseminations*, B. Johnson tr., Chicago, University of Chicago Press, 1981, for a detailed discussion of the polysemy of *pharmakon* in *Phaedrus*.

24. Paul Plass, "The Unity of the *Phaedrus*," in Erickson, *Plato*, p. 220.

25. Thomas Gould, *Platonic Love*, New York, Free Press of Glencoe, 1963, p. 1.

26. Vlastos points out the otherworldliness and inhumanity of *eros* in most of the dialogues without acknowledging its compensating personification in Socrates. (Gregory Vlastos, *Platonic Studies*, Princeton, New Jersey, Princeton University Press, 1973, p. 30)

27. Stanley Rosen, "The Non-Lover in Plato's *Phaedrus*," in Erickson, *Plato*, p. 224.

28. Martha Nussbaum, " 'This Story Isn't True': Poetry, Goodness, and Understanding in Plato's *Phaedrus*," in J. Moravcik and P. Temko eds., *Plato: On Beauty, Wisdom, and the Arts*, Totowa, New Jersey, Rowman and Littlefield, 1982, pp. 87-88)

29. Alexander Sesonske, "To Make the Weaker Argument Defeat the Stronger," in Erickson, *Plato*, p. 78. See also Eric Havelock, *Preface to Plato*, Cambridge, Massachusetts, Harvard University Press, 1963.

30. Sallis, *Being and Logos*, p. 95.

31. Findlay, *Plato The Written and Unwritten Doctrines*, pp. 90-91.

32. This distinction is discussed in Jean-François Lyotard, *The Postmodern Condition: A Report on Knowledge;* G. Bennington and B. Massumi trs., Minneapolis, University of Minnesota Press, 1984, p. 10.

33. J. C. B. Gosling, *Plato*, London and Boston, Routledge & Kegan Paul, 1973, ch. I.

34. See Sallis, *Being and Logos*, ch. V, for a discussion of the images of Hades in *Republic*.

35. Socrates cannot and will not escape the city in *Phaedrus*; the philosopher-king cannot escape the city of human life in *Republic*.

36. Iris Murdoch reads Plato as a puritan. Gregory Vlastos reads him as subjecting human *aretē* entirely to the ideal. Both neglect the ironies and inversions. (Iris Murdoch, *The Fire and the Sun: Why Plato Banished the Artists*, Oxford, Oxford University Press, 1977, pp. 12-13; Vlastos, *Platonic Studies*, ch. I)

37. Sallis, *Being and Logos*, p. 134.

38. John Herman Randall Jr. offers a reading of *Republic* closely related to the one given here. It may be salutary to consider the important differences.

> How far can you carry the ideal of organization, of Justice, if, because it is so obvious and essential a good, you take it as the supreme and only good, if you let the mind play with it as men do in discussion, and push it as far as you possibly can? . . .
>
> It is clear, you can carry the ideal out to the bitter end, in imagination; and Plato shows the end is bitter! So Plato has Socrates, maliciously and ironically, elaborate, shall we say, Protagoras' scheme for a perfectly organized state—a perfectly planned society, we moderns put it—till in the end we have a picture of . . . "Justice Itself," Pure Justice—the Perfect City, from which every other consideration has dropped away, which exists for the sake of efficient organization, and efficient organization alone. . . .
>
> The answer, for anyone in his senses, and certainly for any perceptive and imaginative reader of the *Republic*, is clear. Justice, organization, efficiency, is only one element in the Good Life, or in the Good Society. (John Herman Randall Jr., *Plato: Dramatist of the Life of Reason*, New York, Columbia University Press, 1970, pp. 162-63)

If we pay attention to the ironic displacements and dramatic excesses of *Republic*, we must be led to agree with Randall that *Republic* is not to be taken seriously as a portrait of an ideal, but to the contrary, is a self-ironizing portrait of an autocratic society absurdly ruled by those who think they have a supreme vision of the good. Yet, there is something profoundly misconceived about taking this instead to be Plato's doctrine. It is nicely expressed by Randall himself in another context.

> The most important and basic fact about the philosophy of the Platonic dialogues is that it is the philosophy of a man who *had* to write imaginative dialogues, a philosophy such as only a writer of dialogues could have worked out, and a philosophy capable of expression only in dialogue—that is, in *dramatic* form. (p. 134)

> Platonic myths are not ways of stating what is hard to say in literal words—they are not allegories. Plato is perfectly capable of stating in precise terms what he wants to state. . . . Platonic myths are rather ways of making us *see* something; and of expressing and communicating what the seeing does to us. That is, the myths are ways of communicating what the artist sees and feels: myths do not state anything, they do something to us. (p. 199)

However, in relation to *Republic*, Randall makes the distinction he is here opposing, between what Plato states and what Plato shows. To the contrary, the heretical reading is that what Plato says is what Plato shows and conversely: that is
what it means to say that the dramatic dialogue form is the only philosophy
Plato writes. To translate Plato into nondramatic prose is to interpret his philosophy but not to re-present it.

39. The two relevant descriptions of method are both profoundly and
unceasingly aporetic. In the one case, the "what is not" is inexhaustible; in the
other, the intermediate forms—measure and number—pass away into the unlimit.

> . . . there is something noble and inspired in your passion
> for argument, but you must make an effort and submit yourself,
> while you are still young, to a severer training in what the world
> calls idle talk and condemns as useless. Otherwise, the truth will
> escape you.
> . . . you would not allow the survey to be confined to visible
> things or to range only over that field; it was to extend to those
> objects which are specially apprehended by discourse and can be
> regarded as forms.
> . . . But there is one more thing you must do. If you want to
> be thoroughly exercised, you must not merely make the supposi-
> tion that such and such a thing *is* and then consider the conse-
> quences; you must also take the supposition that that same thing is
> not. (*Parmenides*, 135de)

> All things, so it ran, that are ever said to be consist of a one and a
> many, and have in their nature a conjunction of limit and unlimited-
> ness. This then being the ordering of things we ought, they said,
> whatever it be that we are dealing with, to assume a single form and
> search for it, for we shall find it there contained; then, if we have
> laid hold of that, we must go on from one form to look for two, if
> the case admits of their being two, otherwise for three or some other
> number of forms. And we must do the same again with each of the
> "ones" thus reached, until we come to see not merely that the one
> that we started with is a one and an unlimited many, but also just
> how many it is. But we are not to apply the character of unlimited-
> ness to our plurality until we have discerned the total number of
> forms the thing in question has intermediate between its one and
> its unlimited number. It is only then, when we have done that, that
> we may let each one of all these intermediate forms pass away into
> the unlimited and cease bothering about them. There then, that is
> how the gods, as I told you, have committed to us the task of inquiry,
> of learning, and of teaching one another, . . . it is recognition of
> those intermediates that makes all the difference between a philo-
> sophical and a contentious discussion. (*Philebus*, 16de-17)

40. Aristotle, *Metaphysics*, 988.

Chapter 4

1. I identify his orthodoxy finally with what Edel calls the "taming of the indeterminate." (Abraham Edel, *Aristotle and his Philosophy*, Chapel Hill, University of North Carolina Press, 1982, pp. 101-102) Heidegger calls it "ontotheology." (Heidegger, "The Onto-Theo-Logical Constitution of Metaphysics") Dewey calls it a quest for certainty. (Dewey, *The Quest for Certainty*.) All these views neglect Aristotle's aporetic heresies.

2. Giovanni Reale, *The Concept of First Philosophy and the Unity of the Metaphysics of Aristotle*, J. C. Catan tr., Albany, SUNY Press, 1980. Reale finds in *Metaphysics* a consistent concern with what he calls ontology, theology, ousiology, and aetiology. See also G. Patzig, "Theology and Ontology in Aristotle's *Metaphysics*," J. Barnes, M. Schofield, R. Sorabji eds., *Articles on Aristotle*, vol 3, London, Duckworth, 1979, pp. 33-49.

3.   The body is *archē kinēseōs*. What an *archē kinēseōs* in this manner is, is *physis*, the original mode of emergence, which, however, remains limited solely to pure movement in space. Herein appears an essential transformation of the concept of *physis*. The body moves according to its nature. A moving body, which is itself an *archē kinēseōs*, is a natural body. . . . Each body has *its* place *according to its kind*, and it strives toward that place. Around the earth is water, around this, the air, and around this, fire—the four elements. When a body moves toward its place this motion accords with nature, *kata physin*. . . . All motions against nature are *biai*, violent. (Martin Heidegger, "Modern Science, Metaphysics, and Mathematics," in *Basic Writings*, p. 260)

4.   6. . . . the difference between natural and against nature, i.e., violent, is also eliminated; . . . .
    7. Therefore the concept of nature in general changes. Nature is no longer the *inner* principle out of which the body follows; rather, nature is the mode of the variety of the changing relative positions of bodies, ...
    8. Thereby the manner of questioning nature also changes and, in a certain respect, becomes opposite. (Ibid., p. 264)

5. Quotations are from *The Basic Works of Aristotle*, Richard McKeon ed., New York, Random House, 1941.

6. John Hermann Randall, Jr., *Aristotle*, New York, Columbia University Press, 1960, p. 2.

7. See for example, Foucault, *The Archaeology of Knowledge*, pt. IV, ch. 6.

8. Randall, *Aristotle*, p. 1.

9. See Richard Robinson, "Aristotle on Akrasia," in *Articles on Aristotle*, vol. II, pp. 79-91, for the claim that Aristotle does seek to resolve the aporias.

"Refuting the objections" and resolving the aporias are to be understood as quite different activities.

10. See Werner Jaeger, *Aristotle: Fundamentals of the History of His Development*, 2nd ed., R. Robinson tr., London, Oxford University Press, 1962; Reale, *The Concept of First Philosophy and the Unity of the* Metaphysics *of Aristotle*; Joseph Owens, *The Doctrine of Being in the Aristotelian Metaphysics: A Study in the Greek Background of Medieval Thought*, 2nd ed., Toronto, Pontifical Institute of Medieval Studies, 1951; W. D. Ross, *Aristotle: A Complete Exposition of His Works and Thought*, Cleveland, Meridian, 1955 (still the standard against which all interpretations of Aristotle are tested).

11. See Walter Leszl, *Aristotle's Conception of Ontology*, Padova, Editrice Antenore, 1975, pp. 71-73 for an excellent discussion of this point.

12. See Lyotard, *The Postmodern Condition*, for an explanation of this notion, in relation to what he calls "metanarratives."

13. Edel calls it "startling." (Edel, *Aristotle and his Philosophy*, p. 162)

14. See Randall, *Aristotle*, pp. 91-92.

15. In his attack on Aristotle's historical accuracy, Cherniss presents a striking account of the relationship between *apeiron* and *protē hylē*. (Harold Cherniss, *Aristotle's Criticism of Plato and the Academy*, Baltimore, Maryland, Johns Hopkins Press, 1944, pp. 83-174)

16. See Whitehead, *Process and Reality*, pt. IV.

17. See John Searle, *Speech Acts*, Cambridge, Cambridge University Press, 1969, p. 19. See my *The Limits of Language*, New York, Fordham University Press, forthcoming, for a detailed discussion of the inexhaustibility of language.

18. Nelson Goodman, *Languages of Art*, Indianapolis, Hackett, 1976.

19. Gadamer, *Truth and Method*, p. 498.

20. Hans-Georg Gadamer, *Philosophical Hermeneutics*, D. E. Linge tr., Berkeley, University of California Press, 1976, pp. 15-16.

21. See E. Weil, "The Place of Logic in Aristotle's Thought," *Articles on Aristotle*, vol. I, pp. 91-92.

22. Samuel Coleridge, *Biographia Litteraria*, vol. I, closing paragraphs.

23. We come, here, to such contemporary views as Piaget's neo-Kantian principle that "to understand is to invent," (Jean Piaget, *To Understand is to Invent*, New York, Grossman, 1973), as well as to the views of both Merleau-Ponty and Whitehead.

24. In Randall's perspicuous phrase, contemplation is the activity of *nous nousing nous*.

25. I would argue that this activity in reason makes it impossible to "take away" all practical and fabricative judgment. It is impossible to judge, actively and creatively, without influencing events and achieving something.

26. For a discussion of ontological priority and ontological parity, see Justus Buchler, *Metaphysics of Natural Complexes*, New York, Columbia University Press, 1966; and Stephen David Ross, *Transition to an Ordinal Metaphysics*, Albany, SUNY Press, 1980.

27. "The suggestion that all actions have a single end is one which Aristotle several times considers, but never opts for." (Anthony Kenny, "Aristotle on Happiness," *Articles on Aristotle*, Vol. 2, p. 28)

28. Starting always with what things can be said to be, and with the careful analysis of that saying—starting, that is, with an analysis of the language in which things are talked about and stated—he always finds that this linguistic analysis reaches a point where it raises questions that cannot be answered through the analysis of language alone. He then asks, "Well, how did this come into being?" (Randall, *Aristotle*, p. 60)

29. See W. Wieland, "The Problem of Teleology," *Articles on Aristotle*, vol. 1, pp. 140-60. See also Richard Sorabji, *Necessity, Cause, and Blame*, Ithaca, New York, Cornell University Press, 1980 for a discussion of how incidental causes disrupt the causal, explanatory chain. (p. 8)

30. Thus, though we can state of attributeness and substanceness that they are, Being is not a universal of which they are differentiations, nor is Being a universal of which they are particulars. (John Cook Wilson, "Categories in Aristotle and in Kant," *Aristotle: A Collection of Critical Essays*, J. M. E. Moravcsik ed., Garden City, Doubleday, 1967, p. 77)

31. Again, Reale, *The Concept of First Philosophy and the Unity of the Metaphysics of Aristotle*; G. E. L. Owen, "Logic and Metaphysics in Some Earlier Works of Aristotle," *Articles on Aristotle*, vol. 3:

> The new treatment of *to on* and other cognate expressions as *pros hen kai mian tina phusin legomena*, "said relative to one thing and to a single character"—or, as I shall henceforth say, as having *focal meaning*—has enabled Aristotle to convert a special science of substance into the universal science of being, "universal just inasmuch as it is primary." (p. 17)

An excellent treatment of the complexity of being *qua* being and its relation to the aporias of one and many is to be found in Leszl, *Aristotle's Conception of Ontology*, pt. IV.

CHAPTER 5

1.　　　The heads of the Ecclesiastical Council hereby make known that already well assured of the vile opinions and doings of Baruch de Espinoza, they have endeavored in sundry ways and by various promises to turn him from his evil courses. But as they have been unable to bring him to any better way of thinking; on the contrary, as they are every day better certified of the horrible heresies entertained and avowed by him, and of the insolence with which these heresies are promulgated and spread abroad, and many persons worth of credit having borne witness to these in the presence of the said Espinoza, he has been held fully convicted of the same. (Abraham Wolfson, *Spinoza: A Life of Reason*, New York, Modern Classics, 1932, p. 74)

2. Harry A. Wolfson, *The Philosophy of Spinoza*, vol. I, New York, Schocken, 1969, p.3.

3. Wolfson, *The Philosophy of Spinoza*, vol. II, p. 331.

4. Spinoza's mathematical way of looking at things means only the denial of design in nature and freedom in man, and this need not necessarily be written in the geometrical literary form. (Wolfson, *The Philosophy of Spinoza*, vol. I, p. 45)

5. Such an orthodox view is common among Spinoza's commentators. See, for example, Efraim Schmueli, "The Geometrical Method, Personal Caution, and the Ideal of Tolerance," and Douglas Lewis, "On the Aims and Method of Spinoza's Thought," in R. W. Shahan and J. I. Biro eds., *Spinoza: New Perspectives*, Norman, University of Oklahoma, 1978.

6. Quotations are from Spinoza's *Ethics*, adapted by J. Gutmann from the translations by W. H. White (1883) and A. H. Stirling (1894, 1899), New York, Hafner, 1949. Quotations from the letters are from Baruch Spinoza, *The Ethics and Selected Letters*, S. Shirley tr., Indianapolis, Hackett, 1982. Quotations from the *Short Treatise* are from Curley (see note 9).

7. See here Raphael Demos' equivalent characterization of the paradoxes within Spinoza's view of moral consciousness, "Spinoza's Doctrine of Privation," S. Paul Kashap ed., *Studies in Spinoza: Critical and Interpretive Essays*, Berkeley, University of California Press, 1972, pp. 283-84.

8. Hallett denies that finite modes are the durational things of our experience. (H. F. Hallett, *Benedict de Spinoza*, London, Athlone Press, 1957) Many readers are awed by Hallett. I include myself, for I find a remarkable view of the universe in his writing. I simply am not convinced it is Spinoza's.

9. In Curley's apt phrase,

What Spinoza's philosophy seems to require, for finite things, is both an infinite series of finite causes and a finite series of infinite causes terminating in God. (E. M. Curley, *Spinoza's Metaphysics: an Essay in Interpretation*, Cambridge, Massachusetts, Harvard University Press, 1969, p. 64)

10. Spinoza goes so far as to treat the infinite sequence of causes as an eternal fact.

> ... if someone asks by what cause a body determined in a certain way is moved, we may reply that it is determined to such a motion by another body, and this one again by another, and so on to infinity. This, I say, is a possible reply because the question is only about motion, and by continually positing another body, we assign a sufficient and eternal cause of its motion. (Letter 40)

11. See here Martial Gueroult:

> The antinomy opposing infinity and divisibility, resolved in the *Ethics* on the level of substance by excluding the divisible, reappears on the level of the mode, where we must affirm infinite divisibility, that is, both the infinite and the divisible. ("Spinoza's Letter on the Infinite," in M. Grene ed., *Spinoza: A Collection of Critical Essays*, Garden City, Doubleday, 1973, p. 182)

12. Jonathan Bennett rejects the "logical" view of ideas, insisting on a psychological component. (*A Study of Spinoza's* Ethics, Indianapolis, Hackett, 1984, ch. 6) He does not consider the possibility that Spinoza means for ideas to be *both* divine and psychological.

13. Bennett's "field-metaphysics" (*A Study of Spinoza's* Ethics, pp. 88-92) is a useful heuristic analogy here, supplementing the analogy of mechanism. At this point, we must emphasize that both are analogies: Spinoza's God is absolutely infinite in all ways.

14. For a striking alternative point of view, see James Collins, *Spinoza on Nature*, Carbondale, Southern Illinois University Press, 1984, ch. 8, in which nature is regarded as a "community of communities."

15. To Curley, in another striking passage, the purpose of these proofs is "not to prove the existence of a being whose existence is questionable, namely, God, but to justify the deification of a being whose existence no one doubts, namely, Nature." (Curley, *Spinoza's Metaphysics*, p. 41)

16. Whitehead, *Modes of Thought*, p. 66.

17. This is true despite Spinoza's claim to have proved the most difficult and obscure of his propositions, that concerning the number of attributes and our knowledge of them. See letter 9 on whether there is more than one attribute, and letter 64 on our knowledge of only two attributes.

18. Nevertheless, Spinoza does claim that things are as perfect as they can be, and follow with necessity from God. " . . . it clearly follows that things have been produced by God in the highest degree of perfection, since they have necessarily followed from the existence of a most perfect nature." (I, Prop. XXXIII, Note 2)

19. See Curley, *Spinoza's Metaphysics*, for a similar interpretation.

20. Bennett points out, in relation to suicide, that Spinoza cannot avoid teleology. (Bennett, *A Study of Spinoza's* Ethics, pp. 277-40) But neither can he avoid teleology in relation to salvation. See also Collins, *Spinoza on Nature*, pp. 269-78)

CHAPTER 6

1. The approach here will be almost entirely metaphysical, rejecting the interpretation in most contemporary discussions of Leibniz, in Russell and Couturat, for example, basing his metaphysics on his logical principles. (Bertrand Russell, *A Critical Exposition of the Philosophy of Leibniz*, London, Allen & Unwin, 1900; Louis Couturat, *La Logique de Leibniz*, Paris, 1901; see also Louis Couturat, "On Leibniz's Metaphysics," R. A. Ryan tr., in H. G. Frankfurt ed., *Leibniz: A Collection of Critical Essays*, Garden City, Doubleday, 1972) I do not mean thereby to deny connections between logic and metaphysics, but to emphasize the remarkable heresies in Leibniz's view of rationality and intelligibility that do not find expression in a logical interpretation.

2. Parkinson identifies the principle of sufficient reason with the principle of perfection. (G. H. R. Parkinson, *Logic and Reality in Leibniz's Metaphysics*, London, Oxford University Press, 1965, p. 286) I do not accept this identification, although I recognize the close relationship between the principles. What I think is important is that the surplus in each principle includes the other. I might mention also that I would be inclined to call the principle of perfection, of the best, the principle of *plenitude* except for Lovejoy's famous definition of that principle as the actualization of all possibilities. The principle of perfection is a principle of maximal richness—variety balanced with economy—thereby a principle of plenitude though not of mere variety.

3. See Dennis Fried, "Necessity and Contingency in Leibniz," in R. S. Woolhouse, *Leibniz: Metaphysics and Philosophy of Science*, London, Oxford University Press, 1981, p. 55; Benson Mates, *The Philosophy of Leibniz*, New York, Oxford University Press, 1986, ch. VI; Nicholas Rescher, *Leibniz's Metaphysics of Nature*, Dordrecht, Reidel, 1981, ch. IV. Contingency remains but all propositions are analytic. It is one of Leibniz's most heretical suggestions that the distinction between necessary and contingent propositions rests on the finiteness of the analysis whereby the predicate is shown to be contained in the subject. Mates finds no "intuitive plausibility in the proposed solution." (p. 108) Rescher offers an ingenious analysis in terms of the principle of perfection (pp.

42-55) Fried denies that a plausible theory of contingency can be developed in the context of Leibniz's view that every predicate is contained in the subject. Contingency is aporetic in Leibniz's theory. What may be added is that the deeper aporia is that of identity. If there are contingent truths, then some properties of a being are irrelevant to its identity.

What almost no one appears to have considered is that, despite their different languages, Leibniz and Spinoza share a common view of finite contingency. For finite contingent things, an infinite analysis in terms of causes and conditions—internal representations—is necessary. For infinite, necessary things, a formal, deductive analysis is possible, presumably in a finite number of steps. The distinction corresponds to that in Spinoza between what follows directly from God and what follows under qualification by (infinite numbers of) finite modes.

4. I am not including here as fundamental to Leibniz's metaphysics either the principle of plenitude, made famous by Lovejoy in the form that every possibility is actualized—because I do not find it congenial in this form with the principle of perfection—or the logical principle that every subject contains all its predicates, equivalent with the principle that every true proposition is analytic—because that principle can be given a metaphysical analogue more important for our purposes: that every state of every substance follows from its nature, essential to its independence.

5. Quotations except where noted are from *Leibniz: Selections*, P. P. Wiener ed., New York, Scribner's, 1951.

6. See Leroy E. Loemker, "On Substance and Process in Leibniz," in *The Philosophy of Leibniz and the Modern World*, I. Leclerc ed., Nashville, Vanderbilt University Press, 1973, p. 54. " . . . Leibniz offers a compact definition of substance. In essence, it is a permanent law determining a temporal sequence or series of events."

> That there is a certain persisting law which involves the future states of that which we conceive as the same—this itself is what I say constitutes the same substance. (Leibniz to de Volder, January 21, 1704)

Parkinson relates the identity of substance to the principle of indiscernibles (*Logic and Reality in Leibniz's Metaphysics*, p. 134):

> In sum, Leibniz seems to mean by the principle of the identity of indiscernibles what he should mean if he is to be consistent: namely, that it is self-contradictory to suppose two indiscernible substances.

See also Mates, *The Philosophy of Leibniz*, p. 122:

> If any single topic lies at the very heart of Leibniz's philosophy, it is that of identity . . . . and on one crucial point he never changed his mind: things are individuated by their "whole being": Every property of a thing is essential to its identity.

Anything less makes identity aporetic. As it stands, nevertheless, identity is aporetic.

7. See Nicholas Rescher, "Logical Difficulties in Leibniz's Metaphysics," in Leclerc ed., *The Philosophy of Leibniz and the Modern World*, pp. 179-84.

8. See above, ch. 2, p. 78.

9. In Whitehead, *nexūs* are not and cannot be actual entities.

10. Mondadori regards Leibniz's system as "a grand circular design," effectively denying ontological priority despite the simplicity of monads. (Fabrizio Mondadori, "Solipsistic Perception in a World of Monads," in *Leibniz: Critical and Interpretive Essays*, M. Hooker ed., Minneapolis, University of Minnesota Press, 1982, p. 22.

11. In saying, therefore, that things are not good according to any standard of goodness, but simply by the will of God, it seems to me that one destroys, without realizing it, all the love of God and all his glory; for why praise him for what he has done, if he would be equally praiseworthy in doing the contrary? (*Discourse on Metaphysics*, II)

Leibniz rejects an arbitrariness in which God might do anything. There is a different arbitrariness in sufficient reason: that of reason itself.

12. Bradley, *Appearance and Reality*, p. 120.

13. As a consequence, therefore, the law of noncontradiction is not trivial and innocuous, but obscures covert and far-reaching expressions of arbitrariness and aporia.

14. Bradley, *Appearance and Reality*, p. 505.

15. This is, of course, a Heideggerian expression of the limits of every reason. Fundamental here is the indeterminateness in every determination.

16. See also the argument:

36. But there must also be a *sufficient reason* for *contingent truths*, or those *of fact*,—that is, for the sequence of things diffused through the universe of created objects ....

37. And as all this *detail* only involves other contingents, anterior or more detailed, each one of which needs a like analysis for its explanation, we make no advance: and the sufficient or final reason must be outside of the sequence or *series* of this detail of contingencies, however infinite it may be.

38. And thus it is that the final reason of things must be found in a necessary substance, in which the detail of changes exists only eminently, as in their source; and this is what we call God.

39. Now this substance, being a sufficient reason of all this detail, which also is linked together throughout, *there is but one God, and this God is sufficient*. (*Monadology*)

17. Leibniz sometimes speaks of the principle of perfection as a free choice of God among infinitely many possible worlds. See Rescher, *Leibniz's Metaphysics of Nature*, p. 3:

> ... it is only because God—in view of his *moral* perfection—has *chosen* to subscribe to a certain standard of *metaphysical* perfection in selecting a possible world for actualization that possible substances come to have (figurative) "claim" to existence.

Yet God's choice cannot be arbitrary. "Leibniz again and again insisted that there is an independent standard of the perfection of things . . . . (Rescher, p. 3) See also John W. Nason, "Leibniz and the Logical Argument for Individual Substances," in Woolhouse, *Leibniz: Metaphysics and Philosophy of Science*, p. 26:

> In short, God must act upon some reason. Being perfectly wise and perfectly good, he must choose to create the best possible world.

The point here is more that God is not unconditioned than that his freedom makes finite events free from necessity.

18. See note 11.

19. See Rescher, *Leibniz's Metaphysics of Nature*, p. 10.

20. See Leroy E. Loemker, "The Ethical Import of Leibniz's System," in Leclerc, *The Philosophy of Leibniz and the Modern Period*, p. 220.

21. See my *A Theory of Art: Inexhaustibility by Contrast*, Albany, SUNY Press, 1982, pp. 99-107.

22. See Milič Čapek, "Leibniz on Matter and Memory," in Leclerc ed., *The Philosophy of Leibniz and the Modern World*, p. 79. In Leibniz's words:

> For every body is a momentary mind, or one lacking recollection, because it does not retain its own conatus and the other contrary one together for longer than a moment. (*Theoria motus abstracti seu rationes motuum universales a sensu et phaenomenis independentes.*)

23. Leibniz maintained accordingly that it is necessary to distinguish two kinds of entity, which are distinct and different in ontological status. There are, on the one hand, the ontologically ultimate or primitive existents—which he termed "monads," and which in themselves are nonextensive; and, on the other hand, there are the material bodies which are extensive. (Ivor Leclerc, "Leibniz and the Analysis of Matter and Motion," in Leclerc, *The Philosophy of Leibniz and the Modern World*, p. 127)

See also Whitehead's similar denial that actual entities are intrinsically extended, although they may be analyzed coordinately.

... in every act of becoming there is the becoming of something with temporal extension; but that the act itself is not extensive, in the sense that it is divisible into earlier and late acts of becoming which correspond to the extensive divisibility of what has become. (Whitehead, *Process and Reality*, p. 69)

24. Nason regards this as a contradiction rather than an aporia. See Nason, "Leibniz and the Logical Argument for Individual Substances," p. 26.

25. See Rescher, *Leibniz's Metaphysics of Nature*, p. 86:

For Leibniz, every world has its own space. There is no superspace in which distinct possible worlds are co-located with one another. Leibniz, as we may say, was a "one-world, one-space" theorist.

26. Letter to Tschirnhaus, May 1678, *Akademie*, 2nd series, vol. 1, p. 411; quoted in Hidé Ishiguro, *Leibniz's Philosophy of Logic and Language*, Ithaca, New York, Cornell University Press, 1972, p. 35.

CHAPTER 7

1. Quotations are from John Locke, *An Essay Concerning Human Understanding*, New York, Dover, 1959; David Hume, *A Treatise of Human Nature*, London, Oxford, 1888; David Hume, *An Enquiry Concerning Human Understanding*, New York, Liberal Arts, 1955; Francis Bacon, *Novum Organum*, George Berkeley, *Principles Concerning Human Understanding*, Thomas Hobbes, *Leviathan*, David Hume, *Dialogues Concerning Natural Religion,* all from *The English Philosophers from Bacon to Mill*, New York, Modern Library, 1939.

2. In "Some Puzzles in Hobbes," *Thomas Hobbes in his Time*, R. Ross, H. W. Schneider, T. Waldman eds., Minneapolis, University of Minnesota Press, 1974, Ralph Ross notes Hobbes' own metaphysical heresy:

A strange materialist this, a strange mechanist, a strange determinist, when measured by the doctrines to which we give those names today . . . . If Hobbes "reduced" everything to body, body included everything. (p. 48)

3. See Derrida's discussion of Saussure (*Of Grammatology*; Ferdinand de Saussure, *Course in General Linguistics*, W. Baskin tr., New York, McGraw-Hill, 1959). See also my *The Limits of Language*, especially Chs. I and II.

4. A common distinction in the literature is between innate *ideas* and innate *knowledge*. (See R. S. Woolhouse, *Locke*, Brighton, Harvester Press, 1983, pp. 16ff.) Where ideas are representational, this distinction cannot be maintained.

5. Yet Locke's resolution of skepticism has a skeptical side. See Woolhouse, *Locke*, p. 8. Similarly, Locke emphasizes the meagreness of human knowledge.

See Richard Ashcraft, "Faith and Knowledge in Locke's Philosophy," *John Locke: Problems and Perspectives*, J. Yolton ed., London, Cambridge University Press, 1969, p. 194.

6. There are nevertheless plenty of implausible theories. See Jerry Fodor, *Representations*, Cambridge, Massachusetts, M.I.T. University Press, 1981.

7. See Noam Chomsky, *Cartesian Linguistics*, New York, University Press of America, 1966.

8. Cowley emphasizes Locke's repudiation of the "natural attitude" that we live and act among things and thereby ignores the positive side of the skepticism in empiricism. (Fraser Cowley, *A Critique of British Empiricism*, New York, St. Martin's, 1968, p. 21.) The "natural attitude" is not sufficiently aware of its aporias.

9. Whitehead, *Process and Reality*, pt. II, Ch. VIII

10. See Cowley, *A Critique of British Empiricism*, p. 140.

11. Jonathan Bennett, *Locke, Berkeley, Hume*, Oxford, Clarendon, 1971, p. 61.

12. In Cowley's words:

> The primordial thesis, unreasoned, unargued, on which all enquiry and investigation and discovery is founded, is that there is a world and that it is in itself, independent of our being in it, and of our seeing anything of it or knowing anything about it. (Cowley, *A Critique of British Empiricism*, p. 165.)

The "unreasoned" nature of this thesis both affirms the importance of an "other" to reason and argument, in lived experience, and denies any possibility of subjecting such a thesis to criticism. The conjunction is aporetic.

13. In "Berkeley, Perception, and Common Sense," (*Berkeley: Critical and Interpretive Essays*, C. Turbayne ed., Minneapolis, University of Minnesota Press, 1982) George Pappas presents several theses definitive of common sense and several others normally ascribed to Berkeley, raising the question of whether they can be reconciled. His ingenious attempt to do so overlooks the importance in Berkeley of the aporias found to be characteristic of common sense.

14. See notes 8, 10, and 12 above.

15.　　　All the perceptions of the human mind resolve themselves into two distinct kinds, which I shall call IMPRESSIONS and IDEAS. The difference betwixt these consists in the degrees of force and liveliness with which they strike upon the mind, ... Those perceptions, which enter with most force and violence, we may name *impressions*; . . . . By *ideas* I mean the faint images of these in thinking and reasoning; . . . .

There is another division of our perceptions, which it will be convenient to observe, and which extends itself both to our impressions and ideas. This division is into SIMPLE and COMPLEX. Simple perceptions or impressions and ideas are such as admit of no distinction nor separation. The complex are the contrary to these, and may be distinguished into parts.

That all our simple ideas in their first appearance are deriv'd from simple impressions which are correspondent to them, and which they exactly represent. (Hume, *Treatise*, I, I, I, pp. 1, 2, 4)

16. This is true despite the "bewildering complexity" of the *Treatise*, commented on by Kemp Smith and Passmore. (Norman Kemp Smith, *The Philosophy of David Hume*, London, St. Martin's, 1949, p. 3; John Passmore, *Hume's Intentions*, third edition, London, Duckworth, 1980, p. 1) Some of this complexity is the heresy of aporia, typically in the name of skepticism.

17.   'Tis therefore by EXPERIENCE only, that we can infer the existence of one object from that of another. The nature of experience is this. We remember to have had frequent instances of the existence of one species of objects; and also remember, that the individuals of another species of objects have always attended them, and have existed in a regular order of contiguity and succession with regard to them. (Hume *Treatise*, I, III, VI, p. 87)

18.   'Tis therefore certain, that the imagination reaches a *minimum*, and may raise up to itself an idea, of which it cannot conceive any sub-division, and which cannot be diminished without a total annihilation. When you tell me of the thousandth and ten thousandth part of a grain of sand, I have a distinct idea of these numbers and of their different proportions; but the images, which I form in my mind to represent the things themselves, are nothing different from each other, ... What consists of parts is distinguishable into them, and what is distinguishable is separable. But whatever we may imagine of the thing, the idea of a grain of sand is not distinguishable, nor separable into twenty, much less into a thousand, ten thousand, or an infinite number of different ideas. (Ibid., I, II, I, p. 27)

19. . . . *the idea of space or extension is nothing but the idea of visible or tangible points distributed in a certain order;* . . . . (Ibid., I, II, V, p. 53)

20. George Pitcher notes that "Berkeley sometimes speaks as though he thinks that all images must be determinate in all respects." (George Pitcher, *Berkeley*, London, Routledge & Kegan Paul, 1977, p. 71)

21. This is effectively the criticism that most views of artificial intelligence are far too restricted, based on a deficient epistemology. Until machines can experience emotions, they can never be said to *know*.

22.   I had entertain'd some hopes, that however deficient our theory of the intellectual world might be, it wou'd be free from those contradictions, and absurdities, which seem to attend every explication, that human reason can give of the material world. But upon a more strict review of the section concerning *personal identity*, I find myself involv'd in such a labyrinth, that, I must confess, I neither know how to correct my former opinions, nor how to render them consistent. (Hume, *Treatise*, Appendix, p. 633)

When I turn my reflexion on *myself*, I never can perceive this *self* without some one or more perceptions; nor can I ever perceive any thing but the perceptions. 'Tis the composition of these, therefore, which forms the self. (Ibid., p. 634)

If perceptions are distinct existences, they form a whole only by being connected together. But no connexions among distinct existences are ever discoverable by human understanding. (Ibid., p. 635)

23. For from what impression cou'd this idea be deriv'd? . . . It must be some one impression, that gives rise to every real idea. But self or person is not any one impression, but that to which our several impressions and idea are suppos'd to have a reference. (Ibid., I, IV, VI, p. 251)

24. See Donald Livingston, "Time and Value in Hume's Social and Political Philosophy," *McGill Hume Studies*, D. F. Norton, N. Capaldi, W. L. Robison eds., San Diego, Austin Hill Press, 1979, pp. 186ff. Hume, here, bears a largely unacknowledged similarity to Gadamer's hermeneutic theory in *Truth and Method*. Similarly, what we take to be true is a function of our capacity for fiction. See Ian Ross, "Philosophy and Fiction. The Challenge of David Hume," *Hume and the Enlightenment*, W. B. Todd ed., Edinburgh and Austin, University of Edinburgh Press and University of Texas Press, 1974, pp. 60 ff. Here Hume is a forerunner of postmodernism. These anticipations are inherent in the aporetic side of Hume's skepticism.

25. . . . in the course of his writings Hume uses other sceptical arguments such as those which show that we hold mutually contradictory beliefs, or that the principles we operate upon in determining one indispensable belief will oppose the principles we operate upon in determining another indispensable belief. In fact it is this inability to generalise the natural principles of the understanding which is the source of Hume's famous statement of scepticism in in the conclusion to the first book of the *Treatise*. (John P. Wright, *The Sceptical Realism of David Hume*, Manchester, Manchester University Press, 1983, p. 31.)

26.   Since morals, therefore, have an influence on the actions and affections, it follows, that they cannot be deriv'd from reason; and that because reason alone, as we have already prov'd, can never

have any such influence. Morals excite passions, and produce or prevent actions. Reason of itself is utterly impotent in this particular. The rules of morality, therefore, are not conclusions of our reason. (Hume, *Treatise*, III, I, I, p. 457)

27.   Reason is the discovery of truth or falshood. Truth or falshood consists in an agreement or disagreement either to the *real* relations of ideas, or to *real* existence and matter of fact. Whatever, therefore, is not susceptible of this agreement or disagreement, is incapable of being true or false, and can never be an object of our reason. Now 'tis evident our passions, volitions, and actions, are not susceptible of any such agreement or disagreement; being original facts and realities, compleat in themselves, and implying no reference to other passions, volitions, and actions. 'Tis impossible, therefore, they can be pronounced either true or false, and be either contrary or conformable to reason. (Ibid., p. 458)

28. Perhaps the only philosopher who fully understood this aspect of representation is Charles Sanders Peirce.

29. The critical literature on Hume reaches virtual consensus that he did not intend to reject metaphysics *altogether*, but only certain forms of established theology. (See Robert L. Armstrong, *Metaphysics and British Empiricism*, Lincoln, University of Nebraska Press, 1970, Introduction) Nevertheless, Passmore's suggestion is plausible that Hume sought to replace dogmatic metaphysics with a science of human nature. (Passmore, *Hume's Intentions*, p. 71) However, Passmore does not take Hume's skepticism seriously, entirely neglecting the aporetic side of his thought. (p. 137)

30. See Passmore, *Hume's Intentions*: "But, in fact, our irrationality preserves our Reason." (p. 137)

31. It must be noted that Kemp Smith denies Hume's skepticism. (Kemp Smith, *The Philosophy of David Hume*, p. 443)

32. In "Why Should Probability be the Guide of Life?," D. C. Stove suggests that Hume's fallibilism is far more devastating than his skepticism. (*Hume: A Re-Evaluation*, D. W. Livingston and J. T King eds., New York, Fordham University Press, 1976, p. 57)

Chapter 8

1. Quotations are from Immanuel Kant, *Critique of Pure Reason* (CPR), N. Kemp Smith tr., New York, St. Martin's, 1956; *Kant's Critique of Practical Reason and Other Works on the Theory of Ethics* (CPrR), T. K. Abbott tr., London, Longman's, Green, 1954; *Critique of Judgment* (CJ), J. H. Bernard tr., New York, Hafner, 1951

2. Gram argues that the antinomy—or aporia—is not destructive to the idea of the world. (Moltke S. Gram, "Kant's First Antinomy," *Kant Studies Today*, Lewis W. Beck ed., La Salle, Open Court, 1969, p. 215) William H. Baumer notes, in the same volume, that Kant rejected all cosmological arguments. ("Kant on Cosmological Arguments," p. 392) Yet Kant also emphasizes that science demands a unity in thought that is deeply cosmological: nature as a whole under regulative principles.

3. McTaggart, *The Nature of Existence*, vol. II, ch. 33.

4. See Henry Allison, *Kant's Transcendental Idealism*, New Haven, Connecticut, Yale University Press, 1983, p. 128, for a discussion of the completeness of the transcendental conditions in Kant's system.

5. The relationship between phenomena and noumena—one of "affection" if not causality—is one of the most controversial issues in the interpretation of Kant. Vaihinger interprets the arguments that define this relationship as a "patchwork." (Hans Vaihinger, *Commentar zu Kants Kritik der reinen Vernunft*, 2 vols., Stuttgart, Spemann, 1881-92; see also Hans Vaihinger, "The Transcendental Deduction of the Categories in the First Edition of the *Critique of Pure Reason*," *Kant: Disputed Questions*, M. S. Gram ed., Chicago, Quadrangle, 1967, pp. 23-61) He criticizes Kant's argument in terms of a trilemma:

> 1. Either one understands by the affecting objects the things in themselves; in which case one falls into the contradiction discovered by Jacobi, Aenesidemus and others that one must apply beyond experience the categories of substantiality and causality which are only supposed to have meaning and significance within experience.
>
> 2. Or one understands by affecting objects the objects in space; but since these are only appearances according to Kant, and thus our representations, one falls into the contradiction that the same appearances, which we first have on the basis of affection, should be the source of that very affection.
>
> 3. Or one accepts a double affection, a transcendent through things in themselves and an empirical through objects in space. In this case, however, one falls into the contradiction that a representation for the transcendental ego should afterwards serve as a thing in itself for the empirical ego, the affection of which produces in the ego, above and beyond that transcendental representation of the object, an empirical representation of the very same object. (Vaihinger, p. 53; quoted in Allison, *Kant's Transcendental Idealism*, pp. 247-48)

See also Norman Kemp Smith, *A Commentary on Kant's 'Critique of Pure Reason.'* London, Macmillan, 1979, pp. 408-10. Gram continues the discussion in great detail. (Gram, *Kant: Disputed Questions*; Moltke S. Gram, *The Transcen-*

dental Turn: the Foundation of Kant's Idealism, Gainesville, University of Florida Press, 1984) Strawson has criticized Kant for incoherence on this subject. (Peter Strawson, *The Bounds of Sense: an Essay on Kant's* Critique of Pure Reason, London, Methuen, 1966)

All insist that the relationship between noumena and phenomena be free from "contradiction"—i.e., aporia. Gram's "Concluding Aporetical Postscript" is no exception. (Gram, *The Transcendental Turn*, pp. 181-95) Allison offers an alternative interpretation in which some of the contradictions are manifest (Allison, p. 244), although he, too, would avoid aporia.

None takes seriously the possibility that the relationship is profoundly and intrinsically aporetic, that this aporia is at the center of the critical enterprise, that aporia is not incoherence.

6. See my *Transition to an Ordinal Metaphysics*, Albany, SUNY Press, 1980; *Philosophical Mysteries*, Albany, SUNY Press, 1981; *Perspective in Whitehead's Metaphysics*, Albany, SUNY Press, 1983.

7.   Even physics, therefore, owes the beneficent revolution in its point of view entirely to the happy thought, that while reason must seek in nature, not fictitiously ascribe to it, whatever as not being knowable through reason's own resources has to be learnt, if learnt at all, only from nature, it must adopt as its guide, in so seeking, that which it has itself put into nature. (CPR, p. 20)

8. This aporia lies behind the endless controversies over the relationship between noumena and phenomena. The former can neither "cause" nor guarantee the latter, although they must provide their foundation. See H. W. Cassirer, *Kant's First Critique*, London, George Allen & Unwin, 1954, p. 43.

9. See Gilles Deleuze, *Kant's Critical Philosophy: the Doctrine of the Faculties*, H. Tomlinson and B. Habberjam trs., Minneapolis, University of Minnesota Press, 1984, p. 74: "The accomplishment of freedom and of the good Sovereign in the sensible world thus implies an original synthetic activity of man: *History* is this accomplishment, and thus it must not be confused with a simple development of nature."

10. Kant argues that the self is *both* noumenal and phenomenal. To deny the disjunction on the ground of contradiction—aporia—is no less aporetic because there is no third term. (See Cassirer, *Kant's First Critique*, p. 255)

11. This question of the relationship of the finite to the infinite is the pervasive aporia of the "metaphysical tradition": its "ontotheology." Allison equates Kant's theocentric views with transcendental realism, minimizing the absolutist tendencies in Kant's own theory. (Allison, *Kant's Transcendental Idealism*, pp. 14-16) What Heidegger finds in Kant, the origin of the infinite in the finite (Martin Heidegger, *Kant and the Problem of Metaphysics*, J. S. Churchill tr., Bloomington, Indiana University Press, 1962), is indeed a Copernican Revolution, although it is, as Ernst Cassirer points out, overstated as a thesis about

Kant. (Ernst Cassirer, "Kant and the Problem of Metaphysics," in Gram, *Kant: Disputed Questions*, pp. 131-57) The absolute plays a role even within the critical enterprise, in relation, for example, to divine intuition (see John Sallis, *The Gathering of Reason*, Athens, Ohio University Press, 1980, pp. 20-22) and to a permanent substrate (see Jonathan Bennett, *Kant's Analytic*, London, Cambridge University Press, 1966, pp. 181-210); see also Allison, *Kant's Transcendental Idealism*, p. 66). Deleuze repeats the Heideggerian emphasis on finiteness without acknowledgment of its aporetic side. (Deleuze, *Kant's Critical Philosophy*, p. 68)

Far more important here in Kant is the transformation of the aporia of the finite in relation to the infinite into the aporia of the determinateness of experience and practice, especially, the aporia of the freedom—consequently, the indeterminateness—of the imagination.

12. At best, the "Refutation of Idealism" offers a reply to the most global forms of skepticism, and none whatever to doubts about the efficacy of scientific methods.

13.   Obviously there must be some third thing, which is homogeneous on the one hand with the category, and on the other hand with the appearance, and which thus makes the application of the former to the latter possible. This mediating representation must be pure, that is, void of all empirical content, and yet at the same time, while it must in one respect be *intellectual*, it must in another be *sensible*. Such a representation is the *transcendental schema*.

. . . Now a transcendental determination of time is so far homogeneous with the category, which constitutes its unity, in that it is universal and rests upon an *a priori* rule. But, on the other hand, it is so far homogeneous with appearance, in that time is contained in every empirical representation of the manifold. Thus an application of the category to appearances becomes possible by means of the transcendental determination of time, which, as the schema of the concepts of understanding, mediates the subsumption of the appearances under the category. (CPR, p. 181)

14.   Reality, in the pure concept of understanding, is that which corresponds to a sensation in general; it is that, therefore, the concept of which in itself points to being (in time). . . .

The schema of substance is permanence of the real in time, ...

The schema of cause, and of the causality of a thing in general, . . . consists, therefore, in the succession of the manifold, in so far as that succession is subject to a rule. . . .

The schema of community or reciprocity, . . . is the coexistence, according to a universal rule, of the determinations of one substance with those of the other. . . .

The schema of possibility is the agreement of the synthesis of different representations with the conditions of time in general. . . .

The schema of actuality is existence in some determinate time. . . .

The schema of necessity is existence of an object at all times. (Ibid., pp. 184-85)

15.   A magnitude which is apprehended only as unity, and in which multiplicity can be represented only through approximation to negation $= 0$, I entitle an *intensive* magnitude. (Ibid., pp. 203; see Bennett, *Kant's Analytic*, pp. 170-75)

16. See the discussions in Gram, *The Transcendental Turn*, and Kemp Smith, *A Commentary to Kant's 'Critique of Pure Reason,'* concerning the distinctions that pertain to noumena, things in themselves, and transcendental objects.

17.   Now all pure concepts in general are concerned with the synthetic unity of representations, but [those of them which are] concepts of pure reason (transcendental ideas) are concerned with the unconditioned synthetic unity of all conditions in general. All transcendental ideas can therefore be arranged in three classes, the *first* containing the absolute (unconditioned) *unity* of the *thinking subject*, the *second* the absolute *unity of the series of conditions of appearance*, the *third* the absolute *unity of the condition of all objects of thought in general*. (CPR, p. 323)

18. Transcendental paralogism produced a purely one-sided illusion in regard to the idea of the subject of our thought. No illusion which will even in the slightest degree support the opposing assertion is caused by the concepts of reason. . . .
    A completely different situation arises when reason is applied to the *objective* synthesis of appearances. For in this domain, . . . it soon falls into such contradictions that it is constrained, in this cosmological field, to desist from any such pretensions. (Ibid., pp. 384-85)

19. Bennett dismisses part two of the first *Critique* as of little value, in part because its aporias are not compatible with his largely anti-aporetic reading. (Bennett, *Kant's Analytic*, p. 4)

20.   With this faculty [of reason], transcendental *freedom* is also established; freedom, namely, in that absolute sense in which speculative reason required it in its use of the concept of causality in order to escape the antinomy into which it inevitably falls, when in the chain of cause and effect it tries to think the *unconditioned*. . . .
    Inasmuch as the reality of freedom is proved by an apodictic law of practical reason, it is the *keystone* of the whole system of pure reason, even the speculative, . . . (CPrR, pp. 87-88)

21.   Freedom, however, is the only one of all the ideas of the speculative reason of which we *know* the possibility *a priori* (with-

out, however, understanding it), because it is the condition of the moral law which we know. (Ibid., p. 88)

22. See Deleuze, *Kant's Critical Philosophy*, p. 6:

The faculty of desire is thus a higher faculty, and the practical synthesis which corresponds to it is *a priori* when the will is no longer determined by pleasure, but by the simple form of law.

23.   In the *summum bonum* which is practical for us, *i.e.* to be realized by our will, virtue and happiness are thought as necessarily combined, so that the one cannot be assumed by pure reason without the other also being attached to it. (CPrR, p. 209)

24. . . . either the desire of happiness must be the motive to maxims of virtue, or the maxim of virtue must be the efficient cause of happiness. The first is *absolutely* impossible, because (as was proved in the Analytic) maxims which place the determining principle of the will in the desire of personal happiness are not moral at all, and no virtue can be founded on them. But the second is *also impossible*, because the practical connexion of causes and effects in the world, as the result of the determination of the will, does not depend upon the moral dispositions of the will, but on the knowledge of the laws of nature and the physical power to use them for one's purposes; . . . . (Ibid., pp. 209-10)

25. Now, the perfect accordance of the will with the moral law is *holiness*, a perfection of which no rational being of the sensible world is capable at any moment of his existence. Since, nevertheless, it is required as practically necessary, it can only be found in a *progress in infinitum* toward that perfect accordance, ...
. . . The *summum bonum*, then, practically is only possible on the supposition of the immortality of the soul; . . . . (Ibid., pp. 218-19)

Now it was seen to be a duty for us to promote the *summum bonum*; consequently it is not merely allowable, but it is a necessity connected with duty as a requisite, that we should presuppose the possibility of this *summum bonum*; and as this is possible only on condition of the existence of God, it inseparably connects the supposition of this with duty; that is, it is morally necessary to assume the existence of God. (p. 222)

26. Continental European writers raise this aporia of the task of practical reason—which demands its temporality although we cannot think of the a priori in relation to time—to the forefront of their understanding of the critical enterprise. See Cassirer, *Kant's Life and Thought*, p. 257; Lucien Goldmann, *Immanuel Kant*, London, NLB, 1971, p. 131; Deleuze, *Kant's Critical Philosophy*, pp. 73-75.

27. See Cassirer, *Kant's Life and Thought*, pp. 218-19.

28. See quotation, pp. 238-39.

29. It is this remarkable feature that Susanne Langer rejects as "paradoxical" in most theories of art including Kant's.

> ... a more radical difficulty is their inveterate tendency to paradox. Most of the dominant ideas, even taken all alone, carry with them some danger of self-defeat. As soon as we develop them we find ourselves with dialectical concepts on our hands. We have Significant Form that must not, at any price, be permitted to signify anything—illusion that is the highest truth—disciplined spontaneity—concrete ideal structures—impersonal feeling, "pleasure objectified" —and public dreaming. (Susanne Langer, *Feeling and Form*, New York, Scribner's, 1953, p. 25)

That these "paradoxes" are aporias is indicated by Langer's reference to the relevant concepts as "dialectical." They reflect most profoundly the aporia that is art. On the one hand, as Langer herself claims,

> It is a curious fact that people who spend their lives in closest contact with the arts—artists, to whom the appreciation of beauty is certainly a continual and "immediate" experience—do not assume and cultivate the "aesthetic attitude." To them, the artistic value of a work is its most obvious property. (p. 45)

On the other hand, however, every attempt to understand this "obvious property" falls into aporia. There is no room for beauty or art, except negatively, in an experience completely filled by freedom and necessity. Langer's theory is no exception.

30.   *Taste* is the faculty of judging of an object or a method of representing it by an *entirely disinterested* satisfaction or dissatisfaction. The object of such satisfaction is called *beautiful*. (CJ, p. 45)

The *beautiful* is that which pleases universally without [requiring] a concept. (p. 54)

Beauty is the form of the *purposiveness* of an object, so far as this is perceived in it *without any representation of a purpose*. (p. 73)

The *beautiful* is that which without any concepts is cognized as the object of a *necessary* satisfaction. (p. 77)

31.   We thus see (1) that genius is a *talent* for producing that for which no definite rule can be given; it is not a mere aptitude for what can be learned by a rule. Hence *originality* must be its first property. (2) But since it also can produce original nonsense, its products must be models, i.e. *exemplary*, and they consequently ought not to spring from imitation, but must serve as a standard of rule of judgment for others. (3) It cannot describe or indicate sci-

entifically how it brings about its products, but it gives the rule just as nature does . . . . (4) Nature, by the medium of genius, does not prescribe rules to science but to art, and to it only in so far as it is to be beautiful art. (Ibid., p. 150-51)

32.   Taste, like the judgment in general, is the discipline (or training) of genius; it clips its wings, it makes it cultured and polished; but, at the same time, it gives guidance as to where and how far it may extend itself if is to remain purposive. (Ibid., p. 163)

33. And by an aesthetical idea I understand that representation of the imagination which occasions much thought, without however any definite thought, i.e. a *concept*, being capable of being adequate to it; it consequently cannot be completely compassed and made intelligible by language. (Ibid., p. 157)

34.   We may describe the sublime thus: it is an object (of nature) *the representation of which determines the mind to think the unattainability of nature regarded as a presentation of ideas.* (Ibid., p. 108)

Such is the—discordant—accord of imagination and reason: not only reason, *but also the imagination*, has a 'suprasensible destination.' (Deleuze, *Kant's Critical Philosophy*, p. 51)

35. See my *Learning and Discovery*, London, Gordon & Breach, 1981, especially Part III, for a discussion of the paradigmatic nature of all knowing.

36.   . . . this intellectual purposiveness . . . can only be conceived as purposiveness in general without any [definite] purpose being assumed as its basis, and consequently without teleology being needed for it. . . . This purposiveness does not imply a *purpose* or any other ground whatever. (CJ, p. 210)

37.   In order to see that a thing is only possible as a purpose, that is to be forced to seek the causality of its origin, not in the mechanism of nature, but in a cause whose faculty of action is not possible according to mere natural laws, it is requisite that its form be not possible according to mere natural laws, ... (Ibid., p. 216)

38. The last question is: How is the final end also the last end of nature? That is to say: How can man, who is only final end in his suprasensible existence and as noumenon, be the last end of *sensible nature*? (Deleuze, *Kant's Critical Philosophy*, pp. 73-74)

39. I take this to be Aristotle's view of chance and coincidence.

Chapter 9

1. A striking example is Charles Taylor's claim that Hegel resolves the

aporia in Kant's view of freedom—the disruption of natural necessity—as if any view of freedom could be free from aporia in a world of necessity.

> Thus the major task of philosophy for Hegel can be expressed as that of over-coming opposition. The oppositions are those which arise from the breaking up of the original expressive unity. (Charles Taylor, *Hegel*, Cambridge and New York, Cambridge University Press, 1975, pp. 76-77)

Taylor's reading of *Geist* as "cosmic spirit" (p. 80) is almost entirely blind to its finiteness and partiality, though it does retain an important sense of aporia.

> Contradiction is thus fatal to partial realities, but not to the whole. But this is not because the whole escapes contradiction. Rather the whole as Hegel understands it lives on contradiction. It is really because it incorporates it, and reconciles it with identity that it survives. (p. 107)

A salutary contrast is with Stanley Rosen's view that:

> . . . the Absolute is not a "thing," whether in the sense of subject or object. The Absolute is the formation-process of subjects and objects. (Stanley Rosen, *G. W. F. Hegel: An Introduction to the Science of Wisdom*, New Haven and London, Yale University Press, 1974, p. 42)

2. Many examples could be cited, but an explicit claim that Hegel over-comes all aporias is made by Gasché in his treatment of Derrida.

> Hegel's philosophy must be described as an attempt to overcome the aporias of traditional philosophical positions, which arise from a naive adoption of a set of inherited conceptual oppositions, by constructively destroying them in a purely conceptual genesis. (Rodolphe Gasché, *The Tain of the Mirror*, Cambridge and London, Harvard University Press, 1986, p. 125)

This assumption surely lies behind Gasché's interpretation of Derrida's radical relation to the tradition. The question is whether aporia cries out for aporetic or nonaporetic resolution. The former alternative is supported by the notion of "heterology": the thought of radical difference.

> Opening the discourse of philosophy to an Other that is no longer simply *its* Other, an Other in which philosophy becomes inscribed, and which limits its ultimate pretension to self-foundation (a pretension independent of philosophical orientation), is an accomplishment that marks not the end but the structural limits of philosophy's autonomy and autarchy. Philosophy comes to a close, paradoxically, because its heterological presuppositions constitute it as, necessarily, always incomplete. (p. 251)

These notions of philosophy's "ultimate pretension to self-foundation," its "autonomy and autarchy," are the notions around which its "close" can be defined. Such an idea presupposes the *absolute* limits of philosophical thought, an idea incompatible with both radical difference and inexhaustible aporia.

What is at stake in heterology is inexhaustibility, manifested by Gasché in his discussion of the "analogy of being": the multiple aporetic senses of being realized only in analogy; being as difference. (pp. 296-98)

3. In Merleau-Ponty's words:

> Hegel had already identified [history and philosophy] by making philosophy the understanding of historical experience, and history the becoming of philosophy. But the conflict was only masked, since for Hegel philosophy is absolute knowledge, system, totality, whereas the history of which the philosopher speaks is not really history, that is to say, something which one does. It is rather universal history, fully comprehended, finished, dead. But, on the other hand, history as pure fact or event, introduces into the system in which it is incorporated an eternal movement which tears it to pieces. These two points of view both remain true for Hegel, and we know that he carefully maintained this equivocation. (Maurice Merleau-Ponty, *In Praise of Philosophy*, J. Wild and J. Edie trs, Evanston, Illinois, Northwestern University Press, 1963, pp. 48-49; quoted in Jan Van der Veken, "A Plea for an Open, Humble Hegelianism," in George R. Lucas ed., *Hegel and Whitehead*, Albany, SUNY Press, 1986, p. 112)

What Van der Veken calls an "open, humble Hegelianism," somewhat paradoxically, resolves its aporias by dissipating them into humility.

4. Walter Kaufmann translates *aufheben* as "sublimation," which in its psychoanalytic resonances has come to suggest replacement more than preservation (and certainly not surpassing). Nevertheless, the same issues of preservation in substitution remain in Freud. (Walter Kaufmann, *Hegel*, Garden City, Doubleday, 1965, p. 52) Kaufmann adds that sublation includes not only cancellation and preservation but lifting up, a notion difficult to associate with sublimation.

5. References to Hegel are to the *Phenomenology of Mind* (PM), J. Baillie tr., London, George Allen & Unwin, 1931; *The Logic of Hegel* (from the *Encyclopaedia*) (LL), W. Wallace tr., Oxford, Oxford University Press, 1892; *Hegel's Science of Logic* (L), A. V. Miller tr., London, George Allen & Unwin, 1969; *Hegel's Philosophy of Nature* (PN), A. V. Miller tr., Oxford, Oxford University Press, 1970; *Hegel's Philosophy of Right* (PR), Oxford, Oxford University Press, 1952.

6. For the real subject-matter is not exhausted in its purpose, but in working the matter out; nor is the mere result attained the concrete whole itself, but the result along with the process of arriving at it. The purpose by itself is a lifeless universal. (PM, p. 69)

7. The absolute spirit is "the infinite sorrow," which has chosen individual agents in religious, artistic, and philosophical forms of self-knowledge. It is rooted in the truth that there is no absolute wisdom in the world.

Man is essentially temporal or mortal; this truth and its knowledge is absolute and not merely temporal. In this absolute truth man has reached "absolute knowledge." (Gustav Emil Müller, "The Interdependence of the *Phenomenology, Logic*, and *Encyclopedia*," in Warren E. Steinkraus ed., *New Studies in Hegel's Philosophy*, New York, Holt, Rinehart and Winston, 1971, pp. 22, 23)

Absolute knowledge is that there is no perfection, and this consciousness of finiteness is tragic. Müller's is the most finite reading I have encountered, in that way resolving the aporias of absolute knowledge. See, however, Hyppolite:

Unhappy consciousness is the fundamental theme of the *Phenomenology*. Consciousness, as such, is in principle always unhappy consciousness, for it has not yet reached the concrete identity of certainty and truth, and therefore it aims at something beyond itself. (Jean Hyppolite, *Genesis and Structure of Hegel's* Phenomenology of Spirit, S. Cherniak and J. Heckman trs., Evanston, Northwestern University Press, 1974, p. 190)

The "not yet" is aporetic.

8.   This is the crucial point about Hegel's theory of consciousness as the "concept of spirit." It is essentially human, because it *must* be embodied; but the *embodiment is never* properly singular — for in singular embodiment there is no freedom. *Consciousness is a communal medium.* (H. S. Harris, *Hegel's Development: Night Thoughts (Jena 1801-1806)*, Oxford, Clarendon, 1983, p. 308)

This public embodiment of consciousness is a forerunner of Wittgenstein's arguments against a private language (extended to consciousness in general). The question is how a public embodiment can be *universal*.

9.   Something becomes an other; this other is itself somewhat: therefore it likewise becomes an other, and so on *ad infinitum*. (LL, p. 174)

. . . We lay down a limit: then we pass it: next we have a limit once more, and so on for ever. All this is but superficial alternation, which never leaves the region of the finite behind. (LL [*Zusatz*], p. 175)

10. . . . according to this way of working each determination, each mode, can be applied as form or schematic element in the case of every other, and each will thankfully perform the same service for any other. With a circle of reciprocities of this sort it is impossible

to make out what the real fact in question is, or what the one or the
other is. (PM, p. 108)

11.   The onward movement of the notion is no longer either a
transition into, or a reflection on something else, but Development.
For in the notion, the elements distinguished are without more ado
at the same time declared to be identical with one another and
with the whole, and the specific character of each is a free being of
the whole notion. . . .

Transition into something else is the dialectical process within
the range of Being: reflection (bringing something else into light),
in the range of Essence. The movement of the Notion is *development*: by which that only is explicit which is already implicitly present. (LL [*Zusatz*], p. 289)

12. See Schlomo Avineri, "Consciousness and History: *List der Vernunft*
in Hegel and Marx," in Steinkraus, *New Studies in Hegel's Philosophy*, pp. 108-18.

13. Every reader of the *Phenomenology* has doubtless puzzled over
the significance of the "wir" and the "für uns" which periodically
come into view and break up the flow of experience described.
(Kenley Royce Dove, "Hegel's Phenomenological Method," in
Steinkraus, *New Studies in Hegel's Philosophy*, p. 44)

See also Jean Hyppolite, "Hegel's Phenomenology and Psychoanalysis," in Steinkraus, p. 60: "Who is the 'we' which sees so clearly in a consciousness that does
not see itself?"; Avineri, "Consciousness and History," p. 111: "Who, then, *is*
aware of history's progress if the historical figures themselves are, to say the
least, in such an ambivalent position as we have just noted?"

14. Alexandre Kojève, *Introduction to the Reading of Hegel*, assembled
by Raymond Queneau, A. Bloom ed., J. H. Nichols, Jr. tr., New York, Basic
Books, 1969, Editor's Introduction, p. xi. It is no accident that this list of "free-
doms" corresponds almost precisely to Heidegger's list of originary truths.
(Martin Heidegger, *The Origin of the Work of Art*, in *Poetry, Language, Thought*,
A. Hofstadter tr., New York, Harper, 1971, p. 59)

15. Whatever happens, every individual is a child of his time; so philosophy too is its time apprehended in thoughts. It is just as absurd to
fancy that a philosophy can transcend its contemporary world as it
is to fancy that an individual can overleap his own age. (PR, p. 11)

It follows that absolute Spirit too can be of its time and no other.

16. Hannah Arendt, *Between Past and Future*, New York, Meridian, 1963,
p. 24.

17. The aporias persist even in those writers who appear most concerned
with resolving it.

The otherness of the Infinite Self is overcome in the discovery that the divine is nothing but this "nation of men related to one another by love." Here, too, otherness does not simply disappear. But it loses that strangeness which leaves man estranged rather than at home in the presence of the other. (Merold Westphal, *History and Truth in Hegel's* Phenomenology, Atlantic Highlands, Humanities Press, 1979, p. 213)

18. This last form into which Spirit passes, *Nature*, is its living immediate process of development. Nature—Spirit divested of self (externalized)—is, in its actual existence, nothing but this eternal process of abandoning its (Nature's) own independent subsistence, and the movement which reinstates Subject. (PM, p. 807)

In this reinstatement, absolute Spirit negates itself.

19. Nature is not the concept but only the concept's past, and reason cannot truly satisfy itself by observing it. . . . For this reason, though the philosophy of nature and more generally all the natural sciences must play a part in the phenomenological development in which consciousness learns to discover itself and to rediscover itself as spirit, it cannot have (as Schelling and, for a time in Jena, Hegel thought it could) a preponderant role. (Hyppolite, *Genesis and Structure*, p. 233)

20. "Self-consciousness is desire in general." (PM, p. 220)

21. Kojève suggests that the development of Spirit be read as the progression of the slave to freedom, for the master's freedom is degenerate, entirely dependent on the presence of the slave. Hyppolite suggests that the slave is the mediation in the tautologous I = I that constitutes mastery. (Hyppolite, *Genesis and Structure*, p. 171) What we must ask, if Kojève and Hyppolite are correct, is what kind of future could exist in which knowledge and truth might be independent of desire and power.

22. According to Harris, Hegel does not emphasize or advocate mastery. (H. S. Harris, *Hegel's Development: Toward the Sunlight 1770-1801*, Oxford, Clarendon, 1972, p. 310) He is in this sense far removed from the Enlightenment sense of dominance over nature. Why, then, do we think he exhibits such a view? Why do we find a Faustian theme in his sense of absolute Spirit? The answer, I believe, is that we fail to take the sacrifices required by sublation seriously (as we may also fail to take seriously the sacrifices Faust both experiences and imposes).

23. As Kenley Royce Dove points out, there is no dialectical Method in Hegel, but a dialectic of consciousness that comprises history. "Hegel's method is radically *un*dialectical. It is the experience of consciousness itself which is dialectical." (Dove, "Hegel's Phenomenological Method," p. 40)

24. Kaufmann offers an extraordinarily weak interpretation of necessity, far too weak to be taken seriously as the basis of science.

Hegel uses "necessary" as an inclusive antonym of "arbitrary," as if everything for which good reasons can be given and which was not, therefore, arbitrary could be reasonably called "necessary." (Kaufmann, *Hegel*, p. 85)

25. Time, as the negative unity of self-externality, is similarly an out-and-out abstract, ideal being. It is that being which, inasmuch as it *is*, is *not*, and inasmuch as it is *not*, *is*: it is Becoming directly *intuited*; this means that differences, which admittedly are purely *momentary*, i.e. directly self-sublating, are determined as *external*, i.e. as external to *themselves*. (PN, p. 34)

26. This interpretation is clearly critical of Heidegger's early critique in *Being and Time* of Hegel's view of time.

No detailed discussion is needed to make plain that in Hegel's Interpretation of time he is moving wholly in the direction of the way time is ordinarily understood. When he characterizes time in terms of the "now," this presupposes that in its full structure the "now" remains levelled off and covered up, so that it can be intuited as something present-at-hand, though present-at-hand only "ideally." (Heidegger, *Being and Time*, p. 483)

The time that devolves from the "now" is nature's time, history (with its aporias) outside of itself. What is suggested is that the "present-at-hand" is human being outside of itself: outside of historicity and the future.

27. The dimensions of time, *present, future,* and *past*, are the *becoming* of externality as such, and the resolution of it into the differences of being as passing over into nothing, and of nothing as passing over into being. (PN, p. 37)

28.   Idea is essentially a process, because its identity is the absolute and free identity of the notion, only in so far as it is absolute negativity and for that reason dialectical. It is the round of movement, in which the notion, in the capacity of universality which is individuality, gives itself the character of objectivity and of the antithesis thereto; and this externality which has the notion for its substance, finds its way back to subjectivity through its immanent dialectic. (LL, p. 357)

29.   Seeing that there is in it no transition, or presupposition, and in general no specific character other than what is fluid and transparent, the Absolute Idea is for itself the pure form of the notion, which contemplates its content as its own self. (Ibid., p. 374)

30. This recognition constitutes a rejection of what Whitehead calls "simple location." (Alfred North Whitehead, *Science and the Modern World*, Macmillan, New York, 1925, pp. 69-70)

31. See also, emphasizing transition:

> Logic shows that the subjective which is to be subjective only, the finite which would be finite only, the infinite which would be infinite only, and so on, have no truth, but contradict themselves, and pass over into their opposites. Hence this transition, and the unity in which the extremes are merged and become factors, each with a merely reflected existence, reveals itself as their truth. (LL, pp. 355-56)

32. The Idea, which by itself is no doubt the truth, really never gets any farther than just where it began, as long as the development of it consists in nothing else than such a repetition of the same formula. (PM, p. 78)

> This monotonous and abstract universality are maintained to be the Absolute. This formalism insists that to be dissatisfied therewith argues an incapacity to grasp the standpoint of the Absolute, and keep a firm hold on it. (pp. 78-79)

> To pit this single assertion, that "in the Absolute all is one," against the organized whole of determinate and complete knowledge, or of knowledge which at least aims at and demands complete development—to give out its Absolute as the night in which, as we say, all cows are black—that is the very *naïveté* of emptiness of knowledge. (p. 79)

33. The Spirit manifested in revealed religion has not as yet surmounted its attitude of consciousness as such; or, what is the same thing, its actual self-consciousness is not at this stage the object it is aware of. . . . All that remains to be done now is to cancel and transcend this bare form. (PM, p. 689)

34. Man overcomes the brute otherness of the world largely through practical activity, which the mind then tries to grasp. This practical activity basically consists in an exercise of the will, which in turn is free. Consequently practical activity, transforming the world as the result of that will, is also an exercise in the achievement of human freedom. (Raymond Plant, *Hegel*, Bloomington, Indiana University Press, 1973, p. 152)

Indeed, there is a full theory of ideology in Hegel:

> What we have before us is a full-fledged theory of ideology, which can hardly be said to have originated with Marx. For it was Hegel to whom we owe the discovery that "a radical critique of knowledge is possible only as social theory." [Jürgen Habermas, *Knowledge and Human Interests*] (Westphal, *History and Truth in Hegel's* Phenomenology, p. 42)

35.   Sentience is the immediate unification at once of the processes of the body and of the whole of nature. It becomes mediated in consciousness as the awareness of self and of the world. (Errol E. Harris, "Hegel's Theory of Feeling," in Steinkraus, *New Essays in Hegel's Philosophy*, p. 83)

36. Through work and labour, . . . this consciousness of the bondsman comes to itself. . . . Desire has reserved to itself the pure negating of the object and thereby unalloyed feeling of self. This satisfaction, however, just for that reason is itself only a state of evanescence, for it lacks objectivity or subsistence. Labour, on the other hand, is desire restrained and checked, evanescence delayed and postponed; in other words, labour shapes and fashions the thing. (PM, p. 238)

37. "Self-consciousness is essentially practical; it is the consciousness of transcending the knowledge of the other." (Hyppolite, *Genesis and Structure*, p. 146)

38.   In Becoming the Being which is one with Nothing, and the Nothing which is one with Being, are only vanishing factors; they are and they are not. Thus by its inherent contradiction Becoming collapses into the unity in which the two elements are absorbed. This result is accordingly Being Determinate (Being there and so). (LL, p. 169)

It is through the determinate characteristic that the thing excludes other things. Things themselves are thus determinate in and for themselves. (PM, p. 170)

CHAPTER 10

1. Heidegger, "The End of Philosophy and the Task of Thinking," p. 373

2. Jacques Derrida, "*Ousia* and *Grammē*," E. Casey tr., *Phenomenology in Perspective*, F. J. Smith ed., The Hague, Nijhoff, 1970, p. 93. See also:

By taking the classical exigencies of philosophy to their logical end, without, however, giving in to its ethico-theoretical, ethico-ontological, ethico-teleological, or ethico-political decisions, Derrida brings philosophy to a certain close. This, however, is an accomplishment in a unheard-of sense. Opening the discourse of philosophy to an Other that is no longer simply *its* Other, an Other in which philosophy becomes inscribed, and which limits its ultimate pretension to self-foundation (a pretension independent of philosophical orientation), is an accomplishment that marks not merely the end but the structural limits of philosophy's autonomy and autarchy. Philosophy comes to a close, paradoxically, because its heterological presuppositions constitute it as, necessarily, always incomplete. (Gasché, *The Tain of the Mirror*, p. 251)

Like Rorty, Gasché dismisses the tradition as foundational:

> To the extent that transcendental philosophy lays claim to reflecting the a priori conditions of all knowledge, it must reflect on the ground proper of philosophy, and thus become the medium of the self-reflection of philosophy. In the thinking of thinking—what Aristotle called *noēsis noēseōs*—reflexivity serves at once as a medium, the method, and the foundation by which philosophy grounds itself within itself. Through such a reflection upon itself, in the philosophy of philosophy, the philosophical discourse seeks to achieve complete clarity concerning its own essence and complete freedom from any assumptions, thereby confirming its claim to be the "first" philosophy, the philosophy of philosophy, the philosophy capable of furnishing the foundation of all other sciences. In other words, self-reflection grounds the autonomy of philosophy as the knowledge that is most free. Here, one can best grasp that self-reflection is not only method or medium but foundation as well. All modern philosophy has an essential relation to itself such that all reflexive analyses are analyses of the essential nature of things themselves, ... (p. 25)

3. Heidegger, "The End of Philosophy and the Task of Thinking," p. 377.

4. Ibid., p. 379.

5. Carnap, *The Logical Syntax of Language*, p. 279.

6. Heidegger, "The End of Philosophy and the Task of Thinking," p. 375

7. Michael Polanyi, *Personal Knowledge*, Chicago, University of Chicago Press, 1958.

8. The quest for certainty is a quest for a peace which is assured, an object which is unqualified by risk and the shadow of fear which action casts. For it is not uncertainty *per se* which men dislike, but the fact that uncertainty involves us in peril of evils. . . . Quest for complete certainty can be fulfilled in pure knowing alone. Such is the verdict of our most enduring philosophic tradition. (Dewey, *The Quest for Certainty*, p. 8.)

9. Wittgenstein, Heidegger, and Dewey are in agreement that the notion of knowledge as accurate representation, made possible by special mental processes, and intelligible through a general theory of representation, needs to be abandoned. For all three, the notions of "foundations of knowledge" and of philosophy as revolving around the Cartesian attempt to answer the epistemological skeptic are set aside. . . . Rather, they glimpse the possibility of a form of intellec-

tual life in which the vocabulary of philosophical reflection inherited from the seventeenth century would seem as pointless as the thirteenth-century philosophic vocabulary had seemed to the Enlightenment. (Rorty, *Philosophy and the Mirror of Nature*, p. 6)

10.   I myself would join Reichenbach in dismissing classical Husserlian phenomenology, Bergson, Whitehead, the Dewey of *Experience and Nature*, the James of *Radical Empiricism*, neo-Thomist epistemological realism, and a variety of other late nineteenth-and early twentieth-century systems. Bergson and Whitehead, and the bad ("metaphysical") parts of Dewey and James, seem to me merely weakened versions of idealism . . . . Phenomenology and neo-Thomism . . . tried in vain to isolate a *Fach* for themselves, distinct from science and its self-clarification, by giving sense to the notion of a distinctively "philosophical," super-scientific knowledge. (Rorty, *Consequences of Pragmatism*, pp. 213-14)

Systematic philosophy is either foundational or metaphysical, both in a pejorative sense.

11. Rorty, *Philosophy and the Mirror of Nature*, p. xl.

12. Friedrich Nietzsche, *Gay Science*, W. Kaufman tr., New York, Random House, 1974, par. 34.

13. John Dewey, *Reconstruction in Philosophy*, Boston, Beacon, 1957, p. 26.

14. John Dewey, *Philosophy and Civilization*, New York, Minton, Balch, 1931, p. 8.

15. Gadamer, *Truth and Method*, p. 167.

16. Ibid., pp. 235-36.

17. Ibid., p. 236.

18. Ibid., p. 236.

19. Ibid., p. xxiii.

20. Ibid., pp. 261-62.

21. Ibid., p. xxv.

22. Ibid. A similar denial of aporia and heresy is to be found in Habermas. See Jürgen Habermas, *Communication and the Evolution of Society*, T. McCarthy tr., Boston, Beacon, 1976; *The Theory of Communicative Action*, vol. I, T. McCarthy tr., Boston, Beacon, 1981.

23. Martin Heidegger, *On the Way to Language*, P. D. Hertz tr., New York, Harper & Row, 1971, p. 108.

24. Gadamer, *Truth and Method*, p. xxv.

25. Ibid., p. 259.

26. Ibid., p. 489.

27. John Dewey, "Context and Thought," *On Experience, Nature and Freedom*, R. Bernstein ed., Indianapolis, Bobbs-Merrill, 1960, p. 92.

28. Ibid., p. 93.

29. Ibid., p. 107.

30. Ibid., pp. 108-09.

31. Heidegger, "The End of Philosophy and the Task of Thinking," p. 374.

32. Heidegger, *On the Way to Language*, p. 76.

33. Ibid., p. 58.

34. Heidegger, "The Onto-Theo-Logical Constitution of Metaphysics," p. 61.

35. Gadamer, *Truth and Method*, p. 483.

36. Heidegger, "The Onto-Theo-Logical Constitution of Metaphysics," p. 43.

37. Ibid., p. 47.

38. Ibid., p. 48.

39. Ibid., p. 51.

40. Heidegger, "The End of Philosophy and the Task of Thinking," p. 375.

41. Ibid., p. 377.

42. John Dewey, *Experience and Nature*, 2nd ed., New York, Dover, 1958, pp. 97-98.

43. Derrida denies the "homogeneity" of the metaphysical tradition that is to be "brought to its end," though he retains the figure of enclosure.

> ... I have also frequently, elsewhere but even in "White Mythology," advanced the proposition that there could not be "one" metaphysics—"closure" here being not the circular limit bordering a homogeneous field but a more twisted structure that I would be tempted to call today, according to another figure: "invaginated." (Jacques Derrida, "Le retrait de la métaphore," *Analecta Husserliana*, vol. 14, A-T. Tymieniecka ed., Dordrecht, Reidel, 1983, p. 281 [my translation])

The notions of end and closure are all aporetic.

44. Heidegger, "The Onto-Theo-Logical Constitution of Metaphysics," p. 54.

45. Ibid., p. 58.

46. This "radical" alterity thus marks a "space" of exteriority at the border of philosophy, whether or not philosophy is explicitly phenomenological. It is situated on the margin of what can be meaningfully totalized. Yet, although it does not bend to the concept of presence, neither does it for that matter lend itself to the conceptual grip of absence, since, lacking all meaning, it is also void of the meaning conferred by an absence of meaning.

   But as we shall see, this border is not simply external to philosophy. It does not encompass philosophy like a circle but traverses it within. Although this "radical" alterity does not present itself *as such*, the history of philosophy in its entirety is, indeed, the uninterrupted attempt to domesticate it in the form of its delegates. In presenting it in negative images—as the opposites of valorized metaphysical concepts—specular reflection seeks to account for, and do away with, the sort of alterity that subverts its hope of reflexive or speculative self-foundation. This alterity forever undermines, but also makes possible, the dream of autonomy achieved through a reflexive coiling upon self, since it names a structural preconditon of such a desired state, a precondition that represents the limit of such a possibility. (Gaschē, *The Tain of the Mirror*, p. 105)

47. Heidegger, "The End of Philosophy and the Task of Thinking," p. 391.

48. Ibid., p. 392.

49. See quotation above, note 2. According to Gasché, Derrida leaves philosophy as it is. Why should we desire to do so? How can a thought be heretical without transforming thought itself?

50. Michel Foucault, *The Order of Things*, Vintage, New York, 1973, p. 315.

51. Ibid., p. 317.

52. Foucault, *The Archaeology of Knowledge*, p. 8.

53. Ibid., p. 9.

54. Ibid., p. 25.

55. Ibid., p. 209.

56. Ibid., p. 131.

57. Heidegger, "The Origin of the Work of Art," p. 62.

58. Foucault, *The Order of Things*, pp. 385-87.

59. Derrida, *On Grammatology*, pp. 4, 5.

60. Lyotard, *The Postmodern Condition*, p. xxiv.

61. Ibid.

62. Ibid., p. 81.

63. Technology is among the major disruptive forces in the contemporary world. If there is postmodernism, if we face the possibility of a radically different future, it will be as a consequence of the transformations wrought by contemporary technology. See my discussions in "Technology and Practical Judgment," *Logos*, VII, 1986, pp. 125-39; *Locality and Practical Judgment: Charity and Sacrifice*, New York, Fordham University Press, forthcoming, ch. VI.

Chapter 11

1. William James, *A Pluralistic Universe*, New York, Longmans, Green, 1909, p. 321.

2. John Dewey, "The Need for a Recovery of Philosophy," *On Experience, Nature, and Freedom*, p. 59.

3. Power is everywhere, not because it embraces everything, but because it comes from everywhere.

—Where there is power, there is resistance. (Michel Foucault, *History of Sexuality, vol. I*, pp. 93, 95)

4. This multiplicity of being is reflected in the medieval tradition's discussion of the "analogies of being." See the discussion in Gasché, *The Tain of the Mirror*, pp. 296-300.

5. See my *Locality and Practical Judgment: Charity and Sacrifice*, forthcoming.

6. See Rorty, *Philosophy and the Mirror of Nature*; Paul Feyerabend, *Against Method*, Atlantic Highlands, Humanities Press, 1975.

Chapter 12

1. Kuhn, *The Structure of Scientific Revolutions*.

2. Charles Sanders Peirce, "The Fixation of Belief," *Collected Papers* (CP), P. Weiss and C. Hartshorne eds., Cambridge, Massachusetts, Harvard University Press, 1931-35, 5.358-87.

3. Peirce, "How to Make Our Ideas Clear," CP 5.388-410.

4. See my *The Limits of Language*.

5. Foucault, *The Order of Things*, p. 386.

INDEX

389